Symbols

pers   Make the nouns and pronouns consistent in person. **9g(1),** p. 293

prin pt   Use the correct principal part of this verb. **7c-7d,** p. 169

pr phr   Phrase this idea more precisely. **14c(2),** p. 394

pr wd   Try to find a more precise word. **17c(9),** p. 458

ref   Make this pronoun refer clearly to a particular word. **9c,** p. 262

sent log   Make the parts of your sentence relate to each other more logically. **15b-15c,** p. 400

s/mood   Use the subjunctive mood here. **7i(3),** p. 194

sp   Spell this word correctly. **16b,** p. 421

S/V agr   Make this verb agree with its singular or plural subject. **9a,** p. 238

tns   Make the tenses of these verbs consistent. **9f(1),** p. 287

var   Work on sentence variety in this paragraph. **12b-12c,** p. 372

voice   Use the active voice unless the situation calls for the passive. **7e(3),** p. 178

WDWW   Make your sentence more direct and clear by telling "Who Did What to What." **15a,** p. 398

wdy   Wordy: try to say the same thing in fewer words. **17c(7),** p. 456

w wd   Wrong word: replace it with a better one. **14c(1),** p. 394

English

H A N D B O O K

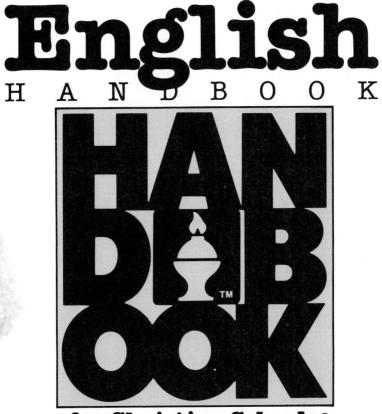

for Christian Schools®

Grace C. Collins

This textbook was written by members of the faculty and staff of Bob Jones University. Standing for the "old-time religion" and the absolute authority of the Bible since 1927, Bob Jones University is the world's leading Fundamentalist Christian university. The staff of the University is devoted to educating Christian men and women to be servants of Jesus Christ in all walks of life.

Providing unparalleled academic excellence, Bob Jones University prepares its students through its offering of over one hundred majors, while its fervent spiritual emphasis prepares their minds and hearts for service and devotion to the Lord Jesus Christ.

If you would like more information about the spiritual and academic opportunities available at Bob Jones University, please call
1-800-BJ-AND-ME (1-800-252-6363).
www.bju.edu

NOTE:
The fact that materials produced by other publishers may be referred to in this volume does not constitute an endorsement by Bob Jones University Press of the content or theological position of materials produced by such publishers. The position of the Bob Jones University Press, and the University itself, is well known. Any references and ancillary materials are listed as an aid to the student or the teacher and in an attempt to maintain the accepted academic standards of the publishing industry.

ENGLISH HANDBOOK for Christian Schools®

Produced in cooperation with the Bob Jones University School of Education, the Department of English, and Bob Jones Academy.

for Christian Schools is a registered trademark of Bob Jones University Press.

© 1985, 1999 Bob Jones University Press
Greenville, South Carolina 29614

Printed in the United States of America

ISBN 0-89084-279-5

15   14   13

Short Contents

Contents

Acknowledgments

Of the following persons for their advice and assistance:

Bruce A. Byers, M.A.
Ronald A. Horton, Ph.D.
Elizabeth E. Kitching, B.S., pilot teacher
Raymond A. St. John, Ph.D.
Edith E. Smith, M.A., grade-level consultant
Geraldine Stratton, B.S., pilot teacher

Of the following publishers:

E. P. Dutton, Inc.: Excerpt from *A Precocious Autobiography* by Yevgeny Yevtushenko. Reprinted with permission of E. P. Dutton, Inc.

Houghton Mifflin Company: Excerpt from *The American Heritage Dictionary.* Copyright 1982. Houghton Mifflin Company. Reprinted by permission of *The American Heritage Dictionary of the English Language,* pp. 475-79, 484. All rights reserved.

Simon and Schuster: Excerpt from *We Seven* by M. Scott Carpenter. Reprinted with permission of Simon and Schuster.

Preface: To the Teacher

Because some aspects of our approach to the parts of speech may be new to you or to your students, a word about rationale may be helpful.

English words have been classified into parts of speech in various ways, some more satisfactory than others. Although many of us think of "the eight parts of speech," traditional descriptions have varied surprisingly even in the number of parts of speech. One recent grammar of current English, an exceptionally thorough and scholarly one,[1] lists these ten as the "commonly

---

[1] Randolph Quirk, *et al., A Grammar of Contemporary English* (London: Longman, 1972), 1120 pages.

distinguished" parts of speech: noun, adjective, adverb, and verb as the four large classes; and article, demonstrative, pronoun, preposition, conjunction, and interjection as the small classes (pp. 44-45). The authors go on to comment (p. 47) that in spite of the simple labels, "the parts of speech tend in fact to be rather heterogeneous. The adverb and the verb are perhaps especially mixed classes, each having small and fairly well defined" sets of small-class words inside them. The most obvious of these sets, they suggest, is the small group of verbal auxiliaries, often lumped together with the large group of true verbs.

The approach taken in this handbook aims at both simplicity and accuracy. Of course, the complexity of any language requires that there be some compromise between these two goals. The working principles have been these: to keep the terms as simple and familiar as possible; to present accurately the facts and concepts that will be the most helpful tools for practical use in the improvement of writing; and to reveal the basic order and system of the language.

If you have not already done so, you may wish to read section **3a** now. It provides an overview of the parts of speech as they are presented in this handbook.

A central concept is that of the *major* and *minor* parts of speech. The major parts of speech are the large groups of words that convey most of the content meaning of our sentences. The minor parts of speech are the small groups of words whose meaning is mainly grammatical. That is, the minor parts of speech provide the "grammatical glue" for the sentence, relating the content words to one another correctly. The major parts of speech are "open" classes in the sense that we can easily add new members to these classes. The minor parts of speech, however, have a relatively closed membership. For instance, it is much easier to add a new noun to the language than a new pronoun.

The table on page 17 shows that for each of the major parts of speech there is a related minor part of speech. These four minor classes can be considered part of the related major classes if one prefers. In every case, however, the minor class is distinct in function, and nearly all the pairs are distinct in form changes as well. (In fact, it is significantly easier to distinguish auxiliaries from verbs, determiners from adjectives, and qualifiers from adverbs than it is to state the familiar distinction between pronouns and nouns.) For the sake of clarity and usefulness, the major and minor classes of words are described in this handbook as separate groups of words.

Some students will come to this text from a system in which, for example, determiners are called adjectives. These students should be told that this idea is indeed very common, and that the two groups of words do share the characteristic of modifying the noun. But now these students are ready to learn the striking differences between true adjectives and the determiners—differences in form and differences in their placement as modifiers. Then the students will also be ready to learn the punctuation rule that solves the perennial student problem of when to use (and especially when not to use) commas with modifiers before the noun. The rule, stated in **10d(7.4),** is simple once the students can recognize determiners and true adjectives.

The point is not that this system is right and that another one is wrong. This system simply goes a bit farther down the road toward accurate description of the language.[2] And better description of the language gives you better tools to use in helping students express their ideas effectively.

---

[2] In presenting the advantages of this approach we make no claims of originality. Systematic grammar, the approach here, represents a consensus of older and more recent studies of the structure of English.

Chapter 1

English for Many Purposes

1a Questions about what to say
1b What is the situation?
1c How should I adjust for formality?
1d The path ahead

One of the most amazing gifts God has given us is the gift of language. With no noticeable effort, we can use our language to talk about a game we went to, to understand directions for a fire drill, to read a story about missionaries in Mexico, or even to imagine how it would be to float in air like a fish in water. That is, through language we can tell—or learn—about old things and new things, and things that never have been. And most of the time we give no thought to the sounds and words and sentences we use to do all this.

1a Questions About What to Say

Sometimes, though, we do have questions about what to say or what to write. For instance, we may have questions about words: when do I use *good* and when do I use *well?* Is it "different *from*" or "different *than*"?

1

Or we may have questions about how to put words together: would it be better in a certain letter to say "they haven't got a plan" or "they don't have any plan" or "they have no plan"? Then again, we may wonder how to say something more clearly, more interestingly, or more forcefully.

One of the main purposes of this book is to answer questions like these. Answers about certain words, like those mentioned above, can be found in the Glossary of Usage on pages 536-38. Pointers about how to make your writing more clear, interesting, and forceful come in various parts of the book—especially in sections like Chapter 9 (Clear Links), Chapter 14 (Lively Sentences), and Chapter 15 (Logical Sentences). These chapters, though, will help you most after you have mastered the fundamental concepts found in Part I, especially Chapters 2-5 on sentences, parts of speech, and the basic sentence patterns.

Now let's go back to the question about what to say in your letter: "they haven't got a plan" or "they don't have any plan" or "they have no plan." The answer will partly depend on the rest of your paragraph. Shorter is often better, and so you might choose the third version. However, you might choose something else because of the rhythm of your paragraph or because of what you want to emphasize.

"But wait a minute," you say. "What about those contractions? Are they really all right to use?"

Well, that depends. Certainly, contractions are used less often in writing than in speaking. Beyond that, "don't have" somehow seems more appropriate in writing than does "haven't got," even though "haven't got" is a perfectly good conversational form. The key word here is *appropriate*. What kind of letter are you writing? Is it a personal letter to a close friend or, say, a letter to the editor of a national news magazine?

1b What Is the Situation?

We do use language in different ways, depending on the situation. Part of maturing in our use of English is observing some of these differences and then learning to make them ourselves. Doing so will keep us from sounding stiff when we talk with close friends, and it will keep us from sounding disrespectful when we apply for a job.

There are four aspects of the situation that adults normally adjust for, almost without thinking:

1. **The medium.** Am I writing or speaking? And am I doing it quickly with no opportunity for planning, or am I expected to plan carefully?
2. **The audience.** How large is my audience—one person, several, or many? In general, how much do they know? What is their relationship to me? Are they people to whom I owe special respect, or are they more or less my equals? How well do I know them?
3. **The occasion.** Is it private or public? If it is public, how formal is this kind of occasion expected to be? What is my subject? Have I already established an understanding with this audience about this subject?
4. **The speaker.** How do I want to present myself to others through my use of language? What is my background? What are my age and my position in life?

Fortunately, we do not have to adjust for all of these things individually. In general, all of these factors affect what we call the **formality** of our writing and speaking. A history textbook, for example, is usually more formal than a newspaper. A newspaper may be about as formal as a political speech, which would be more formal than the conversations afterward.

Some factors tend to reduce formality, and others to increase it. Up to a point, formality tends to increase with such factors as these:

3

a written medium;

an audience of higher status than the speaker or writer;

an audience that is not well known by the writer or speaker;

a large audience;

a public occasion;

a serious subject, especially when there is not already a background of shared understanding on it;

a speaker or writer who is in a position of responsibility, especially among those who are educated.

As you might guess, some of these factors are stronger than others as causes of greater formality.

LEVELS OF USAGE

Nonstandard	Standard		
	Informal	General	Formal
Mostly spoken	Spoken more than written	Both spoken and written	Mostly written
Used by people not much affected by education	Used by educated people in relaxed situations; might include some slang or certain local expressions	Used by educated people in most situations, both public and private; has broadest use	Used by educated people in certain formalized situations
Used for the same purposes as educated people use informal and general standard English; also used at home by some who use standard English in public	Casual conversation; letters between close friends	Much conversation; most business letters; public talks to general audiences; most articles in newspapers and magazines; books on subjects of general interest; most popular literature; most student writing in high school, and some in college	Academic writing; lectures to scholars or other special audiences; reports for professionals; some literary works; student papers in many college courses; legal documents; formal correspondence such as graduation and wedding invitations

The table "Levels of Usage" presents three main varieties of standard English and puts nonstandard English beside them for comparison. The table simplifies the facts by dividing the whole range of formality differences into just three parts. This division is useful as long as we remember that there is no clean break between the types and that there are some formality differences within them. For example, in its oral uses general English usually contains some contractions, but these are less likely in written general English. A well-educated person is "at home" with all the formality levels of standard English, using each one as appropriate.

1c How Should I Adjust for Formality?

Formality in writing and speaking partly limits our choices, and partly widens our choices. For example, in somewhat formal writing we avoid contractions, certain personal pronouns, and certain colloquial (conversational-sounding) words and expressions. However, formal writing also allows us to use certain words, expressions, and constructions that would sound out of place in more casual surroundings. It is simply a matter of choice, and of appropriateness—saying it in the best way for the situation.

At this point, you may wonder: "Is all this just a matter of convenience, or is it something I have a duty to do?" Certainly there is no eleventh commandment, "Thou shalt not say *ain't*"; but then neither is there a specific commandment not to eat potatoes and gravy with the fingers. As Christians we should avoid giving offense and should do all things "to the glory of God" (I Cor. 10:31-32 and II Cor. 6:3-6). We please our Saviour not only by loving Him and living for Him but also by not offending people unnecessarily. Part of that responsibility is what we could call "language manners"—correctness and appropriateness in speaking and writing.

Compared with the whole English language, the problem areas are few. We still have much freedom of choice as we look for the best way of saying the things we want to say.

Your English studies will continue to help you increase your understanding of the many varieties and uses of our language. You no doubt already know what sounds right for conversations in your neighborhood. In your English classes you have learned how to change certain words and phrases to the standard ones used, for instance, in downtown offices across the country. As you continue reading, writing, and studying English, you will also develop skill with the more formal varieties of English used by educated adults.

1d The Path Ahead

God's gift of language is well worth studying in its own right. Every language is both powerful and flexible, allowing for generous amounts of creativity. Languages also reflect God's nature in being reasonable and orderly.

The basic structure of the orderliness of English is presented in the first part of this handbook (Chapters 1-8). A knowledge of this grammatical structure will not automatically make you a better writer, but it will certainly help you understand a great deal of good advice about writing.

Some of that good advice will come from your teachers and other sources, and some of it will be found in the second part of this handbook (Chapters 9-15). In those chapters you will learn more about avoiding errors and making wise use of the many choices that English gives us. Then the final section (Chapters 16-19) contains other helps toward good writing. A major goal of all these materials is to help you express your ideas with greater clarity, strength, and confidence.

One

Understanding Grammar

Chapter 2
The Simple Sentence

2a What are sentences?
2b Finding the complete subject and the complete predicate
2c Finding the simple subject and the simple predicate
2d What do sentences do?

What is the English language for? The basic purpose of any language is to express meaning—to say something to someone. Words (and sometimes parts of words) have little bits of meaning attached to them, but we need more than that. To express ideas, or thoughts, we need to combine words into sentences. The sentence is the most important thing we build with words.

2a What Are Sentences?

There are several ways of explaining what a sentence is. One way would be to say, for example, that everything on this page that ends with a period or a question mark is a sentence. That is true, but not much of a definition. After all, people do make mistakes in where they put periods.

Another way is to say that **a sentence expresses a complete thought,** or a whole thought. That is not very exact, but it may help. Smaller groups of words (phrases) like "in the house" and "as fast as possible" seem to express pieces of thoughts rather than whole thoughts. Of course, it sometimes takes several sentences before we really understand what a person is talking about. But still, each sentence is a thought-link in the chain of ideas.

We can also notice that **a sentence sounds complete.** At the end of a spoken sentence a person's voice usually falls, sometimes very quickly, going down to a "low note" and then pausing briefly. At the end of some questions, the voice goes up instead and then pauses. Without looking at your book, listen to a good reader read the paragraph below. While he reads, see whether you can count how many sentences there are. Notice that the sentences have a "complete" sound to them.

> Diamonds are the hardest stones there are. They are valued because of their beauty and their hardness. They are also very rare. The richest diamond mines in the world are in South Africa. Even there, an average of twenty-three tons of rock must be crushed to find one medium-sized diamond. Then the diamond must be carefully cut to show its beauty. It's no wonder that diamonds are expensive! *(seven sentences)*

However, in a conversation something less than a sentence (a fragment) can have that same "complete" sound; so this test is not foolproof. Fragments can work all right in a conversation, as long as the rest of the conversation makes the meaning clear. Notice these examples:

Randy:	Why did you do that?	Sentence
Peter:	Do what?	Fragment 1
Randy:	Move my ball.	Fragment 2
Peter:	Oh—sorry.	Fragment 3
	I didn't mean to.	Sentence
Randy:	That's OK.	Sentence
	Say, who gave you the croquet set?	Sentence
Peter:	My uncle.	Fragment 4
Randy:	It's a nice one.	Sentence

Fragments are appropriate in conversations, but not usually in written paragraphs. In writing, complete sentences are expected.

Finally, here is a definition that you can actually use to test whether or not a group of words is a sentence:

A sentence is a group of words that has a subject and a predicate and nothing that makes it part of another sentence.

First, a sentence has a **subject,** something the sentence is about. Then it has a **predicate,** that is, a verb and perhaps other words that say something about the subject. Look again at the conversation. Fragment 1 has a verb (*do*), but it has no subject. Which other fragment has a verb but no subject? _____ Which fragment has a subject but no verb? _____ And which fragment has neither subject nor verb? _____ Check your answers: fragments 2, 4, 3.

Another kind of fragment has a subject and a verb, but also something that makes it part of another sentence. Here are some examples: *whether he will go, that it will rain, what he likes, because they said so.* In these examples the first word changes the word group from a possible sentence to a part of another sentence.

What at first seems to be an exception to this definition is a kind of sentence that has its own rule. When we give a command, we usually leave the subject (the doer) unmentioned but clearly understood. For instance, when we say "Shut the door, please," the subject *you* is understood. If we include this understood *you,* we can still say that the normal sentence has both a subject and a predicate.

● **Practice 2-1**   Write down the numbers of the word groups that can be complete sentences by themselves. (Answers to all exercises are in the back of the book.)
   1. A glacier is like a river of ice.
   2. Many miles long.
   3. It moves very slowly.
   4. Usually a few inches a day.
   5. Formed from deep snow.
   6. Slowly turns into ice and begins to move.
   7. Some glaciers reach the ocean.
   8. Big chunks of ice.
   9. May fall off into the ocean.
   10. These huge floating chunks are icebergs.

2b Finding the Complete Subject and the Complete Predicate

The typical simple sentence has just two main parts, the complete subject and the complete predicate. The complete subject is the part that tells what the sentence is about. It usually comes at or near the beginning of the sentence, and it may be one word or many. In each of the following sentences, everything up to the dividing line is the complete subject.

The Lord │ is my shepherd.

I │ shall not want. (Ps. 23:1)

| The word of the Lord | endureth forever. (I Pet. 1:25) |

After the complete subject has been divided off, then the rest of the sentence is the complete predicate (or, "the predicate"). The predicate is the part that tells something about the subject. Notice how that works in the sentences above. What does the first sentence say about the Lord? He *is my shepherd.* What is said about me in the second sentence? I *shall not want.* And what is said about the word of the Lord? It *endures forever.* As you can see, the complete predicate either describes the subject in some way or tells about an action of the subject.

● **Practice 2-2** Check your understanding by dividing the following sentences between the complete subject and the complete predicate.
1. The rainbow reminds us of God's promise in Genesis 9:11-17.
2. Rainbows are produced by sunlight and raindrops.
3. Many drops of water reflect the sun's rays.
4. A bright arch of colors appears in the sky.
5. Every rainbow has the same colors, from true red through violet.

2c Finding the Simple Subject and the Simple Predicate

Whenever a complete subject or a complete predicate consists of several words, it always has a main part—usually just a single word—that is most important. This is easiest to see in the complete subject.

Often the complete subject consists of a main word and other words that tell more about it. The main word is the **simple subject.** (Of course, when the complete subject is just one word or one proper noun, the simple subject and the complete subject are the same.) The underlined words below are the simple subjects:

The <u>Lord</u>	**is** my shepherd.
<u>I</u>	**shall** not **want.**
The <u>word</u> of the Lord	**endureth** forever.

Notice that "the word of the Lord" tells whose *word* it is that endures forever. The simple subject is always part (or all) of the complete subject.

In each sample sentence the word or words in bold print make up the **simple predicate,** more often called the verb (or complete verb). The verb is the foundation stone of the complete predicate. The complete verb can be either a single word (*is, endureth*) or two or more words (*shall want*).

A simple test can help you be sure you have found the simple subject and the simple predicate. In the present tense the verb has different forms depending on whether the subject is singular or plural—that is, whether it stands for one person or thing, or many. To make sure you have made the simple present-tense form, put the words "every day now" in the sentence. Then see whether the present-tense verb changes form according to whether the noun subject is singular or plural. (If the subject is a pronoun or a proper noun, test the verb instead with *he* [or *it*] and *they* as subjects.) Let's try that with the three sentences we have used:

Every day now (he *is,* they *are*) my shepherd(s).
Every day now (he *wants,* they *want*).
Every day now (the word *endures,* the words *endure*).

This change in the present verb form to match singular and plural subjects is called "subject-verb agreement." It happens with every present-tense verb. If the word does not change form in this way, it is not a true verb.

● **Practice 2-3** Check your understanding by finding the complete subjects and predicates and

the simple subjects and predicates in the following
five sentences.
1. Glass has many uses.
2. Glass jars preserve food safely.
3. Bullet-resisting glass can stop even heavy
   bullets.
4. Glass windows admit light.
5. Art objects of fine glass have a special beauty.

2d What Do Sentences Do?

Sentences can be classified by their purpose, that is,
by what they do.

1. *Declarative* sentences make a statement.
   Sam caught the ball.
   He will probably catch the ball again.
2. *Interrogative* sentences ask a question.
   Can Sam catch the ball?
   Why did he catch the ball?
   Who will catch the ball?
   He caught it, didn't he? (tag question)
3. *Imperative* sentences give a command or a
   request.
   Please try to catch the ball.
   Quick, catch the ball!
4. *Exclamatory* sentences exclaim about some-
   thing, expressing strong feeling.
   He actually caught the ball!
   What a catch that was!

You will notice that the end punctuation of these four
types follows a pattern. Declarative sentences always
end with a period, interrogative with a question mark,
and exclamatory with an exclamation mark. Imperative
sentences usually end with a period, although sometimes
one is strong enough to require an exclamation mark.

Chapter 3
The Major Parts of Speech

Sentences are made up of words, but not just any words in any place. In order for our sentences to make sense, we have to put the right kinds of words in the right places. These "kinds of words" are what we call the **parts of speech.** Thinking about the different kinds of words, and learning labels to call them by, is basic to learning something about how our language works.

3a Survey of Major and Minor Parts of Speech

There are two types of parts of speech. First, there are the four very large classes of words that we call *major* parts of speech. Then there are several small but important classes of words, called *minor* parts of speech.

Most of the words in the English language are found in the four **major parts of speech.** The largest group of words is nouns, then verbs, then adjectives, then adverbs.

Major Parts of Speech
(content words)

Nouns
man, house, Ohio, tree, idea
Verbs
return, have, think, be
Adjectives
big, beautiful, blue
Adverbs
well, nicely, now

There are thousands of words in each group, and more can easily be added. New words can be added to these classes by invention, by changing or combining other words, or by taking them from another language. In any complete sentence it is the nouns, verbs, adjectives, and adverbs that carry most of the meaning-content of the sentence. For that reason they can be called "content words."

Notice how much of the meaning of II Timothy 1:7 is contained in the major parts of speech, the words in bold print below.

> "For **God** hath **not given** us the **spirit** of **fear;** but of **power,** and of **love,** and of a **sound mind.** "

We can get some idea of the verse's total meaning from "God not given spirit fear power love sound mind." However, we get very little meaning from "For hath us the of but of and of a ." It is also obvious that we need both kinds of words in order to fully understand the meaning.

In the **minor parts of speech** are fewer words, but they are the necessary words that show how the nouns, verbs, adjectives, and adverbs are related one to another. For example, the verse above does not say, "God has not given a spirit of fear, or power, or love, or a sound mind." It says the very opposite: He *has* given a spirit of power, love, and a sound mind, *instead of* fear. The meaning of the words in the minor parts of speech has less to do with content (things and actions and qualities in the real world) than with grammatical matters (how the content words are related to each other). For that reason they can be called "grammatical words."

Below are both the major and the minor parts of speech, as they are presented in this chapter and the next.

MAJOR (content words)	**MINOR** (grammatical words)
Noun ⟵————————⟶	Pronoun
house, idea	*he, anyone, who*
Verb ⟵————————⟶	Auxiliary
go, think	*may, can, have*
Adjective ⟵————————⟶	Determiner (including the article)
big, beautiful	*the, some, this*
Adverb (modifies verb) ⟵———⟶	Qualifier (modifies adjective and
well, nicely	adverb) *very, almost, too*
	Preposition
	by, into
	Conjunction
	and, because
	Isolate
	oh, please, yes, hello

As indicated by the arrows, each of the first four minor parts of speech is related to one of the major parts of speech. In some texts the major part of speech and the related minor part of speech are grouped together as one part of speech. In this book, however, we try to keep things clear by speaking of them separately. As you will see, in each case there are distinct differences between the minor group and the major group, even

MAJOR PARTS OF SPEECH

NOUN 3b	The name of a person, place, thing, or idea. Can be made plural or possessive or both. (Cannot be made comparative or superlative.)	man, Paul, Chicago, book, water, truth
VERB 3c	A word that expresses action or state of being. Can have form ending in *-ing* and has special form for third-person singular in the present tense.	smile, think, see, be, become
	Fills at least one blank: They will ____ . They will ____ it. They will ____ good.	
ADJECTIVE 3d	A word that usually modifies a noun and that can be made comparative and superlative, using *-er/-est* or *more/most*.	happy, big, faithful, attractive
	Fills both blanks: The ____ thing (person) is very ____ .	
ADVERB 3e	A word that usually modifies a verb. (Some adverbs can be made comparative and superlative.)	soon, slowly, well, now, here, not

though the pairs do have certain things in common. As is explained more fully in the Preface to the Teacher, other approaches to the parts of speech are not necessarily wrong—but they are perhaps less explanatory and less useful.

The major parts of speech are presented in sections **3b** through **3e.** Notice that the major parts of speech can usually be identified by how they change in form as well as by how they are normally used.

MINOR PARTS OF SPEECH

PRONOUN 4a	A word that substitutes for a noun or for an entire noun phrase. (Similar to the noun in some ways.)	we, who, this, someone, himself, which, each, other
AUXILIARY 4b	A word that may join the true verb in making up the complete verb of a sentence. (Similar to the verb in some ways. Could be considered a special type of verb, but in this book is always treated separately.)	will, have, be, can, might
DETERMINER 4c	A word that signals that a noun is coming. Modifies a noun but cannot be made comparative or superlative. Precedes adjectives in the noun phrase. (Similar to the adjective in function. Could be considered a special type of adjective, but in this book is always treated separately.)	the, a, our, this, some, every, first, all
QUALIFIER 4d	A word that usually modifies an adjective or an adverb, either strengthening or weakening its meaning. (Could be considered a special type of adverb, but in this book is always treated separately.)	very, quite, somewhat, too, more, extremely
PREPOSITION 4e	A word that relates its object to another word in the sentence. The object is usually a noun or a pronoun.	at, by, for, from, in, of, within, instead of
CONJUNCTION 4f	A connecting word that joins words or groups of words in a sentence. Includes coordinating and subordinating conjunctions.	and, but, or; because, although
ISOLATE 4g	A word that takes no real part in a sentence. Can sometimes stand alone punctuated as a sentence. Includes interjections and other independent words.	oh, ouch, yes, hello, please

3b Nouns

(1) Identifying the noun
(2) Forms of the noun
(3) Types of nouns
(4) Making nouns

(1) Identifying the noun

Meaning	A noun names a person, place, thing, or idea.
Form	Most nouns can be made plural or possessive or both, by a change in form.
Usual function	Nouns can function (act) in sentences as subjects, direct objects, and so on. (See **6b** on noun functions.)

Example: The *man* laughed heartily.

1. *Man* names a person.
2. *Man* could be made plural, possessive, or both (*men, man's, men's*).
3. *Man* functions as the simple subject of the sentence.

● **Practice 3-1** Find all the nouns in the paragraph below, listing each one only once. This paragraph from John Bunyan's *Pilgrim's Progress* comes soon after Christian's companion Faithful dies for the Lord in the worldly city of Vanity Fair.

Now I saw in my dream that Christian went not forth [from Vanity Fair] alone, for . . . Hopeful . . . joined himself unto him, and . . . told him that he would be his companion. Thus one [person] died to bear testimony to the truth, and another [rose] out of his ashes to be a companion with

Christian in his pilgrimage. This Hopeful also told
Christian that there were many more . . . men
in the fair, that would take their time to follow
after.

(2) Forms of the noun

Most nouns have four possible forms: singular, singular
possessive, plural, and plural possessive.

	Regular		Irregular	
Singular	girl	fox	mouse	child
Singular possessive	girl's	fox's	mouse's	child's
Plural	girls	foxes	mice	children
Plural possessive	girls'	foxes	mice's	children's

Plural indicates that there are two or more of the
thing named by the noun.

Regular plurals	Boy/boys, dish/dishes. See **16b(2)**.
Irregular plurals	Man/men, goose/geese, child/children, alumnus/alumni, stratum/strata, sheep/sheep, etc.

Any irregular form will be part of the entry in a good
dictionary.

Possessive expresses ownership or some kind of "belongingness." The possessive is formed by adding *-'s*
or just an apostrophe, according to the rules of **16c(2.1)**.

● **Practice 3-2** Copy the following box and fill in
the missing forms. Use a dictionary to check
irregular plurals if you need to. The answers are
in the back of the book.

Singular	man			
Singular Possessive			wife's	
Plural		boys		
Plural Possessive				runners'

(3) Types of nouns

(3.1) Common and proper
(3.2) Count and noncount
(3.3) Collective
(3.4) Concrete and abstract

(3.1) Common and proper All nouns are either common or proper.

Common nouns	General words for persons, places, things, or ideas: *person, father, city, apple, truth*
Proper nouns	Specific names for certain persons, places, or things: *Abraham Lincoln, Chicago,* the *White House*

Proper nouns, unlike common nouns, are always capitalized.

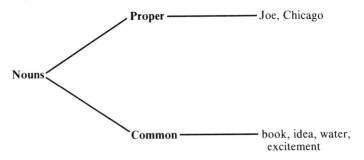

Proper ——————— Joe, Chicago

Nouns

Common ——————— book, idea, water, excitement

(3.2) Count and noncount   Every common noun is either count or noncount.

Count nouns	Can be made plural (can be counted): *the bean, the beans, some beans, five beans, plenty of beans*
Noncount nouns	Cannot be made plural (cannot be counted): *the rice, some rice, plenty of rice*

We cannot say "the rices" or "five rices." If we want to talk about the individual grains, we have to use a phrase like "five grains of rice." In other words, the difference between count and noncount is a difference in how words like *rice* and *bean* are used in sentences, not a matter of whether beans or grains of rice can in fact be counted.

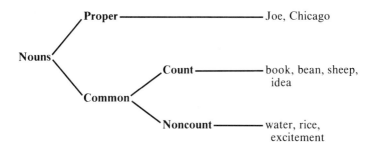

A few words can be used as either count or noncount nouns, but always with a difference in meaning.

As noncount noun	We drank some water (a lot of water, much water).
As count noun	The waitress said, "I need four waters for the last table."

Obviously here the waitress means "four glasses of water," as the rest of us would usually say it. In any one sentence, however, a word is always either definitely a count noun or definitely a noncount noun. Section **11c** explains that certain other words in the sentence are chosen to harmonize with our selection of a count noun or a noncount noun.

- **Practice 3-3** Using the words in bold print below, list four count nouns and three noncount nouns. Check your answers when you have finished.

  The Prator **family** was moving. The moving **van** had already taken their **furniture;** and all that remained was their **luggage,** filled with the things they would need on their **trip** to Maine. They got in the car, slammed the doors, and crunched over the **gravel** of the driveway for the last time. So long, little green **house!**

(3.3) Collective Collective nouns are words like *family* and *jury* that refer to groups. Because a collective noun refers to a group, even when it is singular in form it can be treated as a plural.

Collective noun treated as singular	The jury *has* not yet been dismissed.
Collective noun treated as plural	The jury *were* divided in *their* opinions.

In the first example the focus is on the group as a whole, but in the second it is on the members of the group. (Section **9a(3.2)** deals with collective nouns in subject-verb agreement, and **9b(5)** in pronoun-antecedent agreement.) Collective nouns function like other count nouns except for this one peculiarity.

(3.4) Concrete and abstract All common nouns can be considered either concrete or abstract in meaning.

Concrete nouns	Refer to physical, material things. (Most are count nouns.)
Abstract nouns	Refer to mental, nonmaterial things. (Most are noncount nouns.)

The difference here is just one of meaning; it does not affect how the words are used. This difference applies to both count and noncount nouns.

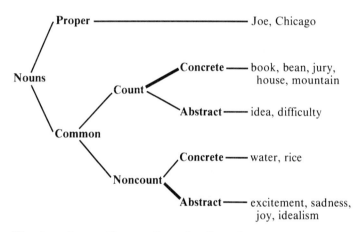

The two heavy lines reflect the fact that most concrete nouns are count nouns and most abstract nouns are noncount nouns.

(4) Making nouns

(4.1) Compounding
(4.2) Using noun-forming suffixes

Some nouns are made from other words.

(4.1) Compounding One way of making nouns is by joining together two or more words to make a new word, called a compound (or "compound noun").

| basketball | (noun + noun) |
| earthquake | (noun + verb) |

crybaby	(verb + noun)
hotspot	(adjective + noun)
cutback	(verb + adverb)
underpass	(adverb + verb)

Many compound nouns are written solid (without hyphens), like the ones above. Others are written with hyphens.

by-product daughter-in-law kilowatt-hour

See **16d(5)** for hyphenated compounds, solid compounds, and open compounds.

(4.2) Using noun-forming suffixes Nouns can be formed by adding suffixes to other words. Some common suffixes are listed below, divided into three general categories according to their meanings.

A person (or thing) that _____s	{ -er	speaker, teacher
	{ -or	sailor, advisor
An act or the result of an act	-ment	appointment, achievement
	{ -ion	action, decision
	{ -ation	formation, relaxation
	{ -ance	admittance, performance
	{ -ence	emergence, dependence
	-y	discovery, inquiry
A quality or a condition	-ness	sadness, happiness
	-ship	companionship, leadership
	-ism	realism, paganism
	-th	warmth, truth, width
	{ -ity	reality, conformity
	{ -ty	loyalty, realty
	-y	difficulty, jealousy

In this list, braces join pairs of suffixes that can be considered just different forms (or different spellings) of the same suffix.

Notice that adding a suffix from this list may change the pronunciation and sometimes the spelling of the basic word (*act* becomes *action; decide* becomes *decision; long* becomes *length*).

3c Verbs

(1) Identifying the verb
(2) Making verbs

(1) Identifying the verb

This section describes true verbs only. See **4b** for auxiliaries.

Meaning	Verbs express action or state of being.
Form	True verbs can take the *-ing* suffix, and they have a special form for the third-person singular in the present tense. He is **being** good, **having** fun, **walking** to school. He **is** good, **has** fun, **walks** to school.
Usual function	A verb is the main word in the predicate of any sentence or clause.
Test frame	Any true verb can fill the blank in at least one of the following test-frame sentences: They will _____ . They will _____ it. They will _____ good. These frame sentences give us the simplest form of the verb, with no suffix. They will **walk.** They will **have** it. They will **be** good.

● **Practice** 3-4 Find the verbs in the following sentences.
1. The cat strolled leisurely across the lawn.
2. The puppy yearned for some activity.
3. He barked loudly in the cat's face.
4. The cat's paw landed firmly on the puppy's nose.
5. He quickly learned a valuable lesson in discretion.

(2) Making verbs

(2.1) Using verb-forming prefixes and suffixes
(2.2) Shifting the accent
(2.3) Compounding

(2.1) Using verb-forming prefixes and suffixes
Certain prefixes and suffixes can turn adjectives and nouns into verbs. (These affixes often have the meaning "to make" or "to produce.")

Verb from adjective	Black**en,** national**ize,** activ**ate**
Verb from noun	Glori**fy, be**friend, **en**rage

(2.2) Shifting the accent We can turn some nouns and adjectives into verbs by shifting the accent to the end of the word or by adding another accent at the end of the word.

| Noun to verb | PERmit ⟹ perMIT |
| | PRESent ⟹ preSENT |

| Adjective to verb | PERfect ⟹ perFECT |
| | SEParate ⟹ SEParATE |

(2.3) Compounding A few verbs are made by combining words: *uproot, overflow, whitewash.*

Types and forms of verbs
See Chapter 7 for further information on verbs.

3d Adjectives

(1) Identifying the adjective
(2) Positions of the adjective
(3) Forms of the adjective
(4) Making adjectives

(1) Identifying the adjective

Function	An adjective is a word that usually modifies a noun. She is a nice person.
Meaning	An adjective adds to the meaning of the noun it modifies.
Form	An adjective can have changes in form to show comparison, normally by using either *-er* and *-est* or *more* and *most*.
	nice beautiful
	nicer more beautiful
	nicest most beautiful

There are a few adjectives, however, that according to logic should not be used in comparisons: how can something be rounder than round? or more perfect than perfect? The structure of the language allows it, but logic does not. In careful writing we should say that one thing is "more nearly perfect" than the other. In addition to *round* and *perfect,* some other common adjectives that should not be compared are *dead, unique, excellent, square,* and *eternal.*

Summary definition	An adjective is a word that (1) usually modifies a noun and (2) can be compared using *-er* and *-est* or *more* and *most.*
Test frame	Any word that fits *both* blanks in this sentence is an adjective: The _____ thing (person) is very _____ .

● **Practice 3-5** Find the adjectives in the following sentences, using the test frame or the summary definition of the adjective.
1. The cold white flakes fluttered to the ground.
2. Small round faces gathered at the windows.
3. Hungry sparrows congregated at the bird feeder.
4. Children slid noisily down the icy hill.
5. Warm soup for lunch simmered on the old stove.

(2) Positions of the adjective

(2.1) The three most common positions
(2.2) Two other adjective positions

(2.1) The three most common positions

Before the noun	Typically, an adjective modifies a following noun.
	     two happy smiles
	     some big, ugly weeds

After the indefinite pronoun	An adjective may also modify a preceding indefinite pronoun.

something nice

nothing better

As a predicate adjective	An adjective can appear in the predicate, after the verb, and yet describe the subject in some way. An adjective in this position is called a predicate adjective, PA. (See **5c** for S LV PA.)

$$\text{S} \quad \text{LV} \quad \text{PA}$$
The art exhibit is popular.

$$\text{S} \quad \text{LV} \quad \text{PA}$$
The paintings look good.

(2.2) Two other adjective positions

After the noun	An adjective that is part of a longer modifying phrase comes after the noun it modifies.

an idea agreeable to all of us

Two adjectives joined by a conjunction can come either before or after the noun.

the tired but happy runner

the runner, tired but happy,

Certain restrictive adjectives can come either before or after the noun.

the necessary money

the money necessary

As an objective complement	An adjective can appear after the direct object, describing the direct object because of the action of the verb. (See **5g** for the sentence pattern S TrV DO OC.)

$$\text{S} \qquad \text{TrV} \qquad\qquad \text{DO} \quad \text{OC}$$
We will paint this room yellow.

(3) Forms of the adjective

(3.1) The meanings of comparative and superlative
(3.2) The forms for comparative and superlative
(3.3) The absolute comparative and superlative

(3.1) The meanings of comparative and superlative

Positive degree—no comparison made.
- John is *tall.*
- I thought I was *observant.*

Comparative degree—comparison of two things.
- John is *taller* than Jack.
- You were *more observant* than I was.

Superlative degree—comparison of three or more.
- Steve is the *tallest* in the class.
- This time Mr. Steptoe was the *most observant.*

(3.2) The forms for comparative and superlative

Some adjectives take -er and -est, and other adjectives take *more* and *most.*

Nearly all one-syllable adjectives are compared with -er and -est.

Positive	Comparative	Superlative
nice	nicer	nicest
tall	taller	tallest
big	bigger	biggest

Also, some two-syllable adjectives take *-er* and *-est,* especially adjectives that end in *-y, -ly,* and *-le:*

busy	busier	busiest
messy	messier	messiest
early	earlier	earliest
friendly	friendlier	friendliest
noble	nobler	noblest
simple	simpler	simplest

Otherwise, you can expect the adjective to be compared with *more* and *most:*

careful	more careful	most careful
famous	more famous	most famous
beautiful	more beautiful	most beautiful

There are some exceptions to these rules. (1) A few adjectives, such as *red* and *common,* can use either *-er/-est* or *more/most.* (2) Some adjectives are irregular. When in doubt, check a dictionary.

good	better	best
bad	worse	worst

● **Practice 3-6** To make sure you know how to form comparatives and superlatives, write down the comparative form that would go in the blank of each sentence below. Then check your answers.
1. This one was early, but that one was _____ .
2. This one is practical, but that one is _____ .
3. This one is bad, but that one is _____ .
4. This one is helpful, but that one is _____ .
5. This one is dirty, but that one is _____ .

● **Practice 3-7** In this practice exercise you can see whether you know when to use the three degrees of the adjective. For each blank write down the correct form of the adjective given.

The lime is a green citrus fruit related to the lemon. However, it is *(1)* _____ than the lemon. The lime grows on a fairly *(2)* _____ tree native to southeast Asia. Limes, like other citrus fruits, are *(3)* _____ in vitamin C. They also have a *(4)* _____ flavor. Many people think that a creamy lime pie is *(5)* _____ than lemon cream pie. And have you ever tried limeade? Some people think it is the *(6)* _____ drink there is.

1. small	3. rich	5. good
2. short	4. tangy	6. refreshing

(3.3) The absolute comparative and superlative
The comparative and the superlative are sometimes used in an "absolute" sense—that is, without any intention of specific comparison to other things.

Absolute comparative (mostly a few set phrases)	My cousin, who teaches college English, has always been involved in *higher education*. (There is no phrase "high education" for the level just before college.)
Absolute superlative for emphasis	He gave me the *strangest look*. (No comparison intended, just the meaning "a very strange look.")

Although the absolute superlative is perfectly legitimate, when written it is likely to be misunderstood for normal comparison with something unnamed. For that reason it should be used in written material only with caution. And in a sentence like "She wore the most beautiful dress yesterday," the emphasis of the absolute superlative can easily become a gushy overemphasis.

(4) Making adjectives

(4.1) Compounding
(4.2) Using adjective-forming suffixes

Although many adjectives are simple words like *big* and *small,* some adjectives are made from other words.

(4.1) Compounding Two or more words can be joined to make a single adjective (a compound word).

$$\underset{}{\text{She bought a }\underline{\text{waterproof}}\overset{\text{S LV}}{\underline{\text{jacket}}}\text{, but it was not}}$$

very $\underset{\text{PA}}{\underline{\text{waterproof}}}$.

A $\underline{\text{wedge-shaped}}$ piece of cheese was served with the

apple pie. The $\overset{\text{S}}{\underline{\text{piece}}}$ of pie $\overset{\text{LV}}{\underline{\text{was}}}$ also $\overset{\text{PA}}{\underline{\text{wedge-shaped}}}$.

In these examples the spelling remains the same whether the compound word is used before the noun or as a predicate adjective.

With some compounds, however, the position makes a difference.

We waited for an $\underline{\text{up-to-date}}$ weather report, but

not even the radio station was $\underline{\text{up to date}}$ on the

storm.

When a compound adjective is used before a noun, its parts must always be joined in some way. That principle is the reason for the hyphens in "an up-to-date weather report." However, if the strongest accent inside the hyphenated compound changes position when the compound becomes a predicate adjective, often the hyphens can then be dropped.

The $\underline{\text{UP-to-date}}$ report was not really $\underline{\text{up to DATE}}$.

(4.2) Using adjective-forming suffixes Many adjectives are made from other words by the use of certain suffixes.

One common adjective-forming suffix has two spellings, *-able* and *-ible*. These two spellings are normally pronounced the same way, so we must learn the spelling for each word.

	-able spelling	*-ible* spelling
Added to verbs: "capable of"	avoidable enviable breakable	collapsible collectible
Added to nouns: "inclined to, tending toward"	peaceable comfortable fashionable	sensible

The adjective-forming suffixes listed below almost always make adjectives out of nouns.

"charac-terized by"	-ful	peaceful, powerful, joyful, beautiful
	-ous	poisonous, envious, glorious; covetous
	-y	messy, cloudy, dirty, icy, lumpy; jumpy
"charac-teristic of"	-ish	childish, boyish, foolish, mulish
	-ly	manly, womanly, friendly, heavenly
"made of"	-en	wooden, silken, earthen, woolen
"not having"	-less	sleepless, penniless, blameless

Notice that when a final *y* follows a consonant in the source word, it changes to *i* before several of these suffixes (*envy* + *able* = *enviable*).

Remember that these suffixes are used to make certain adjectives in the first place. Then when we have these "made" adjectives, we can add *-er/-est* or *more/ most* to make the comparative and superlative forms— just as we do for simple adjectives like *nice:*

Positive	Comparative	Superlative
nice	nic-*er*	nic-*est*
cloud-y	cloud-i-*er*	cloud-i-*est*
fool-ish	*more* foolish	*most* foolish

3e Adverbs

(1) Identifying the adverb
(2) Common positions of the adverb
(3) Some meanings of the adverb
(4) Forms of the adverb
(5) Making adverbs
(6) Verb-adverb combinations
(7) Special types of adverbs

(1) Identifying the adverb

Adverbs are best defined by function.

Function	An adverb is a word that usually modifies a verb.
Meaning	The adverb normally adds information about the action or state of being expressed by the verb. (See **3e(3)** for adverbial meanings.)

Form	There is no consistent adverb form. Many adverbs end in *-ly,* but so do some adjectives, like *manly.* *

See "Qualifiers," section **4d,** for most modifiers of adjectives and adverbs.

(2) Common positions of the adverb

Adverbs are usually movable in the sentence, some adverbs more so than others. Here are four of their frequent positions:

After the verb (and direct object, if any)	He will come *soon.* She will answer the question *soon.*
Between auxiliary and verb	He will *soon* come.
Before the complete verb	He *soon* will come.
Beginning the sentence	*Soon* he will come.

This mobility can often help you recognize adverbs.

(3) Some meanings of the adverb

(3.1) Basic meanings
(3.2) Two additional meanings

---

* Adjective + *-ly* = adverb. Noun + *-ly* = adjective.

(3.1) Basic meanings

Manner (including extent and number)—slowly, well, somehow; completely, almost, even; once, twice

Place (including direction and order)—here, below, outside, somewhere, everywhere, nowhere; down, northward; first, second

Time (including frequency)—now, later, sometime, never; often, usually, seldom, sometimes

Negative only (pure negative meaning)—not

A sentence can have several adverbs, often with each one coming from a different meaning group.

              (manner) (place) (time)
  The rescue team worked slowly here yesterday.

If two adverbs from a single group are used, usually they are joined with *and:*

    (time)   (manner)
Yesterday and today the rescue team *carefully and*
              (place)
slowly worked *inside and outside.*

● **Practice 3-8** See how many adverbs you can find in this paragraph. (Look only for actual adverbs, not adverbial prepositional phrases.) Then classify the adverbs according to the four basic meaning groups.

    Astronaut Scott Carpenter peered silently out the window of the spacecraft. Earlier he had been constantly involved with the control of his ship, but now he had time for observation. He had already seen his jettisoned escape tower zip away "like a scalded cat." When he looked around, he could clearly see "little rosettes or clustered circles of fair-weather cumulus" clouds between him and the earth. He was awed by the view. He could not even guess at the miles that fell within the range of his vision. Everywhere he looked, he was deeply moved by the loveliness of the world beneath him.

(3.2) Two additional meanings

> Result and logical conclusion—therefore,
> accordingly, consequently, hence, thus
> Cause—why

Adverbs of result and logical conclusion are frequently useful, especially for the writer who is explaining a process or a logical concept.

> The voltage regulator shorted out and did not allow the battery to be charged properly. *Consequently,* the battery went bad too.

Cause is rarely expressed by one-word adverbs, though it is a common meaning for adverbial prepositional phrases and dependent clauses. *Why* is the only common adverb of cause.

> *Why* did that happen? There was a reason *why* the car wouldn't start yesterday.

(4) Forms of the adverb

Some adverbs have no change in form at all, but others have the same changes for comparison that adjectives have. Most dictionaries give you help as to whether to use *-er* and *-est* or *more* and *most.* One reliable rule is that adverbs made from adjectives by the addition of *-ly* always take *more* and *most,* never *-er* and *-est.*

Positive	Comparative	Superlative
He walked . . .		
soon	sooner	(the) soonest
fast	faster	(the) fastest
often	more often	(the) most often
carefully	more carefully	(the) most carefully
happily	more happily	(the) most happily

One common adverb is irregular:

well	better	(the) best

Section **3d(3.1)** tells how to use the comparative and superlative degrees.

(5) Making adverbs

Although many adverbs are simple words like *here* and *above,* some adverbs are made from other words. Most of these are made by adding *-ly* to the adjective.

> A careful person does things *carefully.*
> A prompt person does things *promptly.*
> An immediate answer comes *immediately.*
> A special case is one treated *specially.*

Adverbs made with *-ly* are so common that most *-ly* words turn out to be adverbs. However, we cannot state this as a rule because there are also some *-ly* adjectives; see **3e(1).**

Besides *-ly,* here are two other adverb-forming suffixes:

-ward or *-wards* "in a certain direction"	Added to nouns: *skyward, earthward, northward, northwards*
	Added to words that are already adverbs: *outward, upward, backwards*
-wise "in the direction, position, or manner of"	Usually added to nouns: *clockwise, slantwise, fanwise*

The *-wise* suffix is questionable when it has the more general meaning "with reference to, or concerning" (*saleswise, moneywise, attendancewise*). Words like these are generally considered to be awkward and overused. They are also frequently unclear:

> Mr. Brown is teacherwise pretty smart.
> (smart for a teacher? smarter than most other teachers? smart in the things teachers know about? smart in the way he teaches?)

How much better to think through the exact meaning and then say it: "Mr. Brown is one of the smartest teachers at my school."

(6) Verb-adverb combinations

(6.1) Recognizing the construction
(6.2) Style: placing the adverb

(6.1) Recognizing the construction Sometimes it seems hard to tell an adverb from a preposition when a noun follows. For instance, notice the two uses of *in* in the two sentences below.

He turned in the street.
He turned in his paper.

The first sentence contains a prepositional phrase.

```
   S   InV
He turned in the strcct.
```

Where did he turn? In the street.

The second sentence contains a verb-adverb combination, *turn in,* meaning "submit."

```
   S   TrV  (Adv)    DO
He turned in his paper.
```

What did he turn IN? His paper.

A verb-adverb combination (VAC) is made up of two words, a verb and a following adverb. The two words often work together to produce a meaning different from the meanings of the two words alone.

back up ("support")	bring about ("cause to happen")
break off ("put an end to")	look over ("inspect casually")

English is rich in such combinations. Many of them express briefly a concept that might otherwise sound complicated.

The two words of a VAC appear either (1) together in the sentence or (2) with the adverb moved to a position right after the direct object. The best way to tell the difference between a verb-adverb combination and a verb followed by a prepositional phrase is to apply the

Movement Test: the adverb of a VAC can be moved so that it comes after the direct object.

Original sentence	S TrV DO He *turned in* his paper yesterday.
Movement Test applied	S TrV DO ADV He *turned* his paper *in* yesterday. S TrV DO He *turned* it *in* yesterday.*
Conclusion	Since *in* can be moved, *turn in* is a verb-adverb combination.

If the sentence cannot pass the Movement Test without a change of meaning, the word in question is a preposition, not an adverb.

- **Practice 3-9** Some of the following sentences contain verb-adverb combinations and direct objects. The others contain verbs followed by prepositional phrases. Use the Movement Test to find the sentences that have verb-adverb combinations. For each of these write down the verb and the adverb.
  1. We called to the children.
  2. He called off the meeting.
  3. The manager looked for a better solution.
  4. Let's look beside the house.
  5. Did you look up the word in the dictionary?
  6. My mother makes up good stories.
  7. Have you filled out the form?
  8. She went into the matter fully.
  9. The children went into the house before dark.
  10. According to I Corinthians 6:7 and 8:13, we should sometimes give up our rights.

  (6.2) Style: placing the adverb As explained above in **3e(6.1),** the adverb of a verb-adverb combination can be moved so that it follows the direct object.

---

* The adverb of a VAC *must* follow any direct object that is a personal pronoun.

However, if the complete direct object is very long, the sentence will sound better with the adverb next to the verb.

Possible but awkward	Yesterday he *turned* the very first term paper of his life *in*.
Better	Yesterday he *turned in* the very first term paper of his life.

Sometimes even with a relatively short noun phrase as direct object, the sentence still sounds better with the VAC adverb next to the verb.

Acceptable	Last week they *drew* a new contract *up*.
Better	Last week they *drew up* a new contract.

Notice that *up* sounds rather weak at the end of the sentence. Section **9h(3)** gives more information about how to end a sentence strongly.

• **Practice 3-10**   Write the six different verb-adverb combinations in this passage. (One of them is used twice.) Then improve the two sentences in which the VAC adverb sounds awkward after the direct object.

Ray Daniels, the executive vice president, was talking to a group of his managers.

"I believe we can bring some changes about in the morale of our workers. I recently found out that several production-line people believe we are interested only in output, and not in them. I found that out by using comment sheets.

"All the production-line workers filled one of the comment sheets out last week. They turned the papers in today, anonymously. Nearly twenty percent feel that we are interested in nothing but productivity.

"Now how can we put a better attitude toward them across? In my opinion, first we must think our attitudes through and make sure that we really do care about our employees."

(7) Special types of adverbs

	Modifies the Verb in—	Does What—	Examples
Interrogative adverb	Direct or indirect question	Asks the question	*When* did he leave? She asked *when* he left. (*when, where, how*)
Conjunctive adverb	Independent clause	By its meaning serves as a link to another independent clause	I'd like to go. *However,* I have some work to do.
Relative adverb	Adjective clause	Introduces a clause that modifies a noun of time, place, or reason	This is the time [*when* anyone can enter]. See **8a(1.2).** (*when, where, why*)
Indefinite relative adverb	Noun clause	Introduces the noun clause, has no definite antecedent (means "the time when" etc.)	I know [*when* it happened]. (*when, where, why, how*)

See **9e(5)** for examples of conjunctive adverbs. All of the single words in the last column there (except *to*) can act as conjunctive adverbs.

Chapter 4

The Minor Parts of Speech

4a Pronouns
4b Auxiliaries
4c Determiners
4d Qualifiers
4e Prepositions
4f Conjunctions
4g Isolates

Peaches and pears are about as similar as the major parts of speech and the minor parts of speech. Both peaches and pears are fruit, but hardly the same kind of fruit. You may remember that the major parts of speech—nouns, verbs, adjectives, and adverbs—include many thousands of words each. These are the words that carry most of the meaning of what we say. The minor parts of speech, however, are much smaller groups of words. These words mainly show how the nouns, verbs, adjectives, and adverbs are related to each other in the sentence. Section **3a** explains the differences more fully and summarizes all the parts of speech in a two-page table.

Even in a sentence we can often recognize the major parts of speech by their form; but we recognize the minor parts of speech like prepositions and conjunctions by the way they are used, and often by knowing the words themselves. Therefore the definition section for each minor part of speech deals with its function in the sentence. Then, usually under subtypes of the part of speech, the actual words are listed and explained.

4a Pronouns

(1) Definition of the pronoun
(2) Personal pronouns
(3) Two problems related to personal pronouns
(4) Interrogative pronouns
(5) Demonstrative pronouns
(6) Indefinite pronouns
(7) Reflexive pronouns
(8) Intensive pronouns
(9) Relative pronouns
(10) Reciprocal pronouns

(1) Definition of the pronoun

Pronouns are usually said to be substitutes for nouns. However, there is more to the story.

A pronoun is a word that substitutes for a noun or for an entire noun phrase.

For example, here we substitute the pronoun *he* for an entire noun phrase:

The energetic old man walked up to the desk, and then *he* asked to see the manager.

As substitutes for noun phrases, pronouns can be used in the various ways that full noun phrases can be— as subjects, direct objects, and so on.

See the accompanying table for an overview of the types of pronouns.

TYPES OF PRONOUNS

	Examples	Functions	Samples of Use
Personal pronouns 4a(2)	I (me, my, mine) we (us, our, ours) *etc.*	Show person and number	*We* gave Ranger a rabies shot today. *I* don't think Fluffy has had *hers* yet.
Interrogative pronouns 4a(4)	who (whom, whose)? what? which?	Ask questions	*Who* was that, and *what* did he want? *Which* is the best?
Demonstrative pronouns 4a(5)	this, these that, those	Point out something	*This* is my father's latest carpentry project, and *that* is his favorite.
Indefinite pronouns 4a(6)	someone, anything, everyone, each, nothing, none, *etc.*	Convey indefinite or general meaning	*Everyone* should learn to do *something* well. *Nothing* is as attractive as cheerfulness.
Reflexive pronouns 4a(7)	myself, yourself, himself, themselves, *etc.*	Show that an object refers to the same person as the subject	Can you see *yourself* in the water? Ethel did not call attention to *herself*.
Intensive pronouns 4a(8)	myself, yourself, himself, themselves, *etc.*	Emphasize (intensify) a preceding noun or pronoun	Have you ever spoken with the teacher *herself* about that? Jeff *himself* cleaned up the mess. (Jeff cleaned up the mess *himself*.)
Relative pronouns 4a(9)	who (whom, whose) which, that	Relate a dependent clause to the main clause	Everyone appreciates Jeff, *who* is always ready to help. This is the gift *that* Mary gave.
Reciprocal pronouns 4a(10)	each other one another	Express a mutual relationship	Those brothers really like *each other*. We'll need to keep track of *one another* at the mall.

All pronouns are substitutes for nouns or noun phrases.

(2) Personal pronouns

(2.1) Person
(2.2) Number
(2.3) Gender
(2.4) Case
(2.5) The archaic second-person pronouns
(2.6) Correct use of pronoun case

Of the various types of pronouns, the most common are the personal pronouns: *I, we, you, he, she, it,* and *they,* along with their other forms. These pronouns are called "personal" because they are divided into three grammatical persons.

Below are the four characteristics of personal pronouns. Person, number, and gender distinguish each personal pronoun from the others, and case describes the form of the pronoun.

(2.1) Person Every personal pronoun is classified by whether it is first, second, or third person.

First person	The speaker (*I*), or the speaker and others (*we*)
Second person	The person or persons spoken to (*you*)
Third person	Any other person or thing (*he, she, it, they*)

Because the third-person pronouns are the ones that substitute for most nouns in sentences, we sometimes speak of nouns as being in the third person also.

(2.2) Number Personal pronouns have singular and plural number.

Singular	Refers to one person or thing
Plural	Refers to more than one person or thing

Combining the three persons and the two numbers gives us a basic six-way division for personal pronouns:

	Singular	*Plural*
First person	I	we
Second person	you	you
Third person	he/she/it	they

(2.3) **Gender** Three genders differentiate the third-person singular pronouns *he, she,* and *it.*

Masculine gender	Normally refers to males (*he*)
Feminine gender	Normally refers to females (*she*)
Neuter gender	Normally refers to things (*it*)

As suggested by the word *normally,* the gender pronouns do not always follow the simple rules above. Certain animals, like pets, are usually referred to as *he* or *she,* but insects and other animals like frogs are usually called *it.* Also, the neuter *it* is sometimes used for infants. On the other hand, countries, ships, and certain other things can be referred to by the feminine pronoun.

(2.4) **Case** Case is the form of a noun or pronoun that reflects the way the noun or pronoun is used in the sentence. Although nouns have only two case forms—common case (like *boy* or *boys*) and possessive case (like *boy's* or *boys'*)—pronouns have three cases.

Subjective case	Used mainly for *subjects* of sentences.

Subjective

I	we
you	you
he/she/it	they

Objective case	Used mainly for *objects:* direct objects, indirect objects, and objects of prepositions.

Objective

me	us
you	you
him/her/it	them

Possessive case	Used to show *possession.* There are two types: • Determiners (modifiers) It was *her* idea. • Independent possessives S *Hers* was the best idea. I like DO *yours,* too.

Possessive Determiners

my	our
your	your
his/her/its	their

Independent Possessives

mine	ours
yours	yours
his/hers/its	theirs

When we combine all of these characteristics—person, number, gender, and case—we are able to account for all the personal pronouns and their forms.

		Subjective	Objective	Possessive Det.	Indep.
Singular					
First person		I	me	my	mine
Second person		you	you	your	yours
Third person	M	he	him	his	his
	F	she	her	her	hers
	N	it	it	its	its
Plural					
First person		we	us	our	ours
Second person		you	you	your	yours
Third person		they	them	their	theirs

(2.5) The archaic second-person pronouns Partly because of the continued influence of the 1611 King James Version of the Bible, it is traditional in many groups to use the older pronouns *thou, thee, thy,* and *thine* in addressing God in prayer.

	Archaic second-person singular	Example
Subjective	thou	*Thou* art my help.
Objective	thee	We love *Thee,* O Lord.
Possessive	thy (Det.)	*Thy* will be done.
	thine (Indep.)	*Thine* be the glory.

These pronouns are called archaic because they are no longer in general use. The subject *thou* is used with archaic verb forms: *art, wast, hast, givest,* and so on.

Today in prayer we might use the possessives *thy* and *thine* in the same way as we use *my* and *mine*—with *thy* as a modifier (determiner) and *thine* as an independent possessive, as illustrated above. However, in older English there was an additional complication for both *my/mine* and *thy/thine.*

	First person	*Second person*
Determiner before a vowel sound	*mine* eyes	*thine* eyes
Determiner before a consonant sound	*my* will	*thy* will
Independent possessive	It is *mine.*	It is *thine.*

Examples can be found in the 1611 version of the Bible, in the works of Shakespeare and other writers of the Early Modern English period (1500-1660), and even in many of the hymns we use today.

The pronouns discussed above are singular pronouns. In the King James Version *thou, thee, thy,* and *thine* are always singular. They show that the speaker was talking to just one person. They contrast with the plural pronouns *ye, you, your,* and *yours.*

	Early Modern English second-person plural	*Example*
Subjective	ye	*Ye* are my friends.
Objective	you	I have called *you* .
Possessive	your (Det.)	For *your* sakes I said it.
	yours (Indep.)	All are *yours.*

Notice that the old subject form was *ye,* not *you.*

(2.6) Correct use of pronoun case The correct case of a pronoun is determined by its use in its own sentence or clause. In the following list, the simplest and most important principles appear first.

You and *it* do not have different subjective and objective case forms, but the correct forms of the other personal pronouns appear in the illustrations for the first and fifth rules below.

Rule 1. Use the subjective case for subjects, and the objective case for objects.

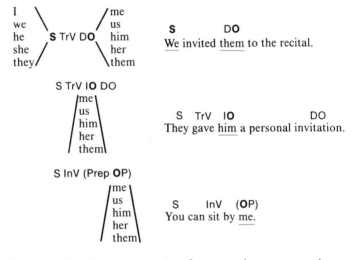

I		me
we		us
he	S TrV DO	him
she		her
they		them

S   DO
We invited them to the recital.

S TrV IO DO
me
us
him
her
them

S   TrV   IO   DO
They gave him a personal invitation.

S InV (Prep OP)
me
us
him
her
them

S   InV   (OP)
You can sit by me.

Rule 2. Use the same rules for case in constructions with conjunctions as in simple constructions.

S   DO
He and **I** invited John and **her** to the recital.

IO
We gave you and **him** personal invitations from

OP
Sam and **me** .

- **Practice 4-1** Choose the correct pronoun forms, based on rules 1 and 2.

1. (He, Him) and George planned an extensive campaign.
2. The race for the office of treasurer was between Tom and (I, me).
3. The votes were counted by Mr. Miller and (she, her).
4. We gave Brad and (he, him) a rousing ovation.

Rule 3. Determine the case of an appositive according to the function of the renamed word.

      S   (App)
The two of us, Joe and **I,** handed out programs.

     S   (App)
No one, not even **I,** expected a crowd as large
as that.

                        O P   (App)
A prize was given to the winners, Todd and **her,**
at the end.

● **Practice 4-2** Choose the correct pronoun forms.
1. We three, James Madison, John Jay, and (I, me), were largely responsible for the ratification of the Constitution.
2. My closest friend was George Washington. I gave my political help and friendship to two leaders of the American Revolution, Lafayette and (he, him).
3. Anyone honorable, especially (I, me), Alexander Hamilton, would put moral principles above political convenience.

Rule 4. Disregard an appositive noun that follows a pronoun. The case of the pronoun is not affected by the presence of an appositive.

   S (App)   S
We boys worked there last Saturday.   (*we* worked)

                         DO (App)
"Have you ever watched *us* experts?" he asked
                       DO
teasingly.   (watched *us*)

● **Practice 4-3** Choose the correct pronoun forms.
1. (We, Us) boys visited New York last spring.
2. Do you boys wonder who it is that (we, us) girls appreciate?
3. Have you ever watched (we, us) players at practice?
4. (We, Us) students taught ceramics in the elementary art classes yesterday.

Rule 5. In formal English, use the subjective case for a pronoun in predicate-noun position. (Informally, especially in speech, the objective case is frequently used.)

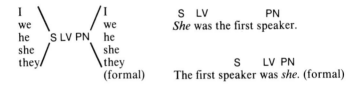

Remember that a linking verb is like an equal sign. In formal English it always has the same case after it as before it.

● **Practice 4-4** Choose the correct formal pronoun forms.
1. I wonder if it was (she, her) who first noticed the error.
2. I observed that it was (they, them) who were always late to class.
3. If the loser last year was (he, him), he certainly has improved.

Rule 6. Use the subjective-case pronouns *who* and *whoever* for subjects.

	S
Interrogative pronoun	*Who* heard the weather report?
Relative pronoun	I know the person [*who* heard the weather report].

All that matters is the function of *who* within its own clause, not how the whole clause is used.

$$\overset{\text{S \quad TrV \quad DO}}{\text{He found out } [who \text{ heard } it \,].}$$

Rule 7. In formal English, use the objective-case pronouns *whom* and *whomever* for objects. (Informally, *who* is often used instead of *whom* at the beginning of a question.)

Interrogative*	^{DO} *Whom* did you see?
	^{OP} To *whom* did you give it?
Relative	^{DO} He is the person [*whom* / *that* you saw].
	^{OP} He is the one [to *whom* you gave it].

In written use of English, *whom* is the proper objective-case pronoun.

● **Practice 4-5** Choose the correct pronoun forms, based on rules 6 and 7.

1. I met a man (who, whom) had lived in Greenland.
2. Can you imagine someone (who, whom) would choose to live on an island that is eighty percent ice?
3. Greenlanders are people (who, whom) obtain most of their wealth from the sea.
4. To (who, whom) does Greenland belong?
5. The country of Denmark makes the laws for the Eskimos and others (who, whom) live on this largest island in the world.

Rule 8. Ignore parenthetical expressions like *do you think, I believe,* or *did they say* when you determine the function and case of *who/whom.*

---

* *Informal speech:* Who did you see? Who did you give it to?

$\overset{\text{S}}{Who}$ $\underset{\text{TrV}}{[\text{do you think}]}$ $\overset{\text{DO}}{\text{won}}$ the election ?

$\overset{\text{DO}}{Whom}$ $[\overset{\text{S}}{\text{did they say}}]\overset{\text{TrV}}{\text{he saw}}$?

He's the one $\left[\overset{\text{S}}{who}\left[\overset{\text{LV PA}}{\text{I feel}}\right]\text{is best}\right]$.

- **Practice 4-6** Choose the correct pronoun forms.
  1. (Who, Whom) do you think is the author of *The Old Man and the Sea?*
  2. Santiago is one hero (who, whom), in my opinion, is truly tragic.
  3. The boy is someone (who, whom) I feel the old man really liked.
  4. He is also the one, I believe, (who, whom) could have helped Santiago succeed.
  5. This novel about a determined old fisherman was written by Ernest Hemingway, (who, whom) I think won a Nobel Prize.

Rule 9. In a comparison, determine the correct case of the pronoun after *than* or *as* according to how the pronoun would function in the full understood clause.

He did better than *I.* $\quad$ $(\text{than } \overset{\text{S InV}}{I} \text{ did})$

You watched Billy more than *me.* $\quad$ $(\text{than } \overset{\text{S}}{\text{you}} \overset{\text{TrV}}{\text{watched}} \overset{\text{DO}}{me})$

Are you as tall as *he?* $\quad$ $(\text{as } \overset{\text{S}}{he} \overset{\text{LV PA}}{\text{is tall}})$

- **Practice 4-7** Choose the correct pronoun forms.
  1. Are you as industrious as (he, him)?
  2. The teacher was shorter than (he, him).
  3. The new girl finished the assignment more quickly than (I, me).
  4. The other team guarded our center more closely than (I, me).

Rule 10. Use the possessive case for the "subject" (doer) of a gerund.

Gerund modified by possessive doer word	*Joe's* singing has improved. ^{S} Were you surprised by *my* cleaning the ^{OP} house?

Do not confuse this construction with the one in which a participle modifies a preceding noun or pronoun.

Participle modifying the doer	Did you see *me* cleaning the house? ^{DO}

The earlier question asked whether the *cleaning* was a surprise. This one asks, "Did you see *me*?"

If the verbal with *-ing* functions like a noun (S, DO, OP, etc.), it is a gerund. The doer pronoun before it, if there is one, should therefore be possessive.

● **Practice 4-8** Choose the correct pronoun forms.
1. Were you impressed by (my, me) singing a solo?
2. (Her, She) laughing is a pleasant sound.
3. I wonder if (he, his) playing has improved.
4. (Him, His) winning the contest is proof of that.

Rule 11. Use the objective case for the "subject" (doer) of the infinitive.

Do you want *us* to sing?
They told *Joe and me* to go ahead.

Objects of infinitives, like all other objects, are also in the objective case.

I want to see *him.*	(direct object of infinitive)
He told me to give *her* the book.	(indirect object of infinitive)

Rule 12. Use the same case after a linking-verb infinitive as before it. That is, a pronoun in predicate-noun position after a linking-verb infinitive should have the same case as the earlier word that it renames.

● A pronoun that renames the subject of the main verb should be subjective in formal English.

⌐———— LV ———⌐
That had to be *he*.

- A pronoun that renames the subject of the infinitive should be objective.

⌐———————— LV ———⌐
Everyone believed the winner to be *him*.

⌐———— LV ———⌐
They thought me to be *her*.

Such constructions, however, may sound awkward. When they do, the sentences can be revised.

That had to be Joe.
Everyone thought he was the winner.
They mistook me for her.

- **Practice 4-9** Choose the correct pronoun forms on the basis of rules 11 and 12. Then you may rewrite any sentence that sounds awkward to you.
1. Did he invite (we, us) to join him?
2. The teacher asked Charles and (I, me) to collect the papers.
3. The next speaker has to be (she, her).
4. I thought it was anticlimactic to give (he, him) the award.
5. No one imagined the loser to be (she, her).

(3) Two problems related to personal pronouns

(3.1) Double subjects
(3.2) Courtesy order of pronouns

(3.1) Double subjects Do not use a phrase like *Joe he* as a subject. Let your pronouns replace nouns, not trail along after them.

| Double subject | Joe he told me to come. |

Either the pronoun or the noun should be omitted:

| Corrected | Joe told me to come. |
| | He told me to come. |

Usually it is the pronoun that is unnecessary.

(3.2) Courtesy order of pronouns Two rules of courtesy govern the order for joining personal pronouns to other pronouns or to nouns.

1. Always mention yourself last. That is, always put the first-person pronoun last.

Say this—	*Not this—*
Jackie and I will . . .	I and Jackie will . . .
Between you and me . . .	Between me and you . . .

2. Unless the emphasis of your sentence suggests otherwise, put the second-person pronoun *you* before third-person pronouns or nouns. The courtesy here is the mention of your hearer before anyone else.

We usually say—	*Rather than—*
You and she could . . .	She and you could . . .
You and Bob were . . .	Bob and you were . . .
I'll go with you or Sue.	I'll go with Sue or you.

In summary, put yourself last, and put your hearer first.

(4) Interrogative pronouns

There are three basic interrogative pronouns:

who (whom, whose)
what
which

Interrogative pronouns ask a question whose answer would be a noun or a pronoun. They may be used in direct or indirect questions.

> *Who* will speak at the meeting tonight?
> She asked *what* he will talk about.

Sometimes, for special emphasis, *-ever* is added to the basic interrogative pronoun:

> Why, Tom! *Whoever* told you that?
> Oh, no, surely not—*whatever* made you think so?

● **Practice 4-10** Pick out the interrogative pronouns in the following sentences from the Bible. Some sentences have more than one interrogative pronoun, and some have none. Apply both of these tests: (1) Is it interrogative?—does it ask a question? (2) Is it a pronoun?—does it stand alone in place of a noun?

1. Whom shall I send, and who will go for us? (Isa. 6:8a)
2. Why do the heathen rage? (Ps. 2:1a)
3. Where the word of a king is, there is power: and who may say unto him, What doest thou? (Eccles. 8:4)
4. What man is he that feareth the Lord? (Ps. 25:12a)
5. Then there arose a reasoning among them, which of them should be greatest. (Luke 9:46)
6. Which of you convinceth me of sin? And if I say the truth, why do ye not believe me? (John 8:46)
7. Whose is this image and superscription? (Matt. 22:20b)

(5) Demonstrative pronouns

There are two singular demonstrative pronouns, *this* and *that,* each with its own plural form.

	Singular	*Plural*
Near	this	these
Far	that	those

A demonstrative pronoun "points out" the position of whatever it refers to. *This* and *these* stand for things that are near in space or time; and *that* and *those* stand for things that are farther away.

> *This* is the week when Grandma will come.

> *That* was a good visit we had last month.

These words are pronouns only when they replace nouns, not when they are modifiers. (When they modify nouns, they are determiners.)

- **Practice 4-11** Pick out the demonstrative pronouns in the following sentences. Some sentences have none.
  1. Look at that!
  2. That building has a snowman on top of it.
  3. This has been a cold winter.
  4. Do you like these flowers?
  5. These are nice, but those are better.

(6) Indefinite pronouns

When we want to speak in general terms, we often use indefinite pronouns.

> *Someone* knocked at the door.

> *Anyone* is welcome.

The indefinite pronouns may be classified according to whether they are singular or plural.

Always singular	Someone, anyone, everyone, no one; somebody, anybody, everybody, nobody; something, anything, everything, nothing; either, neither, another, each, one, much, little, less
Always plural	Many, several, both, few, fewer
Singular or plural	Some, any, more, most, all, none

Knowing whether an indefinite pronoun is singular or plural can be important both for subject-verb agreement (see **9a**) and for pronoun-antecedent agreement (see **9b**). Section **9a(3.3)** gives the special rule for the indefinite pronouns (and certain other words) that may be singular or plural.

Indefinite pronouns are different from nouns in several ways. Nouns, but not indefinite pronouns, can be made plural and can be preceded by determiners and adjectives. (We do not say "anybodies" or "a nice anybody.") However, sometimes one of these words can be used as a noun: "She thinks he's *an absolute nobody*." "We brought *the good ones*."

● **Practice 4-12** Find the indefinite pronouns in the following sentences. Be sure that you choose only pronouns, not modifiers.

1. Everyone that is of the truth heareth my voice. (John 18:37c)
2. Many are called, but few are chosen. (Matt. 22:14)
3. Son, thou art ever with me, and all that I have is thine. (Luke 15:31)
4. For if a man think himself to be something, when he is nothing, he deceiveth himself. (Gal. 6:3)

(7) Reflexive pronouns

Personal pronouns with *-self* or *-selves* added are called **compound personal pronouns.** They have two main uses, reflexive and intensive.

The **reflexive** pronouns are the *-self* pronouns used as objects (or sometimes as predicate nouns), but always referring to the same person or thing as the subject.

Direct object	Susan hurt *herself* on the sharp corner of the table.
Indirect object	John gave *himself* a haircut.
Object of preposition	We listened to *ourselves* on the tape recorder.

A reflexive pronoun is occasionally used in the predicate-noun position, usually in the idiom "to be oneself," meaning to act naturally:

If you will just be *yourself,* you will get along better.

Below is a table of the correct forms of the compound personal pronouns, whether they are reflexive or intensive.

	Singular	*Plural*
First person	myself	ourselves
Second person	yourself (*archaic:* thyself)	yourselves
Third person	himself, herself, itself	themselves

First, notice that the singular pronouns always end in *-self* and the plural ones in *-selves.* Then notice the correct forms *himself* and *themselves.* Avoid the nonstandard forms *hisself, theirself,* and *theirselves.*

● **Practice 4-13** Find the reflexive pronouns in numbers 1-4, and supply the correct reflexive pronouns for numbers 5-8.
1. He tried to figure out the puzzle by himself.
2. They got themselves into a mess.

3. Are you giving yourself a fair chance?
4. Anyone who talks to himself is sure to have an audience.
5. At the touch of a button, the box will open or close _____.
6. Mrs. Perez said to her children, "Look at _____! Are you still clean enough to go downtown?"
7. While on vacation, they sent _____ a package so that they would not have to carry their purchases along.
8. Tom imagined _____ standing behind the pulpit preaching.

(8) Intensive pronouns

The intensive pronouns are the *-self* pronouns used for emphasis. They intensify, or emphasize, some noun or pronoun already in the sentence:

We saw the President *himself*.

I *myself* don't know the answer yet.

Grammatically, an intensive pronoun functions as an appositive; it renames the preceding noun or pronoun. A table of the intensive (and reflexive) pronouns appears above in section **4a(7)**.

At times the intensive pronoun does not appear right after the noun it emphasizes, but later on in the sentence. In such a sentence, though, we can always put the intensive pronoun back next to the noun it emphasizes.

Joe will do it *himself*. = Joe *himself* will do it.

- **Practice 4-14** Find the intensive pronouns in sentences 1-4, and supply the intensive pronouns for sentences 5-7. (Watch for the one sentence in the first group that has a reflexive pronoun in it instead of an intensive pronoun.)
  1. We thought she had won, but Carol herself didn't know for sure.
  2. You yourself could keep it if no one claims it.
  3. She sang "Happy Birthday" to herself.

4. I thought of that myself.
5. Joan _____ thought we should go.
6. We were all going to share the cake, but the little boys ate it _____ .
7. Have you ever spoken with the Secretary of State _____ ?

(9) Relative pronouns

(9.1) Relative pronouns with antecedents
(9.2) Indefinite relative pronouns

A relative pronoun has a noun function (S, DO, etc.) in a dependent clause, and at the same time it relates that clause to the rest of the sentence. Usually, a relative pronoun has an antecedent and is part of an adjective clause.

(9.1) Relative pronouns with antecedents The relative pronoun typically functions as part of an adjective clause, and its antecedent is the word that the whole clause modifies.

who (whom, whose)
which
that

The examples below are marked to show the function of each relative pronoun in its clause and to show the antecedent of each relative pronoun.

It was Paul [*who* was arrested in Acts 21-22].

He saw that situation as a way [in *which* the gospel

could be preached].

He got permission to speak to the great

crowd [*that* he saw before him].

Rules 6 and 7 of section **4a(2.6)** explain that the choice of *who* or *whom* depends on how the pronoun is used within its own clause.

The possessive form *whose* has two uses.

Determiner	"Are you the boy [*whose* yoyo was lost]?" ^S^
Independent possessive pronoun	Mrs. Baker tried to give the yoyo to the child [*whose* it was]. ^PN^

The first use is much more common than the second.

The three basic relative pronouns—*who, which,* and *that*—are used in somewhat different ways.

Rule 1. Use *who/whom/whose* to stand for persons (beings with personality), and use *which* for things and most animals. Use *that* for either type of word.

Persons	I know the man [*who* called last night].
	I know the man [*that* called last night].
Things	The first house, [*which* is very convenient], is actually less expensive.
	They rented the house [*that* I like best].

Rule 2. Use *that* only in restrictive clauses. (Restrictive clauses, described also in **10d(5),** are those that are needed to specifically identify the particular item or items named by the noun.)

Restrictive	I know the man [*that* called last night]. They rented the house [*that* I like best].

Who and *which* can be used in either restrictive or nonrestrictive clauses:

Restrictive	Jane is the person [*who* told me that story].
	The brown gloves [*which* you gave me] are my best ones. *(But see below.)*
Nonrestrictive	Jane Jackson, [*who* told me that story], said that it really happened.
	Those brown gloves, [*which* you gave me last year], are still my best ones.

As a matter of style, however, some writers prefer not to overuse *which* in restrictive clauses.

Acceptable	The brown gloves [*which* you gave me] are my best ones.
Perhaps better	The brown gloves [*that* you gave me] are my best ones.

● **Practice 4-15** Find the relative pronouns in the following sentences. These sentences, somewhat simplified, are based on the account given in John 4:4-42.

1. When Jesus asked her for a drink, the woman of Samaria said, "Since you are a Jew, why do you ask a drink of me, who am a woman of Samaria?"
2. Jesus replied, "If you knew the one who asks for a drink, you would ask him for the living water."
3. The woman asked whether he was greater than Jacob, who gave them that well.
4. Jesus said, "Anyone who drinks of the water that I will give him will never thirst; but the water that I will give him will be in him a well of water springing up into eternal life."

5. Later he told her, "God is a Spirit: and they that worship him must worship him in spirit and in truth."

6. Before long, the woman received the living water, which is salvation in Christ.

(9.2) **Indefinite relative pronouns** An indefinite relative pronoun is a relative pronoun that does not have an antecedent and does not occur in an adjective clause. Usually it is part of a noun clause, though one is occasionally found in an adverb clause.

		Archaic
who (whom, whose)	whoever (whomever, whosever)	whosoever (etc.)
which	whichever	whichsoever
what	whatever	whatsoever

The indefinite relative pronouns, as opposed to the regular relative pronouns and the interrogative pronouns, usually seem to be doing double duty. For example, in *I know who just left,* the *who* seems to mean "the person who" or "the identity of the person who." Similarly, in *I like whatever you like,* the *whatever* means "anything that" or "everything which." Thus these indefinite relative pronouns have a meaning that is both indefinite ("anything, everything") and relative ("that, which").

The following examples, divided by types of clauses, are labeled to show the uses of the indefinite relative pronouns in their own clauses.

Used in noun clauses

Clause as subject	[*Whoever* just left]ᔆ didn't shut the door.
Clause as direct object	Let's ask [*whoever* comes in next]ᔆ.
	I know [*whom* he saw]ᴰᴼ.
	Anyone can see [*whose* this is]ᴾᴺ.

Clause as object of preposition	She gave the permission slip to S [*whoever* was on duty].

Clause as predicate noun	DO Novels are [*what* I usually like best].

Used in adverb clauses

Adverb clause modifying the main clause	DO [*Whatever* you do], don't try to go downtown during the rush hour. S [*Whoever* comes], we will try to do our best.

The correct case of *who* and *whoever* depends only on the pronoun's use in its own clause.

- **Practice 4-16** Find the indefinite relative pronouns in the following sentences. One sentence has none.
  1. Whatever you want to do is all right with me.
  2. I couldn't hear what you said.
  3. I know which is the right house.
  4. Who is coming to the door?
  5. We have apple pie and peach pie. Please take whichever you prefer.

(10) Reciprocal pronouns

The reciprocal pronouns express a mutual relationship among the persons mentioned in the subject. There are two reciprocal pronouns:

    each other
    one another

The reciprocal pronouns are used mostly as direct objects, but they can also be indirect objects and objects of prepositions.

DO

Jane and Bill saw *each other* at the same time.

IO

The committee gave *one another* the benefit of the

doubt.

The Johnsons always choose thoughtful gifts for

OP

one another.

The reciprocal pronouns can also be made into possessive determiners, which modify nouns.

Det

Let's try to stay out of each other's way.

Those children like to play with one another's toys.

The reciprocal pronouns should not be used as subjects of clauses.

Unacceptable | They knew [what *each other* would do].

Corrected | *Each* knew [what *the other* would do].

4b Auxiliaries

(1) Definition of the auxiliary
(2) Auxiliaries for tense
(3) Auxiliaries for the perfect and progressive aspects
(4) Auxiliaries for modal expressions
(5) An auxiliary for passive voice
(6) An auxiliary for emphasis and other uses

(1) Definition of the auxiliary

Auxiliaries, or "helping verbs," are words that may join the true verb in making up the complete verb of a sentence.

Auxiliaries act as grammatical signals and contribute certain minor meanings to the complete verb. See the accompanying table for an overview of auxiliaries.

AUXILIARIES

	Meaning	How Used*	Samples of Use
Will, shall	Future	With the basic present form of the verb	Each of us *will speak* for five minutes. *Shall* I *speak* a word for you?
Have (has, had)	Perfect (present perfect, past perfect, future perfect)	With the past participle	John *has spoken* with the chairman already. When I got there, she *had* just *spoken* with her. In two minutes he *will have spoken* for an hour.
Be (am, are, was, *etc.*)	Progressive	With the present participle	Tom Jackson *was speaking* just then.
	Passive	With the past participle	That word *was spoken* just in time.
Can, could, may, might, should, would, must, ought (to)	Modal expressions of ability, possibility, obligation, necessity, etc.	With the basic present form of the verb	Anyone *can speak* who wants to. We *should speak* up for the Lord.
Do (does, did)	Emphasis, question inversion, negative—all in present or past tense only	With the basic present form of the verb	That parrot *does speak* too much. *Do* you often *speak* in public? Buck *did* not *speak* at our meeting.

---

* Some of these auxiliaries can be combined in a single complete verb. The "How Used" column always gives the form of the next word in the complete verb. For example, with *have* the next word is a past participle: have *spoken,* have *been* speaking.

Some of the auxiliaries in the table are look-alikes for true verbs.

True verbs	Mom's lasagna *is* good.
	We will *have* some tonight.
	We *canned* these tomatoes.
	I will *do* the dishes.

Auxiliaries are different from true verbs in their meanings and in the ways they are used.

(2) Auxiliaries for tense

English has three basic tenses: past, present, and future. Only the future tense requires an auxiliary—usually *will,* but sometimes *shall.*

In earlier English, such as in Shakespeare and the King James Version of the Bible, *shall* was used very commonly for the future tense, perhaps as often as *will.* The two words sometimes had slightly different meanings, according to rather complicated rules. Now, though, the facts are simpler.

Today *will* is the usual sign of the future. *Shall* has two main uses, both of them with the first-person pronouns *I* and *we:*

| Questions to find out another's preference | Shall I get you a glass of water? |
| | Shall we sit here? |

| Statements in formal English (as in some business letters) | I shall be happy to come for an interview at your convenience. |
| | We shall be delighted to serve you in the future. |

In addition, *shall* is used frequently in legal language, sometimes for simple future and sometimes to express obligation:

Any person who shall sell such obscene materials shall be guilty of a misdemeanor.

> The President shall designate one of the members of the commission as chairman.

With these exceptions, the normal sign of any kind of future tense is *will.*

(3) Auxiliaries for the perfect and progressive aspects*

(3.1) The perfect
(3.2) The progressive

The three basic tenses—past, present, and future—can be combined with certain auxiliaries to make the perfect and the progressive forms.

(3.1) The perfect The perfect has to do mainly with actions or states of being that are completed ("perfected"). The perfect tenses today always use some form of the auxiliary *have.*

	Meaning	*Example*
Past perfect	Completed before a certain time in the past	By seven o'clock last night he *had done* all his homework.
Future perfect	To be completed before a certain time in the future	Why should we wait until one o'clock to eat lunch? Probably by 12:15 everyone *will have arrived.*
Present perfect	Often means complete in the present (done within the present time period)	I *have corrected* all my homework today.

---

* Strictly speaking, tense has to do only with time (past, present, and future), and the added meanings of perfect and progressive are **aspects,** having to do with the *kind* of action a verb expresses. The perfect aspect refers basically to *completed* actions and the progressive aspect to *continuing* actions in the past, present, or future. However, for convenience we do often refer to the "present perfect tense," for example.

See **7b** for more information on the meanings of the perfect tenses.

The name of each perfect tense tells which form of *have* it uses:

	Forms of Have	Example
Present perfect	Present of *have*	*have/has* seen
Past perfect	Past of *have*	*had* seen
Future perfect	Future of *have*	*will/shall have* seen

The word after *have* is always a past participle.

One final note will help you understand earlier literature. A few centuries ago, forms of *be* instead of *have* were used with the past participle to make the perfect tenses of certain verbs. One example is found in the translated words of Christ: "I *am come* that they might have life" (John 10:10). Today that would be translated "I *have come*." You can find another example in Luke 24:6 ("is risen"), and two more in II Corinthians 5:17, all in the King James Version. Remember that the earlier *am come* always means *have come,* never *am coming*.

(3.2) The progressive The progressive expresses continuing action (action in progress). The progressive is made by adding some form of the auxiliary *be,* and by putting an *-ing* suffix on the next word in the complete verb.

The name of each progressive tense tells which form of *be* it uses:

	Forms of Be	Example
Present progressive	Present of *be*	*am/are/is* looking
Past progressive	Past of *be*	*was/were* looking
Future progressive	Future of *be*	*will/shall be* looking
Present perfect progressive	Present perfect of *be*	*have/has been* looking

The complete active progressive verb ends with the *-ing* form of the true verb, called the present participle.

● **Practice 4-17** This is a check-up exercise on tenses. If you like, you can first review by looking at the table in **7g.**

A. Classify each italicized verb as present, past, or future.

1. We *visited* Williamsburg, Virginia, last year.
2. The historical buildings and the people in colonial costume *were* very interesting.
3. Next year we *will go* again for a few days.
4. I *like* historical places where we can learn things.

B. Classify each italicized verb as present perfect, past perfect, or future perfect.

1. John *had* always *liked* volleyball until this year.
2. He told me, "I *have tried* long enough to hit that ball over the net."
3. Maybe by next summer at camp he *will have learned* to like it again.

C. Classify each italicized verb as present progressive, past progressive, or future progressive.

1. When I arrived at the Johnsons' house, Jimmy *was washing* their car.
2. Susan *was picking* flowers to put on the table at dinner.
3. All week they *will be helping* more than usual, because their father is away and their mother hurt her ankle.
4. They *are learning* how much their parents usually do at home.

D. In this last section you may find any of the tenses. Each numbered item has one complete verb in italics; give its tense.

1. *Have* you ever *touched* poison ivy?
2. People *are* not sensitive to poison ivy the first time they touch it.
3. Touching it once, though, *makes* most people break out when they touch it again.

4. Stuart *thought* he was not sensitive to poison ivy,
5. because he *had* never *broken* out before.
6. While he *was walking* along two days ago,
7. he *saw* a poison ivy vine with its triple green leaves.
8. He *picked* a leaf to show off.
9. Now his hand really *itches,*
10. and he *has learned* a lesson.
11. He says he *will* not *be doing* that again!
12. Probably this lesson is one he *will remember.*

(4) Auxiliaries for modal expressions

The modal auxiliaries express certain things about the speaker's attitude toward the action or state he is talking about. These auxiliaries show such things as whether the speaker thinks the action or state is possible, doubtful, likely, permitted, or necessary.

I *may learn* a great deal this year.
That man *might be* a dentist.
The common modal auxiliaries are listed below:

can	could
may	might
should	would
must	ought (to)

These auxiliaries always come first in the complete verb, and in standard English only one is used at a time.

- **Practice 4-18** Write down the complete verbs from the following sentences or partial sentences; many of them contain modal auxiliaries. (Ignore *to study* in number 1.)
  1. What would you like to study in college?
  2. I might study Christian missions,
  3. because God is calling me to the mission field.
  4. I may become a medical missionary, though.
  5. If so, I would study medical missions
  6. after I become a nurse or a doctor.

(5) An auxiliary for passive voice

As **7e** explains more fully, when the subject *acts,* the verb is **active;** when the subject is *acted upon,* the verb is **passive.**

Active voice | I *broke* a glass last night.

Passive voice | A glass *was broken* last night.

Both of these sentences are in the past tense, but the passive verb has an extra word in it, a past-tense form of the auxiliary *be.*

Compared with the active, a complete passive verb always has an extra *be*-word in it just before the true verb. Here are a few more examples:

	Active Voice	Passive Voice
Present	breaks	*is* broken
Present progressive	are breaking	are *being* broken
Past perfect	had broken	had *been* broken
Present with modal auxiliary	might break	might *be* broken

In the passive voice the true verb always takes the form of the past participle *(broken).*

- **Practice 4-19** Which of the italicized complete verbs are passive?
  1. Ye *are* the light of the world.
  2. A city that *is set* on an hill
  3. *can*not *be hid.* (Matt. 5:14)
  4. Ask, and it *shall be given* you;
  5. seek, and ye *shall find;*
  6. knock, and it *shall be opened* unto you. (Matt. 7:7)

(6) An auxiliary for emphasis and other uses

(6.1) Emphatic *do*
(6.2) Some other uses of *do*

In the active voice the simple present and past tenses have no auxiliary. However, there are a number of situations in which an auxiliary is needed—to show emphasis, to help make a sentence negative, to form many kinds of questions, and so on. In those situations, if there is not already an auxiliary, one of the simple forms of *do* is added to the verb: *do, does,* or *did.*

(6.1) Emphatic *do* One obvious use of the auxiliary *do* is for emphasis. Have you ever made a statement you were quite sure of and had someone express doubt about what you said? Probably you made the statement again, with a little more emphasis. Notice these two examples:

(1) "I will get the mail tomorrow."
"No you won't—you'll forget."
"Oh yes, I *will* get it. I'll remember."

(2) "Jeff likes the blue plaid best."
"Oh? I'm sure he'd choose the green, as always."
"No, he *does* like the blue best; he told me so."

In the first example, where the auxiliary *will* already appears in the statement, greater stress on the *will* emphasizes the whole statement. In the second example, the verb *likes* has no auxiliary, so it is changed to *does like* and heavy stress is put on the *does* for emphasis.

- **Practice 4-20** Write down the complete verb in each of the following sentences or parts of sentences. If the verb contains the auxiliary *do* for emphasis, write *emphatic* after the verb. (One sentence contains the true verb *do;* that verb is not emphatic, because the auxiliary *do* is not there too).

1. Bill was walking home from school.
2. He thought,
3. "I will do my homework first.
4. Then I will shoot baskets for a while.
5. I certainly do hope
6. that Todd and Joe can come over today.
7. I have really missed them this week.
8. Sometimes Joe is bossy,
9. but they usually do make good company."

(6.2) Some other uses of *do* The auxiliary *do* can perform several functions in addition to showing emphasis. In all these functions it is used only when some other auxiliary is not already present. Notice the parallel between the uses of *did* and *will* in the situations below. The basic sentences are "He finished" and "He will finish."

Negative	He *did* not finish. He will not finish.
Question inversion	*Did* he finish? Will he finish?
Tag question	He finished, *did*n't he? He'll finish, won't he?
Omission of true verb	He finished, and I *did* too. He'll finish, and I will too.

4c Determiners

(1) Definition of the determiner
(2) Articles
(3) Possessives
(4) Demonstratives
(5) Indefinites
(6) Quantity words
(7) Interrogatives
(8) Limiters
(9) Restricters
(10) Arrangement in the noun phrase

(1) Definition of the determiner

Determiners are words that point out, or limit, a following noun and that come before the descriptive adjectives that may modify the same noun. Determiners signal that a noun (or a word used as a noun) is coming in the sentence.

Below are three noun phrases with the determiners and the adjectives marked.

Det Det Adj
these two red leaves

Det Det   Adj
our first small house

Det Det Det   Adj
all the other good players

Determiners and adjectives both modify nouns, but they are different in several ways:

1. Determiners precede adjectives in the noun phrase.
2. Adjectives can be compared, using *-er/-est* or *more/most,* but determiners cannot.
3. Adjectives, but not determiners, can fill both blanks in the following test frame:
   The _____ thing (person) is very _____ .

Adjectives are discussed in **3d.** Some books treat determiners as a type (or as types) of adjectives, but this handbook does not. See **4c(10)** for a table of the common types of determiners.

(2) Articles

English has two articles:

Definite *(the)*	Shows that the noun refers to something already known or already mentioned
Indefinite *(a/an)*	Shows that a singular noun refers to something not named in particular or not mentioned before

(A plural noun used indefinitely has no article: "He collects stamps.")

The form of the indefinite article depends on the sound that follows it: *an* goes before words that begin with a vowel sound and *a* before those beginning with a consonant sound. (In older English sometimes *an* was used instead of *a* before pronounced *h*—compare "an hill" in KJV Matthew 5:14 with "a hole" in Ezekiel 8:7.)

(3) Possessives

When possessives modify nouns, they are determiners. Other possessives are not determiners.

Determiners	John's big apple would not fit into
	my lunchbox.
Independent possessives—not determiners	The apple was John's, and the lunchbox
	was mine.

Remember that a determiner always modifies a following noun.

The forms of possessive personal pronouns are found in **4a(2.4)**, and possessive nouns in **3b(2)**.

Sometimes a possessive noun is part of a **possessive phrase.**

Uncle Henry is my mother's brother.

(= the brother of my mother)

A pastor's job is challenging.

(= the job of a pastor)

The possessive phrase modifies the noun as a unit, acting as a single determiner.

● **Practice 4-21** For practice with two kinds of determiners, find the articles and the possessive determiners in the following sentences. Remember:

(1) do not include any independent possessives; and (2) consider possessive phrases to be single determiners.

1. This is our neighbor's wall.
2. His wall is higher and wider than ours.
3. A wall should be wide enough for sitting.
4. Our other neighbor's yard has a fence in the back.

(4) Demonstratives

Demonstrative determiners have the same meanings and forms as the demonstrative pronouns of **4a(5).**

	Singular	*Plural*
Near	this	these
Far	that	those

A demonstrative determiner always modifies a following noun.

- **Practice 4-22** Look for the demonstrative determiners in the following conversation. To be sure that you have found determiners and not pronouns, write down the whole noun phrase that each demonstrative determiner introduces.
  1. "This cup and that saucer don't fit together very well."
  2. "That's true, but then all of these glass dishes are somewhat odd."
  3. "Oh? How's that?"
  4. "Well, some of the plates are different sizes. Notice how these two plates are a little smaller than those."
  5. "I wonder why that is."
  6. "They were made cheaply in the thirties, back during the Depression. For these smaller plates, a smaller glob of molten glass happened to be put in the press."
  7. "That's interesting. But I thought dishes like these were sort of expensive."
  8. "Well, they are. Collectors really like these dishes, and so their price has gone up. 'Depression glass' is a collector's item these days."

(5) Indefinites

Just as there are indefinite pronouns, there are also indefinite determiners.

He ate *some* ripe strawberries but *no* plums.

Each plum tree produced *much* fruit this summer.

These words are determiners only when they modify nouns.

Modifiers of singular nouns only	Each, either, neither, another, much
Modifiers of singular or plural nouns	Some, any, no, enough

See **4f(1.4)** for the correlative conjunctions *either—or* and *neither—nor*.

(6) Quantity words

For convenience we call the next group of determiners quantity words, since most of them suggest either quantity or numerical ordering. Quantity words are not defined by meaning, however. They are the determiners that can be used after an article, a possessive, a demonstrative, or an indefinite determiner.

Modifiers of singular nouns only	Every, little, less, least
Modifiers of plural nouns only	Few, fewer, fewest, several
Additional examples	One, two, three . . . one hundred . . . ; first, second, third . . . last; many (a), such (a), more, most, other

Note the restrictions on the first two groups, and see the Glossary of Usage for *less* and *fewer*. *Fewer* also shows that some of the quantity words can be compared. In this one way some of these words are like the adjectives, but they are still determiners because of the way they act in the noun phrase.

(7) Interrogatives

Three interrogative words may be used as determiners: *which, what,* and *whose.*

> *Which* book is yours?

> *What* idea did they have?

> *Whose* plan was that?

The interrogative determiners can combine with certain quantity words and with adjectives in the noun phrase:

> Int   Quan   Adj
> *Which other small vase* do you like?

Which, what, and *whose* are determiners only when they modify nouns. Used alone, they are pronouns.

(8) Limiters

The limiters are a very small group of words that can come before any type of determiner presented above, except for the indefinite determiners. We call them limiters because they further limit, or specify, the meaning of the total noun phrase. They combine freely with most other determiners:

	Lim Art		
both	*both* the pages		

	Lim	Int
all	*all*	which houses?

	Lim	Dem	Quan	
all	*all*	these	other	houses

	Lim	Art
half	*half*	a loaf

In more formal language some of these phrases might be restated with an *of* after the first word.*

(9) Restricters

The restricters are a small group of words that are used at the very beginning of the noun phrase. Below are the most common ones:

only	just
even	almost
merely	hardly
exactly	nearly
especially	not

A restricter can often be interpreted either as modifying the rest of the noun phrase or as modifying a specific later determiner. But that really matters little—either way, the words add up to the same information about the main noun.

Res
Only half of my tomato plants have fruit yet.

Res
I planted *only hybrids* this year.

Res   Res
Just three weeks seems like *not enough time.*

Res
I'd be happy to see *almost any progress.*

---

* Adding *of* to these phrases—"half of a loaf" etc.—would turn *half* into a noun (and *both* and *all* into indefinite pronouns) modified by a prepositional phrase.

Outside the noun phrase, these words would usually be adverbs.

(10) Arrangement in the noun phrase

In the noun phrase, determiners come first, then adjectives, then modifying nouns, and then the main noun.

> Det Adj ModN
> the tall brick building

As has already been suggested, the determiners themselves have a set order. Though you need not memorize that order, you may want to look now at the table called "The Noun Phrase: Modifiers Before the Noun" to see how the various kinds of determiners are arranged.

Looks rather involved, doesn't it? Yet we normally use these words without ever thinking of what word goes where. Though languages are complex, God gave to young children the special ability to master them. Certainly this is one way that we are "fearfully and wonderfully made." (See Ps. 139:14.)

You might experiment with using the table to make some noun phrases, beginning toward the left and working your way across. Instructions at the bottom of the table tell you how to combine the words. You can of course add more adjectives, modifying nouns, and main nouns to the lists.

- **Practice 4-23** For practice with the parts of the noun phrase, copy all the noun phrases from the following sentences. In each phrase, underline the main noun and label the modifying words with *Det* for determiner, *Adj* for adjective, and *ModN* for modifying noun.
    1. Though many useful corn varieties are grown in America, one interesting type is popcorn.
    2. When heated, its small pearl kernels explode into delicious white puffs.
    3. Most scientists believe that these tiny explosions are caused by steam pressure.
    4. All the kernels will pop if just enough moisture is present in the corn.

The Noun Phrase: Modifiers Before the Noun

Restricters 4c(9)	Limiters 4c(8)	Determiners 4c	Quantity Words 4c(6)	Adjectives 3d(1)	Modifying Noun 6b(5)	Main Noun
only even merely exactly especially just almost hardly nearly not	both half all	**Articles 4c(2)** the a/an **Possessives 4c(3)** my, our (etc.) Joe's (etc.) **Demonstratives 4c(4)** this, these that, those **Interrogatives 4c(7)** which, what, whose* **Indefinites 4c(5)** some, any, enough, each, either, neither, another, no, much	one, two, three . . . , first, second, third . . . last many (a) such (a) more most other every little (quantity) less least few fewer fewest several	tall short big large little (size) small fat thin smooth rough wooden woolen biblical American French wintery beautiful (etc.)	stone brick wood wool nylon Christmas Sunday winter garden home school university church Bible (etc.)	wall building fence suit jacket dinner service day path visit party class meeting truth patience (etc.)
(One of these may be used to modify either the rest of the noun phrase or a later determiner.)	*(One of these can combine with any word that is above the line in the next column.)*	*(Only one from this whole column is used.)*	*(Usually just one of these is used.)*	*(More than one may be used.)*	*(It is often advisable not to use more than one.)*	*(This is the word that everything else modifies.)*

* *Whose* (and sometimes *which*) may also be a **relative** determiner.

Section **6c** tells more about the noun phrase.

4d Qualifiers

A qualifier is a special kind of word that modifies an adjective or an adverb, either strengthening or weakening the idea of the adjective or adverb.

> He looked *very* funny as he stood there balanced *rather* insecurely on one foot. Then, being *slightly* shy, he tried *even* harder to get down.

In those sentences *very* and *slightly* modify adjectives, and *rather* and *even* modify adverbs. Qualifiers generally tell how or how much: in these two sentences they tell how funny he looked, how insecurely he was balanced, how shy he was, and how much harder he tried.

In the past, grammarians often grouped qualifiers together with the adverbs, probably because a very few words could act either as qualifiers or as modifiers of verbs. (Dictionaries still label qualifiers as adverbs.) However, most qualifiers never modify verbs, and so it seems best to keep qualifiers separate from adverbs.

● **Practice 4-24** Find the qualifiers in the following sentences.
1. President Reagan made a somewhat rapid recovery from the rather serious gunshot wound he received in March, 1981.
2. It was quite remarkable that he was not killed, but the absence of any permanent damage was even greater reason for amazement.
3. His return to work at the White House came much earlier than the doctors had predicted.
4. God's hand of protection was very clear throughout the almost fatal ordeal.

Though most qualifiers are single words, sometimes a word group acts as a qualifier.

> Well, Josie, I felt *kind of* tired yesterday, but today I feel *a great deal* better.

Qualifiers like these tend to be informal, even colloquial.

4e Prepositions

(1) Definition of the preposition
(2) Formation of the preposition
(3) Meanings of the preposition
(4) Included prepositional phrases

(1) Definition of the preposition

A preposition is a word that relates its object (normally a noun or a pronoun) to another word in the sentence.

Consider this simple example:

The pen on the table writes well.

In this sentence the preposition *on* shows the relation between the table and the pen—the pen is *on* the table, not *by* it or *under* it.

If we take a preposition like *on* and ask "what?" after it ("on what?"), we find the object of that preposition. In the example above, the complete object of *on* is *the table*. The simple object is just the noun *table*. A preposition and its complete object make up a **prepositional phrase:**

on the table

Notice that the object is after the preposition.

Prepositional phrases commonly modify nouns, pronouns, or verbs:

Modifying a noun	That pen on the table must be yours.
Modifying a pronoun	Something on the table caught my eye.
Modifying a verb	A squirrel was sitting on the picnic table.

A preposition, then, shows the relationship between its object (*table*) and the word that the whole prepositional phrase modifies (*pen,* etc.) .

There are nearly fifty common one-word prepositions in English, but nine of them are used more than the others: *of, in, to, for, with, on, at, by, from.* However, even some of these common words can at times be adverbs instead of prepositions. **A word is not a preposition if it does not have an object.**

In as preposition	My mother's working in the HOUSE.

In as adverb	The swimmer fell IN.

In the first sentence, *in* is a preposition because it has an object (*house*). In the second sentence, *in* is an adverb (modifying *fell*), because it has no object. Notice also that the preposition is not usually said with a heavy accent, but the adverb usually is. This would normally be true even if other words followed in the sentence:

In as preposition	My mother's working in the HOUSE now.

In as adverb	The swimmer fell IN yesterday.

● **Practice 4-25** Before you read more about prepositions, look for the prepositional phrases in the following five sentences. Write down each prepositional phrase and underline the preposition in it.

1. Fearless Ferdinand, the world's greatest lion tamer, walked to the door of the cage, opened it, and boldly entered.
2. A worried look appeared on his face when the lion bounded forward in the cage.
3. With his wooden chair Ferdinand kept the ferocious beast at a safe distance.
4. Suddenly a roar of laughter burst from the audience.
5. A set of shiny false fangs had fallen from the lion's mouth, revealing an old, rather sickly-looking creature.

(2) Formation of the preposition

Many prepositions are simple little words like *of, with, by, under,* and *through.* Not all prepositions are so simple, however.

Simple words	of, with, over, in, to
Combined words	inside, into, within
Words with prefixes	across, around, beside
Multiple words	according to, in spite of

(3) Meanings of the preposition

Prepositions cover a great many areas of meaning. Here are a few of the most common areas. Other prepositions could be added to these lists.

Location	above, across, against, around, at, behind, below, beneath, beside, between, beyond, by, in, in front of, inside, on, outside, over, past, toward(s), under, upon, within
Direction	down, from, into, off, onto, out, out of, through, to, up (*see also* Location)
Time (including duration)	after, at, before, between, by, during, for, in, on, past, since, until, till, up to
Agency or means	by, by means of, with, of (*archaic*)
Cause	because of, due to, in view of, on account of

Association	about, according to, along with, among, around, as for, besides, for, like, of, with
Opposition or exception	against, apart from, but (*meaning* "except"), despite, except, except for, in spite of, instead of, without

Most prepositions have more than one area of meaning, and almost any of these prepositions could be put on other lists as well.

- **Practice 4-26** In this exercise you will find a wider variety of prepositions than in Practice 4-25. Write down all the prepositional phrases and underline the preposition in each. Do not try to classify the prepositions by meaning.
  1. Thomas A. Edison ranks high among the world's great inventors.
  2. During his lifetime he produced hundreds of useful inventions.
  3. Without a doubt the invention he preferred above all the others was the phonograph.
  4. The first phonograph was a curious device with a cylinder on the top.
  5. Edison wrapped some tinfoil around the cylinder and spun it with a crank.
  6. While the cylinder turned around, he leaned toward the mouthpiece and said, "Mary had a little lamb."
  7. Edison then listened, along with his assistant.
  8. After a brief pause the machine repeated the line.
  9. According to the story, the assistant's face turned white with astonishment.

(4) Included prepositional phrases

It is not unusual for one prepositional phrase to modify a word in another prepositional phrase.

He walked to the door of the cage.

To the door and *of the cage* are prepositional phrases; the simple object of each preposition is marked with OP. Notice, though, how the two phrases work together.

Where did he walk?   To the door of the cage.

The second prepositional phrase is included in the first, since it modifies a word in the first phrase.

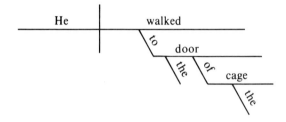

We can use parentheses to show that one prepositional phrase is included in another.

              OP   OP
He walked (to the door (of the cage)).

● **Practice 4-27** Do this and the next exercise on your own paper or as your teacher directs. Place parentheses around the prepositional phrases, showing the included prepositional phrases. Write *OP* over the simple object of each preposition.
1. One of the prettiest things in our yard is our butterfly bush.
2. Its huge spikes of blue flowers are similar to the blooms of the lilac.
3. The flowers are a great attraction to butterflies.
4. In northern winters the bush sometimes dies back to the roots.
5. That does not matter, though, because the butterfly bush blooms only on the new wood of the current year.

    Sometimes one prepositional phrase follows another without the second one being included in the first.

Our butterfly bush gives us an abundance

OP   OP
(of cut flowers) (over the summer).

These two prepositional phrases must be marked separately since *over the summer* modifies *gives,* not *flowers.*
Notice that *over the summer* could be moved in the
sentence without a change of meaning.

OP
(Over the summer) our butterfly bush

OP
gives us an abundance (of cut flowers).

● **Practice 4-28** On your own paper, use parentheses
  and *OP* to indicate the prepositional phrases in
  the following sentences. Show any included
  prepositional phrases. Do not mark a prepositional
  phrase as being included unless it actually does
  modify something in the prepositional phrase just
  before it.

  1. Another name for the butterfly bush is summer
     lilac.
  2. Since all blooms are produced on new wood,
     the bush should be cut back in the winter.
  3. It starts into its new growth in late spring but
     then grows rapidly.
  4. We usually cut back our bush to about six inches
     in the winter.
  5. Except for its winter trim, it requires little care
     from any of us.

4f Conjunctions

(1) Coordinating conjunctions
(2) Subordinating conjunctions

A conjunction is a connecting word that joins words
or groups of words in the sentence.

(1) Coordinating conjunctions

(1.1) Coordinating conjunctions joining single words
(1.2) Coordinating conjunctions joining phrases
(1.3) Coordinating conjunctions joining clauses
(1.4) Correlative conjunctions

A coordinating conjunction joins sentence parts of the same type.

The common coordinating conjunctions are listed below.

and	nor
but	yet
or	for

Those in the first column are used most often.

(1.1) Coordinating conjunctions joining single words

Verbs	The puppies <u>scampered</u> **and** <u>played</u>.
Auxiliaries	I <u>can</u> **and** <u>will</u> help you.
Adjectives	He was <u>tired</u> **but** <u>happy</u> .
Direct objects (nouns)	We saw <u>horses</u>, <u>sheep</u>, **and** <u>goats</u> in the fields.
Prepositions	The robins flew <u>over</u> **or** <u>around</u> the tree.

Other kinds of words may be joined in the sentence also.

When two or more verbs are joined by a conjunction, we say that the sentence has a **compound** verb. Similarly a sentence can have a compound subject, a compound direct object, and so on.

(1.2) Coordinating conjunctions joining phrases A phrase is a word group that does not contain both subject and predicate.

Subject phrases	The preacher **and** the deacons work well together.
Direct object phrases (and other noun phrases)	She ate <u>boiled potatoes</u> **or** <u>wild rice</u> every day.
Preposi-tional phrases	We looked <u>behind the sofa</u> **and** <u>under the chair.</u>
Predicates	I went to the <u>library</u> **and** <u>checked out three books.</u>

Here again, we can use the term *compound:* for instance, the last sentence above has a compound predicate.

(1.3) Coordinating conjunctions joining clauses A clause is a group of words that has both a subject and a predicate. If a clause can stand alone as a sentence, we call it an independent clause.

My yoke is easy.
My burden is light.

Here we have two simple sentences. However, these two independent clauses can instead be joined by a coordinating conjunction, making a compound sentence:

My yoke is easy, and my burden is light.
(Matt. 11:30)

Independent clauses can be joined by *and, but, or, yet, for,* and sometimes *so.*

Dependent clauses too are occasionally joined by coordinating conjunctions. See **8a(5.3)** for an example.

● **Practice 4-29** Find the coordinating conjunctions and also the words or word groups that they join.
1. Watch and pray, that ye enter not into temptation. (Matt. 26:41a)

2. Many are called, but few are chosen. (Matt. 22:14)
3. I behaved myself as though he had been my friend or brother. (Ps. 35:14a)
4. All the rivers run into the sea; yet the sea is not full. (Eccles. 1:7a)
5. Turn not to the right hand nor to the left: remove thy foot from evil. (Prov. 4:27)
6. I am Alpha and Omega, the beginning and the end, the first and the last. (Rev. 22:13)

(1.4) Correlative conjunctions Sometimes a *pair* of words is used to join equal sentence parts together. These two words are called correlative conjunctions. Though they are divided in the sentence, they work together to relate the two sentence parts.

Either I will go at 4:00, **or** we'll both go at 5:00.

He gave it to **both** Jan **and** me.

His so-called friends **neither** called him **nor**

wrote him while he was sick.

She won **not only** the mathematics award **but also**

the science contest.

Correlative conjunctions have three special uses:
(1) to provide emphasis (as in the last two sentences above);
(2) to let the reader know that a second thing will be added to the first; and
(3) to make clear exactly which things are being joined in the sentence.

Confusing | John and Mary or Joe will do it.

One meaning clear	**Either** <u>John and Mary</u> **or** <u>Joe</u> will do it.
Other meaning clear	John and **either** <u>Mary</u> **or** <u>Joe</u> will do it.

Section **9i(5)** gives help with the placement of correlative conjunctions.

● **Practice 4-30** Find the coordinating conjunctions, including correlative conjunctions, and also the words or word groups that they join.

1. Each year millions of people in Paris and in New York admire the work of a Frenchman named Gustave Eiffel.
2. Eiffel designed the framework of both the Eiffel Tower in Paris and the Statue of Liberty in New York.
3. Both monuments were built to help celebrate freedom and brotherhood.
4. Neither the Eiffel Tower nor the Statue of Liberty was fully appreciated at first.
5. The Statue of Liberty was dedicated in 1886, yet it did not become a national monument until 1924.
6. The people of Paris at one time thought that the Eiffel Tower was either too tall or too ugly for their city.
7. The two monuments slowly but surely gained both national and international recognition.

(2) Subordinating conjunctions

(2.1) Subordinating conjunctions for adverb clauses
(2.2) Subordinating conjunctions for noun clauses

A subordinating conjunction joins a dependent clause (a subordinate clause) to an independent clause. A subordinating conjunction is part of the dependent clause, but its only function in that clause is to introduce it.

(2.1) Subordinating conjunctions for adverb clauses Most subordinating conjunctions introduce adverb clauses. Many of these subordinating conjunctions appear on the accompanying table, grouped by areas of meaning. The table is divided into three sections, beginning with the meaning categories that are the most obvious.

SOME COMMON MEANINGS SIGNALED BY SUBORDINATING CONJUNCTIONS IN ADVERB CLAUSES

	Subordinating Conjunctions	Examples
Time	when, while, as, before, after, since, now that, once, until, till, every time (that), whenever	*When* she heard that the famine was over, Naomi decided to go back to Judea.
		Once she had made that decision, she told her two daughters-in-law.
Place	where, wherever, whither (*archaic*)	Orpah remained *where* she was, in Moab.
		Ruth told Naomi, *"Whither* thou goest, I will go."
Cause	because, since, as, inasmuch as, whereas (*legal language*)	*Because* Ruth returned with Naomi, she was blessed by God through the kindness of Boaz.
		Inasmuch as Ruth married Boaz, she became one of the ancestors of Christ.
Condition	if, on condition that, provided that; unless	*If* Ruth had remained in Moab, she would have missed God's best for her life.
		God promises to bless His people, *provided that* they are obedient to His Word. (From Ruth 1-4)
Contrast	whereas, while	*Whereas* most of the people feared Haman, Esther chose to fear only her God.
		While Haman's trust was in human cleverness, Esther trusted in God's power.

Manner	as, as if, as though, however	The king's gift of his ring to Esther and Mordecai was like saying, "Preserve your people *however* you can."
		Queen Esther acted *as though* Haman was a friend, and he came to her dinner with the king.
Purpose	so that, so (*less formal*), that, in order that; lest	Haman had built a gallows *that* he might hang Mordecai.
		God used Esther's courage to defeat Haman's plan, *in order that* He might preserve His people.
Concession	although, even though, though, even if	*Even though* the situation looked hopeless, God gave deliverance.
		(From Esther 2-8)
Comparison and Degree	than, (as . . .) as, (so . . .) as (The word in parentheses is not actually part of the subordinating conjunction. It is a qualifier, modifying the word after it. The clause introduced by as modifies the qualifier.)	In his day Captain John Smith was not *so famous *as* he is now. He served as Jamestown's leader *as long *as* the colonies needed him.
Result	so that, (so . . .) that, (such . . .) that (The word in parentheses is a modifier, not a part of the subordinating conjunction. The word in parentheses is modified by the clause introduced by *that*.)	Smith's leadership ability was *such a positive factor *that* Jamestown colony survived Indian raids, disease, and starvation. He was an able spokesman for the colonies, *so that* many Englishmen came to settle there. His exploits are *so legendary *that* he has become a colorful figure in American history.

The following three practice exercises deal cumulatively with the three sections of the table.

● **Practice 4-31** By first locating the subordinating conjunctions, find the adverb clauses in the following sentences. (Only words from the first section of the table—time, place, cause, and condition—appear here.)
1. Hannah wept before the Lord in prayer, because she desired a son.
2. She vowed to give the boy back to God if He would grant her request.
3. After she had borne Samuel, she gave him to Eli to serve in the Lord's house.
4. When she would come to offer sacrifice, she would visit Samuel and praise God for His goodness to her.
5. God blessed her with five more children, once she had kept her vow.
   (From I Sam. 1-2)

● **Practice 4-32** By locating the subordinating conjunctions, find the adverb clauses in the following sentences. (Words from the first two sections of the table are included here.)
1. The outward beauty of a woman is vain, unless in her heart she fears the Lord.
2. While it is yet night, the virtuous woman rises to provide for her family.
3. She works hard so that their needs will be met.
4. She acts toward her husband as she would act toward the Lord.
5. Since her husband safely trusts in her, he places his heart, his home, and his health in her loving hands.
6. The virtuous woman fears the Lord and acts wisely, so that she is found worthy of the praise of her husband and her children.
   (From Prov. 31 and Eph. 5:18-33)

● **Practice 4-33** By first locating the subordinating conjunctions, find the adverb clauses in the following sentences. (Words from all three sections of the table are included here.)

1. When the Canaanites afflicted Israel, God raised up Deborah to deliver His people.
2. Barak, Israel's captain, begged Deborah to go with him into battle lest he lose courage.
3. The victory was so complete that not one of the enemy escaped.
4. Jael acted as if she were a friend of Sisera, the Canaanite captain, but killed him in his sleep.
5. The outcome was such a deliverance that Deborah and Barak composed a song to commemorate the battle.

(From Judges 4-5)

(2.2) Subordinating conjunctions for noun clauses The most common way of beginning a noun clause is with the subordinating conjunction *that*. Like other subordinating conjunctions, *that* is simply an introducer. It has no other function in its clause.

S   TrV DO   S

Did you know [*that* the Agricultural Revolution

TrV   DO

preceded the Industrial Revolution]?

Here the noun clause is the direct object of *did know*. *That* introduces the noun clause.

The subordinating conjunction *that* should not be confused with the relative pronoun *that*. Relative pronouns, used in adjective clauses, are covered in **4a(9.1).**

Sometimes the subordinating conjunction *that* is not expressed, but simply understood.

Correct | I knew [that we would win].

Also correct | I knew [we would win].

That can often be left out when the sentence is fairly short and uncomplicated. It should not be left out, though, when its omission would cause momentary misreading.

Not immedi- ately clear	I saw my pastor's wife had the situation under control. *(I saw my pastor's wife?)*
Improved	I saw that my pastor's wife had the situation under control.

That is helpful here because it clearly marks the beginning of the noun clause. *That* is also used more often in relatively formal writing.

- **Practice 4-34** Find the noun clauses introduced by *that*. Be sure that the clauses you find are noun clauses, not adjective clauses containing the relative pronoun *that*.
  1. The Agricultural Revolution showed that new farming methods could use less seed and yet produce greater yields.
  2. Lord Townshend proved that root-crop rotation could provide both nitrogen for the soil and winter fodder for livestock.
  3. That Robert Blackwell's cattle-breeding methods worked is shown by the rise of average cattle weight from 370 pounds to 800 pounds.
  4. Jethro Tull's plan for thorough plowing and cultivating required that seeds be planted in rows.
  5. Parliament's landlords enacted "enclosure" laws that forced most small farmers to abandon the land to wealthier farmers.
  6. One reason was that small farmers could not afford to enclose their land with the required fences.
  7. The Agricultural Revolution's modernization meant that unemployed village farmers would become the factory workers for the Industrial Revolution.

An additional subordinating conjunction is *whether*. *Whether* introduces noun clauses involving a choice.

S   TrV DO   (S)   (InV)
I don't know [*whether* he will win].

$\overset{S}{[}Whether$ he will win$\overset{LV}{]}$is not the $\overset{PN}{question}$ now.

Sometimes *if* is substituted informally for this use of *whether*. However, in some sentences *if* is less clear than *whether*. When in doubt, use *whether*.

4g Isolates

An isolate is a word that can stand alone, punctuated as a sentence, or can appear along with a regular sentence in which it takes no real part. An isolate* is not a necessary part of any regular sentence.

One well-known type of isolate is the interjection, a word that expresses strong feeling. However, isolates express several different kinds of things:

1. Strong feeling (these words are called **interjections**): Ouch! Whew! Eek! Yum! Brrr! Hey! Ugh! No! Oh!
2. Agreement and disagreement: yes, yeah, right, okay, sure, uh-huh, maybe, no, nope, huh-uh
3. Greeting and leave-taking: hello, hi, goodbye, bye
4. Politeness: please, thanks, sorry
5. Hesitation or introduction of a subject: uh, well, why, oh

There are also a few phrases that may fulfill the same functions. Here is one example for each of the five groups above: For crying out loud! Sure thing! good morning; thank you; you know.

An isolate can be set off by commas, or it can stand alone followed by an exclamation mark or possibly a period. In the following conversation all the isolates are in bold type. Notice how they are punctuated.

---

* *Isolate* is pronounced EYE-suh-lit, parallel to the nouns *duplicate* and *graduate*.

> Jan: **Hi**, Mary. Did you know that the
> party's been called off?
> Mary: **Oh**, **no**! **Why**, I've even made cookies
> for it! Do you know why it was called
> off?
> Jan: **No**, I don't. Maybe because of exams.
> **Well**, I'd better get to class. **Bye**.

The tone of voice and the situation can have a great
effect on the meaning of certain isolates. For example,
the *no*'s above have different meanings according to how
they are used. The first *no* expresses dismay, and the
second one just gives a negative answer. Sometimes the
punctuation is a clue to such differences in meaning.

● **Practice** 4-35 Look for the isolates in the
following conversation. Remember to judge by the
way the word is used, not just by whether it appears
on the list of possible isolates.

1. "Hello. Do you know this area very well?"
2. "Yes—why do you ask?"
3. "Well, could you tell me how to get to the post
   office from here, please?"
4. "Why, yes, just turn right at the next corner,
   and it's the, uh, third building on the left."
5. "Okay, turn right at the corner and the post
   office is the third building down?"
6. "Right."
7. "Thanks."

Chapter 5
The Basic Sentence Patterns

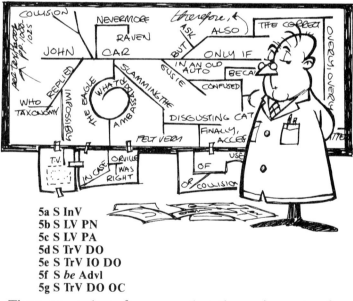

5a S InV
5b S LV PN
5c S LV PA
5d S TrV DO
5e S TrV IO DO
5f S *be* Advl
5g S TrV DO OC

There are only a few ways that the main parts of a simple sentence in English can be put together; we call these ways the **basic sentence patterns** of English. All simple sentences are based on these few sentence patterns—and all other sentences are built from simple sentences. If you can recognize at least the first five of these patterns, you have the basis for understanding some of the most important things about how sentences work.

Here is a listing of the five most common patterns with examples and pattern diagrams:

Pattern	Example	Diagram
S InV	S InV Joe laughed. He was laughing (at Brownie).	$\underline{S \mid InV}$
S_1 LV PN_1	S LV PN Brownie is his dog.	$\underline{S \mid LV \setminus PN}$
S LV PA	S LV PA She looked funny. She was very muddy.	$\underline{S \mid LV \setminus PA}$
S_1 TrV DO_2	S TrV DO Muddy leaves covered her back.	$\underline{S \mid TrV \mid DO}$
S_1 TrV IO_2 DO_3	S TrV IO DO Joe gave Brownie a bath.	$\underline{S \mid TrV \mid DO}$ $\setminus IO$

In the left column the subscript numbers are the same within a pattern whenever the two pattern parts would refer to the same person or thing. The numbers are different whenever the two parts would normally refer to different persons or things.

5a S InV

$$\underline{S \mid InV}$$

The two essential parts of S InV are a subject (S) and a verb. We call the verb an intransitive verb (InV) because it needs nothing to complete it—that is, the sentence can be complete with just the subject and the verb. Here are some examples:

S		*InV*	
Joe		laughed.	
He		was laughing	(at Brownie.)
My friend	(nearly)	fell	(down the stairs.)
Everyone		talked	(loudly.)

Some of these sentences have adverbial words or phrases as modifiers, shown here in parentheses; but the sentences would still be complete and correct if these were left out. Remember to ignore modifying words and phrases when you are identifying a sentence pattern.

● **Practice 5-1** All of the following sentences have the pattern *S InV.* Copy each sentence and write *S* above the simple subject. Write *InV* above the true verb.

>   S   InV
> The crowd was waiting expectantly.

1. The general finally arrived.
2. Now the ceremony could begin.
3. The valiant young lieutenant stepped to the front.
4. He looked into his commander's eyes.
5. A tear rolled down the old general's cheek.
6. Such rewards belong only to the brave.

As always, you will find the answers in the back of the book.

5b S LV PN

> S | LV \ PN

The three parts of S LV PN are the subject (S), the linking verb (LV), and the predicate noun (PN). The **predicate noun** is a noun (or noun-substitute) in the predicate that renames or identifies the subject. (See **2b** for the predicate.) That is, the subject and the predicate noun always refer to the same person or thing. They are linked by the verb, which can be thought of as something like an equal sign:

$$S \overset{(=)}{LV} PN$$

In the examples that follow, notice that the predicate noun always renames the subject:

S	LV		PN
Brownie	is		his dog.
My older brother	has become		a good mechanic.
Sandra	was	(always)	a faithful friend.
An orange	is		a citrus fruit.

The third sentence shows that there can be adverbial modifiers along with the pattern parts.

● **Practice 5-2** The following sentences have only the first two patterns, *S InV* and *S LV PN*. Copy the sentences and write S above every simple subject. If a sentence has a predicate noun (renaming the subject), label the noun *PN* and label the main verb word *LV*. Otherwise label the verb *InV*. In other words, each sentence will have as labels either both parts of *S InV* or all three parts of *S LV PN*.

```
         S         LV      PN
Andrew Carnegie was a poor man in 1853.
```

1. Carnegie was working in the telegraph office of a railroad company.
2. Later he moved into the steel industry.
3. His wealth increased through hard work and wise investments.
4. By 1900 he had become a millionaire.
5. In his later years he was a generous contributor to worthy causes.
6. Carnegie's financial success sprang from America's free-enterprise system.

5c S LV PA

$$S \mid LV \setminus PA$$

The pattern S LV PA has three main parts: a subject, a linking verb, and a predicate adjective. The predicate adjective is an adjective that appears in the predicate but describes the subject. (It describes the subject but does not directly modify it.) As in the pattern S LV PN, the verb is something like an equal sign: it serves mainly to link the subject with an important word in the predicate.

$$S \overset{(=)}{LV} PA$$

In the examples that follow, notice that the predicate adjective describes the subject, not anything in the predicate:

S		LV		PA
Brownie		looked		funny.
My teacher		is	(usually)	early.
A gracious person	(never)	seems		rushed.
That plan		sounds		good.

Again we see that adverbial modifiers may be added without changing the pattern.

● **Practice 5-3** The sentences that follow will give you practice in labeling the first three patterns: *S InV, S LV PN,* and *S LV PA.* Be sure that you use all the parts of a single pattern above each sentence; never mix the patterns. (In number 7, put the same label on *life* as on *resurrection;* these are equal elements joined by *and.*)

        S   LV   PA
    Lazarus was very sick.

1. The doctors were helpless.
2. Finally Lazarus died.
3. After four days the Lord Jesus came to the tomb.
4. Lazarus had been His friend.

5. Jesus called with a loud voice.
6. Lazarus walked out of the grave.
7. Jesus Christ is the resurrection and the life.

(From John 11:1-44)

When you check your work, look carefully to be sure that you have not mixed any of the patterns.

One final note: because predicate adjectives and predicate nouns both are completers of the information about the subject, they can be called **subjective complements.**

PA
PN   =   subjective complements

They *complete* the information about the *subject*.

5d S TrV DO

S | TrV | DO

Some sentences have a word that receives the action of the verb; we call that word the **direct object** of the verb. The direct object always refers to something different from the subject, except when the direct object is a reflexive pronoun ending in *-self* or *-selves*. Because the verb in this pattern has a receiver of action (the direct object), it is called a transitive verb. The most common pattern involving transitive verbs and direct objects is the one presented here, S TrV DO.

S	TrV	DO	
Muddy leaves	covered	her back.	
Mr. Anderson	has (not) read	that book	(yet).
Susan	saw	me	(in the picture).
Susan	saw	herself	(in the picture).

Notice that in the first three sentences the subject and the direct object refer to different things. As the last sentence shows, if we ever want to have a direct object that refers to the same thing as the subject, we make that direct object a *-self* pronoun.

We could represent the difference between this pattern and S LV PN by using subscript numbers to tell us how many people or things are being talked about. With this system we use the same number twice to refer twice to the same thing, but we use different numbers to refer to different things:

$$S_1 \text{ LV PN}_1$$
$$S_1 \text{ TrV DO}_2$$

In other words, a predicate noun always refers to the same thing as the subject, but a direct object refers to something different (unless it is a *-self* pronoun). We identify the patterns by what follows the verb, not by the type of verb. Verb types are defined by the patterns, not the other way around.

> ● **Practice 5-4** Now see whether you can tell the difference between *S LV PN* and *S TrV DO*. On your own paper, label the main words of each sentence with one of these two patterns.
>
> 1. The groundhog saw his shadow on the snow.
> 2. He supposedly became a very worried creature.
> 3. He hid himself in his burrow.
> 4. Afterward the people had six more weeks of winter.
> 5. Today the groundhog story has become a legend.
> 6. The second day of February is Groundhog Day.

5e S TrV IO DO

Sometimes a sentence with a direct object also has an indirect object. An indirect object comes before the direct object and tells *to whom* or *for whom* the action is done. An indirect object does not follow a preposition. As in the pattern S TrV DO, the verb here is transitive, since there is a receiver of action (the direct object).

S	TrV	IO	DO	
Joe	gave	his dog	a bath.	
Tom's mother	will buy	him	some stationery.	
Tom's mother	will buy	herself	some stationery	(too).

As with all the patterns, adverbial modifiers can be added.

As in the first two sample sentences above, the subject and the indirect object and the direct object all usually refer to different things or people:

$$S_1 \text{ TrV IO}_2 \text{ DO}_3$$

If either one of the objects should ever refer to the same thing or person as the subject, it will take the form of a reflexive -*self* pronoun, as in the last example above. The only exception is that in a very relaxed spoken style sometimes a plain personal pronoun is used instead:

Colloquial only	I got me a new notebook.

Always correct	I got myself a new notebook.

Normally, of course, all three nouns or pronouns refer to different things.

Sentences that have indirect objects can usually be restated with prepositional phrases instead. In that case, the sentence pattern changes even though the meaning does not.

	S TrV IO DO
S TrV IO DO	Joe gave Spot a bath.

	S TrV DO
S TrV DO	Joe gave a bath (to Spot).

Remember that an object of a preposition cannot be anything else at the same time. Also remember that in today's English the indirect object always comes before the direct object.

● **Practice 5-5** The following group of sentences includes two patterns: *S TrV DO* and *S TrV IO DO*. Copy the sentences and label the pattern parts.

1. The children took the old radio to school.
2. They showed it to their friends.
3. Jack offered them ten dollars for it.
4. They suggested a higher price.
5. In the end they sold the radio to Jill.

● **Practice 5-6** This exercise includes all of the five common sentence patterns. Copy the sentences and label the pattern parts.

1. One of the worst natural disasters in our history happened in Johnstown in 1889.
2. Johnstown is a city in western Pennsylvania.
3. Joseph Johns gave the city its name.
4. The valley setting of the city is very beautiful.
5. In 1889 a heavy rainfall swelled the reservoir behind the South Fork Dam.
6. The earthen dam finally burst under the pressure.
7. The flood waters covered the city.
8. Approximately 2100 people died in the flood.
9. Clara Barton of the Red Cross offered the survivors her help.
10. High-water markers on certain downtown buildings are reminders of the historic disaster.

5f S *be* Advl

S	be	\\ Advl

A sixth kind of sentence contains either a prepositional phrase or an adverb after some form of the true verb *be*.

S	be		*Advl*	
Sandy	is	(already)	in the house.	
The mailman	was		here	(then).
The game	will be		after lunch.	
The meeting	is		now.	

Advl in this pattern stands for *adverbial,* to include adverbs like *here* and *now* and adverb-like prepositional phrases such as *in the house.* These adverbs and prepositional phrases normally have meanings of place and time.* *Be* is named in the pattern because no other verb is ever used in it. Notice that the word or phrase after *be* seems to be telling us something about the subject, since *be* has no real meaning of its own.

In summary, the last element of the pattern is called *Advl* to recognize its adverb-like qualities, but it is included as part of the sentence pattern because it is not an ordinary, optional modifier of the verb.

When the third element of this pattern is a prepositional phrase, parentheses will help make the labeling clear:

>   S   *be*   Advl
> Sandy is already (in the house).

The interrogative adverbs *where* and *when* can be used in this pattern, as well as along with other patterns.

>   S   *be* Advl   Advl *be*   S
> Sandy is where? ⟹ Where is Sandy?
>
>   S   InV   S InV
> She went where? ⟹ Where did she go?

Notice the reversal of the pattern elements when the interrogative adverb is brought to the beginning of the S *be* Advl sentence.

---

* Occasionally a prepositional phrase unrelated to place or time occurs after *be: This space is for the handicapped; His death was with honor; Her bravery was without equal.* These could be considered examples of either S LV PA or S *be* Advl, according to one's preference. Probably a good rule of thumb, though, is to consider them examples of S *be* Advl unless *seem* could substitute for *be.* By that rule only the last of these would be S LV PA.

• **Practice 5-7** Copy the sentences and label the pattern parts.
1. Where are the mysterious Galapagos Islands?
2. The Galapagos Islands are in the Pacific Ocean.
3. They are a part of Ecuador.
4. Herman Melville gave them a different name, the Enchanted Islands.
5. English buccaneers and whalers first discovered these islands.
6. The land turtles on these islands are gigantic.
7. Sailors used them as a source of fresh meat.
8. Didn't Charles Darwin develop his preposterous theory of evolution after a visit to these islands?
9. When did he visit there?
10. In 1835 he was there.

Some sentences with the pattern S *be* Advl can be said in a different way.

Normal Order	*Inverted Order*

$$\text{S } \textit{be} \quad \text{Advl} \qquad \textit{be} \quad \text{S} \quad \text{Advl}$$
A boy is (at the door). ⟹ There is a boy (at the door).

$$\text{S } \textit{be} \text{ Advl} \qquad \textit{be} \quad \text{S Advl}$$
Two boys are here. ⟹ There are two boys here.

The sentences on the right mean the same thing as the original sentences on the left. The same word is the subject in both versions: the verb agrees with the subject even when the subject and the verb are inverted.

In the inverted sentences, the empty word *there* stands where the subject would usually be. *There,* sometimes called an expletive, is simply a place-holder for the delayed subject.

We often use the inverted form of this pattern when we want to introduce a new topic, and we may even leave out the adverbial part.

$$\qquad\qquad\qquad \textit{be} \qquad\qquad \text{S}$$
Once upon a time, there was a wicked king
$$\quad \text{Advl}$$
(in a rich country.)

Once upon a time, there *be* was a wicked *S* king.

The inversion seems to allow a greater focus on the subject.

5g S TrV DO OC

S	TrV	DO \ OC

Certain sentences with direct objects have some element—usually a noun or an adjective—after the direct object to complete the idea of what the verb does to the direct object.

S	*TrV*	*DO*	*OC*
We	can make	the meeting	longer.
The club	considered	Tanya	very capable.
We	elected	her	president.
We	declared	her	the winner.

In all of these sentences the last element either describes or renames the direct object. Just as predicate adjectives and predicate nouns can be called *subjective* complements (because they complete the information about the subject), the adjectives and nouns here are called *objective* complements.

Objective complements complete the information about the direct object, as a result of the action of the verb. We could even imagine some form of *be* between the direct object and the objective complement:

Ideas understood in the sentences above	The meeting *will be* longer, because we can make it so. Tanya *is* capable, as we consider it. Tanya *is* president, because we elected her. She *is* the winner, because we declared it.

The verb in the pattern S TrV DO OC is transitive, because it is followed by a direct object. Not many verbs can be used in this pattern.

Notice the differences between this pattern and the one with the indirect object. First, the direct object always *follows* an indirect object, but it always *precedes* an objective complement.

S TrV IO **DO**   S TrV **DO** OC

Then consider how many different people or things are normally referred to in the two patterns.

S_1 TrV IO_2 DO_3 S_1 TrV DO_2 OC_2

The left pattern shows that the subject, the indirect object, and the direct object all refer to different people or things. In the new pattern, there are just two people or things, because the objective complement refers to or describes the same thing as the direct object.

IO and DO different |

> S   TrV   IO
> The teacher$_1$ told his students$_2$ a
>   DO
> strange story.$_3$

Noun OC renames DO |

> S   TrV   DO
> The teacher$_1$ called his students$_2$
>   OC
> fine people.$_2$

Adj OC describes DO |

> S   TrV   DO   OC
> The teacher$_1$ called his students$_2$ brilliant.$_2$

- **Practice 5-8** Copy the sentences and label the pattern parts. All of the patterns may be included.
  1. In A.D. 330 Constantine the Great made Constantinople the new capital of the Roman Empire.
  2. During this time Constantine gave the Christians relief from years of persecution.
  3. Constantinople is on the shores of the Bosporus River.
  4. During the Middle Ages this large European city was magnificent.

5. By the tenth century one million people lived in this city.
6. Constantinople's church Hagia Sophia, Holy Wisdom, is one of the supreme architectural masterpieces of the Middle Ages.
7. Historians call this period the Byzantine period.
8. These people, however, considered themselves "Romans."
9. A triple wall of fortification and the use of Greek fire protected this city from most invaders.
10. Eventually, though, the Turks captured the city.
11. They renamed it Istanbul.

Chapter 6
Major Functions in the Sentence

This chapter is a summary of functions—what words and phrases do in the sentence.

6a Function Versus Part of Speech

In any sentence we can ask two very different questions about the words:

> What *kind* of word is this? —part of speech
> What does it *do* in this
> sentence? —function

For example, we can ask both questions about the individual words in the sentence "A wise man prepares for the future."

Part of Speech (kind of word)		Function (what it does)
determiner	A	modifier (of *man*)
adjective	wise	modifier (of *man*)
noun	man	simple subject (of *prepares*)
verb	prepares	simple predicate (of *man*)
preposition	for	relater (of *prepares* and *the future*)
determiner	the	modifier (of *future*)
noun	future.	(simple) object of the preposition (*for*)

Individual words have functions, and phrases (groups of words) also have functions. Labeled below are the functions of the phrases in that same sample sentence.

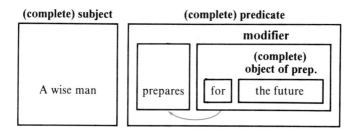

Words of the same part of speech can often be used in different ways. The two nouns in the sample sentence above have different functions—*man* is the simple subject and *future* is the simple object of the preposition. A noun can even be a modifier, as is *Bible* below. And, of course, a pronoun can do nearly anything that a noun can do.

Part of Speech (kind of word)		Function (what it does)
pronoun	She	subject (of *can remember*)
adverb	usually	modifier (of *can remember*)
auxiliary	can ⎫	simple
verb	remember ⎭	predicate (of *she*)
noun	Bible	modifier (of *references*)
noun	references.	direct object (of *can remember*)

How do we know the part of speech and the function of a word? We know its part of speech by applying tests like those found in Chapters 3 and 4. We know its function in a particular sentence by recognizing how it fits into its own group of words (its phrase or clause) within the sentence, and then often by recognizing how that group of words is related to the rest of the sentence. For instance, if a word is an object, it is an object *of* something. If it is a modifier, it is a modifier *of* something.

Function, then, is what a word does in the sentence. And whatever it does, it does in relation to the rest of the sentence.

● **Practice 6-1** Find all the nouns in the following sentences. For each sentence, tell which noun functions as the simple subject.
1. A good spirit makes a successful team.
2. What captain wants a lazy player?
3. In a skillful team, each member helps and depends on his teammates.

6b Functions of Nouns and Pronouns

(1) Subjects, predicate nouns, and the subjective case
(2) Objects and the objective case

(3) Possessives and the possessive case
(4) Appositives
(5) Modifying nouns
(6) Nouns of address
(7) Adverbial nouns
(8) Complements of verbals
(9) "Subjects" of verbals
(10) Objective complements
(11) Complements in passive sentences

Nouns and pronouns can be used in a number of different ways. The most frequent uses—subject, predicate noun, the various objects, and the possessives—are grouped in the first three sections below according to their appropriate case forms. The other "noun functions" (as we call them for short) appear separately.

(1) Subjects, predicate nouns, and the subjective case

Every sentence pattern begins with *S* for the **subject.** The five most common patterns illustrate all the common meanings of the subject.

Pattern	Meaning of Subject	Example
S InV	S = doer of the action	*Joe* smiled.
S LV PN	S = the one identified	*He* was the host.
S LV PA	S = the one described	*He* seemed happy.
S TrV DO	S = doer of the action	*He* opened the door.
S TrV IO DO	S = doer of the action	*We* brought Sue a gift.

Whenever a pronoun is used as the subject, its form is that of the subjective case. For instance, *he* and *we* (not *him* and *us*) are used as subjects in the examples above. Sections **4a(2.4 and 2.6)** give further information on the subjective case.

One pattern, S LV PN, includes a predicate noun.* The **predicate noun** is a noun that appears in the predicate but renames the subject. (It might also be a noun-equivalent, like a pronoun.)

S LV   PN
He was *the host.*   (He = host)

In formal English a pronoun used as a predicate noun is in the subjective case.

S   LV PN
"May I speak with Mary, please?" "This is *she.*"

In an informal setting the subjective form may sound awkward. Some people would use the objective form here, especially in familiar conversation. Others would reword to avoid the problem: "This is Mary."

● **Practice 6-2** The following sentences use the five most common sentence patterns. Copy the sentences and label the pattern parts. Then underline the complete subject in every sentence and the complete predicate noun when there is one.

S   LV   PN
Howler monkeys are the jungle's noisemakers.

1. Howler monkeys abound throughout South and Central America.
2. They make loud, resounding calls.
3. They are the largest New World monkeys.
4. The treetops provide howlers food and protection.

** Predicate nouns are still sometimes called *predicate nominatives,* nominative being the term in Latin grammar for the subjective case. We use the term *predicate noun* as being (1) parallel with the term *predicate adjective* and (2) immediately understandable, since most predicate nouns are in fact nouns. We are then free to use the English-based case terms *subjective, objective,* and *possessive* (rather than nominative, accusative-dative,* and *genitive).*

5. Consequently, they rarely descend to the ground.
6. Howlers can be black, brown, or red.
7. Fifteen to eighteen animals are a typical howler clan.

(2) Objects and the objective case

There are three basic kinds of objects: direct objects, indirect objects, and objects of prepositions. **Direct objects** are found in two common patterns:

Pattern	Meaning of Direct Object	Example
S TrV DO	Receiver of action of verb	I saw *him.*
S TrV IO DO	Receiver of action of verb	He gave me *the news.*

Indirect objects are found in one sentence pattern:

Pattern	Meaning of Indirect Object	Example
S TrV IO DO	The one to whom or for whom an action is done	He gave *me* the news.

Objects of prepositions accompany prepositions in any kind of sentence. In the examples below, the prepositional phrases appear between parentheses. The

patterns are labeled, and an underline shows the extent of every complete noun phrase that is used as an object. The abbreviation *OP* means "object of preposition."

          S   TrV   DO

Our church invited <u>local officials</u> (to <u>our July</u>

       (OP)

  <u>Fourth service</u>).

          S   TrV   IO   DO

The pastor gave <u>all his listeners</u> <u>a challenge.</u>

    Any pronoun used as an object is in the objective case.

                   DO

Our church invited *them* to our service.

              IO

The pastor gave *us* a challenge.

       OP

All (of *us)* should be good citizens.

Section **4a(2.6)** gives specific rules for using the objective case.

- **Practice 6-3** Copy the following sentences and label the pattern elements. Place parentheses around prepositional phrases, using (*OP*) to label the objects of the prepositions. Then underline all the complete objects of any type, following the examples above.
  1. This is our farmhouse on the left.
  2. The house is old-fashioned but comfortable.
  3. Dad built my mother a porch swing.
  4. In late fall, Mom plants tulips along the front walk.
  5. In the spring, Dad plants sweet corn beyond the barn.
  6. He gives us the lawn mowers.
  7. We feel privileged, of course.

(3) Possessives and the possessive case

(3.1) Possessive determiners
(3.2) Independent possessives

Both nouns and pronouns can be used in the possessive case to show some kind of possession or belongingness. Possessives are used in sentences either as determiners or as independent possessives.

(3.1) Possessive determiners Most often, possessives directly modify nouns. When they do, they are determiners, signals that a noun is coming. Determiners come before any true adjectives that may modify the same noun.

Jan's red notebook	*that man's* new car
her red notebook	*his* new car

The first example, *Jan's,* is a simple possessive noun acting as a determiner; it can be replaced by the possessive determiner *her*. The possessive noun *man's,* though, is part of a possessive phrase acting as a determiner. A **possessive phrase** is two or more words working together to show possession. Notice that in the example the possessive *his* would replace the whole possessive phrase, not just the word *man's*. Also, "*that man's* new car" is equivalent to "the new car of *that man.*"

Possessive determiners take these forms:

Made From—		
Personal pronouns	my	our
	your	your
	his, her, its	their
The pronoun *who*	whose (can also serve as the possessive of *which*)	
Indefinite pronouns and proper nouns	everyone's Paul's	
Other noun phrases (forming possessive phrases)	that man's my older brother's	

The spelling rules for possessive nouns and possessive indefinite pronouns are given in **16c(2.1)**.

- **Practice 6-4** Find the possessive determiners in the following sentences.
  1. My brother's hamster escaped last night.
  2. For some reason, its cage doesn't satisfy it.
  3. Maybe Bobby's pet snake in the next cage scares his hamster.
  4. Waking with my brother's hamster nibbling on my ear was unnerving.

(3.2) **Independent possessives** Possessives can stand in place of an entire noun phrase, so that the thing possessed is not named.

> I like your earphones. *Mine*^S^ are too small.

Here the independent possessive *mine* stands alone in the noun position of subject of the sentence. It replaces the understood noun phrase *my earphones*. Independent possessives can occur in all the major noun functions.

> Did you bring your tapes? I brought *mine*.^DO^

> Mary hasn't seen her mother yet, but I told *mine*^IO^
>
> the whole story.

> This is your sweater, but that one is *mine*.^PN^

> He stood beside his bike, and I stood beside *mine*.^OP^

Not only single words but possessive phrases can function as independent possessives.

> I don't see my canteen, but I do see *my sister's*.^DO^

(Possessive phrases are defined in **6b(3.1)** just above.)

Except for some of the possessives made from personal pronouns, the independent possessives have the same form as the possessive determiners. Independent possessives take these forms:

Made From—		
Personal pronouns	mine	ours
	yours	yours
	his, hers, its	theirs
The pronoun *who*	whose	
Indefinite pronouns and proper nouns	everyone's Paul's	
Other noun phrases (forming possessive phrases)	that man's my older brother's	

The spelling rules for possessive nouns and possessive indefinite pronouns are given in **16c(2.1)**.

- **Practice 6-5** Find the independent possessives in the following sentences. Do not confuse them with possessive determiners.
  1. Whose is this?
  2. Is this your aardvark, Caroline?
  3. Not at all—mine is bigger than that.
  4. That one is the teacher's, I think.
  5. My aardvark's snout is longer, too.

- **Practice 6-6** Copy the sentences, label the parts of the sentence patterns, and underline all the possessive words and possessive phrases. If an independent possessive is used as the object of a preposition, label it with *(OP)*.

                 S   InV
  A centurion's servant was suffering from palsy.

  1. The Lord restored the servant's health.
  2. Peter's mother-in-law was sick with a fever.
  3. The Lord healed her with the touch of His hand on hers.
  4. A widow's sobs for her dead son reached the Lord's ears.
  5. His tender heart responded to the widow's.
  6. The young man became alive at the Lord's command.

- **Practice 6-7** Copy the four sentences of Practice 6-6 that contain possessive phrases, substituting a possessive pronoun for each possessive phrase.

(4) Appositives

Sometimes one noun or noun phrase comes right after another that it renames and further identifies. It is the second noun that functions as an appositive.

S   (App)   TrV
The Smiths, my nearest neighbors, have
DO
a beautiful yard.

A noun performing any of the main sentence functions can have an appositive after it.

S   InV   (OP)   (App)
My sister plays with Joyce, the girl next door.

S   TrV IO   (App)   DO
They gave Tiny, Joyce's dog, her first bath.

Occasionally an appositive does not immediately follow the noun it renames; but it *could,* if the sentence were restated.

DO   App
I bought some flowers yesterday, big red roses.

DO   App
Yesterday I bought some flowers, big red roses.

Although most appositives are nouns, occasionally a pronoun may be an appositive. (See **4a(8)** for intensive pronouns.)

Notice that all of the appositive phrases given above are set off by commas. This is the usual punctuation for appositives. However, no commas are used with a "close appositive"—a short appositive that is more important than the noun or pronoun before it. There are two kinds of close appositives:

Noun renaming a personal pronoun	S (App) TrV IO (App) We girls have found you boys DO a good job.
Short proper name needed to identify the one discussed	S InV (OP) Tom was talking to his friend (App) Peter Ames then. *(Surely Tom has more than one friend.)*

If you will read these examples aloud and compare them with the ones in the previous paragraph, you will be able to hear which ones need the commas. Most appositives do need commas.

Finally, let's be sure about the difference between appositives and predicate nouns, since both of these rename a noun or pronoun that comes earlier in the sentence. Predicate nouns, you remember, occur in just one pattern: S LV PN. Therefore a predicate noun always renames the subject of the sentence, with a linking verb in between:

    S   LV   PN
Peter was a fisherman.

Though an appositive may rename a subject, there will not be a linking verb between the two:

    S   (App)   InV
Peter, a fisherman, started toward the Lord on the water.

    S   (App)   LV   PN
Peter, a fisherman, later became a leading apostle.

Finding the parts of the sentence pattern first should make it easy for you to tell the difference between appositives and predicate nouns.

- **Practice 6-8** Copy the sentences, underline the complete appositives, and add commas where needed. (You may find it helpful to label the sentence patterns first.)
  1. Herman Melville the famous American novelist based his stories on his experiences at sea.
  2. In 1841 he became a seaman on the whaling ship *Acushnet*.
  3. Later he spent some time in the Marquesas Islands a group of islands in the South Pacific.
  4. *Typee* Melville's first novel draws its inspiration from his adventures on these islands.
  5. After a month on the islands, he took another whaler an Australian vessel to Tahiti.
  6. His most famous whaling story is the novel *Moby-Dick*.

(5) Modifying nouns

A modifying noun is an individual noun used to modify another noun. Modifying nouns follow any determiners and true adjectives that may be present in the noun phrase.

```
Det  Adj  ModN  N
his warm wool jacket
```

Notice the part-of-speech differences between the adjective *warm* and the noun *wool*. *Warm* passes the adjective tests given in **3d(1)**:

1. *Warm* usually modifies a noun.
2. *Warm* can be compared using *-er/-est* or *more/most: warmer, warmest.*
3. *Warm* can fill both blanks in the test frame: The *warm* thing is very *warm.*

Wool does not pass the set of adjective tests, but instead has the characteristics given in **3b(1)** for nouns:

1. *Wool* names a thing.
2. *Wool* can be made possessive by a change in form: *wool's strength.*
3. *Wool* can function as subject, direct object, and so on: *Wool is warmer than cotton.*

Wool and *warm* are different parts of speech, but the two words have the same function in the phrase *his warm wool jacket*—both words are modifiers. Therefore we call the noun *wool* a **modifying** noun.

- **Practice 6-9** Write down the complete noun phrases. Then label the adjectives and modifying nouns, using *Adj* and *ModN*.

  <pre>
              Adj ModN   Adj
  The cold ocean waves pounded the bleak shoreline.
  </pre>

  1. Gray rain clouds blackened the noonday sun.
  2. Hungry sea gulls and brown pelicans scanned the water for a fish dinner.
  3. An autumn storm lashed the sandy beach.

(6) Nouns of address

Proper names, or sometimes other kinds of noun phrases, can be used in addressing someone. We then call these "nouns (or pronouns) of address." They have no function in the sentence except to identify the person being addressed.

> Well, *Joe,* how's your ankle today?
>
> All right, *you in the back,* sit up and listen.
>
> *Neighbors and friends,* I ask you to vote for me next week.

As in these examples, noun-of-address phrases are set off by commas.

- **Practice 6-10** Find the four nouns of address in Ephesians 6:1-9. Some of them may be phrases.

(7) Adverbial nouns

Nouns (or more accurately, noun phrases) can be used to modify verbs. They frequently have meanings of time, place, or manner.

> I usually work all day,
>
> but this Friday I'm going home early.

I have never done it that way before,

but I'll try it your way the next time.

The main words in all these phrases meet the noun tests given in **3b(1),** but they modify verbs. Anything that modifies a verb is adverbial (adverb-like) in function, and so we call these nouns **adverbial nouns.** (The term *adverbial noun phrase* can be used to specify the whole adverbial phrase.)

- **Practice 6-11** Find the adverbial noun phrases.
  1. Before the end of the school year, I thought I would want to sleep late every morning all summer.
  2. Instead, I woke up early the first day.
  3. In fact, the whole month of June I never slept late.
  4. Well, I *did* get a job the second day.
  5. Who can stay home when a good job is available?

(8) Complements of verbals

Verbals are infinitives *(to run),* participles (a *running* stream), and gerunds (I enjoy *running*). Verbals, also called nonfinite verbs, are explained in **7f.** The present section assumes that you are familiar with simple verbals, as presented in **7f(1, 2.1, 3.1, 4.1).**

First, let's be sure what complements are. All the sentence patterns except S InV require at least one thing after the verb to complete the pattern—PA, DO, and so on. The standard term for these "completers" of the patterns is **complements.**

Although verbals (nonfinite verbs) cannot be the simple predicates of sentences, they are still made from verbs. And because they are made from normal finite verbs, they can have the normal kinds of complements.

Finite verb	S	TrV	IO			DO
	Sandra	showed	people			her photo album.

Infinitive	She likes <u>to show people her album</u>.

(IO)   (DO)

Gerund	She enjoys <u>showing people her album</u>.

(IO)   (DO)

Participle	<u>Showing people her album</u>, Sandra gets very excited.

(IO)   (DO)

In these examples we see direct and indirect objects of an infinitive, a gerund, and a participle.

To decide what kind of complement a verbal has, imagine the verbal as a finite verb in a sentence, and see what the pattern would be.

Infinitive phrase	He wants <u>to be a success</u>.

?

Independent clause	He wants something: S LV PN He will <u>be a success</u>.

Complement identified	He wants <u>to be a success</u>.

(PN)

Here too, the language is systematic: the sentence patterns give us the basic plan not only for independent and dependent clauses, but also for verbal phrases.

- **Practice 6-12** Write down the complete verbal phrases, and in parentheses label the types of complements that they contain.
  1. Charles Francis Adams, grandson of John and Abigail Adams, was selected by Lincoln to be his ambassador to England.
  2. Being sympathetic to the Confederate cause, England considered recognition of the Confederacy as a nation.

3. Adams's diplomatic skill was responsible for preventing British recognition of the South.
4. Faithfully serving the American people was a tradition in the Adams family.

(9) "Subjects" of verbals

Because verbals (infinitives, gerunds, and participles) are made from regular finite verbs, there is always a "subject" understood. In most cases that means that there is an understood doer of the action. Let's look at some examples:

Infinitive phrase	I want *to go home now.*
Understood meaning	I want something: *I* go home now.
Gerund phrase	Jack likes *winning races.*
Understood meaning	Jack likes something: *Jack* wins races.
Participle phrase	Ruth, *walking along behind,* saw something odd.
Understood meaning	Ruth saw something odd. *Ruth* was walking along behind.

Notice that in all of these the understood "subject" of the verbal is the same as the subject of the finite verb (I want, I go; Jack likes, Jack wins; etc.). Therefore the understood subjects of these verbals are not stated in the sentence.

With infinitives and gerunds, though, it is also possible to have a *different* "subject" for the verbal. This "subject" must appear in the sentence. (The quotation marks around *subject* are a reminder that we are speaking of a subject only in meaning, not in its grammatical form.)

Infinitive phrase	I want *him to go home now*.
Understood meaning	I want something: *He* goes home now.
Gerund phrase	Jack likes *my winning races*.
Understood meaning	Jack likes something: *I* win races.

In the first sentence, *him* is the "subject" of the infinitive. It is part of the infinitive phrase. As rule 11 of **4a(2.6)** points out, "subjects" of infinitives are in the objective case. In the second example, *my* modifies the gerund *winning* as its "subject." Rule 10 of **4a(2.6)** points out that "subjects" of gerunds are correct in the possessive case.

● **Practice 6-13** Write down the verbal phrases in the following sentences. If a gerund or an infinitive has an expressed "subject," underline it.

> President John Adams wanted <u>his wife</u> to be influential in his administration.

1. Taking control of the social life of her husband's administration, Abigail Adams enthralled Washington with her graciousness.
2. In rearing her son, John Quincy Adams, she purposely trained him to become a president of the United States.
3. She became a rich source of early American history by her grandson's publishing of her many letters.

4. By contributing to America as a wife, mother, and historian, Abigail Adams became one of America's most distinguished first ladies.

(10) Objective complements

When a noun is an objective complement, it renames the direct object. Objective complements occur in only one sentence pattern.

$$\text{S} \qquad \text{TrV} \qquad \text{DO} \qquad\qquad \text{OC}$$
The coach designated Johnson *the pinch hitter*.

See **5g** for more information on objective complements.

(11) Complements in passive sentences

(11.1) Retained (direct) objects
(11.2) Retained (indirect) objects
(11.3) Subjective complements in passive sentences

The pattern parts that follow the verb are called the **complements** (completers) of the various patterns. When an active sentence has two complements, one of them usually remains in the complement position when the sentence is made passive.

(11.1) Retained (direct) objects

Passives are sometimes made from active sentences that have both indirect and direct objects. Often this is done by making the indirect object of the active sentence into the subject of the passive sentence.

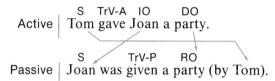

```
              S  TrV-A  IO      DO
   Active │ Tom gave Joan a party.

              S        TrV-P  RO
   Passive │ Joan was given a party (by Tom).
```

Joan becomes the subject, and *Tom* is either left out or made the object of the preposition *by. A party,* though, stays where it was; that is, it is **retained** (kept) in object position. An object that is retained after the verb when a sentence becomes passive is called a **retained object** (RO). Thus retained objects are found only in passive sentences.

● **Practice 6-14** Find the complete retained objects in the following sentences. Not every sentence has one.
1. The attacking Roman Catholic armies were dealt a tremendous defeat by the Hussites of Bohemia.
2. One Catholic army after another had been handed embarrassing setbacks by this ragtag Christian army.
3. The Catholic generals were continually out-maneuvered by John Zizka, the blind leader of the Hussites.
4. Zizka's peasant army used armored farm wagons mounted with small cannons to repulse the superior armies of the Holy Roman Empire.
5. History was given the name of John Zizka to add to the list of great military leaders.
6. By the genius of Zizka the world was given its first hint of modern motorized tank warfare.

(11.2) Retained (indirect) objects Section **6b(11.1),** just above, shows one way of making a passive from an active sentence that has both an indirect and a direct object. As illustrated there, often the indirect object is made the subject. However, we can also make the direct object into the subject of the passive sentence.

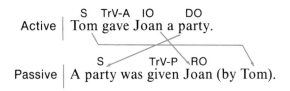

```
            S   TrV-A  IO      DO
Active | Tom gave Joan a party.

            S        TrV-P  RO
Passive | A party was given Joan (by Tom).
```

In this passive sentence the indirect object is retained in object position; it is therefore a **retained object** *(RO)*.

Another way of stating the passive sentence would be to insert the preposition *for* before *Joan*:

```
        S          TrV-P      (OP)
A party was given for Joan.
```

In this version, *Joan* is not a retained object, but the object of a preposition.

- **Practice 6-15** Find the retained objects in the following sentences, regardless of whether they have come from direct objects or from indirect objects. Not every sentence has a retained object.
  1. For years, many literary compliments have been paid Christina Rossetti for her superb poetry.
  2. She has been designated by many literary critics as the greatest female poet of British literature.
  3. Her poetry has been given high marks for its technical perfection.
  4. In addition, we have been provided through the spiritual themes in her poetry a deep insight into her devout Christian character and love for God.
  5. Many spiritual lessons have been given us by Christina Rossetti's unwavering devotion to the will of God.

(11.3) Subjective complements in passive sentences Observe what happens when a sentence with an objective complement is made into a passive sentence.

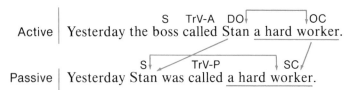

```
                    S   TrV-A  DO        OC
Active | Yesterday the boss called Stan a hard worker.

            S        TrV-P        SC
Passive | Yesterday Stan was called a hard worker.
```

The phrase *a hard worker* was an objective complement in the active sentence; it renamed *Stan,* the direct object. In the passive sentence it still renames *Stan*—but since *Stan* is now the subject, *a hard worker* is now a subjective complement, abbreviated *SC.* (You may remember that predicate nouns and predicate adjectives can be called subjective complements, because they rename or describe the subject.)

The same thing happens when the objective complement is an adjective.

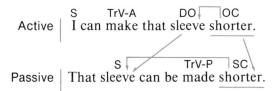

                S   TrV-A   DO   OC
Active │ I can make that sleeve shorter.

                        S   TrV-P   SC
Passive │ That sleeve can be made shorter.

In both sentences *shorter* describes the sleeve. In the active sentence *shorter* is an objective complement, and in the passive sentence it is a subjective complement.

Notice the similarity between a subjective complement with a transitive-passive verb and a subjective complement with a linking verb. Only the verb is different.

Stan was called a hard worker.
Stan has become a hard worker.

That sleeve can be made shorter.
That sleeve is now shorter.

● **Practice 6-16** Label the sentence patterns in the following sentences. Use *TrV-P* for passive verbs, *RO* for retained objects, and *SC* for subjective complements with passive verbs. Use the regular labels for active sentences.
1. The Waldenses were a strictly biblical group who were active during the Middle Ages.
2. They were severely persecuted by the Roman Catholics.
3. Continuous persecution was dealt these people for four centuries.

4. By their own members they were named "The Poor of Christ," on the basis of Christ's teaching in Matthew 5:3.

5. The Bible, translated into the common language, was made available to the people by the Waldenses.

6. The Roman Catholic church was called the "Babylonian house of lies" by these forerunners of the Reformation.

7. Later they gave the Reformation their full support.

6c The Noun Phrase

(1) Definition of the noun phrase
(2) Modifiers before the noun
(3) Modifiers after the noun or pronoun

One of the primary building blocks of the sentence is the noun phrase. An understanding of the noun phrase will help you recognize the main groups of words in the sentence.

This section is about what the noun phrase *is,* not what it does. What the noun phrase does is the same as what its main word does. For instance, consider the first sentence of this paragraph. Just as the noun *section* is the simple subject, the noun phrase *this section* is the complete subject. What *section* does, *this section* does. Thus the functions of noun phrases are described in **6b,** "Functions of Nouns and Pronouns."

(1) Definition of the noun phrase

A noun phrase consists of a noun or a pronoun and any modifiers it may have.

Three clarifications are in order.

1. For practical reasons the term *noun phrase* is used even when the noun or pronoun has no modifiers. Thus a noun phrase sometimes consists of a single word.

My brother likes fresh apples.

John likes apples.

He likes them.

2. The noun phrase contains actual modifiers, not words that are parts of other constructions. Even though a predicate adjective describes the subject, the predicate adjective is part of the predicate, not part of the complete subject.*

                                      S   LV   PA
    His first short novel was not successful.

3. Occasionally an adjective is used like a noun and is the main word of a noun phrase.

    The rich should not despise the poor.

    The poorest sometimes lose hope.

    Our hopeless poor are few.

    Because these phrases include determiners and sometimes others of the usual modifiers of nouns and because they act like noun phrases in the sentence, we do call them noun phrases.
    Notice, though, that their main word is indeed an adjective and not a noun. *Poor* cannot be made plural or possessive like a noun, but it can be compared (the poor*est*) and modified by a qualifier (the *very* poor) like an adjective. An adjective used like a noun can be called a *nominal adjective.*

    ---

    * Strictly speaking, a predicate adjective does not modify the subject, though it does describe whatever is named by the subject. Describing has to do with meaning; modifying has to do with the grammatical function of words in the sentence.

● **Practice 6-17** Find the noun phrases in the following sentences.
1. The old wall surrounded the orchard.
2. The pink blossoms attracted many bees to the orchard.
3. A lizard scurried up the tree.
4. Soon red apples would fill the tree.
5. Each limb would bend with the weight.
6. Men would come and pick the ripe fruit.
7. The harvest would surely be a good one.

(2) Modifiers before the noun

Most nouns are modified by a determiner (see **4c**). Determiners come at the beginning of the noun phrase.

> *the* thick books
> *all her* new science books

Adjectives come next (see **3d**).

> all her *new* science books
> those *thick, heavy* books

Modifying nouns follow adjectives. (See **6b(5)** for modifying nouns.)

> all her new *science* books

In summary, the most frequent modifiers that precede the noun appear in this order:

> Det   Adj   ModN

Section **4c(10)** contains a table of these pre-noun modifiers, including the various types of determiners.

Some noun phrases also contain participles. A participle by itself, with no modifiers or complements, normally comes somewhere before the noun it modifies. It may either follow or precede true adjectives.

	Det Adj Part ModN
After the adjective	a clear, *gurgling* mountain stream
	Det Adj Part
	that old *broken* chair

Before the adjective	a *gurgling* clear mountain stream
	that *broken* old chair

Most often, the participle follows the adjective.

- **Practice 6-18** Write down the noun phrases and label the modifiers of the nouns.
    1. The rusty screen door swung wildly in the wind.
    2. Faded green shutters slapped the decaying walls.
    3. The abandoned shack had once given many hikers some welcome shelter.
    4. Dust whirled up as the first raindrops fell.
    5. Blowing tree limbs noisily scraped the dented tin roof.
    6. The thunderstorm rolled by, and the empty cabin again sat silently in the woods.

One additional note about participles: sometimes a participle before a noun is modified by another word. If so, the participle and the other word are joined by a hyphen:

> an old *broken-down* chair
> those *fast-running* streams
> a *well-written* book

The hyphen shows that the two words modify the noun as a single unit.

(3) Modifiers after the noun or pronoun

(3.1) Prepositional phrases
(3.2) Infinitives and infinitive phrases
(3.3) Participle phrases
(3.4) Modified adjectives
(3.5) Compound adjectives or participles
(3.6) Adverbs
(3.7) Time phrases
(3.8) Appositives
(3.9) Adjective clauses

Both nouns and pronouns can be modified by words or word groups that follow them. These modifiers too are part of the complete noun phrase. That is, they are part of the complete subject, the complete direct object, and so on.

(3.1) Prepositional phrases When a prepositional phrase modifies a noun or a pronoun, the prepositional phrase always follows the word modified.

> S   InV
> Someone on the phone | is asking about our next sale.

The noun phrase *someone on the phone* is the complete subject.

> S TrV   DO
> Do you like the red jacket on the end?

The complete direct object is *the red jacket on the end*.

(3.2) Infinitives and infinitive phrases An infinitive follows a noun or a pronoun that it modifies.

> Who is the man to see?

> Do you need something to do?

An infinitive phrase also follows the noun or pronoun modified, helping to make up the whole noun phrase.

> Do you need something to do for a while?

(3.3) Participle phrases A participle phrase often follows the noun or pronoun. If nonrestrictive, a participle phrase is set off by commas. (See **10d(5)** for restrictive and nonrestrictive elements.)

> The new mayor, walking slowly down the street, |

> looked very satisfied.

A nonrestrictive participle phrase may also precede the rest of the noun phrase.

> Walking slowly down the street, the new mayor |

> looked very satisfied.

If restrictive, however, the participle phrase always follows the noun and uses no commas.

The man walking down the street there is the new

mayor.

Furthermore, a restrictive participle by itself may also follow the noun.

The man yelling is the one they arrested.

This is an exceptional position for the one-word participle, which normally precedes the noun.

(3.4) Modified adjectives An adjective modified by a qualifier may come before or after the noun it modifies. Commas set off the adjective phrase if it follows the noun.

      Qual   Adj
The unusually lively children |

kept the playground supervisor busy.

               Qual   Adj
The young children, unusually lively, |

kept him busy all hour.

If an adjective is modified by several words, it cannot appear in the normal adjective position before the noun. Usually it follows the noun.

The young children, much more lively today, |

kept him busy all hour.

(3.5) Compound adjectives or participles Adjectives or participles joined by a conjunction often come after the noun. The modifying phrase is set off by commas.

The hunters, weary and dirty, | came in late.

Behind them came the dogs, panting and

walking slowly.

A modifying phrase set off by commas could instead come first in the sentence (followed by a comma), as long as it is part of the first noun phrase in the sentence.

Weary and dirty, the hunters |came in.

(3.6) Adverbs Sometimes a noun is modified by an adverb, a word that usually modifies a verb. The adverb follows the noun.

The meeting yesterday was more interesting than

the one now.

Now look at the picture below.

As in these examples, adverbs that modify nouns usually have meanings of time or place.

(3.7) Time phrases

A noun phrase with a meaning of time may modify a preceding noun.

The game last week |was really exciting.

Our vacation this year |will be in August.

(3.8) Appositives An appositive, a renamer* of the preceding noun or pronoun, should be considered part of the complete noun phrase.

$$
\text{My first class, } \underset{\text{(App)}}{\underline{\text{U.S. History,}}} \Big| \text{is usually very}
$$

interesting.

The complete subject of this sentence is *my first class, U.S. History.* In it the simple subject is followed by an appositive.

Appositives themselves are actually noun phrases within larger noun phrases. Notice this example.

$$
\text{The Puritans, } \underset{\text{(App)}}{\underline{\text{early American settlers,}}} \Big| \text{brought}
$$

a godly heritage to America.

The complete subject (a long noun phrase) is *the Puritans, early American settlers;* it contains an appositive noun phrase set off by commas.

(3.9) Adjective clauses An adjective clause follows the word it modifies.

U.S. History is the class that I like best.

Mr. Jackson, who enjoys history, teaches it well.

In the first example, the adjective clause is part of the complete predicate noun. In the second, the clause is

---

* Appositives are included in **6c(3)** because they follow the noun and are clearly part of the complete noun phrase. However, this handbook describes and marks appositives as renamers rather than as modifiers. (In this we join the many grammarians who describe apposition as a noun function rather than as a type of modification.)

part of the complete subject. Notice the main groups of words in the first sentence:

complete subject	complete predicate	
	LV	**complete PN**
S U.S. History	LV is	PN the class that I like the best.

6d Functions of Adjectives and Adverbs

(1) Adjectives
(2) Adverbs
(3) The differences between adjectives and adverbs

Adjectives and adverbs are alike in some ways.

	Adjective	*Adverb*
Function	Modifier (of noun)	Modifier (of verb)
Changes in form	Nearly all have comparative and superlative	Some have comparative and superlative

Certain adjectives and adverbs even have the same form:

Adv   Adj
He does not drive very fast in his fast car.

However, because most adjectives and adverbs do not have the same form, it is important to use each correctly. Sections **6d(1.1, 2.1, and 3)** will help you do so.

(1) Adjectives

(1.1) Common functions of adjectives
(1.2) Adjectives as objective complements
(1.3) Nominal adjectives

As you may remember from **3d(1),** an adjective is a word that usually modifies a noun and that can be compared using *-er/-est* or *more/most*. An adjective fits into both blanks in the test frame:

> The _____ thing (person) is very _____ .

(1.1) Common functions of adjectives Adjectives have two main uses in the sentence. First, an adjective can be used as a modifier of a noun. The adjectives in a noun phrase come after determiners and before any modifying nouns.

```
Det Det Adj  Adj   ModN
all the old gray Royal typewriters
```

Second, an adjective can be used as a predicate adjective in the pattern S LV PA. In this pattern the adjective appears in the predicate after the linking verb; it gives further information about the subject.

```
 S  LV   PA
God is merciful.
```

● **Practice 6-19** The following sentences all contain adjectives. Copy the sentences, label the sentence pattern elements, and find all the adjectives.

1. Five flabby fish flopped from the flat pan into the fierce, fateful fire.
2. Granny's green gourds grew golden in the grassy glen.
3. Happy Harry hands his hefty hounds hearty hamburgers after each hunt.
4. The infamous insects were inactive inside the icy igloos.
5. A jolly jogger jerked the jackrabbit from the jagged jaws of the jumpy jackal.

(1.2) Adjectives as objective complements Adjectives can appear as objective complements in the pattern S TrV DO OC. In this pattern the adjective describes the direct object because of the action of the verb.

```
  S    TrV         DO      OC
We painted the doghouse yellow.
```

See **5g** for further examples.

(1.3) Nominal adjectives As mentioned in **6c(1),** sometimes an adjective is used as if it were a noun.

The Lord knows the way of *the righteous.*
OP

(2) Adverbs

(2.1) Usually modifying the verb
(2.2) Sometimes modifying a verbal
(2.3) Occasionally modifying an adjective
(2.4) Occasionally modifying a noun
(2.5) Sometimes modifying a phrase
(2.6) Sometimes modifying a clause or an entire sentence

(2.1) Usually modifying the verb As section **3e(1)** states, adverbs are words that usually modify verbs. In doing so, an adverb may occur in various places in the sentence.

Quickly he gave his name.
He *quickly* gave his name.
He will *quickly* give his name.
He gave his name *quickly.*

● **Practice 6-20** Find the adverbs in the following sentences. If you copy the sentences, you can also label the sentence patterns and then observe the positions in which these adverbs are found.

1. In 1789 Justin Morgan, a Vermont school-teacher, reluctantly accepted a stubby colt as partial payment from a debtor.
2. He would certainly have preferred cash.
3. This short-legged horse was not Morgan's idea of a good deal.
4. Soon he was thinking differently about his little horse Figure.
5. His sturdy animal's capacity for work clearly surpassed that of other horses.
6. Gradually, Morgan's horse became famous for his tireless strength.
7. Demand for Figure's offspring grew steadily throughout America.
8. During the nineteenth century the Morgan horse served our country faithfully on farms, battlefields, and frontiers.

(2.2) Sometimes modifying a verbal Adverbs usually modify finite verbs (verbs acting as simple predicates), but they can also modify nonfinite verbs (verbals).

Adverbs modifying finite verb	He *always* stands *first.*
Adverbs modifying participle	*Always* standing *first,* he would speak very clearly.
Adverbs modifying gerund	I appreciated his *always* standing *first.*
Adverbs modifying infinitive	He intended to *always* stand *first.* He intended *always* to stand *first.*

Some would object to the first infinitive example, on the grounds that *always* makes a "split infinitive." (A **split infinitive** is an infinitive with a modifier between *to* and the next verb word.) However, the reworded sentence below it is somewhat ambiguous, possibly meaning "He always intended to stand first."

Split infinitives are not ungrammatical in English, but they may be awkward—especially if the modifier is several words long.

Awkward split infinitive	She began to with faltering steps walk toward the front.
Improved sentence	With faltering steps, she began to walk toward the front.

Some people disapprove of all split infinitives, but it is worth noticing that the proposed alternatives are themselves sometimes awkward.

Acceptable split infinitive	To really understand his problem, you should hear what happened yesterday.
Awkward wording	Really to understand his problem, you should hear what happened yesterday.

Often, though, you can improve a sentence by eliminating a split infinitive.

(2.3) Occasionally modifying an adjective Adverbs are words that usually modify verbs, and qualifiers are special words (like *very* and *extremely*) that modify adjectives and adverbs. (As explained in **4d,** qualifiers generally strengthen or weaken the idea of the adjective or adverb modified.) However, there are a few adverbs that can occasionally modify an adjective.

Adverb modifying verb	The class normally became quiet when the bell rang.
Adverb modifying adjective	Today the normally quiet room buzzed with excitement.

(2.4) Occasionally modifying a noun Certain adverbs may on occasion modify a noun. When one does, it follows the noun. See **6c(3.6)** for examples.

(2.5) Sometimes modifying a phrase Adverbs sometimes seem to modify phrases, such as prepositional phrases.

Exactly at noon, the men stopped work.

The dog would go quickly out of the house, more

slowly across the yard, but never into the garage.

(2.6) Sometimes modifying a clause or an entire sentence Certain adverbs can apply to an entire independent or dependent clause, rather than to just the verb. These adverbs usually appear at the beginning of the clause.

Clearly, he was being deceptive.

Happily, the river flooded after we left.

We learned that unfortunately no one had brought

the key.

(3) The differences between adjectives and adverbs

(3.1) Important differences in function
(3.2) Differences in form

(3.1) Important differences in function There are two important differences in the functions of adjectives and adverbs.

Adjectives	**Adverbs**
Modify nouns	Modify verbs
Can be predicate adjectives in the pattern S LV PA:	Can be modifiers at the end of any pattern, including S InV:

S	LV	PA		S	InV	(Adv)
Tom	looks (is, feels, seems, became)	good (sad, nice, bad).		Tom	behaves (does, sings, runs)	well (nicely, sadly).

Notice the difference between the two patterns given above. In the first set of sentences we learn that *Tom* looks good or sad or nice; the subject is described by predicate adjectives. In the second set we learn that he *behaves* or *does* or *sings* well or nicely; the verb is modified by adverbs. Adjectives are correct in the first set, and adverbs in the second.

(3.2) Differences in form

Many adjectives and adverbs are different in form. The information above in **6d(3.1)** will help you use these words correctly.

Adjectives	*Adverbs*
good (*opposite of* bad)	well (*opposite of* badly)
well (*opposite of* sick)	
bad	badly
nice	nicely
sad	sadly
terrible	terribly
eager	eagerly
(etc.)	(etc.)

When adjectives and adverbs differ in form, nearly always the adverb is made by adding *-ly* to the adjective. *Well,* however, is the adverb that matches the adjective *good.* Remember that Tom *feels* good/bad/happy/sick/ well (adjectives after a linking verb), but that he *sings* well/badly/happily (adverbs after any other kind of verb).

Of course, some pairs of adjectives and adverbs have exactly the same form. Many of these adjective/adverb pairs have no ending at all, but others have *-ly* or some other ending.

| Either adjectives or adverbs | fast, hard, far, late, straight; weekly, hourly, only, early; northward |

There are also adjectives (like *red*) that have no related adverb form, and adverbs (like *often*) that have no related adjective form.

A few adverbs have forms with or without *-ly,* such as *slow/slowly.* *Slow* tends to be used in certain expressions ("His watch runs slow") and in very informal or forceful speech ("Go slow around that curve"). In general, however, we use *slowly* ("He walked slowly down the street"). Certain adverbs with *-ly* have a different meaning from those without *-ly*: "He was trying *hard,*" but "I can *hardly* see that kite."

- **Practice 6-21** Use the following sentences to make sure that you can recognize adjectives and adverbs. On your own paper, label the parts of the sentence patterns, and then underline adjectives once and adverbs twice.
  1. Man's greedy craving for gold truly became evident in the gold rushes of the nineteenth century.
  2. In 1849 a sudden flood of humanity in search of the precious metal poured rapidly into California.
  3. A similar event briefly shook Australia during the 1850s.
  4. Later, the desire for easy wealth drew many eager prospectors northward during the Alaskan gold rush.
  5. These frenzied rushes never brought their participants any permanent satisfaction.
  6. Certainly God's eternal Word is more desirable than "much fine gold."

- **Practice 6-22** Choose between the adjective and the adverb given for each section; any word may be used more than once.

(nice, nicely)

1. Marcy has a _____ manner of speaking.
2. Some people, unfortunately, are _____ only to their friends; but she speaks _____ to her family, too.

(good, well)

3. Brett did _____ on his history test because he studied _____ .
4. He has a _____ knowledge of the Civil War.
5. He likes history very _____ .

If the answer key shows that you have made a mistake, first try to understand the reason for the right answer. Then practice saying the sentence the right way until it *sounds* right to you. That's the best way to conquer a problem with adverbs and adjectives.

Chapter 7

Types and Forms of Verbs

Probably there is no more important word in the sentence than the verb. Verbs give life to most sentences, and they connect with other words in important ways. For example, in "Joey's foot crushed the dry leaves," *crushed* not only describes the type of action but it also tells two other things: what Joey's foot did and what happened to the dry leaves. And of course we know that without the verb there is no sentence. Understanding these important words—both the types of verbs and the various forms that they can take—will help you use them wisely and correctly.

7a Verb Types as Identified by Sentence Patterns

(1) Transitive verbs
(2) Intransitive verbs
(3) Linking verbs
(4) Verbs of more than one type

An important way of classifying verbs is based on the sentence patterns presented in Chapter 5. (This section assumes that you are already familiar with the first five sentence patterns found in that chapter.) As the sentence pattern labels show, each sentence pattern uses just one type of verb. Therefore, if we recognize the sentence pattern, we know the verb type.

There are just three basic types of verbs: transitive, intransitive, and linking. Some verbs can be only one of these, but other verbs can fit into several sentence patterns and thus can fall into more than one type. In section **7a(4)** you will see examples of this flexibility.

(1) Transitive verbs

Transitive verbs are those that occur in the patterns that have direct objects.

    S   TrV   DO
    We called the fire department.

    S   TrV   IO   DO
    We gave them the address.

Because the direct object "receives" the action of the verb, we can say that a transitive verb is "a verb that has a receiver of action." Notice that this means the same as what you have just learned: a transitive verb is a verb that occurs in one of the patterns that include a direct object.

Only transitive verbs can be made passive; see **7e** for the passive voice.

(2) Intransitive verbs

Intransitive verbs are verbs that are used in the one pattern that does not require anything after the verb: S InV.

            S   InV
The sirens blew loudly.

Intransitive verbs, then, have no receiver of action. Indeed, they have no completer at all. (See **19a(2.2),** however, for the way dictionaries use the term when they label verb meanings.)

(3) Linking verbs

A linking verb is a verb used in either of these two patterns: S LV PN, S LV PA.

The verb links the subject with the predicate noun or predicate adjective:

    S   LV   PN
The building was an old store.

  S   LV   PA
It looked empty.

- **Practice 7-1** Classify the italicized verb in each of the following sentences as transitive, intransitive, or linking. Remember that you can do so only by first identifying the sentence pattern.
    1. Every day the shepherd boy *guarded* his father's sheep.
    2. The mountain pasture *was* a lonely place.
    3. One day he *wanted* some excitement.
    4. He *ran* down to the town, crying "Wolf! Wolf!"
    5. The villagers quickly *rushed* up to the pasture with guns and clubs.
    6. However, the sheep *were eating* quietly, with no wolf in sight.
    7. The shepherd boy *laughed* at the villagers.
    8. He *played* his trick on them several times.
    9. One day a wolf really *came.*

10. The shepherd boy *was* afraid.
11. He *called* loudly to the villagers,
12. but no one *believed* him.
13. The wolf *killed* the helpless sheep.
14. Moral: no one *believes* a liar,
15. even when he *tells* the truth.

(Based on one of Aesop's fables)

(4) Verbs of more than one type

Many verbs—indeed, probably most verbs—can be used in several sentence patterns, so that they can fall under more than one verb type. As an example, consider the verb *sound:*

                  S   TrV   DO
Transitive | They sounded the alarm.

                     S   InV
Intransitive | The siren sounds at noon every day.

             S   LV   PA
Linking | She sounds happy.

Sound is slightly unusual in being used in all three ways, but many verbs can be either transitive or intransitive. *Eat* and *read* are two examples.

                S   TrV   DO
Transitive | Jessica ate her hamburger slowly.

                   S TrV   DO
Have you read today's *News* headline yet?

                S InV
Intransitive | We ate late today.

                S   InV
She can read fast.

Some verbs can be either linking or intransitive. Most notable of these are five verbs of the senses: *look, taste, smell, feel,* and *sound.*

                S   LV   PA
Linking | You looked busy last night.

                S   InV
Intransitive | They looked at the drawing.

Three of these verbs of the senses can also be transitive: "He tasted (smelled, felt) the peach."

7b Tenses and Their Uses

(1) The present-tense family
(2) The past-tense family
(3) The future-tense family

English tenses are sufficiently complicated that whole books have been written on some of them, but below is a systematic summary of the basic tense meanings. These meanings have to do mainly with time.

Verbs, as you know, express action or state of being. (For short, we will call state-of-being verbs **state verbs.** These are the verbs used to describe a state or a condition. They are not necessarily linking verbs.) The difference between action verbs and state verbs turns out to be important for some tenses. For example, present time is expressed by the plain present tense for state verbs:

I *like* band music.
I *have* a new coat.

For action verbs, though, we must use the present progressive to express present time:

He *is walking* to school (right now).

If we try to use the plain present tense with action verbs, we get instead a statement of what normally happens:

He *walks* to school (every day).

And notice that we do not use the present progressive for state verbs:

| Ungram-matical | I *am liking* band music (today). |
| | I *am having* a new coat (this year). |

The point is that tense forms sometimes depend on which kind of verb is used.

Certain verbs can be used either as action verbs or as state verbs. We have just used *have* as a state verb meaning "to possess" ("I *have* a new coat"). *Have* can also be used as an action verb, and in that sense it can take the present progressive:

>She *is having* a party tonight.

In other words, whether a verb expresses an action or a state may depend on the rest of the sentence.

The three "tense families" below also appear in the table in **7g**, which gives all the tense forms of a typical verb.

(1) The present-tense family

The difference between action verbs and state verbs (explained just above) is particularly important in understanding the uses and meanings of the present-tense family of tenses.

1. The **present** tense expresses present time for state verbs.

    >Our school *has* two soccer teams.
    >I *like* band music.

    For action verbs, the present tense expresses habitual action, telling what normally happens:

    >He *walks* to school every day, but he *rides* the bus home.
    >The sun *rises* in the east.

2. The **present progressive** expresses present time for verbs that show action.

    >He *is walking* to school right now.
    >The sun *is rising*.

    (The progressive is not ordinarily used with verbs that describe a state. For instance, we do not say "I *am liking* band music today.")

3. The **present perfect** expresses an action or state completed during the present time period or one that has continued up to the present moment.

    >It *has rained* a lot this year.
    >He *has studied* all evening.

> I *have done* my homework.
> I *have* always *liked* band music.

4. The **present perfect progressive** expresses a continuing action that was done during the present time period. It emphasizes that the action has continued over a period of time.

> He *has been studying* all evening.
> It *has been raining* all day.
> *Have* you *been listening* to the radio?

(2) The past-tense family

1. The **past** tense expresses past time—either an action that was done in an earlier time period or a state that existed in an earlier time period.

> It *rained* a lot last year.
> He *studied* all day yesterday.
> We *had* two soccer teams.

2. The **past progressive** expresses a continuing action in past time. It is used especially to show that the action was in progress at the time of another event.

> It *was raining* when I left the house.
> I *was sleeping* when the sun rose.
> At seven o'clock we *were doing* our homework.

3. The **past perfect** expresses an action that was completed (or a state that existed) before a certain time in the past.

> When the sun rose, we *had been* awake for an hour already.
> We learned that it *had rained* (during the night).

4. The **past perfect progressive** expresses a continuing action that was completed before a certain time in the past. It emphasizes that the action was a continuing one.

When the sun rose, we *had been working*
for an hour already.
We learned that it *had been raining* (all
night).

(3) The future-tense family

1. The **future** tense expresses future time, for
   either an action or a state.
   > Maybe it *will rain* this afternoon.
   > I *will study* it again before the test.
   > Next year we *will have* two soccer teams.
2. The **future progressive** expresses continuing
   action in the future.
   > Do you think it *will* still *be raining* at four
   > o'clock?
   > We *will be writing* letters when Marcy
   > walks in.
3. The **future perfect** expresses an action that will
   be completed (or a state that will exist) by or
   before a certain time in the future:
   > Don't worry—by test time I *will have
   > studied* it two more times.
   > By this time tomorrow she *will have taken*
   > that medicine for a whole week.
   > In early October we *will have had* our first
   > soccer team just one month.

4.　The **future perfect progressive** expresses a continuing action that will be completed by or before a certain time in the future.

> When you get back from the store, I *will* probably *have been working* on the car for quite a while.

> In another ten minutes it *will have been raining* for an hour.

7c How to Use the Principal Parts of a Verb

All the forms of nearly every English verb can be made from just three basic forms, or **principal parts,** of the verb. That is, if you know the three principal parts of a verb and how to use them, you can make any form of that verb. (*Principal* here means "main.")

Some verbs have three different principal parts:

break	broke	broken

Many others have two that are the same:

want	wanted	wanted
bring	brought	brought

And for a few verbs all three principal parts are the same:

put	put	put

Notice that the second and third principal parts of *want* are made by adding *-ed* to the first principal part: *want, wanted, wanted*. Because there are so many verbs like *want*, we call these the regular verbs. Both regular and irregular verbs follow the same system in using the principal parts to form the tenses.

The table "Uses of the Principal Parts" is marked with underlines, boxes, and shading to show how the three principal parts are used to form the various tenses. To find the correct tense form for any other verb—such as the verbs listed in **7d**—just substitute the principal part that corresponds to *break, broke,* or *broken.*

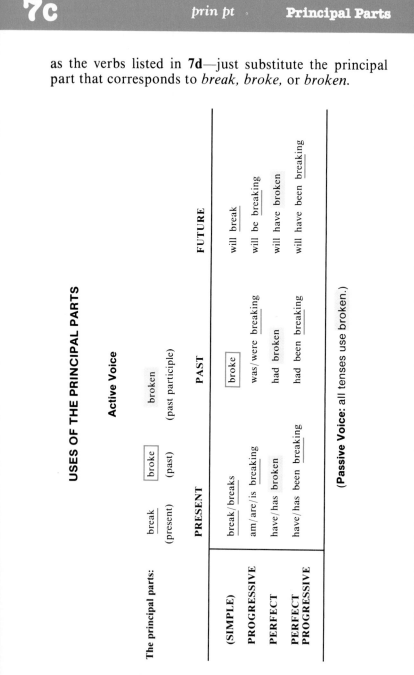

USES OF THE PRINCIPAL PARTS

Active Voice

The principal parts:

break	broke	broken
(present)	(past)	(past participle)

	PRESENT	PAST	FUTURE
(SIMPLE)	break/breaks	broke	will break
PROGRESSIVE	am/are/is breaking	was/were breaking	will be breaking
PERFECT	have/has broken	had broken	will have broken
PERFECT PROGRESSIVE	have/has been breaking	had been breaking	will have been breaking

(**Passive Voice:** all tenses use broken.)

Notice that although the third principal part is used with *have, has,* and *had,* the second principal part never is.

Only four true verbs have any exceptional forms not covered by this table. Two verbs, *do* and *say,* have an irregular third-person singular form only in speaking: *does* is pronounced *duz,* not *dooz;* and *says* is pronounced *sez,* not so as to rhyme with *days.* For *have* we say "he has," not "he haves." However, the most commonly used verb of English, the verb *be,* is so irregular that we cannot very well speak of it as having principal parts. A table of all the forms of *be* is given in **7h.**

Apart from the forms of *be* and the minor exceptions of *does, says,* and *has,* the table here may be used for every English verb, as long as you have the principal parts. You can find the principal parts of a verb by looking in the dictionary entry or in the list of troublesome verbs in the next section.

● **Practice 7-2** Use the table to give the tense form requested. The principal parts of each verb are given within parentheses.

Example: future perfect of *sing* (sing, sang, sung): *will have sung*

1. Past of *bring* (bring, brought, brought)
2. Past perfect of *go* (go, went, gone)
3. Future progressive of *help* (help, helped, helped)
4. Present perfect of *fall* (fall, fell, fallen)
5. Present of *lie* (lie, lay, lain)

7d Troublesome Verbs

Although most English verbs are regular (like *want, wanted, wanted*), many common verbs are irregular. Some of these are so well known that they are no problem, but others seem less easy. Listed below for easy reference are the principal parts of verbs that are likely to be a problem. By knowing the principal parts of any of these verbs (and the material in **7c** on how to use the principal parts), you will be able to make all the tense forms correctly. Of course, the principal parts of any verb not listed here may be found by looking in a good desk dictionary.

Present	Past	Past Participle
begin	began	begun
bite	bit	bitten
blow	blew	blown
break	broke	broken
bring	brought	brought
burst	burst	burst
buy	bought	bought
catch	caught	caught
choose	chose	chosen
climb	climbed	climbed
cling	clung	clung
come	came	come
dig	dug	dug
dive	dived (*or* dove*)	dived
do	did	done
drag	dragged	dragged
draw	drew	drawn
drink	drank	drunk
drive	drove	driven
drown	drowned	drowned
eat	ate	eaten
fall	fell	fallen
fly	flew	flown
forget	forgot	forgotten *or* forgot
freeze	froze	frozen
get	got	gotten *or* got
give	gave	given
go	went	gone
grow	grew	grown
hang (by the neck)	hanged	hanged

———————

* *Dove* is considered informal by some.

hang (other meanings)	hung	hung
hide	hid	hidden
kneel	knelt *or* kneeled	knelt *or* kneeled
know	knew	known
lay "place"	laid	laid
lead	led	led
lie "recline"	lay	lain
light	lighted *or* lit	lighted *or* lit
loose "release"	loosed	loosed
lose "mislay"	lost	lost
raise "lift up"	raised	raised
ride	rode	ridden
ring	rang	rung
rise "go up"	rose	risen
run	ran	run
see	saw	seen
set	set	set
shake	shook	shaken
shine "polish"	shined	shined
shine "beam, glisten"	shone *or* shined	shone *or* shined
show	showed	shown *or* showed
shrink	shrank *or* shrunk	shrunk
sing	sang	sung
sink	sank *or* sunk	sunk
sit	sat	sat
sneak	sneaked	sneaked
speak	spoke	spoken
spring	sprang *or* sprung	sprung
steal	stole	stolen
strive	strove	striven *or* strived
swim	swam	swum
swing	swung	swung
throw	threw	thrown
tread	trod	trodden *or* trod
weep	wept	wept
wring	wrung	wrung
write	wrote	written

7e Active and Passive Voice

(1) Defining active and passive
(2) Making active and passive sentences
(3) Using active and passive sentences
(4) Making passives with complements

(1) Defining active and passive

In most sentences the subject does something or is something:

> The twins slept.
> Your uncle is an effective preacher.
> My new friend chose a good story today.

In sentences like these, when the subject either "is" or *acts,* the verb is **active,** and the sentence is active. As a matter of fact, all the basic sentence patterns are for active sentences. Some sentences, though, can be restated in such a way that something is done *to* the subject:

> A good story was chosen.
> *or*
> A good story was chosen by my new friend.

When the subject is *acted upon,* as in these sentences, the verb is **passive.** Only transitive verbs—those that have direct objects—can be made passive. (See **7a(1)** for transitives.)

(2) Making active and passive sentences

To make a passive sentence, we start with an active sentence that has a transitive verb and a direct object.

>   S   TrV-A   DO
> My new friend chose a good story today.

The label TrV-A shows that this is the normal, active form of the transitive verb. (We will use TrV-P for the passive form.) First, we move the direct object to the subject position.

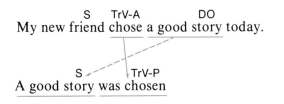

Then we change the verb from active to passive, keeping the same tense. Here the past active verb *chose* becomes the past passive verb *was chosen.*

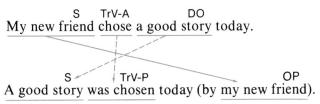

If we mention the doer, it becomes the object of the preposition *by*. Here we will put the *by*-phrase inside parentheses to show that it can either be there or not. Adverbial modifiers like *today* stay in the same general part of the sentence.

```
               S    TrV-A           DO
My new friend chose a good story today.


        S  ⌐ TrV-P                                OP
A good story was chosen today (by my new friend).
```

The resulting sentence, as well as the complete verb, can be called passive. The sentence is passive because the subject is not the doer, but the receiver of action. That is, it is *acted upon.*

We could also start with a passive sentence and change it to active. In that case we would just do all the steps in reverse. We would take the object of the preposition *by* and make it the subject (leaving out the *by*), and we would change the verb back to active voice.

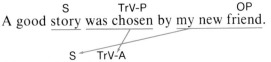

Then we would take the passive subject and make it the direct object:

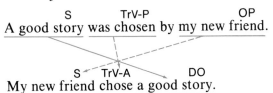

Notice that the active sentence here seems more "active" and interesting.

If you ever want to make an active sentence out of a passive sentence that does not mention the doer, then you have to either figure out who the doer is or use an indefinite word like *someone*.

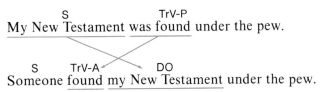

It is usually best not to use *they* as an indefinite subject.

Poor	They teach piano at this school.
Improved	Piano is taught at this school.
	We can take piano at this school.
	Miss Solberg teaches piano here after school.

Are you wondering how to be sure about the form of passive verbs? Section **7g** gives all the active and passive forms of the sample *break*, with the active table and the passive table arranged in exactly the same way for easy comparison. Another way to know the passive forms is to remember that the passive tenses are made up of the regular tense forms of *be,* added to the past participle (the third principal part) of the verb in question.

● **Practice 7-3** In this true story (which is continued in the next two practices), you are to decide whether each sentence is active or passive.

1. Every summer loggers and woodsmen hold a two-day festival in northern Pennsylvania.
2. Lumberjacks come from all over the eastern United States to compete in log-pulling and wood-chopping contests.
3. Teams of huge workhorses are driven by expert loggers in the pulling contests.
4. One summer a rather small pair of bay horses was entered in the contest by a young woodsman named John Brown.
5. Four bigger teams tried first to pull the heavy oak logs to the finish line.
6. The other loggers yelled at their horses and kept them struggling without a break for the entire allotted time.
7. Because the horses were nervous from all the yelling, none of the teams could pull the logs more than fifty yards.
8. Brown's quiet team was brought around by his small sons.
9. Brown picked up the reins, clicked his tongue, and watched his horses lean into their harness together.
10. The crowd, seeing the surprisingly small horses, watched anxiously.

Check your answers and then go on to the next practice exercise.

● **Practice 7-4** The story of John Brown and his horses continues here with five passive sentences. Change the sentences to the active form, reviewing this section if you need to. (If there is no *by*-phrase for the doer of a sentence, you can supply the doer from your knowledge of the story.)

1. First the logs were pulled about twenty yards.
2. Then the horses were stopped for a rest.
3. During the break, stones were thrown out of the way by the horses' considerate owner.
4. The horses were petted on their noses, and then they were told to pull again.
5. All the while, not a word was said by the watching crowd.

(3) Using active and passive sentences

(3.1) Advantages of active sentences
(3.2) Advantages of passive sentences

Most of the time we just write or talk without thinking about actives and passives. However, sometimes what we have written can be improved by changing an active to a passive, or a passive to an active.

(3.1) Advantages of active sentences Although the passive can be useful, the best general advice is this: **do not overuse the passive.** Your writing will be more lively and strong if you normally mention the doer first, then the action, and then the receiver of action. An occasional passive sentence is fine, but too many of them hang weights on your writing. Notice the difference:

Too many passives	He was first discouraged by the thought of all that work. Then he was reminded that he would be helped by God, and he was cheered up.
Better	At first the thought of all that work discouraged him. Then he remembered that God would help him, and he cheered up.

Besides being more direct and vivid, the second version is also shorter. Shortness and directness often go together.

(3.2) Advantages of passive sentences Even though we want to avoid using the passive too much, sometimes the passive is useful.

1. The passive is a handy way to avoid mentioning the doer of an action. For instance, the doer may be unimportant or unknown.

| Good use of passives | The money was kept in the store's safe overnight.
The doors to the Sunday School rooms are opened before 9:00 a.m. on Sunday. |

2. You may also use the passive to keep your subjects the same for several verbs in a row. Doing so may help your sentences flow more smoothly.

| Acceptable (different subjects) | When *parents* ask children to help in the home, *the children* learn responsibility. If *parents* expect children to do their share, *these children* will also be more thoughtful when they grow up. |

| Better (consistent subjects) | When *children* are asked to help in the home, *they* learn responsibility. If *they* are expected to do their share as children, *they* will also be more thoughtful as adults. |

Again, the better version also turns out to be shorter.

3. Finally, the passive lets us move certain kinds of things from the subject position to the end of the sentence. For example, it is often awkward to have a long phrase as a subject.

179

| Awkwardly long subject | *Parents, brothers and sisters, other relatives, and even friends* teach the young child. |

| Better | *The young child* is taught by parents, brothers and sisters, other relatives, and even friends. |

Also, it is usually better to save the new or more important information for the end of the sentence, putting the old information at the beginning. The end of the sentence, you see, is *a naturally strong position*. Therefore we are wise to put at the end what we want to *emphasize*.

| Passive used to move a phrase to the end | Emphasis can be obtained by *several methods*. |

See **9h(2-3)** for good use of the end of the sentence.

- **Practice 7-5** The story of John Brown and his horses ends with the following five active sentences. One of the sentences has an awkwardly long subject. Find that sentence and change it to the passive form.
  1. With a simple "whoa," John Brown stopped his horses twice more to rest.
  2. During the final pull, the calm logger with the soft but firm voice kept the horses to their work.
  3. The team finally pulled the front end of the logs across the finish line, with time to spare.
  4. The entire crowd rose and cheered.
  5. John Brown proved that patience and consistency get good results.

(4) Making passives with complements

Complements, you remember, are the "completers" of the various patterns—the pattern parts that follow the verb. If an active sentence has two complements, one of them may be left behind in complement position when the sentence is made passive. See **6b(11)** for complements in passive sentences.

7f Nonfinite Forms

(1) Finite and nonfinite verbs
(2) Infinitives
(3) Participles
(4) Gerunds

(1) Finite and nonfinite verbs

Finite verbs are verbs that can be used as simple predicates. Their form allows them to fill the verb position in sentence patterns. They have subjects, and in the present tense they change form according to whether a noun subject is singular or plural.

My sister *likes* music.
My sisters *like* music.

Nonfinite verb forms are the special forms that let a verb be used as if it were a noun, an adjective, or an adverb. (Nonfinite forms, or nonfinite verbs, can also be called **verbals.**) The three kinds of nonfinite verbs are infinitives, participles, and gerunds.

(2) Infinitives

(2.1) The simple infinitive
(2.2) The passive infinitive
(2.3) The perfect infinitive
(2.4) The perfect passive and other infinitives

(2.1) The simple infinitive The simple infinitive of a verb is made up of the word *to* followed by the first principal part (basic form) of the verb: *to run, to see, to be,* and so on. We call the *to* here "the sign of the infinitive." Remember that *to* plus the first principal part of a verb is never a prepositional phrase, but always an infinitive. (*To the house* and *to church* are prepositional phrases, but *to go* is an infinitive.)

Infinitives can be used in the same ways as nouns, adjectives, and adverbs.

Infinitive as verbal noun	S TrV DO Jeremy likes <u>to sing</u>.
Infinitive as verbal adjective	S LV PN (Adj) Harry is the person <u>to ask</u>.
Infinitive as verbal adverb	S InV (Adv) I'll go there <u>to see</u>.

In all these cases we have a verb form being used as one of the other major parts of speech, not as the simple predicate.

Even though infinitives act in some ways other than as verbs, they are still made from verbs and may be modified by adverbs or by prepositional phrases.

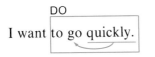

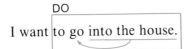

Because they are made from verbs, they may also have objects or other completers.

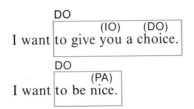

The infinitive and its modifiers and completers together make up the whole infinitive phrase. Infinitive phrases are very common in English.

DO
Jeremy likes to sing the old hymns.

Adj
Harry is the person to ask about that.

Adv
I'll go there to see for myself.

(2.2) The passive infinitive The simple infinitive, discussed above, has an active meaning.

Active | I want *to choose* the next song. (I will *choose* it.)

Because transitive verbs can be made passive, they can have passive infinitives.

Passive | I want *to be chosen.* (I will *be chosen;* they will choose me.)

The passive infinitive is made up of the following parts:

1. The sign of the infinitive   *(to)*
2. The passive auxiliary   *(be)*
3. The third principal part of the true verb   *(chosen)*

Passive infinitives can be used in the same ways as other infinitives.

(2.3) The perfect infinitive *Have,* the auxiliary that makes the perfect tenses, can also be part of an infinitive. An infinitive with *have* is called a perfect infinitive.

I am very glad *to have met* you.

A perfect infinitive always makes it clear that the action of that infinitive took place before the action of the main verb of the clause. Thus the example means, "I am glad now that I met you earlier." By contrast, "I am very glad to meet you" puts the being glad and the meeting in the same (present) time.

Use a perfect infinitive only when you intend to put the time of the infinitive before that of the main verb.

Wrong	I would have liked to have gone.
Right	I would have liked to go. *(both in past time)* I would like to have gone. *(liking present, going past)*

A sentence with *have* in both the main verb and the infinitive is probably wrong.

(2.4) The perfect passive and other infinitives Just as there are passive infinitives and perfect infinitives, there are also perfect passive infinitives.

I am happy *to have been chosen.* (I am happy that I was chosen.)

Have makes it perfect, and so the time is before that of the main verb. *Been,* from *be,* makes it passive, and so the implied subject ("I") is acted upon.

Progressive infinitives are another possibility:

I'll try *to be waiting* for you at five o'clock.

Progressive infinitives emphasize the continuing nature of an action.

Finally, you will sometimes see an infinitive without a *to.* If the infinitive would also sound right with the *to,* the *to* will be used in more formal English.

Correct	What he did was *jump* the fence.
More formal	What he did was *to jump* the fence.

Sometimes, though, the *to* would sound odd.

| Correct at any level | With his background, he can do nothing except *succeed.* |

(3) Participles

(3.1) The present participle
(3.2) The "past" (passive) participle
(3.3) The perfect participle
(3.4) Other participles

A participle is a verbal adjective.

(3.1) The present participle The present participle consists of the first principal part of the verb, with *-ing* added to it. As a verbal adjective, a participle modifies a noun (or sometimes a pronoun):

The laughing children didn't hear their mother.

Like a regular adjective, a participle by itself usually comes before the noun it modifies.

Because the participle is made from a verb, it too can have modifiers or completers or both. The participle and its modifiers and completers together make up a participle phrase (or "participial phrase"). A participle phrase often follows the noun it modifies.

The children laughing at the joke didn't hear their

mother.

The man giving the speech had a pleasant voice.

Who were the ones talking loudly?

Sometimes the participle phrase comes first, set off by a comma.

Laughing at the joke, the children didn't hear their

mother.

Notice that the *-ing* form of the verb can be used either as part of a progressive finite verb or as a participle, a verbal adjective.

Progressive finite verb	He was laughing softly.
Participle	The laughing doll sounded strange.

Do not be confused by another possible meaning of the term *participle*. In traditional terminology the progressive verb is sometimes described as being made up of "a form of *be* and the present participle of the verb." However, usually *participle* means a verbal adjective.

(3.2) The "past" (passive) participle The so-called past participle is the same as the third principal part of the verb. (This is the form that is used with *have* to make the perfect tenses.) When it is a true participle (a verbal adjective), however, it usually has a passive meaning. Passive participles are possible only for transitive verbs.

The broken window lets in the cold air.

(The window was broken by someone.)

A passive participle can be part of a participle phrase.

The window, broken by Al's home-run ball,

still has not been repaired.

(3.3) The perfect participle *Having* can be used with the third principal part of the verb to make a perfect participle.

Having arrived early, I arranged the chairs.

The perfect participle is used to express an action before that of the main verb. (He arrived, and then he arranged the chairs.) By contrast, the present participle expresses action simultaneous with that of the main verb:

Arriving early, I turned into the snowy driveway

carefully.

(3.4) Other participles The most common participles are the present participle, the passive participle, and the perfect participle. Others, however, are possible. They are recognizable because the first word ends with *-ing* and the whole phrase is used as a verbal adjective.

The door being opened is the door to Mr. Brown's

office.

Being seen through the window, it looked rather

small.

Having been seen as he picked up the costume,

he knew the secret was out.

The first two examples can be called progressive passive participles, and the last one is a perfect passive participle. The names, however, are less important than their usefulness in certain sentences. For instance, see **8b(2.1)** and **8b(3.2)** on reducing clauses to participles.

(4) Gerunds

(4.1) The present gerund
(4.2) The perfect gerund
(4.3) Other gerunds

A gerund is a verbal **noun**.

(4.1) The present gerund The present gerund has the same form as the present participle—the *-ing* form of the verb. As a verbal noun, the gerund is used in the ways nouns are used.

       S   LV   PN
    Swimming is good exercise.

  S   TrV   DO
  I   like *swimming*.

Like other nonfinite verbs, gerunds can have both adverbial modifiers and complements (completers).

                         PN
    His favorite relaxation is *swimming slowly to the*

    point and back.

                            OP
    I need to give the afternoon to *answering letters.*

As a verbal noun, a gerund sometimes has regular noun-modifiers.

             DO
    We did *our best swimming* in the first race.

The whole gerund phrase performs the function marked.

Since a gerund is a verbal noun, it can be used by itself as a modifying noun.

Gerund	Mr. Eaves had the boys in his class over
	ModN
	for a *swimming* party.

Though it may look like a participle, a gerund as a modifying noun has a different "sound" and a different meaning from the participle. In this example it was a party *for* swimming, not a party that was swimming. Notice the difference:

	Part
Participle	We watched the *swimming* turtle.

Here the turtle is doing the swimming. Occasionally the similarity between these two constructions might create ambiguity, as in "a spinning wheel."

(4.2) The perfect gerund *Having* can be used with the third principal part of the verb to make the perfect gerund: for instance, *having met.*

| Perfect gerund | What a name-dropper! His specialty is *having met all the important people.* |

The action of the perfect gerund always takes place before that of the main verb. On the other hand, the action of the present gerund is at the same time as that of the main verb:

| Present gerund | His specialty is *meeting all the important people.* |

(4.3) Other gerunds Besides the present gerund and the perfect gerund, other types of gerunds are possible. Below are two examples, both with a possessive "subject," as covered in **8b(4.1).**

His being seen was good, because they were able
   to help him right away.
His having been seen is fortunate; now we
   know where to look for him.

Both of these gerunds are passive. The second one is a perfect passive gerund: it is now fortunate that he *was* seen.

All gerunds are used as verbal nouns, and all begin with a word ending in *-ing.*

7g A Sample Verb Conjugation

CONJUGATION OF THE VERB *BREAK* (Indicative Mood)

Principal Parts

Present	Past	Past Participle
break	broke	broken

Active Voice

		PRESENT	PAST	FUTURE
(SIMPLE)	I	break	broke	will break*
	you/we/they	break	broke	will break
	he/she/it	breaks	broke	will break
PROGRESSIVE	I	am breaking	was breaking	will be breaking
	you/we/they	are breaking	were breaking	will be breaking
	he/she/it	is breaking	was breaking	will be breaking
PERFECT	I	have broken	had broken	will have broken
	you/we/they	have broken	had broken	will have broken
	he/she/it	has broken	had broken	will have broken
PERFECT PROGRESSIVE	I	have been breaking	had been breaking	will have been breaking
	you/we/they	have been breaking	had been breaking	will have been breaking
	he/she/it	has been breaking	had been breaking	will have been breaking

---

* *Shall* sometimes replaces *will*; see section **4b(2)**.

Passive Voice

		PRESENT	PAST	FUTURE
(SIMPLE)	I	am broken	was broken	will be broken*
	you/we/they	are broken	were broken	will be broken
	he/she/it	is broken	was broken	will be broken
PROGRESSIVE	I	am being broken	was being broken	will be being broken
	you/we/they	are being broken	were being broken	will be being broken
	he/she/it	is being broken	was being broken	will be being broken
PERFECT	I	have been broken	had been broken	will have been broken
	you/we/they	have been broken	had been broken	will have been broken
	he/she/it	has been broken	had been broken	will have been broken
PERFECT PROGRESSIVE	I	have been being broken	had been being broken	will have been being broken
	you/we/they	have been being broken	had been being broken	will have been being broken
	he/she/it	has been being broken	had been being broken	will have been being broken

* *Shall* sometimes replaces *will;* see section **4b(2)**.

7h Conjugation of *Be*

CONJUGATION OF THE VERB *BE* (Indicative Mood)

Active Voice

		PRESENT	PAST	FUTURE
(SIMPLE)	I	am	was	will be*
	you/we/they	are	were	will be
	he/she/it	is	was	will be
PROGRESSIVE	I	am being	was being	will be being
	you/we/they	are being	were being	will be being
	he/she/it	is being	was being	will be being
PERFECT	I	have been	had been	will have been
	you/we/they	have been	had been	will have been
	he/she/it	has been	had been	will have been
PERFECT PROGRESSIVE	I	have been being	had been being	will have been being
	you/we/they	have been being	had been being	will have been being
	he/she/it	has been being	had been being	will have been being

(Passive Voice: because *be* is not transitive, it has no passive voice.)

---

* *Shall* sometimes replaces *will*; see section **4b(2)**.

7i Mood

(1) The indicative mood
(2) The imperative mood
(3) The subjunctive mood

The three moods (or "modes") of English verbs have no simple overall meaning, but they have to do with the speaker's attitude toward what he is saying.

Attitude Toward What Is Said

Indicative mood	Factual, real, or probable
Imperative mood	Commanded
Subjunctive mood	Nonfactual or doubtful

However, the moods are recognized more by their form than by their meaning.

(1) The indicative mood

The indicative mood is the "normal" mood, the one most used. We need the term only to differentiate the normal forms from those of the imperative and subjunctive moods. All the verb forms given in the tables of **7g** and **7h** are in the indicative mood.

(2) The imperative mood

The imperative mood is used to give direct commands. The verb is in its simple present form, with no auxiliary; and the subject *you* is usually omitted except for special emphasis.

Imperative	*Clean* up your plate first. You *do* it right now!

Other, less direct ways of giving commands or making requests are in the indicative mood.

Indicative | You *will* please *bring* your own paper.
| You *must bring* your own paper.

(3) The subjunctive mood

(3.1) Forms of the subjunctive
(3.2) Uses of the subjunctive

The subjunctive mood, used much less today than in former centuries, consists of a set of common verb forms that are used in special ways. In general, the subjunctive expresses the idea that a thing is untrue though perhaps desired. It may also express a wish, a necessity, or an obligation.

Incidentally, the modal auxiliaries—*must, might, would,* and so on—now are used (in the indicative mood) to express some of the ideas that were once expressed by the subjunctive mood. Modal means "expressing mood."

(3.1) Forms of the subjunctive The subjunctive-mood verb forms themselves all look familiar, but they are used differently from the indicative forms. Specifically, we know that they are subjunctive because their time-reference differs from what it would be in the normal indicative mood.

The verb *come* is used below as typical of all true verbs other than *be*.

Subjunctive Form	Time	Example
were	present or future	If he *were* here now, he would tell us. If he *were* here tomorrow at 3:00, we might be able to use his help.
had been	simple past	If he *had been* here last night, he would have told us.

came	present or future	If he *came* now, it might help. If he *came* tomorrow, it would be too late.
had come	simple past	If he *had come,* he would have brought his neighbors.
be	timeless	She insisted that he *be* on time.
come (no *-s*)	timeless	It was (is, will be) necessary that he *come* too.

The two forms marked "timeless" might be considered as unlimited by time (always true), or they may be understood in relation to the time of the main verb.

Notice that the top part of the table contains forms that look like past verbs, and notice that all these are used in clauses with *if.* The last two forms in the table are the same as those used in infinitives (to *be,* to *come*).

(3.2) Uses of the subjunctive   The three main uses of the subjunctive are all illustrated in the table above.

1. **Conditions contrary to fact** are expressed by subjunctive forms in educated general usage. These are clauses that begin with *if* (condition clauses) and that speak of something known to be untrue (contrary to fact). In the table above, the first, third, and sixth examples are conditions contrary to fact. By contrast, when we do not know whether a condition is true or not, we use an indicative verb:

    If he is here now, he will tell us.
    If he was here last night, he probably enjoyed the meeting.

    However, it is not correct to use the indicative in conditions that are contrary to fact; here

195

only the subjunctive is acceptable in standard English. Remember it this way: "I say 'if I *were* you' because I am *not* you."

2. **Doubtful future conditions** may also use the subjunctive, as in the second and fifth examples in the table. These, however, may instead be expressed by the modal auxiliary *would:*

    > If he would be here tomorrow . . .
    > If he would come tomorrow . . .

    The sentences with the subjunctives show perhaps more doubt than the ones with *would,* but either form is correct.

3. **Clauses after expressions of obligation and recommendation** use the subjunctive mood. As the last two examples in the table show, these expressions may be verbs (*insisted*) or adjectives (*necessary*). Sometimes the expression of obligation or recommendation may even be a noun, such as the noun *suggestion:*

    > She made the suggestion that he *be* on time.

    Here are some additional examples.

    > I move that the meeting *be adjourned.*
    > The letter demands (asks, suggests) that she *keep* her dog quiet at night.
    > It is recommended (imperative) that the dog *be given* some meat in its diet.

    Without the subjunctive the idea of obligation would disappear:

    > The letter suggests that she keeps her dog quiet at night.

    Now the letter suggests merely what the fact is, not what she should do.

    Even though the plain indicative cannot substitute for the subjunctive in such sentences, sometimes the sentence can be acceptably reworded with a modal auxiliary like *should.* (This substitution would work with *suggests,* but not with *demands,* for instance.)

4. Finally, certain **set expressions** use the subjunctive. None of these appear on the table, but here are a few.

God be with you.	So be it.
God be praised.	Be that as it may,
Heaven forbid.	Come what may,
Long live the King.	Suffice it to say,

Several of these express desire, as does "Thy kingdom come."

Chapter 8

Expansion and Reduction of Sentences

8a Combining sentence-ideas by using dependent clauses
8b Reducing some combined clauses for flexibility and conciseness
8c Adding detail to adjectives

What if every English sentence were a bare-bones simple sentence? We would need to read many more sentences. And we would likely be bored in the process.

Let's use the term **sentence-idea** for an idea or thought that can conveniently be expressed in a simple sentence. As you know, we can join sentence-ideas in various ways. We can join them on an equal basis, making compound sentences. We can also join them on an unequal basis, pointing up certain ideas as more important.

The ideas that are less important to us we subordinate in a variety of ways. This chapter is mainly about that variety of ways.

8a Combining Sentence-Ideas by Using Dependent Clauses

(1) Adding adjective clauses
(2) Adding adverb clauses
(3) Using noun clauses
(4) Making the proper adjustments in indirect quotations
(5) Classifying sentences by clause structure

Sometimes you can make a sentence interesting by adding another sentence-idea to it in the form of a dependent clause. A dependent clause is like a simple sentence in having a subject and a predicate, but its form has been adjusted enough to make it usable as part of another sentence.

There are three kinds of dependent clauses, based on how the clause is used in the larger sentence:

How Used in the Sentence

Adjective clause	Modifies a noun or pronoun
Adverb clause	Usually modifies a verb
Noun clause	Subject, direct object, etc.

(1) Adding Adjective Clauses

(1.1) Adjective clauses with relative pronouns
(1.2) Adjective clauses with relative adverbs

(1.1) Adjective clauses with relative pronouns Suppose that we want to express the following two ideas in a single sentence, with the first idea as more important:

Jean talked to *a girl.*

who
The girl had stopped to watch her paint.

The link between the two ideas is expressed by the word *girl.* Therefore we may join the sentence-ideas by substituting either *who* or *that* for *the girl* in the second sentence.

$$\text{Jean talked to a girl} \underbrace{[\text{who}/\text{that}}_{\text{S}} \text{ had } \overset{\text{InV}}{\text{stopped}} \text{ to}$$

watch her paint].

The underlined clause tells us something about the girl. Notice three things about the clause:

1. Because it still has a subject and a predicate, it is still a **clause.**
2. Because the clause can no longer stand alone as a sentence, it is now a **dependent** clause.
3. Because the dependent clause modifies a noun (as adjectives usually do), it is an **adjective** clause.

Most adjective clauses contain relative pronouns, like *who* and *that*. These words are pronouns because they can take the place of a noun phrase (in this case *the girl*). They are **relative** because they relate to a word in the main clause (the antecedent, in this case *girl*)— the word that the whole adjective clause modifies.

Here is another example. As before, the main sentence-idea is in the first sentence.

Jean was repainting *the fence.*

Her father had just repaired *the fence.*
(which)

Again we substitute a relative pronoun for the repeated noun phrase. Because a fence is a thing, not a person, our choice is between *which* and *that.*

$$\text{Jean was repainting the fence} \underbrace{[\text{that}/\text{which}}_{} \text{ her father}$$

had just repaired].

This time the order of the words in the adjective clause has been adjusted. The adjustment is needed because a relative pronoun usually comes at the beginning of its clause, no matter what word it has substituted for.

So far there have been no commas between the adjective clauses and the nouns modified. Sometimes, however, a comma does appear there.

> Jean talked to Susan Faron, [who had stopped to watch her paint].
>
> Jean was repainting the front fence, [which her father had just repaired].

As section **10d(5)** explains more fully, a comma is used before adjective clauses in sentences like these two. In these sentences, the clauses are not necessary to identify *which* girl or fence is meant. They simply give us more information about Susan and the front fence. (Commas are used on both sides of such a clause when it comes in the middle of the sentence: Susan Faron, *who had stopped to watch Jean paint*, lives nearby.)

- **Practice 8-1** Find the adjective clause in each sentence.
  1. James Fenimore Cooper was probably the first American who made a living by writing novels.
  2. His famous Leatherstocking Saga, which contains five novels, was written about the fictional frontiersman Natty Bumppo.
  3. A horrible book that he had read to his ailing wife motivated him to write a "better" novel of his own.
  4. One of his best-known books is *The Deerslayer,* which is part of the Leatherstocking Saga.
  5. Cooper's romantic portrayal of the pioneers was criticized by the realists who rose to prominence in the American literary circles of the late nineteenth century.

A relative pronoun can also substitute for an object of a preposition.

> This was *the girl.*

whom
Jean had given a tract to *the girl* last Saturday.

In somewhat formal English *whom* (the objective form of *who*) substitutes for *the girl* in the second sentence, and the whole prepositional phrase (*to whom*) is moved to the beginning of the clause.

(OP)   S   TrV   DO
This was the girl [to whom Jean had given a tract

last Saturday].

In relaxed conversation, the relative pronoun *that* could be the substitute for *the girl.* If so, *that* alone is brought to the beginning, leaving *to* behind.*

(OP) S   TrV   DO
This was the girl [that Jean had given a tract to

last Saturday].

Finally, *whose* (the possessive form of the relative pronoun *who*) can substitute for a possessive word or phrase.

Jean had been praying for *Susan.*

whose
Susan's mother had just been saved.

Since *whose mother* is already at the beginning, no reordering is needed.

Jean had been praying for Susan, [whose mother had just been saved].

See **4a(9.1)** for the three relative pronouns and their use.

---

* The informal aspect of the construction is the separation of the preposition and its object, not the word *that* itself.

● **Practice 8-2** Find the adjective clause in each sentence.

1. Army ants, whose reputation exceeds real life, live in the tropics.
2. These carnivorous insects roam about in swarms that number nearly 150,000 ants.
3. Occasionally deer or even crocodiles that are injured or trapped become victims of these nomadic ants.
4. These ants, which are sensitive to bright light, travel only at night or on cloudy days.
5. They are welcomed by some villagers, for whom they serve as pest exterminators.

One final minor point is that sometimes the relative pronoun *that* is omitted (simply "understood") when it is the direct object or the object of a preposition.

Jean was repainting the fence [her father had just repaired].   (*That* understood, DO)

This was the girl [Jean had given a tract to last Saturday].   (*That* understood, OP)

(1.2) **Adjective clauses with relative adverbs** Sometimes we want to attach extra information to a noun of time, place, or reason. When we do, a relative adverb often works better in the adjective clause than a relative pronoun would.

Jean had prayed for *a quiet place*.

where
She could talk to Susan about the Lord *in that place*.

If the second sentence will become the adjective clause, then we can substitute *where* for *in that place* and move the *where* to the beginning of its clause.

Jean had prayed for a quiet place [where she could talk to Susan about the Lord].

Because *where* substitutes for an adverbial prepositional phrase (*in that place,* modifying *talk*), *where* is an adverb. And because the adverb *where* relates to *a quiet place* in the main clause, it is a **relative** adverb. These three words can be relative adverbs:

when	where	why

They are included in **3e(7),** with other special adverbs.

- **Practice 8-3** Find each adjective clause and the noun it modifies.
  1. Archer fish swim near the surface, where they are constantly on the lookout for insects.
  2. These fish hunt insects that are either at rest nearby or in flight near the water's surface.
  3. An archer fish shoots its prey with drops of water propelled out of its mouth, which it raises above the surface of the lake.
  4. These fish, to whom God has given such a remarkable skill, have perfect accuracy up to four or five feet.
  5. For the archer fish, the best time for lunch is the instant when the "shot" insect hits the surface of the water.

(2) Adding adverb clauses

Sometimes we have two similar sentence-ideas whose relation we would like to make clear.

> Whales have lungs instead of gills.
> Whales come to the surface for air.

In this pair, the fact expressed in the first sentence is the *cause* of the fact in the second. To say so, we can use *because* with the first sentence-idea, joining it to the second.

> *Because whales have lungs instead of gills*, they come to the surface for air.

The word *because* tells us that one fact causes the other, but it also changes the clause to which it is added:

> 1. The word *because* makes the clause into a **dependent** clause—a clause that cannot stand alone as a sentence.

2. The clause tells why the whales *come to the surface,* that is, why they *come.* Because this dependent clause modifies a verb (as adverbs do), it is an **adverb** clause.

Adverb clauses are introduced by **subordinating conjunctions,** words like *because, since, if, while, after,* and *although.* The subordinating conjunction is part of the adverb clause. This kind of conjunction is called "subordinating" because it joins a dependent clause (a "subordinate clause") to an independent clause.

An adverb clause often comes at the beginning of the sentence, as in the example above. When the adverb clause does come first, it is set off by a comma. When the adverb clause comes at the end of the sentence, it may or may not be set off by a comma, depending on the meaning intended. Often there is no comma.

Whales come to the surface for air *because they have lungs instead of gills.*

Whales come to the surface for air, *since they have lungs instead of gills.*

In the first example the adverb clause seems to give important information, but in the second sentence (with a comma) the clause sounds more like an afterthought. Section **10d(5)** discusses this difference.

Here are a few more sample sentences, with the adverb clauses in italics.

If one whale is in distress, the other whales often try to help.

Whales usually try to help *when another whale is in distress.*

A mother whale nurses her calf *until it can survive on its own.*

Although some kinds of whales have teeth, baleen whales are toothless.

The first three examples here are the most common type, in which the adverb clause pretty clearly modifies the verb of the main clause. The last example shows that sometimes the adverb clause seems to modify the whole main clause; we still call it an adverb clause.

See the first part of the table in **4f(2.1)** for four common meanings signaled by subordinating conjunctions. In the same section, Practice 4-31 provides an opportunity to find adverb clauses that begin with some of these words.

(3) Using noun clauses

(3.1) Noun clauses with *that*
(3.2) Noun clauses with other words

(3.1) Noun clauses with *that* Previous sections present adjective clauses and adverb clauses, which are modifiers.

> An *adjective* clause allows a sentence-idea to *modify a noun* in another clause.
> An *adverb* clause allows a sentence-idea to *modify a verb* in another clause.

Sometimes, however, sentence-ideas are related to each other in an even more basic way.

> S TrV   DO
> I know *something*.

> Good men hate the way of the wicked.

If the *something* of the first sentence refers to the second sentence-idea, then we can show that fact by inserting the second sentence-idea in place of *something*.

> S TrV DO
> I know [*that good men hate the way of the wicked*].

Notice two things about the italicized clause:

1. The added word *that* is a sign that this clause is now a **dependent** clause, one used as part of another sentence and not a sentence by itself.
2. Just as the word *something* was the direct object of *know,* so now this clause is the direct object of *know*. And since "direct object" is a

> noun function, we call this kind of dependent clause a **noun** clause. A noun clause is any clause that performs a noun function—S, DO, IO, OP, and so on.

The word *that,* which introduces most noun clauses, is part of the noun clause. Because it introduces a dependent (or "subordinate") clause, it is called a **subordinating conjunction.** A subordinating conjunction does nothing within its clause except to introduce it.

Probably noun clauses are most often used as direct objects. But noun clauses can be used in other ways too.

       S   LV   PA
    Something is also true.

         S   TrV   DO
    Wicked men hate good men.

Again, if *something* refers to the second sentence-idea, then we can let that idea substitute for *something.* As before, we add *that* to introduce the noun clause.

    S   (S) (TrV)   (DO) LV   PA
    [That wicked men hate good men] is also true.

This time the noun clause acts as the subject of the sentence. The noun clause, of course, still has its own subject and verb, as shown by the parenthesized labels.

When a noun clause is the subject of a sentence, we often turn the sentence around, putting the subject last. (That way the reader or hearer does not have to hold the whole noun-clause subject in mind before he knows what is being said about it.)

    LV   PA S
    It is also true [that wicked men hate good men].

The meaning has not changed. The idea in the noun clause is still the thing that "is also true." The noun clause is still the subject, but the word *it* has been added as a "place-holder" for the subject. This *it* is also called a subject substitute (or expletive).

Here are some additional examples of noun clauses.

     S   TrV   DO
Proverbs 29:27 explains [that wicked people and good

people are each uncomfortable in the other's presence].

S
[That Christians cannot always be popular] should not

    TrV   DO
surprise us.

             TrV   DO S
It should not surprise us [that Christians cannot

always be popular].

         S   LV   PN
The good news is [that a humble heart pleases God].

      S   App   InV
The idea [that a humble heart is also restful] appears

in Matthew 11:28-30.

See **4f(2.2)** for the subordinating conjunction *that,* both expressed and "understood," and for practice in finding noun clauses introduced by *that.*

     (3.2) Noun clauses with other words Although most noun clauses begin with the subordinating conjunction *that,* certain other words can also begin noun clauses. The first of these is another subordinating conjunction, *whether.*

     In the following pair of sentence-ideas, the "something" of the first sentence refers to the question asked by the second.

                     DO
     Please find out *something.*

     Can Jill come with us?

We can make the second sentence into a noun clause, substituting it for *something*. Since the second sentence-idea involves a choice (a yes/no question), we add *whether* to it when we make it into a noun clause.

DO
Please find out [whether Jill can come with us].

Compare the noun clause that does not have an implied choice: "I found out [that Jill can come with us]." *Whether* is like *that* in being a **subordinating conjunction**; it introduces a dependent clause and does nothing else in the clause. The subordinating conjunction *if* sometimes substitutes for *whether,* but only when the noun clause is used as a direct object, as it is here. See **4f(2.2)** for a caution about this use of *if.*

The next words that can be used in noun clauses are the **indefinite relative pronouns.** Below are four examples:

Pair of Sentence-Ideas   *Sentence with Noun Clause*

DO
You haven't told me *something.* $\Longrightarrow$ You haven't told me [who came].

who
Someone came.

DO
We have just learned *something.* $\Longrightarrow$ We have just learned [what happened].

what
Something happened.

OP
I will give it to *some person.* $\Longrightarrow$ I will give it to [whomever you promised].

whomever
You promised someone.

S
Some event must be serious. $\Longrightarrow$ [Whatever happened] must be serious.

whatever
Something happened.

In all these examples, the italicized word of the first sentence is replaced by the sentence-idea below it. Instead of the crossed-out indefinite pronoun, the new noun clause contains an indefinite relative pronoun:

1. **Indefinite:** it substitutes for something indefinite (identity unknown) in the noun clause, and it has no antecedent in the main clause.
2. **Relative:** it helps relate the clause to the main clause.
3. **Pronoun:** it functions as a pronoun in its own clause (S, DO, etc.).

The indefinite relative pronouns are covered in section **4a(9.2),** which includes several additional examples of their use in noun clauses.

Finally, **indefinite relative adverbs** can be used in noun clauses. First some examples:

Pair of Sentence-Ideas   *Sentence with Noun Clause*

                          DO   DO
Please announce *something*. ⟹ Please announce [when the program
                                                                          will begin].
                     when
The program will begin at some time.

     S   S
Something is a mystery.   ⟹ [Where the meeting will be held] is a
                                                                          mystery.
                  where
The meeting will be held at some place.

                       DO   DO
No one explained *something*. ⟹ No one explained [why the time was
                                                                          changed].
                   why
The time was changed for some reason.

                 DO   DO
Tell me *something*.   ⟹   Tell me [how we can find the house].
                 how
We can find the house in some way.

In every case the second sentence-idea substitutes for the italicized word in the first sentence. As the second sentence in each pair becomes a noun clause, a single word replaces an adverbial prepositional phrase. The replacement word is an indefinite relative adverb:

1. **Indefinite:** it substitutes for something indefinite (unknown) in the noun clause, and it has no antecedent in the main clause.
2. **Relative:** it helps relate the noun clause to the main clause.
3. **Adverb:** it is used adverbially in its own clause.

The four indefinite relative adverbs are part of section **3e(7)**.

(4) Making the proper adjustments in indirect quotations

There are two ways to report what another person has said. We can report his words exactly, using a direct quotation, or we can reword his statement, using an indirect quotation.

| Direct quotation | He told her, "I am happy to meet you." |

| Indirect quotation | He told her [that he was happy to meet her]. |

In an indirect quotation, what was said is made into a noun clause, often one beginning with *that*.

Changing a direct quotation into an indirect quotation involves two kinds of internal change. First, the **personal pronouns** are changed.

He told her that *he* was happy to meet *her*.

The pronouns are now used from the point of view of the one reporting the speech, rather than from the point of view of the speaker.

The **verb tense** is also adjusted according to the point of view of the one reporting.

He told her that he *was* happy to meet her.

This adjustment of the tense is made when the "reporting verb" (*told, said,* etc.) is in the past tense. In that case the quoted verb would normally change from present to past tense, as in the example. (An exception is often made for indirectly quoted statements that are still true: Galileo observed [that large and small objects *fall* at the same rate].) Below are the common adjustments of tense in indirect quotations when the "reporting verb" is in the past tense.*

Adjustment of Tense in Indirect Quotations	*Example*
Present ⟹ Past	He said, "I'm cold." He said that he *was* cold.
Past ⟹ Past Perfect (often)	He said, "I got the milk." He said that he *had gotten* the milk. He said that he *got* the milk.
will ⟹ would	He said "I will do it." He said that he *would* do it.
can ⟹ could	He said, "I can do it." He said that he *could* do it.
may ⟹ might	He said, "I may go." He said that he *might* go.

These changes are systematic: in every case the past-tense "reporting verb" pushes the quoted verb back one step into the past. (*Would, could,* and *might* were once simply the past tense of *will, can,* and *may.*)

Indirect questions require one additional adjustment.

"When *will* my bus *arrive*?" he asked.
He asked [when his bus *would arrive*].

---

* Any tense in the "past-tense family" of **7b(2)** has the same effect (*said, was saying, had said*). Likewise the indirect-quotation change from present to past actually includes changing present progressive to past progressive, and present perfect to past perfect.

In this indirect question, *my* becomes *his* and *will* becomes *would,* just as in an indirect statement. In addition, the inverted word order of the direct question is set aside, so that once again the entire verb follows the subject. It is generally considered nonstandard or at least highly questionable to use direct-question word order in indirect questions.

Not generally acceptable	He wondered when would his bus come.
Correct	He wondered when his bus would come.
Also correct	He wondered, "When will my bus come?"

● **Practice 8-5** Change the following direct quotations into indirect quotations, rewriting them from the point of view of the reporter mentioned in number 2.
1. "The coach sent in a play with me," the quarterback explained.
2. "Why did you change it?" asked the reporter.
3. "Their defensive backs were in a zone defense," he answered.
4. Mark, the right end, added, "I had been open the whole game against their zone."
5. "Did you notice how much time the linemen gave me to throw?" the quarterback asked happily.
6. "I caught the ball in full stride and just sailed into the end zone," Mark said with a laugh.

(5) Classifying sentences by clause structure

(5.1) Simple sentences
(5.2) Compound sentences
(5.3) Complex sentences
(5.4) Compound-complex sentences

A sentence can be classified according to whether it contains one, or more than one, independent clause, and according to whether it contains any dependent clauses. Classifying your own sentences in this way can help you decide whether you have used a pleasing mixture in a piece of writing. It can also be a way to study the style of a good writer, in order to learn from it.

(5.1) Simple sentences A simple sentence consists of one independent clause only. (An independent clause, you remember, contains one subject-predicate pair, even though the subject or the predicate—or both—may be compound.)

Most shad fishing is done at night.
The fishers and their helpers work with gill nets.

(5.2) Compound sentences A compound sentence consists of two or more independent clauses. The independent clauses are usually joined by a coordinating conjunction, although on occasion a semicolon (or even a colon) alone may be used.

The fish cannot see the nets at night,

and they are easily snared in them.

In this sentence the two independent clauses are underlined. Notice that the coordinating conjunction is not part of either clause.

(5.3) Complex sentences

A complex sentence consists of one independent clause and at least one dependent clause. (Remember that although an independent clause can stand on its own as a sentence, a dependent clause cannot; it is *dependent* on another clause.)

Shad return each year to the river [in which they

were hatched].

[Because the fishing is seasonal] and [because the

men can work at night],

most of the shad fishermen work full-time at other

jobs.

The independent clauses are underlined, and the dependent clauses are enclosed in large brackets. Notice that the relative pronoun *which* and the subordinating conjunction *because* are inside the dependent clauses.

Practice 8-6 Classify the following sentences as simple, compound, or complex.

1. The Dead Sea Scrolls were found by an Arab herdsman who was looking for a goat that he had lost.
2. These scrolls contained the oldest known copies of Old Testament Scriptures, and they also contained various other religious texts.
3. It was one of the greatest discoveries of biblical manuscripts.
4. The scrolls were probably deposited in the caves by men who were fleeing the Roman invasion.

(5.4) Compound-complex sentences A compound-complex sentence contains at least two independent clauses (like a compound sentence) and at least one dependent clause (like a complex sentence).

Fishways, [which allow the shad to pass dams in the rivers], have been built, and an increase in the shad population is likely.

The two independent clauses have been underlined, and the dependent clause has been bracketed. (The clauses are all marked separately, even though a dependent clause is also part of the independent clause to which it is attached.) Compound-complex sentences cannot have fewer clauses than this, but they can easily have more.

● **Practice 8-7** Classify the following sentences as simple, compound, complex, or compound-complex.

1. The earliest papyrus writings still in existence are the Egyptian Books of the Dead.
2. They contain a collection of spells which supposedly helped the dead in the afterlife.
3. The dead had to defend themselves before a jury of the gods, and if they won, they were granted life after death.
4. In every mythical trial that was written down, the dead were found "true of voice" and were allowed to live.
5. These books of magic gave the pharaohs a sense of security, but in reality their hope was false.

8b Reducing Some Combined Clauses for Flexibility and Conciseness

(1) Reducing combined independent clauses
(2) Reducing adjective clauses
(3) Reducing adverb clauses
(4) Reducing noun clauses
(5) Reducing certain complex sentences to simple sentences with adverbs

Often we combine clauses within a sentence in order to make the sentence more interesting and to show the connections between certain ideas. Sometimes, though, we find that the resulting sentence is too complicated, or too heavy, for its setting. Then it is helpful to know some ways of reducing clauses to simpler expressions.

(1) Reducing combined independent clauses

(1.1) Compound sentence to simple sentence with a compound part
(1.2) Ellipsis in a compound sentence

When a compound sentence contains some elements that are the same in two or more clauses, it is often possible to leave out the repetition.

(1.1) Compound sentence to simple sentence with a compound part In certain constructions, we almost always eliminate possible repetition. In fact, with this first group we often perform the process automatically as we originally make the sentence. However, looking at these examples will perhaps make it easier to understand some that may not be quite so obvious.

> Sam *let us out at the entrance* and (~~Sam~~) *then went to park the car.*
> We may *visit the zoo* or (~~we may~~) *spend the afternoon in the park.*
> We drove *by City Hall* and (~~we drove~~) *near the library.*
> I like to watch *the lions* and (~~I like to watch~~) *the tigers.*
> *The lions* (~~seem powerful~~) and *the tigers* seem powerful.

Each of these pairs of ideas can be expressed in a compound sentence. However, as shown by the parenthesized cross-outs, the repeated word or words can be left out. (The process of leaving out of a sentence something that will still be understood is called **ellipsis**.) What remains in each example is a simple sentence that contains some compound part. The italic print shows which parts are joined by the conjunction in the simple sentences.

(1.2) **Ellipsis in a compound sentence** Sometimes when we leave out repeated words in a compound sentence, we do not end up with a simple sentence containing a compound part. Instead we apparently still have a compound sentence, but one now in which some of the words are understood rather than expressed.

> The lion sometimes roars, but I doubt that it will (~~roar~~) today.
> The monkeys do tricks in the morning, and the seals (~~do tricks~~) in the afternoon.
> Jan brought the sandwiches and Dan (~~brought~~) the drinks.
> I have been dieting, and Jan has been (~~dieting~~) too.
> I have been dieting, and Jan has (~~been dieting~~) too.
> Foxes are canines, but goats are not (~~canines~~).
> John is probably at the snake house, and Marcy (~~is probably~~) anywhere else.

The omission of these words can be called ellipsis, and the result is an "elliptical independent clause" in a compound sentence. This kind of ellipsis can be a useful way to eliminate extra words.

● **Practice 8-8** Reduce the amount of repetition in the following compound sentences, but do not leave out anything needed for a natural-sounding sentence. Afterwards indicate which revised sentences have become simple sentences.
   1. Catherine the Great deposed her husband Peter III, and Catherine then became empress of Russia.
   2. She wrote plays and she wrote historical papers.
   3. In wars fought during her reign, Poland was conquered but Turkey was not conquered.
   4. Catherine suppressed the commoners, and she even gave some peasants as gifts to the nobility.
   5. Obviously, the nobility supported Catherine but the commoners did not support her at all.

(2) Reducing adjective clauses

(2.1) Adjective clause to participle
(2.2) Adjective clause to appositive
(2.3) Adjective clause to prepositional phrase
(2.4) Adjective clause to adjective
(2.5) Adjective clause to adjectival adverb

By using an adjective clause we can add significant information to one of the nouns in a sentence. At times, though, we may want to express the information in fewer words.

If the subject of an adjective clause is a relative pronoun, we can usually reduce the clause to just a phrase or even just a word. The usual first step—and often the only step—is to drop both the relative-pronoun subject and either the auxiliary *be* or the verb *be*. What is left of the former adjective clause depends mainly on what was there in the first place.

(2.1) Adjective clause to participle An adjective clause can often be reduced either to a simple participle or to a participle phrase.

> People [who are having problems] should seek biblical advice.

Here we simply leave out *who are:* "People *having problems* should seek biblical advice." All that is left of the former clause is a participle phrase modifying the noun.

> Advice [which is based on God's Word] is worth following.

Back in the first sample sentence, the adjective clause with an active verb produced a present participle. Here the adjective clause with a passive verb produces a past participle. (The past participle is more accurately called a "passive participle.")

So far we have produced participle phrases, and the phrases stayed after the nouns modified. Notice, though, what usually happens when all that remains of the clause is a simple participle:

Everyone appreciates a face [that is smiling].

Don't be a person [who is confused].

We normally move a simple participle around to the left of the noun, as if it were a true adjective.

Everyone appreciates a *smiling* face.
Don't be a *confused* person.

We could not have done so with the participle phrases—for instance, we would never say "*Having problems* people should seek biblical advice." However, a participle modified only by a preceding adverb can usually be moved.

Everyone appreciates a face [that is honestly smiling].

From this we get "Everyone appreciates an *honestly smiling* face." Likewise we can say "Don't be an *easily confused* person."

So far it has appeared that the clause must have a form of *be* in it already. Actually, though, many clauses without *be* could be reworded with *be* and then reduced.

people who have problems (= people who are
  having problems)   ⟹ people having problems

a face that smiles (= a face that is smiling)
               ⟹ a smiling face

anyone who wants an answer
         ⟹ anyone wanting an answer

the cup that he broke (= the cup that was broken)
           ⟹ the broken cup

anyone who laughed ⟹ anyone laughing
anyone who laughs ⟹ anyone laughing

The last two examples show that specific tense reference is missing with participles. They also show that simple participles do not move to the left of indefinite pronouns.

• **Practice 8-9** Reduce the adjective clauses to participles or participle phrases.

1. Easter Island, which is located in the South Pacific, is actually a part of Chile.
2. The island, which was discovered on Easter Sunday in 1722, contains three extinct volcanoes.
3. Hand-carved stone statues that weigh up to seventy tons are found all over the island.
4. Many people visit the island to wonder at these four-story-high lava statues and to speculate about their purpose, which is still unknown.
5. The builders of these eyeless images also left behind wooden tablets that are carved in an undecipherable script.

(2.2) Adjective clause to appositive If the adjective clause contains a predicate noun after *be,* the clause can be reduced to an appositive.

Our pastor, [who is a biblical counselor], does not believe or use the ideas of Freud, Rogers, or Skinner.
Our pastor, *a biblical counselor,* does not believe or use the ideas of Freud, Rogers, or Skinner.

Notice that the commas around the nonrestrictive adjective clause remain around the (nonrestrictive) appositive. A restrictive adjective clause would produce a restrictive appositive:

The apostle [who is Paul] tells us that the Bible will teach us the right way, rebuke us, put us back on the right path, and help us to stay there. (II Tim. 3:16)
The Apostle *Paul* tells us that the Bible will. . . .

(2.3) Adjective clause to prepositional phrase An adjective clause with a prepositional phrase after *be* can be reduced to just the prepositional phrase.

First the Scriptures teach us of salvation through faith [which is in Christ Jesus].
First the Scriptures teach us of salvation through faith *in Christ Jesus.*

Sometimes an adjective clause that has no prepositional phrase in it can nevertheless be converted into a prepositional phrase. The most obvious example is a clause containing the verb *have*.

> People [who have problems] should seek biblical advice.
> People *with problems* should seek biblical advice.

A clause with *have* can usually be converted into a *with*-phrase, and a negative clause with *have* into a *without*-phrase. The preposition *of* is also useful:

> The principle [that is found in Philippians 4:8] is the way to control your thoughts.
> The principle *of Philippians 4:8* is the way to control your thoughts.

● **Practice 8-10** Reduce five of the six adjective clauses to participles, appositives, or prepositional phrases. One adjective clause is probably clearer as it is.

1. The Yoruba, who are the third largest ethnic group in Nigeria, have a common language and culture.
2. Many of these people, who were captured during the Slave Wars, were sent to Brazil.
3. The Yoruba who are in Brazil still speak their native language and worship their old idols.
4. In Africa these people, who have skill in most crafts, are especially well known for their work with bronze.
5. The Yoruba, who were smelting iron, casting bronze, making glass, and weaving cloth even before contact with the Europeans, have given us the greatest wealth of African art treasures.
6. Cacao, which is Nigeria's most important cash crop, is produced primarily by the Yoruba.

(2.4) Adjective clause to adjective If an adjective clause contains a predicate adjective after the linking verb *be,* it can be reduced to just the adjective.

> A heart [that is godly] has God's peace.

A *godly* heart has God's peace.

Just as with a simple participle, a simple adjective nearly always moves to the left of the noun. A qualifier would move with the adjective.

The Christian life is the life [that is really joyful].

The Christian life is the *really joyful* life.

However, if the adjective should happen to be modified by a phrase (as mentioned in **8c**), the adjective and its phrase would not move.

He has a spirit [that is always joyful in the Lord].
He has a spirit *always joyful in the Lord.*

(2.5) Adjective clause to adjectival adverb
Occasionally an adjective clause containing an adverb is reduced in such a way that only the adverb remains to modify the noun.

The lesson [that was taught today] was on
   Philippians 4:6-9.
One principle [which is seen here] is that right
   feelings follow right actions.

Adverbs, unlike adjectives, do not move to the left of nouns.

The lesson *today* was on Philippians 4:6-9.
One principle *here* is that right feelings follow
   right actions.

Usually adverbs used in this way have a meaning of place or time.

> • **Practice 8-11** Reduce each adjective clause in whatever way you think best. Which clause was probably better in its original form?
> 1. The Cavalier Poets, who were fiercely devoted to Charles I, wrote during the seventeenth century.

2. These poets, who were English, were known as the "tribe of Ben" (Jonson).
3. Sir John Suckling, who was in exile at the end of his life, had spent his fortune for the royalist cause.
4. Richard Lovelace, who is possibly the best known Cavalier poet, was even imprisoned for a time.
5. Their poetry, which is often written in a lighter vein, emphasized the pleasures of this world.
6. Their lyrical poems, which are still read today, are considered to be primarily love songs.

(3) Reducing adverb clauses

(3.1) Adverb clause to infinitive
(3.2) Adverb clause to participle
(3.3) Adverb clause to prepositional phrase
(3.4) Adverb clause to absolute phrase
(3.5) Adverb clause to elliptical adverb clause

The information given in an adverb clause can sometimes be expressed more briefly. Though certain clauses should be spelled out fully, it is often useful to be able to reduce a clause to a simpler structure.

(3.1) Adverb clause to infinitive If an adverb clause expressing purpose has the same subject as the main clause, the purpose clause can usually be converted to an infinitive phrase.

We chose this neighborhood [so that we would be close to the church and the school].

(with "to" written above, "so that we would" struck through)

> We chose this neighborhood *to be close to the church and the school.*

When the "purpose" meaning of the infinitive is not fully clear, *in order to* can make it clear.

> We chose it *in order to be close to the church and the school.*

The purpose infinitive, like the purpose clause, is adverbial and can come at the beginning of the sentence.

> *To be near the church,* we looked for a house in this area.
>
> *In order to find a house,* we read the ads and talked to a realtor.

(3.2) Adverb clause to participle If an adverb clause has the same subject as the main clause,* and if it expresses a meaning of time, cause, or condition, it may be reducible to a phrase based on a participle.

> Arriving
> [As/ When we arrived here], we met one of our new
>
> neighbors.

> *Arriving here,* we met one of our new neighbors.

In reducing a time clause, we use a present participle to indicate the same time as in the main clause. To express prior time, we use a perfect participle.

> Having arrived
> [After we arrived here], we tried to meet our other
>
> neighbors.

> *Having arrived here,* we tried to meet our other neighbors.

---

* If an adverb clause with a different subject is reduced to a participle, the result is a dangling modifier: *Arriving here,* the house pleased us. See **9d(3).**

Clauses of cause are reduced in the same way:

               Being
  [Because ~~you are~~ creative], you can surely find a way

  to use our old curtains in this room, can't you?

  Being creative, you can surely find a way, can't
  you?

  [~~Since she was~~ surprised by the question], she
  just looked at him.
  Surprised by the question, she just looked at
  him.

In every case, the participle phrase has a less explicit meaning than the full adverb clause, mainly because the subordinating conjunction is omitted. This reduction in information may be desirable or not, depending on how much we want to say. Usually, of course, the context will allow the reader to figure out the omitted sub-ordinating conjunction (*when, after, because,* etc.). Sometimes a small difference in the main clause signals a significant difference in the implied adverb clause:

  Cleaned up, this house will be attractive.
  Cleaned up, this house would be attractive.

The first participle comes from a time clause ("*When* this house is cleaned up"), but the second from a clause of condition ("*If* this house were cleaned up").

Even though the adverbial meaning can usually be figured out, it is no longer expressly stated. Therefore the participle phrases are generally considered to be adjectival, modifying the subject of the main clause. That is, a participle is considered to modify whatever noun (or pronoun) it tells something about.

  ● **Practice 8-12** In the following sentences, if an
  adverb clause can be reduced easily to a verbal
  phrase (infinitive or participle), make that reduction. One adverb clause should be left as it is.
  1. In the seventeenth century, monarchs stressed
     the divine right of kings so that these kings

could suppress the revolutionary ideas growing in Europe.
2. Because they had become dissatisfied with the Pope's political and religious power, the nobility during the Middle Ages had transferred that authority to their kings.
3. Because the monarchy was supposedly ordained by God, the monarchy could not be abolished.
4. Even if a king was wicked, he should be obeyed.
5. In addition, kings considered themselves to be above the law, since kings thought they were accountable only to God.

(3.3) Adverb clause to prepositional phrase Certain kinds of adverb clauses can be reduced to prepositional phrases.

[Because there was a decrease in humidity], the heat was not oppressive.
Because of a decrease in humidity, the heat was not oppressive.

When the clause contains no noun that can become the object of the preposition, sometimes a noun can be made from another part of speech:

[After it rains in the desert], plants seem to appear by magic.
After a desert rainfall, plants seem to appear by magic.

(3.4) Adverb clause to absolute phrase If the subject of the adverb clause is different from that of the main clause, we may be able to turn the adverb clause into an absolute phrase. Usually the adverb clause expresses some sort of associated circumstance, which might be stated as time or cause.

falling
[Because no rain usually falls there in June], few

desert flowers are expected in midsummer.

No rain usually falling there in June, few desert flowers are expected in midsummer.

We reduce the clause to an absolute phrase by dropping the subordinating conjunction and changing the finite verb to a participle. What remains is a typical absolute phrase, consisting of a noun phrase (*no rain*) modified by a participle phrase (*usually falling there in June*). We call it an **absolute** phrase because it is more or less independent (absolute) in the sentence. An absolute phrase loosely modifies the rest of the sentence.

In the example above, the present participle *falling* indicates about the same time as in the main clause. A perfect participle clearly indicates prior time.

> [Because no rain fell in June], this month's
>   irrigation bill is high.
> *No rain having fallen in June,* this month's
>   irrigation bill is high.

In both examples, the reduction could also be carried one step further, to a prepositional phrase: "With no rain in June."

Although most absolute phrases consist of a noun phrase modified by a participle phrase, occasionally the participle can be omitted.

> [While the sun was low in the west], the desert air
>   quickly grew cool.
> *The sun being low in the west,* the desert air
>   quickly grew cool.
> *The sun low in the west,* the desert air quickly
>   grew cool.

In its shortest version, then, the absolute phrase consists of a noun phrase containing at least one modifier after the noun. This kind of absolute phrase too is considered to modify all of the rest of the sentence.

- **Practice 8-13** Reword four of the following sentences by using absolute phrases. (In normal writing, of course, you would not use so many absolute phrases together.) Use a prepositional phrase to revise the one sentence in which an absolute phrase would not work well.

1. After an earthquake has shifted the ocean's floor, a great wave called a tsunami starts out across the surface.
2. Because the ocean is so large, these hundred-mile-long waves are not easily spotted.
3. Since the waves are of such tremendous size, a tidal effect is produced on the shore.
4. Because they travel at excessive speeds (350 to 500 m.p.h.), and because they reach enormous heights (up to 200 feet), these "tidal waves" are devastating when they reach the shore.
5. When a tsunami has reached the shore, men are helpless before its might.

(3.5) Adverb clause to elliptical adverb clause When we reduce an adverb clause either to a verbal or to an absolute phrase, we drop the subordinating conjunction. However, another way to reduce an adverb clause is to keep the subordinating conjunction and simply drop one or more other words—words that will be clearly understood from the context.

[While (he was) in school], he did best in his math courses.

Because the subordinating conjunction remains, the word group's origin as an adverb clause is still clear and we call it an "elliptical adverb clause." (*Elliptical* simply means that some words have been left out.) An elliptical clause has the same function in the sentence as a full adverb clause.

In the example above, the rest of the sentence makes it plain that *While in school* is short for *While he was in school.* Notice the difference in this one:

While in school, you should learn all you can.

This time the elliptical clause is short for *While you are in school.* A correctly used elliptical clause can always be expanded by the reader in this way.*

---

* Do not reduce an adverb clause whose subject is different from that of the main clause. The result would be a dangling modifier: *While in school,* math was his favorite subject. See **9d(3).**

Some additional examples follow. Notice the kinds of things that can be left out and the various meanings of the clauses.

[Though (he is) not very tall], he is a good
   basketball player.
[When (they are) given a chance], the new players
   do well.
[While (I was) climbing the stairs], I stumbled.
I'll go [if you will (go)].
I'm happy [if you are (happy)].
[Because Mom couldn't (do it)], Cindy is doing
   the shopping.
[Although (he was) sad], he was not grief-stricken.

The second and third examples show that elliptical adverb clauses can include participles, reduced from finite verbs; compare the fourth pair of examples in **8b(3.2).**

We often use elliptical clauses of comparison.

Jack is taller [than Joe is (tall)].
You made more baskets [than I made (baskets)].

In both of these examples, though, further ellipsis is possible.

Jack is taller [than Joe (is tall)].
You made more baskets [than I (made baskets)].

Some short clauses of comparison are fine either with or without ellipsis.

He is less discouraged now [than (he was) before].
I tried to do as well [as he (did)].

Here too, correctly used elliptical clauses can be expanded by the reader.

● **Practice 8-14** Whenever the result will be clear, change the adverb clauses to elliptical adverb clauses.

1. Although he was educated at home, Andrew became one of the best-loved twentieth-century artists.

2. While he was a student at home, his father taught him painting.
3. After his father was killed in an accident, Andrew painted *Winter, 1946.*
4. While he was observing a young crippled girl picking berries in a field, he came up with the idea for his famous painting, *Christina's World.*
5. The rural countrysides and bleak seashores of Andrew Wyeth's paintings are known as well today as they ever were.

(4) Reducing noun clauses

(4.1) Noun clause to gerund or infinitive
(4.2) Noun clause to noun phrase

Many noun clauses cannot be reduced to any simpler construction. When a noun clause can be reduced, however, the sentence usually becomes noticeably more trim.

(4.1) Noun clause to gerund or infinitive Sometimes a noun clause could be reduced to either a gerund or an infinitive.

PN
My preference is [that I would stay with you].

PN
My preference is *staying with you.* (gerund)

PN
My preference is *to stay with you.* (infinitive)

In this particular set of examples, the infinitive may be preferable, since the gerund could possibly be misread as part of a progressive verb ("is staying"). These sentences, though, can be made even more direct:

I prefer *staying with you.*
I prefer *to stay with you.*

In the original sentence above, the subject of the noun clause was the same as the implied actor of the main clause (I prefer, I stay). When the two subjects or actors are different, the subject of the noun clause cannot just be dropped. With a gerund, the pronoun "subject" appears as a possessive modifier:

         DO
I know [that he lived in Spain for a while].

I know about *his living in Spain for a while.*   (gerund OP)

With an infinitive, the former subject of the noun clause appears as an objective-case pronoun.

         PN
The plan is [that we would arrive first and claim the tables].

The plan is *for us to arrive first and claim the tables.*   (infinitive PN)

The "subject" of the infinitive is always introduced by *for,* unless the infinitive phrase is used as a direct object after certain verbs.

         S
It's unbelievable [that the roof would just collapse].

It's unbelievable *for the roof to just collapse.* (infinitive S)

         DO
They requested [that he conduct a full investigation].

They requested *him to conduct a full investigation.*   (infinitive DO)

(4.2) Noun clause to noun phrase At times an entire noun clause can be reduced to a simple noun phrase. Usually this can happen only if a noun exists that is related in meaning to the verb of the noun clause.

         DO
I know [that he lived in Spain for a while].

I know about *his residence in Spain.*   (noun OP)

Less information is given by this noun phrase than by the noun clause, but in some contexts no more would be needed. As with the gerund phrase in **8b(4.1),** *about* is added after *know,* and the former subject of the clause becomes the possessive modifier *his.* Here are two more examples.

[How he will do] depends on [how hard he works].

His success depends on *his diligence.*

I want to see [whoever is in charge].

I want to see *the person in charge.*

Conversions from noun clause to noun phrase often do a great deal to streamline the sentence.

- **Practice 8-15** In these sentences, reduce most of the noun clauses to gerund phrases, infinitive phrases, or simple noun phrases. One sentence is probably best left as it is.
  1. How well a novelist succeeds depends upon his understanding of other people and himself.
  2. Charles Dickens believed that a novelist should be an interpreter of his times.
  3. His goal was that he be a morally and socially responsible novelist.
  4. Dickens' hope was that society would be governed by human compassion and not by commercial interests.
  5. Did you know that Dickens visited America and that he was extremely critical of slavery?
  6. In his later years people asked that he do readings of his own works for the public.

(5) Reducing certain complex sentences to simple sentences with adverbs

Some complex sentences with predicate adjectives can be reduced to simple sentences that contain adverbs as sentence modifiers.

It is fortunate [that no one else had reserved the
    picnic shelter].
Fortunately, no one else had reserved the picnic
    shelter.

The reduced sentence is shorter and usually smoother.

We are happy [that everyone can come this time].
Happily, everyone can come this time.*

8c Adding Detail to Adjectives

Some sentences take on new life when detail is added
to certain adjectives in them. For example, consider this
sentence:

He had thought he was ready, but after three days
    in Tokyo he was tired.

The sentence is correct, but a bit vague. (Ready for what?
And was he just tired, or tired of something?) The
sentence becomes clearer when we add a prepositional
phrase to each of those predicate adjectives.

He had thought he was ready for anything,

but after three days in Tokyo he was tired of the

noise and the rushing traffic.

Some adjectives, then, can be modified by prepositional
phrases.

In addition, some adjectives can be modified by
infinitive phrases. This time we begin with a simple
sentence containing a pair of predicate adjectives.

However, he was still happy and eager.

---

* Unfortunately, the similar use of *hopefully* has become
a bone of contention and is best avoided: "Hopefully, it won't
rain at the picnic."

Infinitive phrases can add helpful information:

> However, he was still happy to be in Japan and
>
> eager to begin his language study.

We see then that predicate adjectives can sometimes be modified by prepositional phrases or infinitive phrases.

An adjective modified by a prepositional phrase or infinitive phrase can also follow a noun.

> The young missionaries, happy to be in Japan at last,
>
> were ready to begin language study.

Notice the commas setting off the whole adjective phrase. The adjective phrase can also come at the beginning of the sentence, as long as it is next to whatever it modifies.

> Happy to be in Japan at last, the young missionaries
>
> were ready to begin language study.

Here too the adjective phrase is set off, this time by a single comma.

Putting Grammar to Work

Chapter 9
Clear Links

One of the best aids toward clear and forceful writing is to have clear links (connections) among sentences and clear links within sentences. Some breakdowns in linkage are serious enough to be called grammatical errors. Others are less serious. But every such breakdown results in at least momentary confusion or distraction from the message intended. Attention to sentence links, then, pays great dividends of clarity and effectiveness.

9a Subject-Verb Agreement

(1) The basic principle of subject-verb agreement
(2) Making sure agreement is with the subject
(3) Determining whether problem nouns and pronouns are singular or plural
(4) Determining whether compound subjects are singular or plural

Subject-verb agreement is a bit like housekeeping. When we do it right, no one notices; but if we do it wrong, nearly everyone notices. For example:

> Subject-verb agreement are a bit like housekeeping. When we does it right, no one notice; but if we does it wrong, nearly everyone notice.

Then, too, nearly anyone can run a dust cloth, except perhaps around those fragile knickknacks on the high shelf. Likewise, most of us do fine with subject-verb agreement about 95 percent of the time. This section should help with that other 5 percent.

(1) The basic principle of subject-verb agreement

Sometimes the verb changes form in order to "agree" (or match up) with certain characteristics of the subject. More specifically, the first word of the complete verb agrees with the person and number of the subject.

If the subject is a noun or a third-person pronoun, the only question is whether the subject is singular or plural.

> Pl Pl
> The wild geese *fly* overhead, and they *seem* to call to us.

> Sg Sg
> The first goose *flies* strongly, and he *seems* to pull the others.

Except for the irregular word *be,* it is mainly the present tense that shows agreement. The specific forms of the complete verb can be seen in section **7g.**

The verb words that show agreement can be summarized under three headings. (*A boy* and *boys* stand for all singular and plural noun subjects.)

1. *Be* (as true verb or as first auxiliary)

	Present	Past
First-person singular (*I*)	am	was
Third-person singular (*a boy; he/she/it*)	is	was
Other (*boys; you/we/they*)	are	were

2. *Have* (As true verb or as first auxiliary)

	Present
Third-person singular (*a boy; he/she/it*)	has
Other (*boys; I/you/we/they*)	have

3. All other true verbs (using *look* as typical)

	Present
Third-person singular (*a boy; he/she/it*)	looks
Other (*boys; I/you/we/they*)	look

Use the next practice exercise to see for yourself how this system works. Just follow your instincts in doing the exercise, check your answers, and then see how they would fit into the displays above.

● **Practice 9-1** For each blank in the paragraph, write down the correct present-tense form of the verb or auxiliary indicated.

As the day *(1)* _____ slowly on this September Saturday, I *(2)* _____ the alarm clock in my sister's room. She *(3)* _____ plans to go apple-picking, but I can lie here and wake up slowly. A faint rose color *(4)* _____ in the sky, and the birds *(5)* _____ chattering loudly. How busy they *(6)* _____! Then the sky *(7)* _____ and just a few chirps can be heard. I *(8)* _____ back the covers, eager to begin this good day.

1. dawn	5. be
2. hear	6. sound
3. have	7. brighten
4. show	8. throw

(2) Making sure agreement is with the subject

(2.1) Ignoring intervening phrases after the subject
(2.2) Ignoring a predicate noun of a different number
(2.3) Ignoring the empty word *there*
(2.4) Ignoring negative phrases with the subject

One problem in subject-verb agreement is that sometimes we may lose track of which word is the subject.

(2.1) Ignoring intervening phrases after the subject Do not be distracted from the real subject by a modifier or other phrase between it and the verb. These sentences are correct:

> The *reasons* for that surprising answer to my question *were* not clear.

> A *collection* of answers to commonly asked questions *is being written*.

To check sentences like these, look for the simple subject and try it with the first word of the complete verb *(reasons were; collection is)*.

(2.2) Ignoring a predicate noun of a different number

Usually both the subject and the predicate noun are singular, or both are plural. However, sometimes only one is plural.

```
            S    LV        PN
```
The first *prize was* two tickets to the next concert.

```
         S                   LV        PN
```
Two *tickets* to the concert *were* the first prize.

Even though sentences with predicate nouns can often be turned around (as these two sentences show), in today's English we consider the subject to be the one before the verb. The verb agrees with the subject, not the predicate noun (*prize was, tickets were*).

- **Practice 9-2** Write down the simple subjects and the correct verb forms. Remember to ignore intervening phrases and predicate nouns.
  1. My reward (is, are) the smiles on your faces.
  2. The department stores, as well as the supermarket, (is, are) supposed to be open until midnight tonight.
  3. The next hour, a mere sixty minutes, (is, are) going to be crucial for the struggling patient.
  4. His words (has, have) become a source of inspiration for a great many people.
  5. The head cook, together with the other cafeteria workers, (has, have) worked especially hard to prepare the Thanksgiving Day meal.
  6. Each of my brothers (wants, want) to join the Navy after graduating from high school.

(2.3) Ignoring the empty word *there* As you learned in **5f,** the sentence pattern S *be* Advl can be turned around, with the empty word *there* taking the position usually filled by the subject.

```
       S   be   Advl                      be   S        Advl
```
Rabbits are in that cage. ⟹ There *are* rabbits in that cage.

```
      S   be  Advl                    be    S      Advl
```
A visitor is here. ⟹ There *is* a visitor here.

Sentences in which a form of *be* is an auxiliary can be changed in a similar way.

```
         S        InV                       S      InV
```
Some dogs are barking. ⟹ There *are* some dogs *barking*.

In either form of such sentences, the verb agrees with the real subject *(rabbits are, visitor is, dogs are)*. In other words, we ignore *there* and look for the real subject.

On the other hand, the verb is always singular after *it,* the other empty word (expletive) that can stand in for a subject.

    LV PA S
It is good [that we finished before dark].

    LV   PN   S
It was a disgrace [for me to forget that].

   be   S   Advl
It was the Palmers at the door.

  (*but:* The Palmers were at the door.)

- **Practice 9-3** Choose the correct verb forms.
  1. It (has, have) been two weeks since I last worked in my garden.
  2. There (is, are) a row of weeds where the corn is supposed to be growing.
  3. It (is, are) the birds that ate all the seeds.
  4. There (is, are) not enough weeks to replant the garden.
  5. Next year there (is, are) going to be a scarecrow where the weeds are now.
  6. It (is, are) too bad that we didn't think of that idea sooner.

    (2.4) Ignoring negative phrases with the subject One way to show a strong contrast is to use *not* with a contrasting word or phrase right after the word in question.

    We were jogging, not walking.
    Joyce, not Susan, is the one to ask about that.

When the word with *not* is a noun (as in the second example), we can call it a negative appositive. Negative appositives do not affect subject-verb agreement at all.

    Exercise, not the things we eat, *has* the greatest effect on what we weigh. (exercise has)
    Detergents and soap, but never bleach, *are* safe to use on the counter top.

The second example shows that negative words other than *not* can also be used in negative appositives.

Another way to make a point strongly is to use a negative subject before the positive subject, in a construction with *not . . . but.* Here also the verb agrees with the positive subject.

> Not I but you are the real winner. (you are)
> Not slides but a film is what she showed yesterday.

With either construction, ignore the negative phrase and make the verb agree with the positive subject.

- **Practice 9-4** Choose the correct verb form to agree with each subject, ignoring negative phrases and other intervening phrases.
  1. The mother cat, but not her kittens, (seems, seem) worried that Claude's dog will learn how to jump over the fence.
  2. That dog, along with his stray friends, (has, have) forced the cat to keep a constant vigil over her tiny offspring.
  3. The sight of canine fangs and the sound of incessant barking (reminds, remind) the mother to keep her kittens from straying.
  4. Without doubt, not the fence but alertness (offers, offer) the greatest insurance against harm.
  5. The knowledge of escape routes (promises, promise) more protection than a low, uncertain fence.
  6. Preparation and wisdom, never blind confidence, (assures, assure) anyone a fair chance at success.

(3) Determining whether problem nouns and pronouns are singular or plural

(3.1) Nouns of plural form
(3.2) Collective nouns
(3.3) Words that can be understood as singular or plural
(3.4) Titles, quotations, and amounts as singular
(3.5) Relative pronouns

Once the subject is clearly identified, subject-verb agreement is usually easy. However, a few kinds of subjects demand special attention.

(3.1) Nouns of plural form Certain nouns have only one form, a form that appears to be plural. Many of these words are used in only one way, either as singular or as plural nouns.

Always singular	The *news is* good today.
Always plural	The *pliers are* in the toolbox. (one or more tools)

Some of the nouns that always require a plural verb can also be used with *a pair of* to make clear how many items are meant. In that case, the subject is *pair* instead of the plural noun.

A pair of pliers *is* in the toolbox.

Two pairs of pliers *are* in the toolbox.

Below are some common plural-form nouns, listed according to whether they require a singular verb or a plural verb. (Check other words in your dictionary.)

Singular	*Plural*	
billiards	clothes	riches
checkers	eyeglasses, glasses	shears
measles		spectacles
molasses	goggles	soapsuds, suds
news	pants, slacks (etc.)	
Niagara Falls (etc.)	pliers	thanks
		tights
United States	proceeds	tweezers

245

The plural-sounding names of teams and organizations, such as the Yankees and the Boy Scouts, usually require a plural verb.

Words ending in *-ics* fall into both groups, depending on the meaning intended:

Singular: Fields of Study	*Plural:* Activities, Products, Characteristics
acoustics	acoustics
acrobatics	acrobatics
athletics	athletics
ceramics	ceramics*
civics	
economics	economics
electronics	
ethics	ethics*
mathematics	
physics	
politics	politics
statistics	statistics*
tactics	tactics*

Here is an *-ics* word used both ways:

Acoustics *is* a very technical science.
The acoustics in this auditorium *are* better than we expected.

A good dictionary will distinguish between the singular meaning and the plural meaning of words like these.

- **Practice 9-5** Choose the correct verb form to agree with each subject.
  1. In rainbowed splendor Niagara Falls (thunders, thunder) a hymn of praise to the Creator. Nearby a naive young artist vainly attempts to reduce the scene to a painting.
  2. His overalls (is, are) damp from the mist rising from the cascading waters.

---

*A related singular word also exists.

3. After five hours of fruitless labor, he turns on his transistor radio for a diversion: the Pittsburgh Pirates (is, are) playing the Braves.
4. On another station, the evening news (blares, blare) a report that measles (has, have) reached epidemic proportions in a local school district.
5. A commercial announces that the Girl Scouts (is, are) selling cookies.
6. The would-be artist switches the radio off. All tactics to divert his thoughts from the obvious (has, have) failed.
7. In his mind, large shears (cut, cuts) his worthless painting to shreds, as he folds his easel and sits down to watch the sunset through the mist.
8. Art courses are enjoyable, but perhaps for him electronics (is, are) a better choice.

(3.2) **Collective nouns** Collective nouns are nouns like *club* and *team* that refer to groups. In American English these words usually take a singular verb.

The committee has made its decision.
Our team is ahead so far.

Sometimes, however, the focus is clearly on the individual members of the group. In that case the collective noun takes a plural verb, or else the sentence is reworded to allow a more natural-sounding plural.

The committee are arguing among themselves.
The committee members are arguing among
themselves.

(Collective nouns take plural verbs much more often in British English than is presented here for American English.)

• **Practice 9-6** Choose the correct verb forms.
1. Our civic club (is, are) sponsoring a public "Meet the Candidates" meeting.
2. The crowd (is, are) entering now.
3. As the audience (takes, take) their places, some of the candidates go to the platform.
4. A team of television reporters scattered around the room (is, are) interviewing several people.

5. One local business (has, have) given its employees time off to attend this meeting.
6. Judging by the size of the crowd, the public (is, are) becoming more interested in state and local politics.

(3.3) Words that can be understood as singular or plural Certain words may be understood as either singular or plural, depending on what modifies them.

Treat them as—

Singular when followed by *of*-phrase with singular object	Part of the cake *is* left. (It is left.)
Plural when followed by *of*-phrase with plural object	Part of the cakes for the sale *are* here already. (They are here.)

This rule governs the words below:

all	most
any	part
more	some
half (and other fractions)	
ten percent (and other percents)	

All of these words subdivide either a group or a single thing. For that reason they are exceptions to the general rule of **9a(2.1)** that the verb agrees only with the simple subject.

Here are a few more examples:

Singular Use	*Plural Use*
Half of it was used.	Half of them were used.
Two-thirds of it is left.	Two-thirds of them are here.
Most of it is good.	Most of them are good.

I wanted the cream,	I wanted the cookies,
but part was gone.	but part were gone.

The last pair shows that the *of*-phrase can be understood only.

The negative word *none* has not yet been mentioned, for it follows the rule only part of the time. *None* is always singular when followed by an *of*-phrase with a singular object.

> None of the cake *is* left.

None may be plural when followed by an *of*-phrase with a plural object, if the meaning seems to be plural.

> None of the cakes *are* left.
> None of the cakes *is/are* just what I wanted.

To most people the two versions of the last sentence could be equally logical and equally correct.

Finally, the word *number* has its own rule:

Always singular	The number of local candidates *was* fairly large.
Always plural	A number of the local candidates *were* present.

In sentences like the second one, there is a strong plural meaning, since *a number* means something like "several."

● **Practice 9-7** Choose the correct verb forms.
1. The number of bones in the human body (totals, total) 206.
2. Thirty-nine percent of these bones (is, are) included in the skull, backbone, ribs, and breastbone.
3. Most of our bones (performs, perform) more than one function.
4. Some (gives, give) structural support to the body.
5. Most of the production of blood cells (occurs, occur) within bone marrow.
6. In addition, a number of organs (is, are) protected from injury by rigid bone structures.

7. More of the body's supply of calcium and phosphorus (is, are) stored in the bones than in any other organ.
8. All of the bones together (forms, form) the skeletal system, the body's framework.

(3.4) Titles, quotations, and amounts as singular Even though key words in the title of a work may be plural, the **title** is treated as singular because it names a single work.

> "Three Blind Mice" is easy for children to sing.
> *The Gleaners* was painted by Millet in 1857.
> "Birches" is one of Robert Frost's best-known poems.

A **quoted (or cited) noun or phrase** is also a single item, even though it may contain a plural.

> To him, "all good books" means just the ones he enjoys.
> *Stories* is a plural noun.

Similarly, **amounts** are treated as singular: measured amounts, amounts of money, and periods of time.

> Two tablespoons of oil is enough.
> Ten dollars is the usual fee.
> Two days is a long time to wait.

In all of these, the verb is singular because the subject refers to a single amount or time period.

● **Practice 9-8**   Choose the correct verb forms.
1. "The Happy Cooks" (is, are) a story about two cooks who are happy only when they are inventing a new dish.
2. The happy cooks (has, have) invented several hundred dishes by the time the story begins.
3. *Dishes* here (means, mean) prepared foods of all sorts.
4. "Braised Spanish Chicken Livers" (was, were) their most recent invention, but now normal-sized dishes seemed dull to them.
5. Three bushels of sifted flour (was, were) the starting point for a giant pyramid of cakes.

6. One problem was that bushels (has, have) holes in them and are not intended for measuring.
7. However, the cooks solved their problems, and "Orange Cakes in Pyramid" (was, were) a huge success.

(3.5) Relative pronouns

Relative pronouns *(who, which, that)* do not change form for singular and plural, but we treat them as if they did—as if a relative pronoun has the same number as its antecedent. Therefore when a relative pronoun is a subject, in effect the verb agrees with the pronoun's antecedent.

She is the person who *has* read the book.

They are the ones who *have* read the book.

In the first example, the antecedent of the relative pronoun *who* is *person,* and so the verb is singular *(person has).* In the second, both antecedent and verb are plural.

Occasionally we have to look carefully to find the antecedent:

I bought a book of stories that *were* of different types.

I bought a book of stories that *was* falling apart.

Sentences with "the one of the" or "one of the" before a noun and a relative pronoun are sometimes a problem.

I bought *the* only one of the books that *was* long

enough.

(I bought the one that was long enough.)

Here the antecedent of *that* is *one*—he bought one, the one that was long enough. The clue is "the . . . one," which suggests a singular verb. The next sentence is different.

I bought one of the books that *were* long enough.

This time several *books* were long enough, and he bought one of them. Usually a plural verb is used after "one of the," when no *the* precedes *one*.

● **Practice 9-9** Choose the correct verb forms.
1. King David and his household were fleeing from Absalom, who (was, were) leading a revolt against him.
2. David said, "Lord, how are they increased that (troubles, trouble) me."
3. "Many are they that (rises, rise) up against me."
4. "But thou, O Lord, art a shield for me," continued this king who (was, were) chosen to lead Israel.
5. One of the men who (was, were) faithful to David stayed in Jerusalem to send news to David.
6. This man, Hushai, was the only one of David's followers who (was, were) given this task.
7. God used Hushai, who (was, were) faithful, to help David regain the kingdom.

(Based on Ps. 3 and II Sam. 16-17)

(4) Determining whether compound subjects are singular or plural
(4.1) Compound subjects with *and*
(4.2) Compound subjects with *or*

The rules for subject-verb agreement with compound subjects depend on whether *and* or *or* is used.

(4.1) Compound subjects with *and*   A compound subject with *and* is normally plural—the two or more things add up to more than one.

John and Mary have the paper.   (they have)

Similar to *and* is the correlative *both—and*.

Both Sue and I are waiting to read it.   (we are)

A compound subject with *both—and* is always plural, because *both—and* always joins separate things.

If the two words joined by *and* refer to the same thing, the subject is considered to be singular and the verb is singular.

Our friend and neighbor was a great help when we had the flu.

Also, if the things named are considered part of a single thing or a single concept, the verb is singular.

Peaches and cream is my favorite dessert.
That crackling and banging was deafening.
His pride and arrogance is repulsive.
     (*or* are repulsive)

Usually, however, *and* joins separate things and requires a plural verb.

(4.2) Compound subjects with *or*   For compound subjects with *or* (also *either—or, neither—nor*), the simple subject near the first verb word is the one that decides the form of the verb.

John or Mary has my copy of *Faith*.   (Mary has)
Are you or I or Sam going to do it?   (are you)
Either John or his sisters were there, it seems.
     (sisters were)

Or always involves a choice of things, not an adding up. Therefore we make thc verb agree with just the one noun or pronoun, the closer one.

● **Practice 9-10** Choose the correct verb forms.
  1. Dad, Mom, Ron, and I (was, were) trying to

decide where to eat to celebrate Dad's promotion.

2. Fish and chips (is, are) my favorite meal, but the others wanted steak.
3. On our budget, steak houses or any fancy restaurant (is, are) normally out of the question.
4. My older brother and self-appointed financial advisor (has, have) always told me to avoid anything too extravagant.
5. Besides, a hamburger place or a hot dog stand (is, are) usually about all we can afford.
6. But in the end the need to celebrate and the appeal of a good steak (was, were) persuasive.

9b Pronoun-Antecedent Agreement

(1) The general principle
(2) Agreement with singular indefinite pronouns
(3) Agreement with singular nouns modified by indefinite determiners
(4) Agreement with compound antecedents joined by *or*
(5) Agreement with collective nouns

An earlier word or phrase that a pronoun relates to is the **antecedent** of that pronoun.

Uncle Henry wrote that he and Aunt Enna will come next month.

The antecedent of the pronoun *he* is *Uncle Henry*.

(1) The general principle

Pronouns must agree with their antecedents in number and gender. Agreement in **number** means that singular pronouns are used with singular antecedents, and plural pronouns with plural antecedents.

My aunt and uncle usually travel in their camper.

(*their,* plural)

Agreement in **gender** means mainly the correct use of the singular pronouns *he* (masculine), *she* (feminine), and *it* (neuter). See **4a(2.3)** for details of this use. Gender agreement can also include the correct use of *who* (for persons only) and *which* (for things only).

Was it your uncle who first took you fishing?

(*who,* for a person)

Yes, and my aunt taught me all she knows about

frying perch.   (*she,* feminine singular)

Not all pronouns have antecedents. First- and second-person pronouns refer to speakers and listeners, who usually have not been mentioned earlier. Certain other pronouns, such as indefinite pronouns, also lack antecedents. But those that have antecedents must agree with them in number and gender (and person, which is usually not a problem).

Most questions of pronoun-antecedent agreement involve a choice among the third-person personal pronouns, including the possessive-pronoun determiners.

Making Third-Person Pronouns
Agree with Their Antecedents

1. Find the antecedent. Do so by asking yourself what earlier word the pronoun represents.
2. Decide whether the antecedent is singular or plural. (The four usual problem areas are dealt with below.) If the antecedent is plural, use the appropriate form of *they.*
3. If the antecedent is singular, decide whether *he, she,* or *it* is called for, according to the gender. If the gender is uncertain, look at the guidelines found below in **9b(2).**

Note that agreement does not involve case; a pronoun is in the subjective, possessive, or objective case strictly according to the way it is used in its own clause.

(2) Agreement with singular indefinite pronouns

The following indefinite pronouns are always singular:

someone	somebody	something
anyone	anybody	anything
everyone	everybody	everything
no one	nobody	nothing
either	each	much
neither	one	little
another		less

In careful English, a singular pronoun is used when one of these indefinite pronouns is the antecedent.

Someone on the boys' team forgot his baseball glove.

On the girl's side of the gym, everyone has her own locker.

Everyone brought his own lunch on the class field trip.

In all the confusion no one could find his place.

To each his own.

One should do his best and trust God for the rest.

Because we need a singular pronoun, as in these sentences, we are forced to make decisions about **gender.** That is, do we use a form of *he* or *she* or *it?* In the first two sentences above, the gender is clear from the rest of the sentence, and so we have no trouble choosing *his* and *her.* In the final four sentences, however, the indefinite pronouns could logically cover males or females or both. Notice that in all four sentences *his* is used.

There is a general rule for agreement with indefinite pronoun antecedents of uncertain gender: use the masculine singular pronoun whenever the antecedent does not clearly refer to females.

Everyone brought *his* notebook with *him.*

It is understood in such a case that both males and females are probably involved.* Use of both masculine and feminine pronouns is also permissible, but it is often awkward.

Everyone brought *his or her* notebook with *him or her.*

Sometimes we can reword the sentence to avoid personal pronouns entirely.

Everyone brought a notebook along.

Normally, though, it is best to go ahead and use the traditional masculine pronoun to include either or both sexes. What is *not* acceptable, especially in written English, is to use *their* instead of *his* in such a case.

---

* In such cases *he/him/his* can be said to express "common gender."

(3) Agreement with singular nouns modified by indefinite determiners

Very similar to agreement with indefinite pronouns is agreement with nouns modified by indefinite determiners. Notice this similarity in the following pairs.

Someone forgot to bring his baseball glove.

Some boy forgot to bring his baseball glove.

Anyone can understand that, if he tries.

Any intelligent person can, if he tries.

I needed something, and she gave it to me.

I needed *some help,* and she gave it to me.

Just as most indefinite pronouns are always singular, so also a singular noun modified by an indefinite determiner is always singular.

Here again, from section **4c(10),** are the indefinite determiners:

Modify Singular or Plural Nouns	Modify Singular Nouns Only
some	each
any	either
no	neither
enough	another
	much

When any of these modify singular nouns, any further references must be singular.

The rule seems obvious, but—as with indefinite pronouns—sometimes the unclear gender misleads us into using a form of *they* instead of a singular pronoun form. The singular pronoun is correct:

Each person took his seat before the meeting began.

As with indefinite pronouns, use the masculine singular pronoun whenever the antecedent does not clearly refer to females. If the gender is clear, use the appropriate pronoun:

Each mother brought her own supplies.

Neither idea has much to recommend it.

The determiner *every* works the same way, even though it is in a different group of determiners because of its position within the noun phrase. It too requires later pronouns to be singular, as in the last verse of the book of Judges:

In those days there was no king in Israel:

every man did that which was right in his own eyes.

● **Practice 9-11** For each sentence write down the antecedent and the correct pronoun.
   1. At our house, everyone is expected to clean (his, their) own room.
   2. Marsha and Kelly are also supposed to help with (her, their) own ironing.
   3. Each person has one other job that is (his, their) responsibility.
   4. I give Lassie (his, her) food and water every morning.
   5. I am the only one who keeps (his, their) same job.
   6. The others have to trade (his, their) jobs every two weeks.

(4) Agreement with compound antecedents joined by *or*

Compound antecedents are considered singular or plural according to the same rules as those given in **9a(4)** for compound subjects. Usually only antecedents joined by *or* raise any questions.

As with subject-verb agreement, pronoun-antecedent agreement is with the **nearer** of the elements joined by *or, either—or,* or *neither—nor.*

Either Sheri or Darla will give her report after yours.

When the two antecedents are different in number or in gender, the rule still holds.

I haven't decided whether to ask Grace or

her friends to do what they can.

Sometimes, though, the result seems awkward.

Either Sheri or Don will give his report next.

Then the only graceful solution may be to reword the sentence.

Either Sheri will give her report next,

or Don will give his.

Either sentence, however, is preferable to the incorrect use of *their* with a singular antecedent.

(5) Agreement with collective nouns

As **9a(3.2)** points out, collective nouns—words that refer to groups—most often are used with singular verbs. When they are used with singular verbs, any later pronoun references must also be singular.

    Sg   Sg
The committee *has* made *its* decision.

    Pl   Pl
The committee *are* arguing among *themselves.*

The first sentence illustrates the more frequent singular use of the word, but that sentence could have been in the plural (and in England it probably would have been):

The committee *have* made *their* decision.

The essential matter here is consistency—if the verb is plural, the pronoun must be plural.

Of course, some verb forms (such as the simple past) cannot show agreement with the collective noun. In that case we are simply guided by the meanings: a singular pronoun for the group as a whole, a plural pronoun for the individual members.

The audience took *their* seats.

The audience showed *its* approval by loud applause.

● **Practice 9-12** Choose the pronouns that agree with the antecedents.

1. Anyone who is too lazy to do (his, their) work should follow the admonition of Proverbs 6:6— "Go to the ant, thou sluggard; consider her ways, and be wise."

2. Indeed, each member of an ant colony has a specific task which (it, they) must perform faithfully for the good of the group.

3. The colony cannot continue to exist if (its, their) individual members fail to perform (his, their) duties.

4. Every colony has at (its, their) center a queen who lays thousands of eggs to assure the continuation of the community.

5. All the food for the colony must be gathered and carried to (its, their) proper place by the worker ants.

6. Neither the queen nor the male ants can hunt for (its, their) own food.

7. All the workers and the males have as (his, their) main job caring for the queen.

8. The ant family perform (its, their) various duties with much energy and cooperation.

9. After closely observing the ants, nobody can go away without being reminded of (his, their) own responsibility to work and not grow "weary in well doing."

9c Pronoun Reference

(1) Clear reference
(2) Reference to a noun, not an implied noun
(3) Reference to a noun that is not a modifier
(4) Definite reference of personal pronouns
(5) Reference to a noun, not a broad idea

Among the most important kinds of links in sentences are those provided by the reference of certain pronouns to earlier words and phrases. When these references are clear, the sentences can be clear. When they are unclear, the sentences will be either puzzling or misleading.

As **9b(1)** mentions, not all pronouns have antecedents. However, we do usually expect antecedents for certain kinds of pronouns: the third-person personal pronouns (*he, she, it, they*), the relative pronouns in adjective clauses (*who, which, that*), and the demonstrative pronouns (*this/these, that/those*). Our expectations of careful reference are highest for the personal pronouns named, second highest for the relative pronouns, but significant even for the demonstrative pronouns.

Two issues are involved in the reference of these pronouns:

1. Is there a clear antecedent? If not, the sentence will be hard to understand. See **9c(1)**.
2. Is there an acceptable type of antecedent? If not, the sentence (especially the written sentence) may seem to be poorly stated. It may also be somewhat unclear. See **9c(2, 5)**.

(1) Clear reference

In the reference of pronouns to antecedents, the absolute essential is that the reference be clear. There should be a single noun or noun-equivalent nearby that is the obvious antecedent of the pronoun.

One kind of problem is having two nearby nouns that are possible antecedents of the pronoun used.

Ambiguous	When Mike shouted at Joe, he looked rather strange.
Clear	When Mike shouted at Joe, Joe looked rather strange.
	Mike looked rather strange when he shouted at Joe.

As these corrections show, sometimes the problem can be solved either by repeating the noun itself instead of using a pronoun or by rewording the sentence so that only the intended antecedent comes before the pronoun. At other times a more specific pronoun can be used:

Ambiguous	Diane told Martha that her friends were planning a party.
Clear	Diane told Martha, "*Your* friends are planning a party."
	Diane told Martha, "*My* friends are planning a party."

In this case the direct quotation makes the reference clear.

Unclear reference is also likely when the pronoun is too far from the antecedent.

Remote	I have been reading the passage in Ecclesiastes 12 about the importance of serving God in our youth. In old age our senses will fail and we will grow feeble. Finally the dust will return to the earth and "the spirit shall return unto God who gave it." *It* is poetic yet powerful.
Clear	. . . unto God who gave it." *The passage* is poetic yet powerful.

● **Practice 9-13** Revise the following sentences to correct unclear pronoun reference.
1. Mr. Varner told Jerry that he could attach the bicycle to the trunk of the car.
2. Put the bicycle on the rack and tie it securely to the bumper.
3. Tom sold Jerry the bicycle that he rode in the "Little 500" race in Bloomington, Indiana.
4. After Linda took Susie to the "Little 500," she decided to go to Europe for the annual "Tour de France" bicycle race.
5. When the cyclists sped by the crowds on the outskirts of Paris, they knew the race was almost over.

(2) Reference to a noun, not an implied noun

In careful speaking, and especially in careful writing, it is expected that pronoun reference will be to nouns actually present in the passage.

Implied reference	On vacation I visited my cousin's church, *and* they really made me feel welcome.
Better	On vacation I visited my cousin's church, and *the people there* really made me feel welcome.

In the first version *they* stands for a noun that is never mentioned. The second version is more specific and is immediately clear. It illustrates the usual correction for implied reference: replacing the unclear pronoun with the specific noun that was implied.

● **Practice 9-14** Revise the following sentences to correct the instances of unclear or implied reference. For two sentences additional information is given in parentheses to help clarify the intended reference.

1. Natasha shouted to her mother as she walked onto the wharf after the long voyage from Russia. (The little girl had arrived at last.)
2. Mr. Raymond told Harvey that he would have to work the late shift tonight. (Harvey was happy because he needed the overtime pay.)
3. In a country dominated by Communism they sometimes put a person in prison for practicing his religion.
4. When I got to the bank window, she said I had waited in the wrong line.

(3) Reference to a noun that is not a modifier

In following the flow of ideas through a passage, we generally expect pronouns to refer to nearby nouns that are used as subjects, direct objects, and so on. Nouns that modify are less noticeable antecedents. Possessives, for instance, make poor antecedents.

Unclear reference to a possessive	Dave found Bob's watch, who had lost it at the track meet.
Better	Dave found the watch that *Bob* had lost at the track meet.
	Dave found the watch belonging to Bob, who had lost it at the meet.

Other modifying nouns also make poor antecedents.

Unclear reference to a modifying noun	They finally decided on a brick house. ? That is easier to maintain than painted siding.
Better	They finally decided on a brick house, because *brick* is easier to maintain than painted siding.
	They finally bought a house made of brick, which is easier to maintain.

The two methods of correction are illustrated twice. Either the intended antecedent can be used in place of the unclear pronoun, or the sentence can be revised so that the intended antecedent is no longer a modifier.

- **Practice 9-15** Revise the following sentences, correcting the pronoun references to possessive nouns or to other nouns that modify.
  1. In Mr. Vent's science class he said that the tornado is the most violent type of storm found in nature.
  2. Last year I found my grandmother's diary and read about how she survived a tornado almost forty years ago.
  3. A neighbor's telephone call warned Grandmother to seek shelter, but he died when the storm destroyed his house.
  4. Her barn roof flew off, but it remained standing with no damage to the wall or contents.
  5. God's power and sovereignty are very evident when He creates a whirlwind.

(4) Definite reference of personal pronouns

(4.1) Indefinite *they*
(4.2) Indefinite *it*
(4.3) Indefinite *you*

Although indefinite pronouns like *someone, one,* and *everybody* are intended to have indefinite reference, personal pronouns are normally expected to have antecedents and to refer to definite individuals or groups. Note the following problems.

(4.1) Indefinite *they* In written English *they* should be used only with definite reference.

	?
Indefinite *they*	In the South they say "you-all" for the plural of *you.*
Corrected	In the South people say "you-all" for the plural of *you.*
More exact	Some Southerners say "you-all" for the plural of *you.*

Usually a specific noun or pronoun can be supplied in place of the indefinite *they.** "Some Southerners," for instance, tells us more than the original version did. However, at times another solution is called for.

	?
Indefinite *they*	Last December they gave us two weeks of vacation from school.
Corrected	Last December we had two weeks of vacation from school.

If the specific noun is unknown or irrelevant, as perhaps in this example, the sentence can be revised to do away with the need for the indefinite *they.*

(4.2) Indefinite *it* In careful writing, *it* should not be used indefinitely in the phrase "it says." Replace *it* with the name of the source of information.

---

* Indefinite *they* is closely related to the problem dealt with in **9c(2).**

	?
Indefinite *it*	In *The Wall Street Journal* it says that interest rates are up again.
Corrected	*The Wall Street Journal* says that interest rates are up again.

The corrected sentence has the added advantage of being shorter and more direct.

(4.3) Indefinite *you*   In conversation and informal writing, *you* is commonly used in an indefinite sense to refer to people in general.

Informal	You can lead a horse to water but you can't make him drink.

A folksy proverb of this sort would probably not be used at all in a very formal context. Some statements, however, might appear in either informal or formal writing, with appropriate adjustments.

Informal	The speaker said that you have to work hard if you want to succeed.
Less informal	. . . we must work hard if we want to succeed. . . . a person must work hard if he wants to succeed.
Most formal	. . . one must work hard if he wants to succeed.*

Notice that *we* can be used in a semi-indefinite sense to include the writer along with the audience. *We* is acceptable when the writer can indeed logically be included, but not otherwise. (It would be odd to read, "In the sixteenth century we had to work hard.")

---

* In England (and sometimes in America) *one* would appear in both clauses, though to Americans this repetition sounds a bit stiff: "One must work hard if one desires to succeed in one's profession."

The *you* in the informal examples above was an indefinite *you,* to be removed in general or formal writing. However, in all but the most formal writing, *you* can be used legitimately to refer definitely to the reader. This use is especially likely when instructions are being given.

| Spoken and general written use | Be sure the test tube is completely dry before you add the chemicals. |

The imperative and the use of *you* are perfectly appropriate here. But in a very formal passage, such as a scholarly study, the second person is avoided completely.

| Very formal | One must be sure that the test tube is completely dry before he adds the chemicals. |

Academic writing, such as for research papers and reports, usually is about topics that do not allow for the use of the second person. In order to learn to do this type of writing, students may be asked to avoid all use of *you* and the imperative in certain of their written compositions.

- **Practice 9-16** Revise the following sentences to eliminate all indefinite uses of *they, it,* and *you.* Do not change any of these pronouns that are used correctly. Write *C* for correct sentences.
  1. It says in my biology lab manual that microscopes should be moved carefully.
  2. In class we were told that if you bump a microscope very hard, you may put its lenses out of adjustment.
  3. The microscopes in our lab are old, but they work well.
  4. "Mr. Bugg, would you please help me focus my microscope?"
  5. In our class they let us prepare our own slides to examine.
  6. You have to know what you are doing in order to prepare slides correctly.

(5) Reference to a noun, not a broad idea

The antecedent of a pronoun should be a noun, not the general idea of a preceding sentence or clause. This requirement is strongest for the personal pronouns and the relative pronouns, but it can also apply to demonstrative pronouns.

Broad reference	Joe won the contest, and it$^?$ surprised me.
	Joe won the contest, which$^?$ surprised me.
	Joe won the contest, and that surprised me.

The first two of these sentences are faulty, and even the last one can perhaps be improved.

Corrected	Joe won the contest, and his victory surprised me.
	I was surprised that Joe won the contest.
	Joe's contest victory surprised me.

Part of the problem with broad pronoun reference is that it often makes the sentence less clear.

| Broad reference | I told Jack that we couldn't all fit into my car. |
| | *This*$^?$ was a surprise to him. |

| Clarified | I told Jack that we couldn't all fit into my car, and he was surprised that so many are going. |
| | I told Jack that we couldn't all fit into my car. He was surprised to learn that I have a compact car. |

Even a demonstrative pronoun should be changed when its meaning is not fully clear.

- **Practice 9-17** Revise the following sentences to correct the overly broad reference of certain pronouns.
  1. Kangaroos are able to thrive and multiply even under very harsh conditions, which creates problems for Australian sheep herders.
  2. Early space voyagers had to eat food pastes and concentrates squeezed from tubes. That was necessary because of the weightless conditions experienced during orbit.
  3. Bob decided to give up a career as an insurance salesman in order to study for the ministry. This came as a surprise to everyone.
  4. Julie jogs four miles before breakfast, which means she has to get up at five o'clock every day.
  5. Larry's dog stands up on his hind legs and begs, but he does it only on rare occasions.

9d Easily Understood Modifiers

(1) Correcting misplaced modifiers
(2) Correcting two-way modifiers
(3) Correcting dangling modifiers

Without modifiers, our bare-bones sentences would be dry and lifeless. But unclear or misleading modifiers can be worse than no modifiers.

(1) Correcting misplaced modifiers

(1.1) Adverb or determiner?
(1.2) Phrases and clauses

A modifier needs to be reasonably close to the word it modifies.

If the position of the modifier makes it seem to modify the wrong word in the sentence, it is **misplaced** and should be moved closer to the word it modifies.

(1.1) Adverb or determiner? There are several words that can be either adverbs or determiners. One of these is *only*.

Adverb	I asked him what he meant, but he only laughed.
Determiner	Only the red berries are any good.
	He wants only the red ones.

In the second and third sentences *only* is a determiner, of the type called a restricter. It modifies the rest of the noun phrase.

In sentences like the third example, there is a very strong tendency in spoken English to move the restricter to the adverbial position before the verb:

Spoken style	He only wants the RED ones.

In spoken English this construction is usually perfectly clear. The strong stress (accent) is on *red,* and so we understand the *only* to apply to the noun phrase. However, in writing there may be a problem, since no spoken stress can be heard.

Ambiguous in writing (misplaced)	He only wants the RED ones. He only WANTS the red ones. } ?

The reader may wonder: Is it that he only *wants* them, and never *takes* them?

In writing, a restricter that appears in adverb position is considered a misplaced modifier. It should be moved next to the word or phrase it is intended to modify.

These are the main words to watch:

almost	just
especially	merely
even	nearly
exactly	only
hardly	simply

Although *not* is more freely movable, it too can cause problems: "All of them were not late." Better would be "Not all of them were late."

●**Practice 9-18** Revise the following sentences to correct the misplaced modifiers.
1. I only bought three books because I could hardly afford any more.
2. She even puts tennis shoes in her new washer.
3. Since he is on a diet, he just wants a small piece of cake.
4. They hardly spent any time grading the road surface before they paved it.
5. My little four-year-old sister can almost write the entire alphabet by herself.

(1.2) Phrases and clauses Phrases and clauses too should be near what they modify. If they are not, confusion or unintended humor may be the result.

Misplaced modifier	Living an average of twenty years, the park guide explained that some grizzly bears prefer to return to the same den each year for hibernation.
Corrected	The park guide explained that some grizzly bears, living an average of twenty years, prefer to return to the same den each year for hibernation.

As we see here, an adjectival phrase that comes before the subject is usually assumed to modify the subject. Move the misplaced modifying phrase next to the word it should modify.

Misplaced modifying phrases may occur elsewhere in the sentence also.

Misplaced modifier	The best-of-breed winner was the French poodle standing in front of the judge with a ribbon around his neck.

Strange decoration for a judge, isn't it?

| Corrected | The best-of-breed winner was the French poodle with a ribbon around his neck, the one standing in front of the judge. |

Furthermore, clauses too may be misplaced:

| Misplaced modifier | Yesterday we saw a hot-air balloon above the lake that was carrying two women. |

| Corrected | Yesterday we saw a hot-air balloon that was carrying two women above the lake. |

Modifiers should always be as close as possible to the word or phrase modified.

● **Practice 9-19** Revise the following sentences to correct the misplaced modifiers.
1. The elephant near the tour guide with the long floppy ears was actually a sculptured plant.
2. Scattered throughout the park, I saw scores of such bushes and trees.
3. Patiently trimming and pruning each plant, our tour guide explained that the park gardeners had become very adept in topiary.
4. He told us about ancient Egypt in the tour bus, where topiary was first practiced.
5. At the end of the tour he pointed out an exotic tree shaped like a dog that had a peculiar bark.

(2) Correcting two-way modifiers

A two-way modifier is unclear because it stands between two sentence elements that it might modify. We cannot tell which of the two it modifies, and so we cannot be sure what meaning was intended.

| Two-way modifier | Our teacher said in the fall we could observe the migration of birds. |

Did she say it in the fall? Or can the observation be done in the fall? The sentence can be corrected to express either meaning.

| Corrected for one meaning | In the fall our teacher said that we could observe the migration of birds. |

| Corrected for other meaning | Our teacher said that in the fall we could observe the migration of birds. |

Two-way modifiers are easy to miss in our own writing, because we think only of the one meaning we intended to express. However, if we let our writing sit at least overnight, we can often come back to it with an eye more alert for this kind of problem.

● **Practice 9-20** Revise the following sentences to correct the two-way modifiers.

1. Scientists who study bird migration constantly admit that they understand little about how birds accurately navigate to distant locations.
2. One species that lives in the Arctic regions during the summer months wings its way to Antarctica to spend the winter.
3. Bird watchers explain when the days begin to grow shorter birds sense the arrival of migration time.
4. Many birds that migrate frequently use the sun and stars for navigation.
5. Christ tells His followers on several occasions God cares for them more than He does the birds:

"Behold the fowls of the air: for they sow not,
neither do they reap, nor gather into barns; yet
your heavenly Father feedeth them. Are ye not
much better than they?" (Matt. 6:26)

(3) Correcting dangling modifiers

Picture dangling modifiers as dangling in space, having
nothing to modify. A dangling modifier cannot be
corrected just by moving it, for the word that it should
modify is not in the sentence.

Dangling modifier	*Coming down the street,* the Wrigley Building appeared on our left.

Who or what was coming down the street? Surely not
the Wrigley Building. The modifier is "dangling" because
the implied subject of *coming* is not the same as the
actual subject of the sentence.

One way to correct a dangling modifier is to change
the modifier into a complete clause that includes the
missing element:

Corrected	*As we were* coming down the street, the Wrigley Building appeared on our left.

Another way is to change the rest of the sentence so
that the missing element is supplied right next to the
modifier:

Corrected	Coming down the street, *we* saw the Wrigley Building on our left.

Let's try those two methods again. First, here is
another problem sentence.

Dangling modifier	*While in the South,* "Swanee River" became one of my favorite songs.

While in the South is a dangling modifier because it should describe *I* but instead seems to describe *"Swanee River."* Now the two ways of correcting it:

Correction by changing the modifier	While *I was living* in the South, "Swanee River" became one of my favorite songs.
Correction by changing the rest of the sentence	While in the South, *I* acquired a new favorite song, "Swanee River."

In this case the first method seems to give the simpler correction.

- **Practice 9-21** Revise the following sentences to eliminate dangling modifiers.
  1. On your toes, the top shelf can easily be reached.
  2. To ride a unicycle, a good sense of balance is needed.
  3. Using an electron microscope, the virus became visible to human eyes for the first time in history.
  4. The matchbook cover should be closed before striking a match.
  5. If left unrefrigerated, Joe will soon have a quart of sour milk and a carton of rotten eggs.
  6. To pilot a commercial airliner, many years of training and flight experience are necessary.

To learn more about implied subjects and their relation to dangling modifiers, see **8b(3.2, 3.4).**

9e Relationships Between Sentence-Ideas

(1) The need for connective words
(2) Coordination and subordination
(3) Ideas of equal importance
(4) Ideas of unequal importance
(5) Summary: ways of expressing certain relations between sentence-ideas

A thought or idea that can conveniently be expressed in a single simple sentence can be called a **sentence-idea.** Sentence-ideas are sometimes expressed in simple sentences, but often they are combined into more complicated sentences. Either way, there is frequently a need to show how the sentence-ideas are related to each other. Connectives like *and, but, because, while, however,* and *for instance* express some of the possible logical relations between sentence-ideas. Section **9e** will help you find the connectives you need in order to express meaning-relations accurately.

(1) The need for connective words

First let's look at a paragraph that is well organized but contains no connective words at all. The sentences are numbered for later comparison with other versions.

No Connectives

[1]Sometimes a concrete sidewalk will crack. [2]A shifting soil base under the sidewalk can cause the cracks. [3]Random cracks on a sidewalk are noticeable and unattractive. [4]Something can be done to prevent this problem. [5]Grooves can be cut in the wet concrete. [6]The finished walk will be relatively weak at these grooves. [7]Any cracks will occur in the grooves. [8]The cracks will be less noticeable in the grooves.

The paragraph is perhaps clear enough, but it is not very interesting. It sounds overly simple, almost babyish, because it has no connecting words. Every clause in it stands by itself as a simple sentence. Since the sentences are fairly short and are very much alike, the paragraph also sounds choppy and monotonous.

In the following sections we will improve the sample paragraph in various ways (keeping the same superscript number with each clause every time).

(2) Coordination and subordination

(2.1) Coordination
(2.2) Subordination

(2.3) Faulty subordination
(2.4) A balanced approach

(2.1) Coordination One way of joining ideas is to use coordinating conjunctions like *and, but,* and *or.* The conjunctions reduce the number of sentences and give us some variety between simple and compound sentences. Notice the result of applying this method to the sample paragraph found in **9e(1).**

Coordination

[2]Sometimes the soil base under a sidewalk shifts and [1]the concrete cracks. [3]Random cracks on a walk are noticeable and unattractive, but [4]something can be done to prevent this problem. [5]Grooves can be cut in the wet concrete. [6]The finished walk will be relatively weak at these grooves, and [7]any cracks will occur in them. [8]There the cracks will be less noticeable.

Now the paragraph reads better, and it is clearer. Some of the logical relations among the sentence-ideas have been pointed out.

(2.2) Subordination Another way to point out the logical relations is to change some of the clauses into dependent clauses, beginning them with words like *because* and *although.*

Subordination

[1]Sometimes a concrete sidewalk will crack [2]because the soil base shifts under it. [3]Although random cracks on a sidewalk are noticeable and unattractive, [4]something can be done to prevent this problem. [5]Grooves can be cut in the wet concrete [6]so that the finished walk will be relatively weak at these grooves. [7]Then any cracks will occur in the grooves, [8]where they will be less noticeable.

Again we note an improvement in our sample paragraph.

Words like *because* and *although* have two advantages. First, they are sometimes the clearest way to express certain relations between sentences. In addition, they subordinate (make less prominent) the sentence-ideas that they introduce; thus they allow other ideas to stand out as more important. The bold numbers in this paragraph appear before the independent clauses. Read these clauses, and notice that they are among the more important ones for the paragraph.

(2.3) Faulty subordination It often makes a difference which clauses we make independent and which ones dependent. For example, we can take the sample paragraph of **9e(2.2)** and reverse which sentences are dependent and independent. Even though the meaning relationships can be kept fairly accurate, the paragraph suffers.

Faulty Subordination

2Sometimes the soil base shifts under a concrete sidewalk, [1]while the concrete cracks. **3**Random cracks on a sidewalk are noticeable and unattractive, [4]although something can be done to prevent this problem. **5**If grooves are cut in the wet concrete, **6**the finished walk will be relatively weak at these grooves. **8**Cracks will be less noticeable in the grooves,[7]where they will now occur.

Read the independent clauses in this version, as indicated by the bold numbers. Notice that these are not the most important ideas in the paragraph. This paragraph is an example of **faulty subordination:** the wrong ideas have been subordinated.

(2.4) A balanced approach Most good paragraphs use both coordination and subordination of clauses. Usually (though not always) the most important ideas should be expressed in the independent clauses.

Here is one final version of the demonstration paragraph, the one that perhaps works best.

Best Version, Using Both Coordination and Subordination

[1]Sometimes a concrete sidewalk cracks [2]because the soil base shifts under it. **3**Random

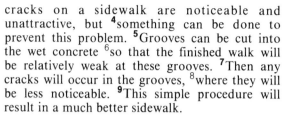
> cracks on a sidewalk are noticeable and unattractive, but [4]something can be done to prevent this problem. [5]Grooves can be cut into the wet concrete [6]so that the finished walk will be relatively weak at these grooves. [7]Then any cracks will occur in the grooves, [8]where they will be less noticeable. [9]This simple procedure will result in a much better sidewalk.

Again, read the independent clauses and notice that they include the most important ideas. A final simple sentence has been added to make clear that simple sentences too have a place in good writing. Not every relationship between sentence-ideas needs to be expressed.

(3) Ideas of equal importance

Ideas of equal importance should usually have equal status in the paragraph. They can stand side-by-side in simple sentences, or they can be joined in a compound sentence.

The top part of the table in **9e(5)** shows the three usual meaning-relationships between ideas of equal importance: similarity and association (*and, also, besides,* etc.); contrast (*but, however,* etc.); and choice (*or, otherwise,* etc.). Listed on the table are a number of words and phrases that may express these ideas—mainly coordinating conjunctions and conjunctive adverbs. Use the table to help you achieve greater variety in expressing these ideas.

(4) Ideas of unequal importance

In any paragraph some ideas are more important than others. As **9e(2.2)** suggests, writers often do well to subordinate the ideas that are less important in a passage. As a rule, less important ideas are best expressed in adjective clauses or adverb clauses. (See **8a(1)** for adjective clauses, and read on for the subordinating conjunctions that introduce adverb clauses.)

The second part of the table in **9e(5)** shows various meaning-relationships between ideas of unequal importance. Usually these meaning-relationships are expressed by subordinating conjunctions (like *because*) or other transitional words (like *therefore*). Use the table to help you find a variety of ways to express the meanings you intend.

(5) Summary: ways of expressing certain relations between sentence-ideas

The following table shows how certain areas of meaning can be translated into various sentence structures using appropriate transitional words. It is divided from top to bottom into categories of meaning, and it is divided from left to right according to types of grammatical structure. Within the table the boldface words are perhaps the most commonly used words for their categories; they are not necessarily better than the other words given.

Because the words in the three columns have different grammatical functions, a reminder about punctuation is in order. The coordinating conjunctions are used in compound sentences, punctuated according to the guidelines in **10c(1).** The subordinating conjunctions create dependent clauses, punctuated according to **10d(3.4)** and **10d(5).** For the punctuation of conjunctive adverbs, see **10d(2, 4.4)** and **10c(3).**

WAYS OF EXPRESSING CERTAIN RELATIONS BETWEEN SENTENCE-IDEAS

	Coordinating Conjunctions	Subordinating Conjunctions	Other Transitional Words and Phrases (Mostly Conjunctive Adverbs)

Coordinate in Meaning (Ideas of Equal Importance)

Similarity and association	**and,** both—and, nor, neither—nor		also, besides, furthermore, likewise, in addition, in the same way, equally important, moreover, similarly, then too, too
Contrast	**but,** yet	whereas, while	**however,** instead, nevertheless, on the contrary, on the other hand, still, by contrast, though
Choice	**or,** or else, either—or		otherwise, alternatively, instead

Noncoordinate in Meaning (Ideas of Unequal Importance)

Cause or reason	for	**because,** since, for the reason that	
Result or consequence or logical conclusion	and so, so *(somewhat less formal)*		**therefore,** accordingly, consequently, hence, thus, as a result, as a consequence
Purpose		**so that,** so, in order that, lest *(negative purpose,* "so that . . . not")	in order to *(infinitive phrase),* to *(infinitive phrase)*
Simple condition		**if,** only if, on condition that, under the condition that, provided that	
Negative condition		**unless** ("if . . . not")	
Concession (condition with exceptional or unexpected result)		**although,** even if, even though, regardless of the fact that	

	Coordinating Conjunctions	Subordinating Conjunctions	Other Transitional Words and Phrases (Mostly Conjunctive Adverbs)
Same time		**as,** while, when, whenever	at that time, at the same time, meanwhile
Sequence of time		**after,** since	**then,** next, later, at last, finally
		before, until	**first,** earlier, already
Place		**where,** wherever	**there,** in that place in that direction, nearby, far away
Example			**for instance,** for example, that is, to illustrate
Logical ordering			first, in the first place, second, next, finally, in conclusion, in summary, to sum up
Manner		as, however, in whatever way	
Greater degree			indeed, even, in fact, as a matter of fact

● **Practice 9-22** Choose a conjunctive adverb from the last column of the table to express the type of relationship that is indicated. Do not use any word twice.

1. Moses had been given a glimpse of God's glory at the burning bush; _____ , he had witnessed God's power at the Red Sea. (similarity and association)

2. _____ , Moses had learned God's righteous commandments on Mount Sinai. (similarity and association)

3. God's revelation of Himself on Mount Sinai had been awesome. Moses _____ desired to see and know God more clearly. (contrast)

4. _____ , all Christians should desire to pray as Moses did, "Shew me thy glory" (Exod. 33:18). (greater degree)

5. God granted Moses' request in part _____ . _____ Moses _____ beheld God's glory on the Mount of Transfiguration as he looked into the face of Christ. (same time; sequence of time; similarity and association)

● **Practice 9-23** Combine each of the following groups of sentences, creating subordinate and coordinate clauses according to the instructions in parentheses.

1. The nation faced a huge financial deficit. Congress raised taxes substantially. It was unfortunate that they cut hardly any spending plans. (Include a subordinate clause showing cause, and a coordinate clause showing contrast.)

2. William McKinley was assassinated in 1901. Then the leadership of the United States fell into the hands of Theodore Roosevelt. (Include a subordinate clause showing sequence of time.)

3. You can observe a short meteor shower. You need to get up at three o'clock tomorrow morning and watch the northeastern sky. (Include a subordinate clause showing simple condition.)

4. Leaders of oil-rich countries appear unified in their desire to raise the price of oil. They often

quarrel among themselves over how to attain their goal. (Include a subordinate clause showing concession.)

5. The Lord sent prophets to the land of Israel. The people could learn about the coming judgment and turn from their idolatry. (Include a subordinate clause showing purpose.)

● **Practice 9-24** Combine the sentence-ideas below into one good paragraph. Revise and link the clauses as you think best, but do not change the order of operations mentioned. Use the table for ideas, and revise toward clarity and a pleasing sound.

- Each completed auto body is chemically cleaned.
- The lower part of the body is dipped into an anti-corrosion primer.
- The joints in the sheet metal are sealed.
- The sealing prevents corrosion caused by leaks.
- Two coats of primer are applied and baked on the whole car body.
- Sometimes an anti-chip vinyl material is applied to the lower body sides.
- The vinyl material gives protection against stone chips.
- Two coats of color are applied and baked.

9f Consistent Verb Forms

(1) Tense
(2) Voice

Verb forms that do not work well together can create disjointedness or confusion in a piece of writing.

John told us that he will do it, when up comes Carol with a new idea. She says that if we didn't mind, she and Sandy will order the food for everyone. If the food is ordered by them, then they can keep track of the prices too.

Making the verb forms consistent can bring order out of confusion.

> John had told us that he would do it, but then Carol came up with a new idea. She said that if we didn't mind, she and Sandy would order the food for everyone. If they order the food, then they can keep track of the prices too.

This section will help you avoid needless shifts in tense and voice.

(1) Tense

(1.1) Consistency of tenses
(1.2) Sequence of tenses
(1.3) An exception: present tense for a universal truth

Correct tenses are especially important for clarity, so that the reader will know the time and the order of the events being described.

(1.1) Consistency of tenses Sometimes we have a choice of possible tenses for a passage, but we must not jump around aimlessly from one tense to another.

For example, the present tense can be used to tell about the events in someone's story or other literary work. This fictional present time is sometimes called the "literary present." In a present-tense passage, the present perfect tense is used for earlier events.

Literary present | After he *has been* on the island for a while, Crusoe *sees* footprints on the beach.   (present perfect, present)

The past (and past perfect) can also be used to tell a story.

Normal past | After he *had been* on the island for a while, Crusoe *saw* footprints on the beach.   (past perfect, past)

Either system of tenses is correct, but the two should not be mixed.

| Mixed tenses (incorrect) | Crusoe *has been* on the island for a while. Then one day he *saw* footprints on the beach.
Crusoe *had been* on the island for a while. Then one day he *sees* footprints on the beach. |

Mixed tense systems make the writing seem carelessly done.

In conversation sometimes we tell about an ordinary series of past events in the present tense to make it more vivid.

| Oral | "So then the manager comes into the room and asks us what we want." |

In writing, however, the past tense is usually expected.

| Written | Then the manager came into the room and asked us what we wanted. |

Again, it is important not to mix the two.

| Mixed (incorrect) | Then the manager comes into the room and asked us what we want. |

This kind of error may be easy to make, but it is also easy to correct. The key is to reread your writing and look for the problem.

- **Practice 9-25** Correct the following sentences to make the tenses consistent. (This and the next two practice exercises are based on a passage from the autobiography of the dissident Russian writer Yevgeny Yevtushenko. In the passage he tells of a lesson he learned about Stalinism, that is, about the authoritarianism of the ruthless dictator Joseph Stalin.)
  1. I was in the crowd in Trubnaya Square going to see Stalin's coffin. Tens of thousands of people were jammed against one another. New streams flow into the human flood from behind, increasing the pressure.

2. The crowd turned into a monstrous whirlpool. I realize that I am being carried straight toward a traffic-light pole.
3. A girl in front of me is crushed to death against the pole. Totally helpless, I could do nothing. I closed my eyes and was swept past.
4. I am horrified to feel a body under my feet. I picked up my feet under me and am carried along by the crowd. For a long time I was afraid to put my feet down again.
5. The crowd closed tighter and tighter. I am saved by my height from being crushed and smothered alive.

(1.2) Sequence of tenses The concern with "sequence of tenses" has to do with how the tenses of two clauses work together to relate the times of two events.

The past perfect is the proper tense to use for an action that precedes another action in the past. Do not use the plain past tense for both of them.

| Imprecise | After he *spent* some time there, he *left.* |
| Better | *After he had spent* some time there, he *left.* |

Notice the tenses in Acts 18:22-23.

> And when he *had landed* at Caesarea . . . he *went* down to Antioch.
> And after he *had spent* some time there, he *departed,* and *went* over all the country of Galatia and Phrygia . . . .

In both sentences, the first clause uses the past perfect tense for an action already completed before the past event of the second clause.

Sometimes the second clause portrays the earlier action.

> He *misplaced* the book that he *had read.*

Of course, two verbs in the plain past tense properly describe two things that happened (or were true) at the same time.

He *misplaced* the book that he *liked* the best.

See section **8a(4)** for the special adjustments needed in indirect discourse.

- **Practice 9-26** The adaptation of Yevtushenko's true story continues. In each numbered item there is one past-tense verb that would be better as a past perfect, to represent earlier action. Make those five changes.

  1. The crowd was caught between the walls of houses on one side and a row of army trucks on the other. "Get those trucks out of the way!" people howled. "Get them out of here."

     "I can't do it! I have no instructions," a young police officer shouted back from one of the trucks, almost crying with helplessness. After he shouted that, I saw that people were being hurtled against the trucks by the crowd, and their heads smashed.

  2. The sides of the trucks were red with the blood of people who died; and people were still dying.

  3. Suddenly I felt a hatred for all that gave birth to that "I have no instructions," shouted at a moment when people were dying because of someone's stupidity.

  4. For the first time in my life I thought with hatred of the man we were burying. Stalin was not innocent of the disaster. It was the "No instructions" that caused the chaos and blood-shed at his funeral.

  5. Now I knew that you must never wait for instructions if human lives are at stake—you must act. After I fully realized that, I myself began to act.

(1.3) An exception: present tense for a universal truth If two things took place or were true at the same time in the past, normally we express both of them in the past tense.

Columbus showed that the world was round.

However, when one of them is an enduring truth—something still true today—we may be dissatisfied with the past tense. After all, the world is still round today. We then have the option of using the present tense for the universal truth.

Columbus showed that the world is round.

Indeed, the present is probably used more than the past in this situation.

(2) Voice

We have much more freedom in varying between active and passive voice than we have in changing from one tense to another. However, even here sometimes a shift is unfortunate.

Try not to shift from one voice to another within the same sentence, especially if that shift prevents the subjects of the verbs from being the same.

Poor shift in voice	In that way our work *could be completed* and we *could go* shopping sooner.

The first verb is passive and the second is active. Notice the improvement when both are made active.

Better	In that way we *could complete* our work and we *could go* shopping sooner.

Better yet	In that way we could complete our work and go shopping sooner.

The final version collapses the two clauses into one.

● **Practice** 9-27 The final adapted segment of Yevtushenko's story will give you an opportunity to review the main points of section **9f.** Revise the passage (1) to produce consistency in the tenses, and (2) to correct the one unjustified shift to the passive voice. Also (3) mark the past perfect verbs found in the passage, noticing that they correctly convey prior action. (One of the past perfect verbs is past perfect progressive.)

I began shouting, "Form chains! Form chains!" I start to join neighboring hands together by force. Some tough young men began to help me. Gradually people understood. They join hands and chains were formed. The crowd was ceasing to be a savage beast.

"Women and children into the trucks!" yelled one of the young men. And women and children, passed from hand to hand, sailed over our heads into the trucks. The whirlpool was slowing down.

The police too finally began to help us.

At last, the tide had turned and everything was calm.

Somehow, I no longer felt like going to see Stalin's remains. Instead, I leave with one of the boys who had been organizing chains. We walked to my place.

"Did you see Stalin?" my mother asks me.

"Yes," I said, too weary to explain.

I hadn't really lied to my mother. I had seen Stalin. Because everything that had just happened—that was Stalin.

9g Consistent Nouns and Pronouns: Person and Number

(1) Shifts in person
(2) Shifts in number

Just as pronouns should agree with their antecedents, other types of repeated reference to the same thing or idea should not needlessly change in person and number.

(1) Shifts in person

In statements of general truths, unnamed people can appear in a number of ways. Some possible words are *people, one,* and *anyone* (all in the third person); sometimes informally *you* (second person); and *we* (first person). A problem comes, though, when there is a shift from one person to another.

| Shift | I learned that *we* can easily make mistakes in arithmetic, so *you* should always check *your* work when *you* add large numbers. |

The statement of general truth begins with *we* (first person) and ends with *you* (second person). We can correct it by changing *you* to *we*, or we can revise more thoroughly for greater formality:

| Corrected | I learned that because it is easy to make mistakes in arithmetic, one should always check his work when he adds large numbers. |

Here is a similar problem sentence.

| Shift | *A person* must work if *you* want to advance. |

The sentence begins with the third person and ends with the second person. *He,* not *you,* would be the correct

pronoun to carry on the person and number of the noun *person*.

(2) Shifts in number

Statements of general truths can also have problems of number. Most general statements can be made in either the singular or the plural.

Correct | The elephant is a very large animal.
Elephants are very large animals.

Mixing the two types of statement, though, can produce strange results.

Shift | Elephants use their trunk for many things.

This sentence seems to be talking about a number of elephants who together have just one trunk. The solution is to make the sentence either singular or plural throughout.

Correct | Elephants use their trunks for many things.
An elephant uses its trunk for many things.

The same kind of problem can appear in directions to a group.

Shift | Now, children, open your Bible to John 3:16.

All the children together have just one Bible? If not, make the sentence plural throughout by using *Bibles*.

- **Practice 9-28** Revise the following sentences to correct the shifts of person and number. Write *C* for any correct sentences.
  1. Tall oaks from a little acorn grow.
  2. You can do anything we ought to do.

3. He who has one enemy will meet them everywhere.
4. On the day of victory no one is tired.
5. Never look gift horses in their mouth.
6. Pygmies placed on the shoulders of giants see more than the giant himself.
7. Train up a child in the way he should go: and when they are old, they will not depart from it. (Prov. 22:6)
8. If you can't say something good, we shouldn't say anything.

9h Placement in the Sentence

(1) Managing the sequence of subjects
(2) Ending sentences with new information
(3) Ending in strength

An important way to link sentences together, creating a natural flow from one to the other, is to make wise use of certain strategic positions in the sentence. Wise use of the end of the sentence will also help you highlight the things that are important.

(1) Managing the sequence of subjects

The subjects of a series of sentences or clauses should fit together well. As an example, the subjects are italicized in the next paragraph.

Subjects are important because *the subject* usually announces what a sentence is about. Since *it* comes near the beginning of the sentence, *the subject* keeps the reader posted about what is being discussed. If *the subjects* jump around from one topic to another, *the reader* has to mentally change directions a number of times in the paragraph. But if *the subjects* fit well together, *the reader* finds the path clear and the countryside familiar.

Compare the paragraph revised as a poor example:

Subjects are important because *the sentence* tells about the subject. Since *the beginning of the sentence* is the usual place for the subject, *the reader* is told early what the sentence is about. If *first one topic and then another* is found in the subject position, *several mental changes in direction* are necessary in the paragraph. But if there is *a good fit of the subjects, the path* is clear and *the countryside* is familiar.

With subjects jumping around from one topic to another, the paragraph flows less smoothly. By contrast, the original paragraph had just two basic subjects: *the subject* and *the reader*.

We have here a principle, not a rigid rule, for the sequence of subjects:

> Within a paragraph, try to make the subjects of your sentences fit well together. Do not jump around needlessly from one topic to another.

It is not always possible to tie subjects together in this way, but doing so is often a help.

- **Practice 9-29** Try to improve the following paragraph by making the subjects shift less often.

> One of the world's most common species is the spider. Spiders can be found from the Arctic to the Antarctic. The tropics, however, are where they are the most abundant. We picture them as brown or black, but green, yellow, red, and white are also spider colors. Insects are their main food source, but wasps are their greatest enemy. Although people like spiders for killing bugs in the garden, we do not appreciate them in our homes.

(2) Ending sentences with new information

Often in good writing the end of one sentence introduces a new idea that is taken up toward the beginning of the next. The next sentence is thus linked to it by the repetition.

> . . . toward the beginning of *the next. The next sentence* is . . .

This kind of link is not always possible, but it is sometimes a good way to tie sentences together.

There are several ways to get the new information to the end of the sentence:

1. Reverse the subject and the predicate noun.

    Bergamot is another kind of flower that hummingbirds like. *Bergamot* is also called bee balm.

    Another kind of flower that hummingbirds like is *bergamot. Bergamot* is also called bee balm.

2. Move other things out of the way at the end of the sentence.

    Bergamot flowers may be red or white or *pink,* and somewhat ragged-looking. *The pink-flowered bergamot* grows well in shady places, but the others prefer sun.

    The somewhat ragged-looking flowers of bergamot may be red or white or *pink. The pink-flowered bergamot* grows well in shady places, but the others prefer sun.

3. Change active to passive or vice versa.

    Reddish bracts surround the flowers of our red bergamot. *The bracts* look like small brightly colored leaves.

    The flowers of our red bergamot are surrounded by *reddish bracts. They* look like brightly colored leaves.

Certainly not every pair of sentences should be tied together in this way. Sometimes, for instance, you will prefer to use the method suggested above in **9h(1).** However, at times this technique will provide just the link needed.

● **Practice 9-30** Link the following pairs of sentences by revising the first sentence of each pair. Put the new information at the end, ready to be picked up by the second sentence.

1. Coins were first minted by the Chinese. Coins were introduced into the western world by the ancient Lydians.
2. Coins have been made from silver, nickel, platinum, and gold, as well as from nonmetals like porcelain and plastic. Gold was the worldwide standard by the nineteenth century.
3. Lead was used by the American colonies to make the continental dollar. Lead is used today by counterfeiters to produce phony coins.
4. The United States first used nickel to mint coins in 1865. It was used to produce a three-cent piece.
5. Silver has been the main metal used for coinage throughout the centuries. Silver coins were minted in the United States until 1964.

(3) Ending in strength

(3.1) Important information
(3.2) Solid words

Partly because final impressions are lasting impressions, it is good to end sentences strongly.

(3.1) Important information Psychologically it is often natural to move in the sentence from familiar information to new information, and from less important to more important. Even our normal pronunciation of the sentence puts the greatest stress (emphasis) on its last significant word. Good writing usually follows this tendency by putting the important information last.

Whatever comes last is most likely to be remembered. As **9h(2)** points out, whatever is last is also in a good position to be picked up in the next sentence for further discussion.

If you find the important information buried in the middle of your sentence, you can usually move other things away from the end of the sentence. If the important information is stranded at the beginning of the sentence, you can often move it out of the subject and into the predicate. Specific suggestions are listed, with examples, in **9h(2)**.

● **Practice 9-31** Revise the following sentences to move the italicized phrases to the end.

1. The nickname *"The Great Commoner"* was given to William Jennings Bryan.
2. Three times he *lost* when he ran for the presidency of the United States.
3. *A godlessness promoted by the theory of evolution* was the cause of World War I according to Bryan.
4. In Bryan's opinion, *a public vote should be taken* before the nation could go to war.
5. *He was hated by many scientists* because of his belief in a literal interpretation of the Bible.

(3.2) Solid words Just as we expect to find important information at the end of most sentences, we also prefer sentences that end with solid words. Weak wording can water down a strong idea.

Weaker	His ideas may be brilliant, but they are rather hard *to get hold of.*
Stronger	His ideas may be brilliant, but they are rather hard *to grasp.*

Compared with the solid word *grasp, of* is a rather flimsy word. Verbs are nearly always more solid than prepositions. Now compare an adverb and a noun:

Adequate	A key sentence should end *strongly.*
Stronger	A key sentence should end *in strength.*

The adverb *strongly* is perfectly acceptable, but the noun *strength* gives the ending a special solidity. The most solid nouns are often those that are derived from other words.

Derived Noun	*Source Word*
strength	strong
solidity	solid
discussion	discuss

Sometimes, then, we can give greater force to a sentence by ending it with a more solid word. The more solid words seem to be those with full and definite meaning content. For example, *thing* is less solid than *tractor;* and *was* is less solid than *parked.*

Below is a listing of some common parts of speech according to how solid or how flimsy they tend to be.

Solid ↑ ↓ Flimsy	• Nouns, especially derived nouns • True verbs • Adjectives and adverbs • Personal pronouns • Prepositions, adverbs (like *in*) that sound like prepositions, and other minor parts of speech

Do not feel that you must tinker with the ending of every sentence. It is probably best to use this information for two purposes:

1. To improve a sentence that ends with an especially flimsy word
2. To give special strength to a key sentence

Practice 9-32 Revise the following sentences to increase the strength of their endings.
1. The book of Judges is a picture of the misery that spiritual compromise results in.
2. It was not spiritual knowledge that the people lacked, but the ability to reason wisely.
3. Their sin of spiritual apathy was difficult to get rid of.
4. God left some of their enemies in the land to test whether Israel would live faithfully.
5. The result of their worldly associations was their living unrighteously.

9i Parallel Structures

(1) Advantages of parallel structures
(2) Using parallelism only for parallel ideas
(3) Using the same part of speech
(4) Using the same type of structure
(5) Placing correlative conjunctions correctly
(6) Clarifying parallelism

Parallel structures are used for concepts of the same type. The structures are **parallel** when they have the same form and are joined by a coordinating conjunction.

(1) Advantages of parallel structures

Using parallel structures can help you improve the "sound" of your writing as well as show the relationship between certain ideas. For instance, we can start with these acceptable sentences:

> This year Jack had good success in growing tomatoes. Even his watermelons did well, and so did his cantaloupes.

Then we can improve them by using parallelism.

This year Jack had good success	in growing tomatoes	
	and	
	even in growing	watermelons
		and
		cantaloupes.

Because the second version puts similar things together, it is both shorter and easier to read. For a second example, we start with these sentences:

> To Joyce the dress appeared almost antique.
> However, her sister thought it was right in style.

Revision produces a single sentence with parallel structures.

$$
\text{The dress appeared}
\begin{Vmatrix}
\text{to Joyce} \\
\quad \| \text{ as almost antique} \\
\\
\qquad\quad \text{but} \\
\\
\text{to her sister} \\
\quad \| \text{ as right in style.}
\end{Vmatrix}
$$

It would certainly be possible to overdo the use of parallel structures—anything gets monotonous after a while. However, the occasional use of parallel structures can be a very useful way to improve the clarity and even the rhythm of your writing.

- **Practice 9-33** Try to combine and improve the following pairs of sentences by using parallel structures.
  1. Basketball teams know the importance of being aggressive on offense. They should also be aggressive when playing defense.
  2. Good offensive basketball is evidenced by a well-balanced attack. It also includes patient self-discipline and precise execution.
  3. A good defensive team knows the value of tenacity. They realize that effective defense is simply intensity and hard work.
  4. An effective defensive player is always aware of the position of the ball. He must know where his opponent and the basket are.
  5. Winning basketball teams usually are characterized by a respect for teammates and coaches. They show respect for their opponent and the officials as well.

(2) Using parallelism only for parallel ideas

Parallelism is a very useful device, but it should be used only for ideas that are truly of the same type.

| Illogical parallelism | The Bible portrays Ruth as faithful, industrious, and fairly young. |
| Corrected | The Bible portrays Ruth as faithful and industrious. |

The comment about Ruth's age does not fit in with the two character traits, so it is removed from the parallel construction.

The next example illustrates the problem of having one item that is either more general or less general than the others.

| Illogical parallelism | We bought seeds for lettuce, carrots, and garden vegetables. |
| Corrected | We bought seeds for lettuce, carrots, and *other* garden vegetables. |

Inserting the word *other* avoids here the logical problem of having one item that includes other items in the series.

In our final example the writer actually did have in mind two parallel ideas, but something else ended up being expressed in the parallel construction.

| Illogical parallelism | My sister has had six college roommates, including those living with her last year and living with her now. |
| Corrected | My sister has had six college roommates, including those living with her last year and *those* living with her now. |

The correction properly draws the parallel between two groups of people rather than two activities of one group.

- **Practice 9-34** Find and correct the instances of illogical parallelism in the following sentences. Write *C* if a sentence is correct.
  1. President Grover Cleveland is portrayed as courageous, ingenious, strong-minded, and very overweight.
  2. In 1893 he endured a cancer operation in secret in order to avoid public panic and political sabotage.
  3. To perform the necessary surgery, the doctors had to sneak scalpels, retractors, and operating instruments onto a yacht.
  4. President Cleveland needed an artificial jaw so that he could speak clearly enough to be understood and loudly enough to be heard.
  5. The facts about the operation were known by just a few men, including those who performed the surgery and who guarded the yacht.

(3) Using the same part of speech

Sentence parts joined by coordinating conjunctions must be of the same grammatical type. Most important, they must represent the same part of speech.

Not parallel	Adj Adj She is intelligent, pleasant, and a good N neighbor.
Corrected	Adj Adj Adj She is intelligent, pleasant, and neighborly.
Apparently nonparallel	Adj TrV A good friend is faithful and helps you.
Corrected	Adj Adj A good friend is faithful and helpful.

The second nonparallel example could instead be interpreted as coordinating the two verbs *is* and *helps*. However, with any form of *be* we usually expect the coordination to be on the more important word that follows, in this case *faithful*.

Modifiers too should be the same part of speech:

Adj   ModN
Not parallel | I like both factual and fiction books.

Adj   Adj
Corrected | I like both factual and fictional books.

In these examples and most others, the problem word or phrase can be changed to the correct part of speech. When you cannot think of a better solution, however, you can take the offending element out of the attempted parallel construction.

Adj   Adj   TrV
Not parallel | She is intelligent, pleasant, and likes children.

Indep. Clause
Corrected | [She is intelligent and pleasant],

Indep. Clause
and [she likes children].

● **Practice 9-35** Correct any faulty parallelism that you find. Write *C* for correct sentences.
1. The American grizzly bear is pictured as aggressive, voracious, and makes us afraid.
2. The existence of the grizzly bear is threatened by exploration, exploitation, and always building roads and towns.
3. Grizzly cubs wrestle, somersault, and explore.
4. Grizzlies are intelligent, strong, and can move quickly.
5. They eat meat, grasses, shrubs, and flowers.
6. Immediately after hibernation, the bears are lazy, passive, and like to sleep.
7. Grizzly bears are expert diggers, climbers, and hunt efficiently.

(4) Using the same type of structure

(4.1) Word or phrase, kind of phrase
(4.2) Kind of verbal
(4.3) Phrase or clause, kind of clause

Not only should parallel elements represent the same part of speech, but when possible they should also be of the same general type of structure.

(4.1) Word or phrase, kind of phrase Certain kinds of phrases should not usually be joined to other kinds of words or phrases.

Not fully parallel | N   N
I enjoy novels, short stories, and
Gerund Phrase
daily reading of the newspaper.

Better | N   N
I enjoy novels, short stories, and
N
the daily newspaper.

Not fully parallel | Adj   Prep. Phrase
The ad was too wide, of excessive length,
Adj
and possibly too late.

Better | Adj   Adj
The ad was too wide, too long, and
Adj
possibly too late.

Sentences like the "not fully parallel" examples are not absolutely wrong; but when they *can* be improved, they should be.

- **Practice 9-36** Improve the parallelism.
  1. Many of the great minds of America's past thought cities to be loathsome, fearful, and of no redeeming value.
  2. Thomas Jefferson feared the city because it produced dependence, ambition, and corrupting of its citizens.
  3. Herman Melville perceived the city people as shameful, decadent, and without any aspects of civilization.
  4. What a contrast to the praise for the city of God in Psalm 48 and its being loved in Psalm 87!

(4.2) Kind of verbal Gerunds, participles, and infinitives should not be mixed in the same construction.

Not parallel | At their ceremonies American Indians
Ger — Inf
liked smoking peace pipes and to perform ritual dances.

Corrected |
Ger
. . . liked smoking peace pipes and
Ger
performing ritual dances.
Inf
. . . liked to smoke peace pipes and
Inf
to perform ritual dances.

Not parallel | Southern African rain taboos included
Ger
burying certain people improperly,
N — Part — N
witchcraft, and disturbed ancestors.

Corrected |
Ger
. . . included burying certain people
Ger
improperly, practicing witchcraft,
Ger
and disturbing the ancestors.

- **Practice 9-37** Correct the parallelism of these sentences.
  1. The men who fight forest fires must learn to parachute into trees, to work sixteen-hour days, and putting up with intense heat.
  2. These firefighters become experts at digging fire lanes, felling burning trees, and first aid.

3. Firefighters learn to accept parachuting into creeks on a cold day, untangling themselves from treetops after a bad jump, and to sleep in holes in the chilly ground.
4. The hot air and the updraft from a forest fire have been known to blister firefighters' lungs, to produce 35,000-foot smoke columns, and uproot entire trees.
5. Helicopters are used for transporting firefighters to the blaze, to bombard "hot spots" with water, and transferring gear for the crews.

(4.3) Phrase or clause, kind of clause A phrase and a clause should not normally be joined by a coordinating conjunction.

Not fully parallel	Noun Phrase The report showed *an improvement in average attendance* Dependent Clause but [that average grades had dropped].
Corrected	The report showed [that Noun Clause average attendance had improved] Noun Clause but [that average grades had dropped].
Perhaps even better	Noun Phrase The report showed *an improvement in average attendance* Noun phrase but *a drop in average grades*.

An independent clause and a dependent clause should never be joined by a coordinating conjunction.

Not parallel	Indep. Clause [It was a hard game], and [which Dependent Clause we could not have won without you].
Corrected	It was a hard game, [which Dependent Clause we could not have won without you]. Indep. Clause [It was a hard game], and [we could Indep Clause not have won it without you].

● **Practice 9-38** Correct the faulty parallelism. Write *C* if a sentence is correct.

1. Samson's parents demonstrated not only a desire to please the Lord but also that they desired to oppose the Philistines.
2. Samson demonstrated great personal courage, and which he could not have succeeded without.
3. Samson never saw the need for self-discipline or for wholehearted commitment.
4. The Philistines tried to assimilate the Israelites by trading with them and that they encouraged intermarriage.
5. Samson chose the wrong company, and which he ended up in failure.
6. Samson overcame his failure by asking God to forgive him and by trusting God to use him.
7. God's discipline of Samson shows His desire to restore us completely and that He longs to make us useful.

(From Judges 13-16)

(5) Placing correlative conjunctions correctly

Correlative conjunctions are pairs like *both—and, either—or, neither—nor,* and *not only—but (also)*. As **4f(1.4)** points out, correlative conjunctions can be very useful in the sentence. However, they must be used carefully:

> The sentence element that immediately follows the first correlative conjunction must be of the same type as the element that immediately follows the second correlative conjunction.

Let's look at some examples.

	TrV
Not parallel	Egyptian hieroglyphics **both** included

DO   DO
phonetic symbols **and** symbols

that represented words.

	TrV
Corrected	Egyptian hieroglyphics included **both**

DO   DO
phonetic symbols **and** symbols

that represented words.

The incorrect sentence has different elements after the two conjunctions. The problem can be corrected by moving the first conjunction.

	LV
Not parallel	A phonetic symbol could **either** be

PA   PA
alphabetic (for a single sound) **or** syllabic

(for a whole syllable).

Corrected | A phonetic symbol could be **either** (LV) **alphabetic** (PA) (for a single sound) **or** **syllabic** (PA) (for a whole syllable).

So far, the corrections have been made by moving the first conjunction. However, other adjustments may also be possible.

Not parallel | **Not only** has (Aux) this (S) third of the Al Murrah tribe **continued** (Verb) with camel-herding, **but also** **faced** (Verb) the inhospitable deserts to care for the herds.

Corrected | **Not only** has this third of the Al Murrah tribe continued with camel-herding, **but** *it has* also faced the inhospitable deserts to care for the herds.

Adding a subject and an auxiliary makes the two parts parallel as independent clauses.

This kind of parallelism error is very easy to make, but usually it is also very easy to correct. Just be aware of the problem and look for the location of the correlative conjunctions.

● **Practice 9-39** Correct the faulty parallelism. Write *C* for a correct sentence.

1. The wild turkey was not only Ben Franklin's choice for our national symbol but also John J. Audubon's choice for his first color plate in *Birds of America.*

2. By the time of the Civil War the wild turkey was faced with the loss both of woodland habitat and the danger of extinction.
3. The Civil War sent many farmers to the West, making possible the restoration both of the Eastern woodlands and the revival of the wild turkey population.
4. Since turkeys both are elusive and intelligent, hunters sometimes spend hours trying to bring a gobbler within shooting range.
5. Devices either named wing-bone yelpers or peg-and-slate scratchers can be used to call turkeys toward a hunter.

(6) Clarifying parallelism

Sometimes in a written sentence the reader cannot be sure just what sentence parts are intended to be joined by the conjunction. To clarify such a sentence, try one of these methods:

1. Using correlative conjunctions
2. Repeating a key word
3. Reordering the joined elements

The first remedy, correlative conjunctions, is discussed in **4f(1.4)** and **9i(5)**.

A second way to make the parallelism clear is to repeat a key word such as a preposition, an auxiliary, or the sign of the infinitive. (If you do repeat a key word, be sure to use it at the beginning of every item in the series.)

Parallelism unclear	In relations with the queen, work arrangements, and judicial matters, the Lovedu people use cooperation. (in relations with work arrangements?)
Improved	In relations with the queen, *in* work arrangements, and *in* judicial matters, the Lovedu people use cooperation.

Parallelism unclear	A new missionary to the Lovedu should learn to speak their language accurately and understand their culture thoroughly. (should understand? or should learn to understand?)
Improved	A new missionary to the Lovedu should learn to speak their language accurately and *to* understand their culture thoroughly.

A third way is to reverse the order of the confusing elements, putting the simpler element first.

Parallelism unclear	The people's method of governing themselves and their religion are closely related. (governing themselves and their religion?)
Improved	The people's religion and their method of governing themselves are closely related.

● **Practice 9-40** Solve the problem of unclear parallelism in each of the following sentences. Use any of the three methods listed above.

1. In dealings with the general public, medical diagnosis, and "cures" prescribed, the medical quack totally ignored honesty.
2. The traveling medicine show of the past used tales of miraculous cures or testimonials of personal healings to sell its so-called medicines.
3. The medicine man's system of appealing to the emotions and his financial success were clearly connected.
4. A medicine show quack would learn to "diagnose" known ailments and invent diseases that did not even exist.
5. We deplore these quacks' unscrupulous methods that endangered the health of others and their thievery.

Chapter 10
Correct and Helpful Punctuation

A paragraph that is not punctuated is hard to read of course if there were no capital letters either it would be even harder capital letters and punctuation work together to set off sentences besides that punctuation often tells us how the sentences are divided into groups of words

Let's try that again:

> A paragraph that is not punctuated is hard to read. Of course, if there were no capital letters either, it would be even harder. Capital letters and punctuation work together to set off sentences.

Besides that, punctuation often tells us how the sentences are divided into groups of words.

Obviously, punctuation does make a difference.

10a Punctuation for Clarity

Punctuation has one main purpose: to help make written material clear. Consider the difference between speaking and writing. In listening to someone speak, we hear more than just words. We also hear the voice as it gets louder and softer, rises and falls in tone, speeds up and slows down, and sometimes even pauses. These changes help us know how we should understand the words we hear. When we read, we depend on punctuation to help us mentally "hear" the right pauses and the right tone of voice.

Let's color Mrs. Bixby.
Let's color, Mrs. Bixby.

If we want our readers to get the right "sound"—and therefore the right meaning—we have to be careful about punctuation.

10b Ends of Sentences, Other Periods

(1) The period
(2) The question mark
(3) The exclamation mark
(4) Other uses of the period

Sentences end with periods, question marks, and exclamation marks. These end-punctuation marks depend almost completely on the type of sentence: declarative, imperative, interrogative, and exclamatory.

(1) The period

Most sentences end with a period. Periods end all declarative sentences (stating a fact) and most imperative sentences (giving a command). For examples, just look at most sentences on this page.

(2) The question mark

Direct questions end with question marks.

> Is it cold outside this morning?
> And no one knew the answer?
> Why did you buy another newspaper?

Elliptical questions in a series use question marks.

> Does this affect you? your family? your church?

Indirect questions do not use a question mark.

> She asked whether it was cold outside.
> I wondered why he bought another newspaper.

Requests courteously stated like questions do not use question marks.

> Would you please get some bread on your way home.

(3) The exclamation mark

The exclamation mark (or "exclamation point") is used to show strong feeling. It can be found at the end of brief exclamations, exclamatory sentences, and some imperative sentences.

> Wow! How wonderful!
> What a crazy idea that was!
> Stop that right now!

The exclamation mark should be used mainly in quoting spoken exclamations. Even so, it should not be overused. A page sprinkled with exclamation marks usually seems overly emotional.

- **Practice 10-1** Supply the correct punctuation at the end of each sentence.
  1. I will be your guide on this tour through Monticello
  2. What a beautiful estate this is
  3. Who built it

4. Monticello was designed and built by Thomas Jefferson

5. Jefferson, our third president, worked on his home between 1768 and 1809

(4) Other uses of the period

(4.1) Abbreviations and initials
(4.2) Numbers in a list
(4.3) Numbers and letters in an outline

(4.1) Abbreviations and initials

Use periods after most abbreviations and initials.

Dr., Mr., Mrs., Rev.	Calif., W. Va., S. C.
(*but* Miss)	(or W.Va., S.C.)
9:15 a.m. (*or* 9:15 A.M.)	H. K. Barbe
A.D. 476, 586 B.C.	John Cooper, Jr.
in., tsp., oz., lb.	Rev. 3:20, Ps. 19:14

Do not use periods after shortened forms of names and of some other words.

> *Tom* and *Ed* hurried from the *gym* to the *lab* for their biology class.

Do not use periods after the two-letter post office abbreviations of states. (Use these abbreviations only in addressing mail, with Zip Codes.)

CA	WV	SC

Do not use periods after certain initials or words made from initials. When in doubt, check your dictionary.

CBS   NASA   OPEC

Section **16f** gives more information about abbreviations.

(4.2) Numbers in a list In a list that is arranged from top to bottom on the page, use periods with the numbers. For example, here are four steps in planning a paper:

1. Gathering information and ideas
2. Determining the purpose
3. Choosing the main idea
4. Outlining the paper

(4.3) Numbers and letters in an outline Use periods with the numbers and letters that identify the points of an outline.

I. Homes of rabbits
   A. Shallow holes
   B. Connected burrows
II. Enemies of rabbits
   A. Hunters
   B. Animals
      1. Wild animals
         a. Foxes
         b. Hawks
      2. Domestic animals

- **Practice 10-2** Supply the periods needed for certain initials and abbreviations and for numbers in a list. (Can you find the list?)
  1 Dr and Mrs Winston will be speaking to the science lab classes at 3:10 p m
  2 The Winstons arrived from Richmond, Va , about 7 a m
  3 T F Winston, Jr , is an expert in archaeology, especially archaeology of the Middle East from 586 B C to A D 476.
  4 Mrs Winston has worked at NASA.
  5 They open every lecture by reading II Pet 3:4.

10c The Compound Sentence

(1) Coordinating conjunction
(2) Semicolon only
(3) Semicolon, conjunctive adverb
(4) Colon only

A compound sentence consists of at least two independent clauses. These clauses, which could have made up two separate sentences, can be joined in various ways.

(1) Coordinating conjunction

Most compound sentences are made up of two independent clauses joined by a coordinating conjunction. Usually a comma precedes the conjunction.

| Independent Clause |, conj. | Independent Clause |

The air is warm today, but the water is cold.

When the two independent clauses are very short, the comma may be omitted before the conjunction.

The air is warm and the water is calm.

If a compound sentence contains three or more independent clauses, a comma is used after all except the last.

| Independent Clause |, | Independent Clause |,

conj. | Independent Clause |

The air is warm, the sky is clear, and

the water is calm.

The commas and the conjunction are used here just as they are when they join any series of things: potatoes, peanuts, and onions.

● **Practice 10-3** Make a compound sentence out of each pair of simple sentences. Do so by connecting the two simple sentences with a comma and the coordinating conjunction that fits the meaning best. Choose from *and, but, or,* and *for*.

1. I want to learn all about caves. My brother and I recently discovered one nearby.
2. Perry wanted to explore it immediately. I reminded him of the danger.
3. In his opinion I could wait outside. I could go in right away with him.
4. Just inside the entrance, water dripped on our heads. Strange noises echoed in the darkness.
5. We weren't afraid. We both decided to call off our exploration.

Section **10h(2)** explains the occasional use of a semicolon before the coordinating conjunction in a compound sentence.

(2) Semicolon only

When the second independent clause reinforces the first, a semicolon alone may be used to join the two clauses. (No more than two clauses should be joined in this manner.)

> Independent Clause ; Independent Clause
>
> Africa is the second largest continent in the world;
>
> it contains about a fifth of the world's land area.

- **Practice 10-4** Revise the following compound sentences by replacing the comma and coordinating conjunction with a semicolon.
  1. Visitors to Africa may explore the Sahara Desert or the Nile River, or they may even go on a big-game hunting expedition.
  2. Africa used to be called the Dark Continent, for many parts of it were mysterious and unknown to outsiders.

(3) Semicolon, conjunctive adverb

When two independent clauses are joined by a semicolon, often a conjunctive adverb helps to show the exact relationship between the clauses. The conjunctive adverb is usually set off by one or more commas, depending on where the conjunctive adverb comes in the second clause.

> Africa is rich in natural resources; **however,** many of the African countries cannot afford to develop them.

> Africa is rich in natural resources; many of the African countries, **however,** cannot afford to develop them.

Notice that the conjunctive adverb *(however)* is part of the second clause. A conjunctive adverb is a kind of *adverb,* not a conjunction. (Like most other adverbs, a conjunctive adverb can be moved within its sentence or clause.) It is called "conjunctive" because its meaning provides a thought-link to another independent clause. Here are a few common conjunctive adverbs:

also	in fact
besides	instead
for example	nevertheless
furthermore	then
however	therefore

Others are given in the last column of the table in **9e(5).**

- **Practice 10-5** Revise each of the following sentences by replacing the period or the coordinating conjunction with the conjunctive adverb that best shows the relationship between the clauses. Choose from *however, therefore, also,* and *furthermore.* Supply the correct capitalization and punctuation for the revised sentences.
  1. Most of the world's diamonds come from Africa's mines, and a large amount of the world's cacao, palm oil, peanuts, and sisal comes from Africa's farms.
  2. Cocoa and chocolate come from cacao. Cacao is a popular export.
  3. Many people have never seen a sisal plant. Everyone has used its products, rope and twine.

(4) Colon only

Rarely, a colon is used to join two independent clauses. The colon shows that the second clause explains the first. Normally no conjunctive adverb is present.

| Independent Clause | : | Independent Clause |

The sisal plant yields a very useful product: fibers from its large leaves are made into rope and twine.

● **Practice 10-6** Join each pair of sentences into a compound sentence, using a comma and a coordinating conjunction, a semicolon (with or without a conjunctive adverb), or a colon. Try to use each of these methods at least once.

1. In order to find moisture, prairie grasses must sink their roots deep into the soil. There is only moderate to low rainfall on the prairie.
2. These grasslands support running and clustering animals like antelope. They provide homes for burrowing animals like prairie dogs and gophers.
3. Prairie farms and farm ponds provide a suitable habitat for woodland animals. Such forest creatures as raccoons and opossums are being attracted to these locations.
4. In earlier years people called America's vast grasslands the "great American desert." Today the area produces much of our country's food.

10d The Comma

     (1) Commas for clarity
     (2) How to use commas to set off sentence elements
     (3) Commas after introductory elements
     (4) Commas to set off other elements anywhere in the sentence
     (5) Restrictive and nonrestrictive elements
     (6) Other uses of the comma
     (7) Incorrect commas

The comma is probably the most important mark of punctuation used inside the sentence. It is certainly the one used most often.

(1) Commas for clarity

Commas show something about how the words are grouped inside the sentence, and so they help to make the sentence clear.

> When Jesus came to Bethany after Lazarus'
> death Mary sat still in the house.

A comma would let us see immediately that *after Lazarus' death* is part of the first clause, not the second.

> When Jesus came to Bethany after Lazarus'
> death, Mary sat still in the house.

Other examples appear in the following practice exercise.

- **Practice 10-7** Add commas to clarify the meaning of the following sentences.
  1. When Hank passed Phil slowed down.
  2. For dessert we had harvest cake sweet potato pie and gingersnaps.
  3. When the teacher asked for John Mark came forward instead.
  4. It is your turn to cook Cheryl.
  5. Dad our accounting teacher stressed the need for a calculator.
  6. Just beyond the dark cave water could be heard roaring over the falls.
  7. For inspecting George will use a flashlight tape measure and operating manual.

(2) How to use commas to set off sentence elements

Commas often set off a word or a group of words from the rest of the sentence. The number of commas needed depends on where the word or word group is—at the beginning, in the middle, or at the end of the sentence.

> However, I'd tell you to wait awhile.
> I'd tell you, however, to wait awhile.
> I'd tell you to wait awhile, however.

At the beginning and at the end just one comma is needed. In the middle two commas are needed—regardless of whether or not you can "hear" them both.

(3) Commas after introductory elements

(3.1) Introductory participle phrases
(3.2) Long introductory prepositional phrases
(3.3) Introductory numbering words
(3.4) Introductory adverb clauses
(3.5) Other introductory elements

We use a comma to set off certain kinds of elements when they come first in the sentence.

(3.1) Introductory participle phrases An introductory participle or participle phrase should be set off by a comma.

> Knowing your ability, I think you can do better.

(3.2) Long introductory prepositional phrases A long or multiple prepositional phrase at the beginning of a sentence should be set off by a comma.

> In comparison with a month, a week does not seem long.

There is no definite rule for "how long is long." Often, as here, a phrase of five or more words seems long enough to merit a comma.

(3.3) Introductory numbering words Commas are often used after numbering words like *first, second, next, finally,* and *last.*

> First, you should revise your story.

(3.4) Introductory adverb clauses An introductory adverb clause nearly always requires a comma.

> If you will work on it, that story can be really good.

(3.5) Other introductory elements Other introductory elements that may require commas include modifiers of the sentence as a whole.

> To see it with fresh eyes, read it again after a week.

When the introductory phrase contains a verbal, a comma is often needed.

> After rereading your story, you will probably see some ways to improve it.

(4) Commas to set off other elements anywhere in the sentence

(4.1) Appositives
(4.2) Isolates
(4.3) Nouns of address
(4.4) Conjunctive adverbs
(4.5) Parenthetical expressions
(4.6) Tag questions
(4.7) Phrases that show contrast

Certain sentence elements are set off by commas wherever they come in the sentence.

(4.1) Appositives Most appositives are set off by commas.

> Miss Campbell, our English teacher, would advise the same thing.

The exception is that no comma is used with a "close appositive"—a short appositive that is more important than the noun before it.

> Even the famous poet John Keats did much rewriting.

(4.2) Isolates Most isolates, including interjections, are set off from the rest of the sentence by commas.

> Yes, I know the contest closes in three weeks.
> Well, wouldn't you rather send a better story?

(4.3) Nouns of address Sometimes we call a person by his name or courtesy title when we speak to him. That name or title, called a noun of address, should be set off by commas.

Jon, you are the best writer in the class.
Thank you very much, sir, for your encouragement.

(4.4) Conjunctive adverbs Conjunctive adverbs like *however* and *though* are often said in such a way that there seems to be a pause before and after them. As long as the word does not come between two independent clauses, we indicate those two pauses with a pair of commas.

Your story won't be good, however, if you hurry.

See **10c(3)** for conjunctive adverbs in compound sentences with semicolons.

(4.5) Parenthetical expressions We use commas to set off a phrase that could be left out of the sentence.

Haste, as the saying goes, does make waste.
As the saying goes, haste does make waste.
Haste does make waste, as the saying goes.

(4.6) Tag questions

Each sample sentence below was made into an interrogative sentence by the addition of a tag question. The tag question is separated from the rest of the sentence by a comma.

You did see my suggestions, didn't you?

John has not read the story yet, has he?

(4.7) **Phrases that show contrast** A phrase that shows contrast should be set off by commas, particularly when the phrase begins with a negative word like *not* or *never*.

Short stories, not novels, are his specialty.

He produces his first drafts at the typewriter, never with pencil and paper.

- **Practice 10-8** Each sentence includes at least one word or phrase that should be set off by commas; supply the needed commas.
  1. With my vast understanding of the various problems involved in lawn care I will assume the responsibility of organizing the work projects.
  2. Well the twins may cut the grass after lunch.
  3. Connie our young helper will water the flowers and wash the lawn chairs. *(Assume that Connie is the young helper.)*
  4. Over there Leroy you will find a garden hoe and some fertilizer.
  5. Using the electric trimmer Grover should easily finish the hedges by supper time.
  6. The proper care of a yard as you can see can be quite demanding.
  7. Supervising the whole operation is however the most difficult job don't you think?

(5) Restrictive and nonrestrictive elements

A **restrictive** modifier is one that is necessary to identify (restrict the possibilities to) the particular thing that is meant. Restrictive modifiers use no commas.

A **nonrestrictive** modifier gives extra information but is *not* necessary for identification of the thing modified. Nonrestrictive modifiers are set off by commas.

The examples below include nonrestrictive and restrictive modifiers of various types. Since appositives follow the same punctuation rule, they are included as well.

Nonrestrictive adjective clause	White-water rafting, which we all enjoy greatly, is done with inflatable rubber rafts.
Restrictive adjective clause	The kind of white-water rafting that we like most uses six-person rubber rafts.
Nonrestrictive phrase	Our first guide, with enough experience to make up for our total lack of it, taught us what we needed to know about rafting.
Restrictive phrase	A guide with enough experience and skill can help novices have an exciting yet safe trip.
Nonrestrictive appositives	Inexperienced rafters, people like us, usually go on the easier section of the river, section 3.
Restrictive appositive ("close appositive")	The magazine *Whitewater* did a feature story on the challenging rapids of section 2.
Nonrestrictive adverb clause	A blue sky and the wild forest made a beautiful setting, although the rushing water was what we watched most.
Restrictive adverb clause	Sometimes we would just float along after we had come out of a set of rapids.

● **Practice 10-9** Supply commas for the non-restrictive phrases and adjective clauses.

1. Many of the old legends and myths that we have read and enjoyed since childhood are stories about giants.

2. In classical Greek mythology with all of its fictional superheroes there were giant men who eventually revolted against the gods and were destroyed.

3. The giant lumberjack Paul Bunyan who has always been a favorite American folk hero had a giant blue ox named Babe.
4. We even get the adjective *gargantuan* from *Gargantua and Pantagruel* which is a novel about two giants.

(6) Other uses of the comma

(6.1) With a series of equal elements
(6.2) With coordinate adjectives
(6.3) With direct quotations
(6.4) With the parts of a date
(6.5) With the parts of an address
(6.6) After certain parts of a letter
(6.7) With transposed words and phrases
(6.8) In place of omitted words
(6.9) With certain additions to names

Although commas are used most often to set off certain elements from the rest of the sentence, they do have other customary uses.

(6.1) With a series of equal elements A series of three or more words or groups of words of the same type, joined with a conjunction, should be punctuated as follows:

First, Second, conj. Third

First, Second, Third, conj. Fourth

The items joined might be single words or groups of words.

Marble, quartzite, and slate are metamorphic rocks.

Marble is used for statuary and monuments, for fireproof floors and walls, and for the decoration of buildings.

In some informal writing, the comma before the conjunction is omitted. However, you would be wise to make a habit of always using that comma; it is often needed and is never wrong.

(6.2) With coordinate adjectives Groups of adjectives can modify nouns in two different ways. One adjective may build on another:

a big red balloon   his new gray sweater

Here *big* tells us what kind of red balloon it is; and *new* tells us which gray sweater is meant. This is the usual situation, which does not call for any commas.

However, sometimes two adjectives have a similar meaning, so that both would not really be necessary to identify the thing described. These adjectives, called **coordinate adjectives,** modify the noun separately; we put a comma between them.

> In the lobby of an office building, marble walls can give an elegant , rich appearance.

Participles (verbal adjectives) can be coordinate in the same way:

> That store has a shining , glistening appearance.

There is a test that can help you identify coordinate adjectives: coordinate adjectives can usually have *and* put between them and still sound correct.

> an elegant **and** rich appearance = an elegant, rich appearance
> (but not "his new and gray sweater")

It is important, though, to guard against incorrect commas in the noun phrase. These are listed in **10d(7.4).**

(6.3) With direct quotations A "quotation tag" (*John said, said she,* and so on) is joined to the quoted sentence with one or two commas. One comma is used if the quotation tag comes at the beginning or at the end, and two are used if it comes in the middle of the quoted sentence.

> Young Susan asked, "What is Michelangelo famous for?"

"Well, Susan," answered her father, "the great artist Michelangelo is best known for his powerful marble statues."

"Many of his statues can still be seen in Italy today," he added.

No comma is used at the end of a quotation if a question mark or an exclamation mark is needed there instead.

"When did Michelangelo live?" she asked.

As **10i(5)** explains, commas always go *before* quotation marks:

"Well, Susan," answered her father. . . .
". . . in Italy today," he added.

Section **10d(7.5)** covers the special uses of quotations when commas should not be used.

(6.4) With the parts of a date When using the normal order of month-day-year, put a comma between the day and the year.

Michelangelo was born on March 6, 1475.

If the date does not end the sentence, put a comma also after the year.

On February 18, 1564, he died in Rome.

(6.5) With the parts of an address Use a comma between the parts of an address. Also use a comma after the last word in the address if the sentence is not yet finished.

He was born in the village of Caprese, Tuscany,
Italy, to a family from Florence, Italy.

Do not use a comma between the state and the Zip Code.

Our new address is 15 Gray Green Road,
Greenville, South Carolina 29647.

(6.6) After certain parts of a letter A comma is used after the salutation in a friendly letter.

Dear Dad,   Dear Pastor Davis,

In either a business letter or a friendly letter, a comma is used after the complimentary closing.

Love,   Sincerely yours,
Susan   Susan Smith

● **Practice 10-10** This exercise includes the six uses of the comma covered above in **10d(6.1-6.6).** Supply the commas needed in the letter below. (If you copy the letter, circle the commas you add so that you can more easily check them later.)

> 518 Windbrook Street
> Millerton Vermont 05999
> June 4 19—

Dear Sarah

Matthew Cheryl and I are still planning to come up to your house at the end of the month. All three of us look forward to the quiet calm atmosphere of the country.

When we checked with Dad about being away at the end of June, he said "I really wish I could take my vacation then!"

"To go with us?" I asked.

"No " he said "to stay home to enjoy the silence!" We all laughed.

By the way, our address is *518* Windbrook Street Millerton Vermont not 815. However, our town is so small that the address hardly matters; we got your note anyway.

We can't wait to see you your family and (of course) the horses!

> Sincerely yours
> Kathy

(6.7) With transposed words and phrases A comma can signal that words or phrases are out of the normal order. For instance, a direct object might be put first in a sentence for special emphasis.

> The big red motorcycle, he really liked.

This is similar to the comma that signals that a person's last name is given first.

> Stapleton, Albert C.

(6.8) In place of omitted words A comma can show the omission of what would otherwise be a repeated word in a parallel construction.

> Brent collects stamps and old postcards; his brother, autographs of famous preachers.

(6.9) With certain additions to names Use a comma between a personal name and a following abbreviated degree or the abbreviations *Jr.* or *Sr.* Do not use a comma before numerals that follow any kind of name.

Janice Jackson, M.A.	Arthur Lane IV, Ph.D.
Harold B. Jackson, Jr.	*Pioneer 10*
Harold Jackson III	Psalm 100

(7) Incorrect commas

(7.1) Before a conjunction that joins only two elements
(7.2) Between a subject and a verb
(7.3) After a conjunction
(7.4) In most positions in the simple noun phrase
(7.5) With quotations used in certain ways

Commas in the wrong places can be distracting and even confusing.

(7.1) Before a conjunction that joins only two elements Normally no comma should be used when only two words, phrases, or dependent clauses are joined by a conjunction.

Wrong	Tammy ⸒ and her sister are in the yard.
Right	Tammy and her sister are in the yard.

In section **10c(1)** you learned to use a comma before a conjunction that joins two *independent clauses;* notice that the present rule deals instead with joining two *words* or *phrases* or *dependent clauses.*

The rule in **10c(1):**

$$\boxed{\text{Independent Clause}} \text{ , conj. } \boxed{\text{Independent Clause}}$$

The present rule:

$$\boxed{\text{Other Element}} \text{ conj. } \boxed{\text{Other Element}}$$

See **8a(5.3)** for a correct example of dependent clauses joined by a coordinating conjunction.

(7.2) Between a subject and a verb Do not put a comma between a subject and a verb.

	S Verb
Wrong	Anyone ⸒ really should know better than that.
	S Verb
Right	Anyone really should know better than that.

However, a *pair* of commas (not just one) may set off an item between the subject and the verb.

	S
Right	Absolutely anyone, it seems,
	Verb
	should know better than that.

Do not try to use a comma to salvage a sentence that has an awkwardly long subject. Revise the sentence instead.

334

Awkward	Checking with the Sunday School superintendent before you moved the tables was wise.
Better	It was wise of you to check with the Sunday School superintendent before you moved the tables.

(7.3) After a conjunction A comma should not ordinarily follow a conjunction.

	Conj
Wrong	We wanted to do the right thing, and ⸴ we thought we knew how to do it.

	Conj
Right	We wanted to do the right thing, and we thought we knew how to do it.

Of course, a *pair* of commas may set off an item after a conjunction as well as anywhere else.

	Conj
Right	We wanted to do the right thing; and, surprisingly, we thought we knew how to do it.

(Here the comma before *and* has become a semicolon because other commas are used in this compound sentence.)

(7.4) In most positions in the simple noun phrase For present purposes we will define the simple noun phrase as a phrase that begins with at least one determiner and ends with a noun; between these it may contain other modifiers (adjectives, one-word participles, and modifying nouns). As explained in **10d(6.2),** a comma is used with coordinate adjectives (or coordinate participles). Otherwise, a comma should not be used in a simple noun phrase.

You can eliminate most incorrect commas in the noun phrase if you can recognize determiners, adjectives, and modifying nouns.

Do *not* use a comma in any of the following positions:

	Wrong	Right
Between the noun and its modifiers	a big ,tree	a big tree
Before a modifying noun	ModN a tall ,stone wall	a tall stone wall
After a determiner	Det Det the ,first ,white house	the first white house
After an adjective that modifies the *combined* following words	Adj the best ,social system	the best social system

● **Practice 10-11** All but one of the following sentences have an incorrect comma. Find the commas that need to be removed, and tell why each one is wrong.
   1. "It's never right to do wrong, even to get a chance to do right," as the evangelist stressed.
   2. Not even the best, reasons can make sin all right.
   3. God usually tells us what to do, and how to do it.
   4. No one, ever found lasting happiness by looking for it.
   5. We stumble over true happiness, and contentment on the path of duty.
   6. We do what's right, and, then we know God's peace and joy.

(7.5) With quotations used in certain ways When a quotation functions as either the subject or the predicate noun of the sentence, it should not be set off by commas.

Subject	"Trust God and work hard" was his motto.
Predicate noun	His motto was "Trust God and work hard."

Like other restrictive appositives, a quoted restrictive appositive is not set off by commas. (See **10d(5)** for restrictive appositives.)

Restrictive appositive	His motto "Trust God and work hard" carried him through the hard times successfully.

10e The Dash

(1) Interrupting phrase or clause
(2) Emphasis
(3) Interrupted speech
(4) Internal appositive series
(5) Summarizing statement after an introductory list

The dash—a rather informal mark—is used mainly for interrupting elements, for emphasis, and for abrupt changes in thought. It should be used sparingly. In appearance a dash is about twice as long as a hyphen, such as the hyphen in *two-thirds*. It is typed as an unspaced pair of hyphens--like this.

(1) Interrupting phrase or clause
An interrupting phrase or clause is commonly set off by a pair of dashes.

> John Derham was one of the many Black Americans—and, indeed, there were many—who made positive contributions to our society.

However, interrupting elements of this type should not be overused.

See **10f(3)** for the different uses of commas, dashes, and parentheses for setting off material within the sentence.

(2) Emphasis

A dash can be used occasionally to give special emphasis to a phrase or a clause. Often this phrase or clause appears at the end of a sentence.

Normal Punctuation	Derham was a slave in eighteenth-century America, when slavery was on the increase.
Emphatic	Derham was a slave in eighteenth-century America—when slavery was on the increase.
	Derham was an American slave in the eighteenth century—a century of increasing slavery.

Such emphasis can be very effective if it is not attempted too often.

Elements within the sentence may also be emphasized by the use of dashes. Notice that the interrupting element given in the preceding section (*—and, indeed, there were many—*) was somewhat emphasized by the dashes around it. Similarly, the appositive in the first sentence of **10e** was emphasized by the use of dashes rather than commas.

- **Practice 10-12** Although in actual writing you would not use dashes in two sentences in a row, in this exercise you are to supply dashes in all three sentences. One dash will simply give emphasis, and the others will set off interrupting elements.

1. Derham was owned at various times by different medical doctors a situation he used to his advantage.
2. His last owner his name has been forgotten allowed him to purchase his freedom.
3. Shortly afterwards John Derham and this is important became America's first Black doctor.

(3) Interrupted speech

The dash is used to show various kinds of interruption in speech.

Faltering speech	"But he—he wasn't the one who told me." "Then I went to get the—uh— capacitor at the parts department."
Abrupt breaking off of a sentence	"But I thought—" Sandra interrupted.
Abrupt change in thought	"Well, you see, he first—oh, I can't explain it."

● **Practice 10-13** Copy the sentences, supplying dashes where they are needed to show interrupted speech. One comma should also be added.

1. "But you you really should pay attention to where your horse is going," Sue yelled into the wind.
2. "I can't I can't hear you. What did you say?" he called back, turning his mount down a forest trail.
3. "Look out for the oh no look out for that branch, Ron!" she shouted.
4. "What? Look at the ranch? I don't see a ."

(4) Internal appositive series

Normally an appositive is set off by commas, as in **10d(4.1)**. Sometimes, however, the appositive is a series of items. Because commas are required within a series of three or more items, something stronger than commas is needed to set off the whole appositive clearly. In that case, a pair of dashes is used.

I need to cut up three more fruits—peaches, green grapes, and bananas—before I can finish the salad.

(5) Summarizing statement after an introductory list

If a sentence begins with a list and then continues with a grammatically-complete summary statement, a dash is used to connect the two parts.

Peaches, green grapes, and bananas—these were all I needed to complete the salad.

- **Practice 10-14** Copy the sentences, supplying dashes where they are needed for any reason.
  1. The handsome new science teacher and believe me, the number of coeds taking biology had greatly increased was a strong believer in lab work.
  2. "Today," he began, "we are going to begin dissecting and is something wrong, Sharon?"
  3. "Okay. Pigs, cats, and frogs these are the three types of animals we will be dissecting in the lab."

4. "Dissecting these animals this will be one of our most important experiments will teach us much about the marvelous structure and workings of the body. Let's begin, shall we?"
5. The three students who turned green the boys' basketball star, the soccer goalie, and Sharon were all quickly excused from the lab.

10f Parentheses

(1) Supplementary elements
(2) Placement of other punctuation with parentheses
(3) Comparison of parentheses with pairs of commas and dashes
(4) Numbers or letters that identify divisions within a sentence

Parentheses are used to enclose extra information, information that is clearly less important than the rest of the sentence. Parentheses (singular, *parenthesis*) are always used in pairs, regardless of whether the extra information comes in the middle or at the end of the sentence.

(1) Supplementary elements

Parentheses are most often used to enclose words, phrases, or clauses that give additional, often explanatory information.

Our next meeting (the annual election of officers) will be held on March 19.

Next month's meeting has been postponed for one week (see enclosed schedule).

Sometimes an entire sentence appears within parentheses.

Next month's meeting has been postponed for one week. (The enclosed schedule gives the dates of our next six meetings.)

(2) Placement of other punctuation with parentheses

Notice the examples just above. When an entire sentence is parenthesized, the end punctuation comes before the final parenthesis. Otherwise, **sentence punctuation stays on the outside of the parentheses.**

The only partial exception is that a question mark or an exclamation mark would go inside if the parenthetical material itself is a question or an exclamation.

Terry, I hear that our next meeting (can you come?) will be on March 19.

Because a parenthesized Bible reference in a paragraph is considered part of the sentence to which it refers, it follows the general rule.

The passage begins by commanding, "Let every soul be subject unto the higher powers" (Rom. 13:1).

The appropriate sentence punctuation goes after the final parenthesis, not at the end of the quotation. Of course, if the quotation is itself a question or an exclamation, it is punctuated appropriately:

Jesus asked John's two disciples, "What seek ye?" (John 1:38).

(3) Comparison of parentheses with pairs of commas and dashes

Pairs of commas, dashes, and parentheses can all be used to set off extra information in the sentence:

1. **Commas** are the normal, neutral punctuation for setting off short phrases or clauses.
   The first step toward clear writing, as I told you yesterday, is clear thinking.
2. **Dashes** make the enclosed material appear important. They also tend to be less formal.
   The first step toward clear writing—as I told you yesterday—is clear thinking.

3. **Parentheses** indicate that the enclosed material is rather unimportant.

> The first step toward clear writing (as I told you yesterday) is clear thinking.

(4) Numbers or letters that identify divisions within a sentence

Parentheses enclose numbers or letters used as in the following sentences:

> In order to participate, you will need to bring (1) a pen or a pencil, (2) several sheets of notebook paper, and (3) the ten-dollar fee in cash.

> The writing contest included three categories: (a) short story; (b) personal essay, editorial, or letter to the editor; and (c) short poetry.

● **Practice 10-15** Insert parentheses where they are needed.
1. The American poet Robert Frost 1874-1963 read two of his poems at the inauguration of President Kennedy in 1961.
2. Although more will be said about the dinosaur see below, we must now focus our attention on the duckbilled platypus.
3. According to Senator Strom Thurmond South Carolina, the announcement was to be made at a news conference.
4. Sodium chloride NaCl is the chemical name for common salt.
5. You have a choice of 1 Algebra II first hour or 2 American History or Personal Typing third hour.

10g The Colon

(1) In Bible references and expressions of time
(2) After the salutation of a business letter
(3) Before a series at the end of a sentence
(4) Before a long or formal direct quotation
(5) Between the title and the subtitle of a book
(6) In certain compound sentences

The colon is a strong mark of punctuation, separating elements almost as definitely as the period. The colon often points up what follows it, marking it as being important, explanatory, or more specific. Two blank spaces should be left after any typed colon that is used as in **10g(2-4, 6).**

(1) In Bible references and expressions of time

An unspaced colon separates the chapter and the verse in Bible references.

> I Corinthians 10:13   Joshua 1:8-9

An unspaced colon also separates the hour and the minute in expressions of time.

> 7:30 a.m. (*or* 7:30 A.M.)

(2) After the salutation of a business letter

A colon follows the salutation of a business letter.

> Dear Sir: Dear Senator Smith:

(3) Before a series at the end of a sentence

A colon can introduce a series that comes at the end of a sentence. Often *the following* or *as follows* appears somewhere before the colon, as in the second example below.

> There are three main types of rocks: igneous, sedimentary, and metamorphic.

> Crystals can easily be seen in the following
> igneous rocks: granite, gabbro, and syenite.

A colon can introduce such a series *only* if the series
is not part of the basic structure of the sentence. That
is, we do not put a colon before a direct object, an
object of a preposition, a predicate adjective, or a
predicate noun.

Wrong	OP Crystals can be seen in: granite, OP OP gabbro, and syenite.
Right	OP OP Crystals can be seen in granite, gabbro, OP and syenite. Crystals can be seen in certain igneous OP rocks: granite, gabbro, and syenite.

Similarly, for emphasis, a colon can introduce a single
appositive at the end of a sentence.

> He has one dominant trait: honesty.

(4) Before a long or formal direct quotation

A colon is often used before a long or formal direct
quotation, especially if the introduction to it is rather
formal.

> Assistant Secretary of War Charles A. Dana made
> the following personal observation of President
> Lincoln: "He was calm, equable, uncomplaining.
> In the discussion of important questions, whatever
> he said showed the profoundest thought, even
> when he was joking. He seemed to see every side
> of every question."

The quotation after the colon must be last in the sentence,
as it is in this example.

● **Practice 10-16** Supply the colons needed in the following set of sentences. Write *C* if a sentence is correct.

1. In Proverbs 31 we read about the characteristics of a virtuous woman.
2. She is good to her family, and according to Proverbs 31 20 she is kind to the poor "She stretcheth out her hand to the poor; yea, she reacheth forth her hands to the needy."
3. My mother gets up at 5 30 to start her day's activities.
4. By the time we leave for school at ten after seven, Mother has already done five things read her Bible, prayed, prepared breakfast, packed our lunches, and made sure we were dressed on time.
5. My mother truly obeys God's counsel to women in Titus 2 4 to "love their children."

(5) Between the title and the subtitle of a book

A book's subtitle appears on the title page below the title; usually it is unpunctuated. However, when you refer to the book by both its title and its subtitle, you should supply a colon between the two parts.

> He bought a copy of Joseph M. Williams' recent book, *Style: Ten Lessons in Clarity & Grace.*

The colon is also used for this purpose in reference notes and in bibliographies. (In a typed paper, only one space is needed after it, rather than the usual two.)

(6) In certain compound sentences

A colon can be used between two independent clauses when the second explains, expands, or illustrates the point made in the first.

> Charles Dana said that President Lincoln was a calm person: Lincoln never seemed impatient or hurried, and "he never tried to hurry anybody else."

Another example and a practice exercise appear in **10c(4).**

10h The Semicolon

(1) Between two independent clauses
(2) Before the conjunction in a long compound sentence
(3) Between word groups containing commas
(4) Used incorrectly

The semicolon signals a more important break in the sentence than does the comma. Though the semicolon has several uses, it always joins equal elements.

A fairly strong mark of punctuation, the semicolon should not be overused.

(1) Between two independent clauses

As **10c(2-3)** explains more fully, two closely related independent clauses may be connected by a semicolon.

> The Romance languages developed from Latin. Latin, of course, was the language of Rome; thus, we call these languages *Romance* languages.

There may or may not be a transitional word like *thus* or *therefore* within the second independent clause.

(2) Before the conjunction in a long compound sentence

Usually a compound sentence has a comma before the coordinating conjunction. However, a semicolon is often substituted for that comma when the sentence contains other commas.

> Nearly everyone knows that Spanish, French, and Italian are Romance languages; but not many know that Rumanian is also a Romance language.

(3) Between word groups containing commas

Because it is a stronger mark of punctuation than the comma, the semicolon is used to separate word groups in a series when any of the word groups contain internal commas. However, the series must be at the end of the sentence.

> Sitting on the platform were the new mayor, Robert D. Workman; the chairman of City Council, David Eaves; and the three new members of City Council.

Even if a list does not have internal commas, it may still have semicolons if (1) the whole list is introduced by a colon and (2) the items on the list are somewhat long:

> On the platform were the following officials: Mayor Robert D. Workman; City Council Chairman David Eaves; and the three new members of City Council.

Semicolons also separate references when any of the references contain commas or other punctuation.

> Genesis 10:5, 18, 25; 11:1-9

Because of the colon ("other punctuation") in Bible references, a semicolon is generally used whenever a new chapter is mentioned (Ps. 4:5; 47:6; 40:6; 51:17).

- **Practice 10-17** In most of the sentences below, at least one comma is incorrectly used. Find these commas and replace them with semicolons. Write *C* for a correct sentence.
  1. Jesus called twelve men to be his disciples, these men came from varied backgrounds and occupations.
  2. Many were fishermen, such as Peter, Andrew, James, and John, and Matthew, the Levite, was a tax collector.
  3. We remember Thomas because of the times he questioned Jesus, consequently, he is often referred to as Doubting Thomas (John 11:16, 14:5, 20:25).
  4. The most infamous was Judas Iscariot, for he was the one who betrayed Jesus.

5. The others are not as familiar to us: Nathaniel, sometimes called Bartholomew, Philip, friend of Peter and Andrew, Simon Zelotes, Jude, and James, son of Alphaeus.

(4) Used incorrectly

The correct uses of the semicolon are given in the three sections above. When a semicolon is used incorrectly, the result is almost always a semicolon fragment. See **13a(3)** for this problem and its solution.

10i Quotation Marks, Ellipses, and Brackets

(1) Quotations
(2) Titles of short works
(3) Words used in a special sense
(4) Single quotation marks
(5) Other punctuation in combination with quotation marks
(6) Ellipses
(7) Brackets

Quotation marks have two main uses: to enclose direct quotations and to indicate the titles of shorter works. Quotation marks are always used in pairs. The correct use or omission of commas with quoted material is covered in **10d(6.3)** and **10d(7.5).**

Ellipses and brackets are used mainly in direct quotations—ellipses to mark an omission, and brackets to mark an insertion.

(1) Quotations

(1.1) Indicating direct quotations
(1.2) Paragraphing dialogue
(1.3) Writing indirect quotations

(1.1) Indicating direct quotations Quotation marks indicate that the exact words of a writer or speaker are being reported.*

"Have you seen my new books?" asked Mark.

Sometimes the quotation tag (such as *he said*) comes in the middle of the quoted sentence. In that case commas surround the quotation tag, and both halves of the divided quotation are enclosed in quotation marks.

"If you just got them," Dale replied, "probably I haven't seen them yet."

(In American usage, commas and periods always come before quotation marks.)

(1.2) Paragraphing dialogue In reporting dialogue, we normally begin a new paragraph every time a new person speaks. (We can therefore sometimes leave out the quotation tag: often the reader already knows who is speaking.)

"I bought these three old books at that garage sale," Mark explained to Dale. "The man who had the sale used to be a lawyer."
"Let me see the third book, Mark. Did you get a bargain?"

In this example, a period is used after the quotation tag *(Mark explained to Dale)* because the preceding quotation is a complete sentence.

---

* There are two common exceptions to the usual need for quotation marks around someone's exact words. (1) Quotation marks are not used within a play for the speeches of the dramatic characters. (2) They are often not used for well-known proverbs (including certain biblical sayings): *She remembered too late that a stitch in time saves nine.*

(1.3) Writing indirect quotations An indirect quotation gives the idea but not the exact words of the speaker or writer. Indirect quotations should not have quotation marks.

| Direct quotation | Mark said, "I paid a quarter apiece for the books." |
| Indirect quotation | Mark said **that he** paid a quarter apiece for the books. |

- **Practice 10-18** Supply the needed quotation marks, remembering to place them after periods and commas.
  1. A neighbor told us that something was happening at the city wall.
  2. There is nothing more thrilling to me than sitting on a wall, declared Humpty.
  3. It gives me a feeling of superiority, he said proudly.
  4. When I'm up here, he continued, everyone has to look up to me.
  5. It appears that we will have scrambled eggs for supper tonight, said one of the king's men.
  6. It is always true, added another gravely, that pride goes before a fall.

(2) Titles of short works

Titles of short works are normally enclosed in quotation marks. A piece of writing is considered a short work if it is part of a larger work or is too short to be a book by itself. Short works include articles, chapters of a book, short stories, essays, songs, and most poems. Quotation marks are also usually used for the titles of radio or television programs.

One of Mark's new books included a chapter entitled "Where Did We Get That Phrase?" Another book was a collection of essays. The first essay, called "The Teachings of Television," was about such programs as "Father Knows Best."

An exception is that we use only capitalization—no quotation marks—with the major subdivisions of the Bible:

> For his devotions that day, he read the Twenty-fourth Psalm from the Old Testament and the sixth chapter of Ephesians from the New Testament.

Another exception is that no quotation marks are used with a title when it stands as the heading of the work itself.

● **Practice 10-19** Supply quotation marks around the titles of short works.
 1. For Monday we will read The Necklace, a short story by the French author Maupassant.
 2. The Raven and The Bells are two of Edgar Allan Poe's best-known poems.
 3. Frank Gauche's article entitled Politics as Usual presents a one-sided view.
 4. The final examination will cover all the chapters from Climates and Weather to the end of the book.

(3) Words used in a special sense

Quotation marks can be used occasionally to signal a special sense of a word. For instance, a word may be used ironically to mean its opposite.

> The "peaceful discussion" required clean-up by two squad cars and an ambulance.

The same result can be obtained by the use of *so-called*.

> The so-called peaceful discussion required clean-up by two squad cars and an ambulance.

Quotation marks may also set off a word that belongs to a noticeably different level of usage from the rest of the passage. For example, there could possibly be reason to use an exceptional slang word in a general or formal passage.

> After his study of inner-city gangs, the anthro-
> pologist returned to the "square" world with
> some new insights.

The word *square* may be appropriate here because of
the gangland subject matter, but normally a nonslang
term would be preferable.

Quotation marks should be used for special senses
very rarely: twice in two or three pages is likely to be
too many times.

(4) Single quotation marks

If you should ever have reason to use quotation marks
inside other quotation marks, the inner set would be
single quotation marks.

> One chapter was called "How to Understand
> Poems like 'The Red Wheelbarrow.'"
> He said to me, "If you keep saying 'I can't do it,'
> people may start to believe you."

(5) Other punctuation in combination with quotation marks

Three rules cover all the combinations.

1. In America, **commas and periods** always go
    before quotation marks, regardless of what
    may seem logical.
    > According to Tom, anyone over
    > twenty-five is "nearly an old man."
    > "If you think that," his older brother
    > told him, "you have a lot to learn."
2. **Colons and semicolons** always go **after** closing
    quotation marks. (Because the colon or
    semicolon is punctuation for the whole
    sentence, it stays outside the quoted item.)
    > Jesus gave great comfort along with His
    > command (in Matthew 28) to go and
    > "teach all nations": first the reminder that

He has "all power" and then the promise, "I am with you always."

    In Luke 16:15 Christ told us more than to "go . . . into all the world"; He also told us to "preach the gospel to every creature."

3. **Question marks and exclamation marks** go before or after quotation marks, **according to the meaning** of the sentence. The whole sentence may be a question:

    Have you read the poem called "The Old Men Admiring Themselves in the Water"?

Or the title may be a question:

    We listened to someone recite the poem "What Then?"

● **Practice 10-20** Copy the sentences, supplying the needed quotation marks. (Position the quotation marks correctly before or after other marks of punctuation, and remember that single quotation marks should be used inside other quoted material.)

1. Well, said Chuck, I read the chapter entitled The Language of Bees last night.
2. What did you think of it? asked Marcia.
3. I was amazed to learn that bees communicate with each other by means of various "dances."
4. What do you mean?
5. To direct other bees to some newly-discovered food, Chuck explained, a bee will perform certain patterned movements on the floor of the hive.
6. How fascinating! exclaimed Marcia.

(6) Ellipses

(6.1) Omission of words in a quotation
(6.2) Halting or unfinished speech

Ellipses (or "ellipsis marks") are three spaced dots that most often indicate the omission of something in quoted matter. The dots look like periods, but there should be a space before and after each one.

(6.1) Omission of words in a quotation

Whenever words are omitted within a sentence, a set of three spaced dots should appear wherever the word or words would have been.

Original	"For God sent not his Son into the world to condemn the world; but that the world through him might be saved" (John 3:17).
With omissions	"For God sent . . . his Son into the world . . . that the world through him might be saved" (John 3:17).

Of course, honesty requires that the omissions not distort the meaning of the original.

Within a quoted passage of two or more sentences, use a period followed by three spaced dots to show the omission of (1) the end of the preceding sentence, or (2) the beginning of the following sentence, or (3) one or more complete intervening sentences. What precedes the four dots must be a grammatically complete sentence, and what follows them must be too.

Original	"Rejoice evermore. Pray without ceasing. In every thing give thanks: for this is the will of God in Christ Jesus concerning you. Quench not the Spirit" (I Thess. 5:16-19).

With omissions	"Rejoice. . . . Pray without ceasing. . . . give thanks . . . . Quench not the Spirit" (I Thess. 5:16-19).
	"Rejoice evermore. . . . Quench not the Spirit" (I Thess. 5:16-19).

In addition, a full line of spaced dots may be used to indicate the omission of one or more lines of poetry.

Ellipsis marks are unnecessary at the beginning or end of a quoted passage.

(6.2) Halting or unfinished speech Ellipses may be used to indicate hesitant pauses in speech, and they may also show that a sentence has just slowly trailed off before completion. Inside a sentence three spaced dots are used, but at the end of the sentence a period precedes the three spaced dots.

> "Well, if you think . . . but on the other
> hand. . . ." She stopped speaking and just looked
> at them.

If instead there is an abrupt interruption or an abrupt end to the sentence, dashes are appropriate; see **10e(3)**.

(7) Brackets

(7.1) For insertions or replacements in quoted material
(7.2) In place of parentheses inside other parentheses

Brackets are not used very often, but they are necessary for an insertion into quoted material. Because most typewriters do not have brackets, they often must be drawn in by hand; parentheses are not a substitute.

(7.1) For insertions or replacements in quoted material It is important that your reader be able to tell the difference between your own words and those of the person being quoted. Therefore brackets are used for your words, whether they add to or replace some part of what was said.

Original	Racial and ethnic minority women should be assured of equality opportunities in life.

An insertion and a correction	"Racial and ethnic minority women ⌈including Hispanics⌋ should be assured of ⌈equal⌋ opportunities in life."

An alternative to correcting an obvious error (or changing what might look like an error) is to add the word *sic* in brackets. *Sic* is Latin for "thus," and it means that you have reproduced the original faithfully even though it may look strange. Because *sic* is a foreign word, you should underline it to indicate italics; see **10j(4)**.

Error noted as from the original	"Racial and ethnic minority women should be assured of equality ⌈*sic*⌋ opportunities in life."

(7.2) In place of parentheses inside other parentheses On rare occasions it is necessary to use brackets as parentheses inside other parentheses.

> Although the division of the sentence into subject and predicate is basic and widely recognized (for instance, see Randolph Quirk *et al., A Grammar of Contemporary English* ⌈London: Longman, 1972⌋, p. 34), Chauncey's curriculum guide ignores the subject entirely.

However, it is best to avoid such a situation when possible. Often the sentence can be rewritten, or the facts of publication can be given in a footnote.

- **Practice 10-21** Suppose that you want to quote parts of two verses from II Chronicles, leaving out some phrases and adding some explanatory remarks. Copy the verses, following the directions given below each one. Use ellipses and brackets as needed.

"And he said, Hearken ye, all Judah, and ye inhabitants of Jerusalem, and thou king Jehoshaphat. Thus saith the Lord unto you, Be not afraid nor dismayed by reason of this great multitude; for the battle is not yours, but God's" (II Chron. 20:15).

1. Insert the word *Jahaziel* after *he* in the first line.
2. Delete everything from *Thus saith* through *for.*

"Ye shall not need to fight in this battle: set yourselves, stand ye still, and see the salvation of the Lord with you, O Judah and Jerusalem: fear not, nor be dismayed; to morrow go out against them: for the Lord will be with you" (II Chron. 20:17).

3. Insert the explanation *against the children of Ammon and Moab* after *battle.*
4. Delete the words *fear not, nor be dismayed.*
5. Insert *sic* after *morrow.*

10j Underlining for Italics

(1) Titles of long works and works of art
(2) Individual names of certain large transport vehicles
(3) Words, letters, and numerals being discussed
(4) Foreign words and phrases
(5) Emphasis

Italic print is special print that leans to the right, *like this.* Italic print is used mainly to indicate titles of books and other long works. In handwritten or typed papers, underlining is used instead of actual italics (italic print).

Handwritten version with underlining for italics	*John Bunyan's Pilgrim's Progress is an all-time best seller.*
Published version with actual italics	John Bunyan's *Pilgrim's Progress* is an all-time best seller.

Because underlining is the handwritten or typed equivalent of italics, the correction symbol *ital* may be used to remind you to underline.

(1) Titles of long works and works of art

Underline (italicize) the title of anything that is long enough to be published by itself. This would include books, magazines, newspapers, and long poems. Also italicize the titles of plays, motion pictures, long musical works, and works of art.

> He reads the *Wall Street Journal* and *Faith for the Family.*
> The hundred-voice choir performed parts of Handel's *Messiah.*

An exception is that we refer to the Bible without using italics.

(2) Individual names of certain large transport vehicles

Underline (italicize) the names of specific ships, aircraft, trains, and spacecraft.

> The first solo flight across the Atlantic was made in 1927 by Charles Lindbergh, flying the *Spirit of St. Louis.*
> In 1961 the U.S.S. *Enterprise* became our first nuclear aircraft carrier.
> Everyone was relieved when the space shuttle *Columbia* returned safely from its maiden voyage.

(3) Words, letters, and numerals being discussed

When we talk about a word as a word, we underline (italicize) it.

> Little two-year-old Joey had a hard time pronouncing *river.*

We do the same when we talk about a letter or a numeral.

> In American use, there is just one *e* in *judgment.*
> His *7* sometimes looks like a *1,* but his *7*s and *9*s
> are clearly different.

Notice that the plural -*s* is not italicized in the last example.

- **Practice 10-22** Underline to indicate italics wherever needed.
  1. The local Morning Sun is the only newspaper published within one hundred miles.
  2. In the first sentence the word within is a preposition.
  3. In 1912 the Titanic, a huge British ocean liner, sank after striking an iceberg.
  4. Stephen Crane's second novel, The Red Badge of Courage, centers on the inner conflicts of a Union soldier during the Civil War.
  5. The American space program progressed rapidly between the suborbital flight of Freedom 7 in 1961 and the landing of the lunar module Eagle in 1969.
  6. After the space capsule splashed into the ocean, it was recovered by seamen aboard the U.S.S. Hornet.
  7. Sharon was able to complete her report with the help of an encyclopedia and the three volumes of Inside Outer Space.

(4) Foreign words and phrases

Words and phrases that are still felt to be foreign should be underlined (italicized). Some dictionaries mark foreign words and phrases in a special way, but others give no guidance. In general, if a word or phrase is in fairly common use in English, do not italicize it.

Italics not needed	His mea culpa did not sound very convincing.
	Their favorite meal was the one they ate in a small trattoria in Venice.

| Italics needed | Karl's father is a *Blumenhändler* in Berlin—a florist, that is. |
| | Your claim of *je ne sais pas* is not very convincing when you have been given the information. |

If a whole sentence in a foreign language is quoted, the sentence should be in quotation marks rather than in italics.

> Even though we thought he knew the answers, Michel kept answering, "Je ne sais pas."

(5) Emphasis

Occasionally underlining (italics) can be used to indicate special emphasis. Normally, however, it is better to obtain the emphasis by placing the important word at the end of the sentence or clause.

| Italics for emphasis | You may attend two performances without extra charge, but only according to *our* choice of times. |

| Emphasis achieved by placement | You may attend two performances without extra charge, but the choice of times will be ours. |

361

Chapter 11

Natural English Wording

11a Idiomatic use of prepositions
11b Idiomatic use of verbs
11c Idiomatic use of count and noncount nouns

A skillful writer or speaker is sensitive to language, aware of the special ways in which certain words can be used. For instance, we part *with* something when we give it away, but we part *from* someone when we leave him. Again, although we can "*hope* that Sandra will come," we cannot "*want* that she will come" but only "want her *to* come."

When words like these correctly follow the special habits of the language, we say that they are used **idiomatically.** The sections below will give some suggestions toward the idiomatic use of prepositions, verbs, and nouns.

11a Idiomatic Use of Prepositions

Many verbs and adjectives, and even some nouns, must be followed by particular prepositions. Most of these combinations, of course, we know from long observation. Some of the others can be discovered in a dictionary entry by observing the phrases that illustrate particular meanings. The reference list below includes many of the prepositional combinations that can be problems.

accuse of
adhere to
agree with (someone), to (a proposal), on (a plan)
alarmed at
angry with (someone), at (something); (*Informal:* mad at)
between (one) and (another)
capable of
compare with (something similar), to (something of a different sort)
comply with (a requirement)
concur with (someone), in (an opinion)
conform to
consist of
consistent with
contend with (someone), for (a principle)
convince (someone) of (a need or a truth)
die of *or* from (a disease), by (violence), to (self, worldly pleasures)
differ with (someone) about *or* over (something), from (something)

different from (something)
disapprove of
equal to
familiar to (someone), with (something)
find fault with
ignorant of
impatient with (someone), at (the delay), for (success)
in search of
independent of
indifferent to
infer from (evidence)
inferior to
influence of (one thing) on (another)
married to
oblivious of *or* to
part with (something), from (someone)
persuade to (do something)
prefer (this) to (that)
preferable to
prior to
refrain from
required of (someone)
responsible to (someone), for (something)
result from (a cause), in (an effect); a result of (a cause)

rewarded by (someone), for (an action), with (a good result)
similar to

succeed in
superior to
wait for (someone) at (a place), on (a customer)

11b Idiomatic Use of Verbs

(1) Transitive and intransitive verbs
(2) Verbs that require personal objects
(3) Verbs that require nouns, not clauses, as direct objects
(4) Verbs that allow gerunds, infinitives, or clauses as direct objects

Verbs should be used with appropriate constructions. Most obviously, some verbs can have direct objects and others cannot. Sometimes it also makes a difference what *kind* of direct object follows the verb.

(1) Transitive and intransitive verbs

Some verbs, normally intransitive, sound odd when they are used transitively, that is, with an object.

Unidiomatic transitive	The programer *vanished* the numbers from the screen.
Corrected	The programer *made the numbers vanish* from the screen. The programer *deleted* the numbers from the screen.

There are also verbs that are always transitive; these sound odd in an intransitive construction.

Unidiomatic intransitive	That explanation just *confuses*.
Corrected	That explanation just confuses *me*.

Unidiomatic intransitive	He tried not to *embarrass*.

Corrected	He tried not to embarrass *his friend*.

Desk dictionaries label verbs as transitive or intransitive or both. (Transitive verbs can have objects and be made passive; in a dictionary, intransitive verbs are all the others.) If a particular verb can be either transitive or intransitive, the meanings will be clearly grouped into the two categories. You can use this information to correct the kinds of problems illustrated above.

(2) Verbs that require personal objects

Certain verbs require personal objects. That is, either the direct or the indirect object must refer to a person in some way.

Unidiomatic	"It won't be hard to use," he *reassured*.

Corrected	"It won't be hard to use," he reassured *them*. "It won't be hard to use," he *said*.

Here is another example.

Unidiomatic	The computer will *enable* better inventory control.

Corrected	The computer will enable *us* to control our inventory better. The computer will *make possible* better inventory control.

As is illustrated here, corrections can be made by supplying the personal object or by replacing the verb.

(3) Verbs that require nouns, not clauses, as direct objects

There are a few verbs that can be followed by nouns or pronouns, but not directly by an object clause.

Unidiomatic	The chairman likes *that we will all help.*
Corrected	The chairman likes the *idea* that we will all help.

Now *idea* is the direct object, and the noun clause is the appositive to *idea*. The next example may be less obvious.

Unidiomatic to most people	She could not accept *that he would do that.*
Corrected	She could not accept the *idea/fact* that he would do that. She could not *believe* that he would do that.

We solve this kind of problem by supplying a noun to be the direct object or by changing the verb.

(4) Verbs that allow gerunds, infinitives, or clauses as direct objects

Relatively few verbs can have gerunds, infinitives, or noun clauses as direct objects. *Prefer* is unusual in allowing all three:

Gerund phrase as object	She prefers *driving alone.* She prefers *our following her.*

Infinitive phrase as object	She prefers *to drive alone.* She prefers *us to follow her.*

Noun clause as object	She prefers *that she would go first.* She prefers *that we (would) follow her.*

Other verbs are less flexible. For instance, *like, love,* and *hate* can be followed by gerunds or infinitives, but not clauses beginning with *that*; compare **11b(3).** *Ask* can be followed by infinitives and clauses but not gerunds. *Want* takes infinitives but not gerunds or clauses. And *declare* and *read* take clauses but not verbals.

Normally these special uses give us no problem; we learned them easily as children. Breaking one of these restrictions, though, would produce an unidiomatic sentence. The remedy is to change either the verb or the following construction.

Unidiomatic	She invited that we would ride back with her.
Corrected	She *suggested* that we ride back with her. She invited us *to* ride back with her.

11c Idiomatic Use of Count and Noncount Nouns

Section **3b(3.2)** points out that every common noun is either a count noun or a noncount noun. A count noun can be made plural and can be "counted."

	Count noun	Noncount noun
Singular	a *bean*	some *rice*
Plural	some *beans,* five *beans*	(no plural)

Notice that count and noncount nouns differ in some of the words that can modify them. Although we say "a bean" and "five beans," we do not say "a rice" or "five rices." Neither would we ask to be served "some BEAN" (with the accent on *bean,* as in "some RICE").

Special idiomatic combinations with count and noncount nouns appear below.

Singular count nouns only	each every either neither	bean, idea, senator
Plural count nouns only	many few/**fewer**/ fewest a few several a **number** of the majority of	beans, ideas, senators

Noncount nouns only	much
	little/**less**/least
	a little
	a great deal of
	a small/large
	   amount of
	a piece/grain/
	   etc. of
		rice, water,
		relief

The words and phrases given here for each type are restricted to that one type.

Notice the result of breaking these restrictions.

Unidiomatic	*A small amount of* children came, and even *less* adults.
Corrected	*A small number of* children came, and even *fewer* adults. *Few* children came, and even *fewer* adults.

The changes are necessary because the words *children* and *adults* are plural count nouns, rather than noncount nouns.

Now here is an error involving a noncount noun:

Unidiomatic | *The majority* of the water had already drained by that time.

Corrected | *Most* of the water had already drained by that time.

"The majority of" (meaning more than half of the individuals in a group) logically requires either a plural count noun like *senators* or a collective noun like *senate*. In this case, we can substitute "most of," which can be used with any type of noun.

Chapter 12

Sentence Variety in the Paragraph

12a Using variety to achieve emphasis
12b Varying the length and complexity of sentences
12c Varying the sentence patterns
12d Making good choices
12e Using uncommon types of sentences

How can you make your writing interesting? Obviously, it helps to have an interesting topic, or at least one that you can make interesting by linking it to something your audience cares about. However, your writing itself—how you express your ideas—should also help maintain the reader's interest. An important key is found in this simple formula:

$$\text{Variety} + \text{Emphasis} \quad \overset{\text{(yields)}}{\Longrightarrow} \quad \text{Interest}$$

First consider how that formula would apply to a style of speaking. A boring voice is one that is always the same. It has the same tone, the same speed, the same loudness—the same everything, on and on and on and on. Nothing seems more important than anything else, and soon to our sleepy ears nothing at all seems important.

In writing, too, variety and emphasis help to create and maintain interest. An effective writer uses a variety of sentence types, making good use of the choices open to him as he builds his sentences. At the same time, he uses those choices to give emphasis to whatever is most important.

> **Good** sentence-construction **choices**
> produce **variety** and **emphasis,**
> resulting in clear, **interesting sentences.**

Variety and emphasis are brothers, then. The present chapter deals mainly with sentence variety, but it can also help you create emphasis.

12a Using Variety to Achieve Emphasis

Four general principles will enable you to draw attention to important ideas in your sentences. The list is ordered from the least to the most powerful principle.

1. A **fuller expression** is often more noticeable, or more emphatic, than a brief one. For instance, in the third sentence of the paragraph just before section **12a,** *give emphasis to* is more noticeable than *emphasize* would be.
2. Certain **kinds of words** are stronger than others. See **9h(3.2)** for an explanation of this principle.
3. A short sentence before or after a series of longer ones can be emphatic because of the **contrast.** Unusual types of sentences can serve the same purpose; several are listed in **12e.**
4. Natural emphasis is attained by putting the important word or phrase at the **end of the sentence.** A similar result comes from putting the important item before a pause elsewhere, such as at the end of a clause or before an interrupting word. (Moving an element to the beginning of the sentence can also give a certain amount of emphasis.) See **9h(3.1)** and

the list in **9h(2)** for some ways of putting the important information at the end of the sentence or clause.

These principles, of course, are helpful only if they are not overused. It is important to emphasize only what needs pointing up, what is truly important.

12b Varying the Length and Complexity of Sentences

A skillful writer avoids both a babyish-sounding series of short sentences and a deadening series of extremely long sentences. The ideal is a comfortable mix of short, medium, and longer sentences. Typically, some of these sentences would be simple, others would be compound, and still others would be complex or compound-complex. (Section **8a(5)** reviews these types.)

Here is a paragraph that needs improvement.

> Genghis Khan was the leader of the Mongols. His name means "universal ruler." He established a vast empire. It stretched from eastern Europe to the Sea of Japan. It included parts of China and Russia. The empire's greatest accomplishment was reopening the Silk Road. Renewed trade led to an East-West cultural exchange. Marco Polo's visit was an eventual result of such action. *(eight simple sentences)*

The style is choppy, and all eight ideas are treated as if they were equally important.

Revised, the paragraph reads better.

> Genghis Khan, whose name means "universal ruler," was the leader of the Mongols. He established a vast empire that stretched from eastern Europe to the Sea of Japan, including parts of China and Russia. The empire's greatest accomplishment was reopening the Silk Road. Renewed trade led to an East-West cultural exchange, and that exchange resulted eventually in the visits of men like Marco Polo. *(four sentences: complex, complex, simple, compound)*

Because only the more important ideas appear in the independent clauses, we can follow the thinking much more easily. You may want to see for yourself just how some of the former simple sentences have been incorporated into the remaining four sentences.

● **Practice 12-1** Improve the following paragraph by combining some of the simple sentences into a variety of other sentence types.

> Genghis Khan was also a great warrior. His Mongol cavalry would quickly surround an enemy and destroy it. The Mongols used other military tactics as well. They used spies. Often they led the enemy into an ambush. This was done by pretending to retreat. They used terror. They spread tales of their viciousness. They even adopted certain methods of their enemies. Although ruthless, they were not like Hitler or Stalin. The Mongols never tried to exterminate any certain group of people.

12c Varying the Sentence Patterns

Good writing seems naturally to include a variety of the basic sentence patterns. Most of the time we need not think about this aspect of writing. Sometimes in the process of revision, though, we may realize that we have overused one or two of the sentence patterns. Then it is time to work consciously for variety.

Notice the following poor example, which uses a high proportion of intransitive verbs.

> Seventeen-year-old Marco Polo traveled from Venice, Italy, to China (s InV). He went there with his father and his uncle (s InV). Kublai Khan was desirous of one hundred Catholic missionaries from the Pope to convert the Khan's people (s LV PA). However, only two friars were willing to go and serve (s LV PA). Both deserted long before the end of the journey (s InV), but the Polo family continued on (s InV). Their journey lasted over three

years (S InV). Marco then served in the Khan's court for seventeen years (S InV). He became fluent in four languages (S LV PA). He ruled over a major city (S InV), and he went on many important missions for the Khan (S InV).

Eleven clauses: (8) S InV, (3) S LV PA

Revision produces much greater variety.

Seventeen-year-old Marco Polo traveled from Venice, Italy, to China with his father and his uncle (S InV). Kublai Khan had asked the Pope for one hundred Catholic missionaries to convert the Khan's people (S TrV DO). Only two friars, however, offered the Pope their services (S TrV IO DO), and they deserted the Polo family long before the end of the three-year journey (S TrV DO). Marco then served in the Khan's court for seventeen years (S InV). He became fluent in four languages (S LV PA). He ruled a major city (S TrV DO), and the Khan sent him on many important missions (S TrV DO).

Eight clauses: (2) S InV, (4) S TrV DO, (1) S TrV IO DO, (1) S LV PA

● **Practice 12-2** Improve the following paragraph by increasing the variety of sentence patterns.

Twenty-four years after leaving Venice, Marco Polo returned. A few years later, he went to jail in Genoa as a prisoner of war. While there, he spoke of his adventures to a fellow-prisoner, a scribe. The scribe was willing to copy them down. He wrote of Marco's adventures using the French language. Until the nineteenth century, many looked at the stories as either fiction or exaggeration. Yet, while reading a copy of Marco's book, Columbus's imagination flared. In 1492, commissioned by the queen of Spain, Columbus sailed in search of Polo's Cathay. Thus the discovery of America came about because of the friendship between a Mongolian ruler and an Italian adventurer.

12d Making Good Choices

(1) Active and passive
(2) Subject substitutes
(3) Indirect object and prepositional phrase
(4) Coordination and subordination
(5) Reduction of coordinate clauses to parallel elements
(6) Reduction of dependent clauses

In expressing our thoughts we routinely choose between certain constructions. These choices are usually automatic, but at times we may wish to think about them in order to improve a piece of writing. The kinds of choices mentioned below can be used for both variety and emphasis.

(1) Active and passive

Section **7e(3)** gives a number of suggestions about good use of the active and passive. Here we simply note two principles.

1. Although an occasional passive may be useful for variety or for some other purpose, it is best not to overuse the passive.
2. Interchanging active and passive can allow a writer to move something to the end of the sentence for emphasis.

● **Practice 12-3** The following paragraph contains a monotonous series of passive sentences. Improve the paragraph by changing passive to active where beneficial.

He was named "Dog" by his parents, who were slaves. When his people were freed from slavery, he was chosen as one of their leaders. He was sent with several others to spy out a land for conquest. The country was found to be as marvelous as they had been told by God that it would be. However, the land was occupied by giants and fierce warriors. This man and a friend were outvoted by the people, who were afraid to attack. They were threatened with execution by their countrymen, but they would not be influenced by the rebellion of God's people against His promises. The people were judged by God and were made wanderers in the desert for forty years. When the land was finally entered, this man at age eighty-five asked for permission to attack the giants. Such a test of God's promises had been his desire for forty years. Is there any doubt who won? He was identified as a man who "wholly followed the Lord God of Israel" (Josh. 14:14). More men like Caleb, God's faithful friend, are needed by Him today.

(2) Subject substitutes

The words *there* and *it* can be used as subject substitutes, mere place-holders for the real subject. The real subject then comes later in the sentence.

Normal order, subject first	S A cake is in the oven. S [That I remembered it] is fortunate.
Reversed order, with *there* or *it*	be　S　Advl *There* is a cake (in the oven). LV　PA　S *It* is fortunate [that I remembered it].

Subject substitutes (expletives) allow us to vary the emphasis of the sentence, and they also let us postpone what might otherwise be an awkwardly long subject. They are discussed further at the end of sections **5f** and **8a(3.1)**.

(3) Indirect object and prepositional phrase

Any sentence with an indirect object can instead be worded with a prepositional phrase.

With indirect object	Brad also brought his mother a dozen yellow roses.
With prepositional phrase	Brad also brought a dozen yellow roses to his mother.

The first sentence focuses on the roses, suggesting perhaps that he had already brought her something else. The second sentence draws more attention to his mother; possibly Brad had already given roses to someone else. Obviously, then, the interchange of these two constructions can allow us to bring either noun phrase to the place of focus, the end of the sentence.

● **Practice 12-4** Improve the following paragraph by creating an indirect object from one of the prepositional phrases and by beginning one of the sentences with *there* as a subject substitute. Rewrite only the two sentences most in need of change.

(1) All North American Indian tribes possessed certain religious beliefs. (2) Many ideas were common to all the tribes, regardless of their environment or customs. (3) For example, all the tribes gave homage to a medicine-man or priest, who was considered to be in close contact with the gods. (4) He also taught the myths and legends of their gods to the tribe. (5) He made amulets, or charms, for them as protection. (6) In addition, he conducted all their special ceremonies.

(4) Coordination and subordination

A pleasing paragraph normally uses both coordination and subordination, resulting in a variety of sentence structures. Of course, the main purpose of coordination and subordination is to show the relations between the ideas being expressed.

In any paragraph, some ideas are more important than others. Ideas of equal importance can be left in separate sentences, or they can be joined on an equal basis, often by a coordinating conjunction.

| Original sentences | Alexander Hamilton came to the American colonies in 1772. From 1773 to 1774 he studied at King's College, now Columbia University. |

Coordinated (compound sentence)	Alexander Hamilton came to the American colonies in 1772, *and then he studied briefly at King's College, now Columbia University.*
(compound predicate)	Alexander Hamilton came to the American colonies in 1772 *and studied briefly at King's College, now Columbia University.*

Ideas of unequal importance for the paragraph can be joined on an unequal basis:

Original sentences	By 1776 he had written several articles and pamphlets. These writings effectively supported the colonial cause.
Subordinated (dependent clause)	By 1776 he had written several articles and pamphlets *that effectively supported the colonial cause.*
(participle phrase)	By 1776 he had written several articles and pamphlets *effectively supporting the colonial cause.*
(adjective, prepositional phrase)	By 1776 he had written several *effective* articles *in support of the colonial cause.*

The choice, then, between coordination and subordination normally depends on the relative importance of the ideas. Section **9e,** especially **9e(2),** gives further information on the coordination and subordination of clauses.

- **Practice 12-5** Improve the following paragraph by good use of coordination and subordination. You may reduce some of the clauses to phrases or single words.

    Aaron Burr was a politician and adventurer. He served under George Washington during the American Revolution. A few years later he became a New York politician. He made a powerful political machine out of the Tammany Society. He used this power base to seek the presidency in 1800. He tied with Thomas Jefferson. Each received seventy-three electoral votes. A special election was held in the House of Representatives. Alexander Hamilton helped Jefferson win. Burr later fought a duel with Hamilton. He killed Hamilton. It was fought over charges made in an election campaign. Several years later Burr was tried for treason. He was accused of planning to start his own empire in the South and West. He was acquitted. He then spent five years in Europe. Finally, he returned to New York. He served as a lawyer until his death.

(5) Reduction of coordinate clauses to parallel elements

The independent clauses in a compound sentence can often be reduced to compound elements in a simpler sentence. (When the compound elements have the same form, as they should have, we say that they are **parallel.**) Reducing coordinate clauses to parallel elements allows us to say the same thing more briefly and perhaps more clearly.

Compound sentence	Among Indians north of Mexico, the Iroquois were the most advanced in political affairs, and they were also foremost militarily.
Compound (parallel) modifiers in a simple sentence	Among Indians north of Mexico, the Iroquois were the most advanced in *political and military* skills.

If, for example, we wanted more emphasis on the military aspect, we could refer to it in a separate phrase.

Parallel prepositional phrases	Among Indians north of Mexico, the Iroquois were the most advanced *in political skills* and *in military prowess.*

Section **8b(1.1)** gives additional examples of reducing compound sentences to parallel elements, and **9i(1)** presents some advantages of using parallel structures.

- **Practice 12-6** Change the following compound sentences into simpler sentences by using parallel constructions.
    1. Some Iroquois crops were planted in flood plains, some were planted in natural clearings, and others were planted in areas cleared by burning.
    2. During the colonial wars, the Iroquois Indians fought for the British twice, and they fought against the French once, and they also fought against the American colonies once.
    3. The Iroquois aided the early English settlers in their struggles for survival, and they also defended those settlers in their wars with the French.

(6) Reduction of dependent clauses

Dependent clauses can often be reduced to phrases (or even single words) that serve the same purpose.

Sentence with dependent clause	Around 1570 five Indian nations formed the Iroquois Confederacy *so that they could eliminate the constant warfare between tribes.*
Sentence with infinitive phrase	Around 1570 five Indian nations formed the Iroquois Confederacy *to eliminate the constant warfare between tribes.*

Not every clause reduces so conveniently, of course. When the reduction can be made without losing important information, the sentence gains the advantage of conciseness. However, either the rhythm or the desired emphasis of the sentence may suggest keeping the full dependent clause. Specific ways of reducing dependent clauses are found in **8b(2-4).**

● **Practice 12-7** Improve the following paragraph by reducing the italicized dependent clauses to lesser elements; make other adjustments as needed. If you need any hints, there is a list of suggested structures for these clauses after the paragraph.

By 1772 the Iroquois Indians, *who were known as the "People of the Longhouse,"* were a loose confederation of six tribes. Maize (corn), beans, and squash were the three crops on which their economy, *which was an agricultural one,* was based. Men cleared the land, but the women did everything else *that needed to be done,* such as the planting, weeding, and harvesting. The men helped to supplement the diet *when they went fishing and hunting.* In addition, *when they would gather berries, mushrooms, and maple sugar,* they added more variety to their menu.

(appositive, adjective, adjective, prepositional phrase with gerunds as objects, gerund phrase as subject)

12e Using Uncommon Types of Sentences

(1) The periodic sentence
(2) The rhetorical question
(3) The inverted sentence
(4) The short fragment

Certain unusual types of sentences can be used sparingly for effect. They obviously contribute to sentence variety, but their primary function is to provide emphasis.

(1) The periodic sentence

A periodic sentence is a fairly long sentence whose main idea is not complete until the end of the sentence. All the less important elements come earlier in the sentence. (A sentence in which some less important ideas trail after the main idea is called a *loose* sentence.)

Loose sentence	There is reason to believe that London was the most populous capital in Europe during the half century before 1685.
Periodic sentence	There is reason to believe that in 1685 London had been, during about half a century, the most populous capital in Europe. *—Thomas Macaulay*

The periodic sentence takes advantage of the natural emphasis found at the end of a sentence. However, the elaborate periodic sentence should not be overused.

● **Practice 12-8** Decide whether each of the following sentences is periodic or loose. Then change each sentence to the other type, and notice the difference in emphasis.

1. We must first admit to being sheep of His pasture in order to claim the Twenty-third Psalm as our own.
2. Sheep are always falling off ledges and placing themselves in hopeless situations because they are oblivious to the dangers around them.
3. Since "baaa" has never yet intimidated a wolf, sheep are also quite defenseless.

(2) The rhetorical question

A rhetorical question is one asked simply for effect, with no answer expected. The rhetorical question can be a means of special emphasis, as long as it is not overused.

Normal sentences	No one else should care whether we get green or gold candles for the banquet. Either color will look good.
Rhetorical question	Why should anyone care whether we get green or gold candles for the banquet? Either color will look good.

(3) The inverted sentence

Special emphasis can come from an occasional inversion of a sentence. Most common is to put the complement at the beginning of the sentence.

>Oyster stew I love.   (DO S TrV)
>A genius he is not.   (PN S LV)

Another possibility is to bring the true verb to the front of the sentence or clause, leaving the auxiliary behind.

>Trotting? That horse may have been cantering or galloping, but TROTTING she was NOT.

The effect of all such inversions is to emphasize both what is brought to the front and what comes last.

- **Practice 12-9** Revise the following paragraph by changing one sentence to a rhetorical question, and by inverting another.

>No one will care if I take another helping. It looks so delicious just sitting there all alone in the middle of that pie pan. I'll bet its feelings will be hurt if it's the only piece not taken. "Pass the lemon meringue pie, please." I am not a paragon of self-control.

(4) The short fragment

Usually we avoid writing fragments, but a rare, skillfully done short fragment can be used for emphasis. It can also express an ironic afterthought, suggesting that all is not as it seemed.

| Emphasis | A ski-jump champion needs nerve and skill. Todd is short on skill, but nerve he has. Therefore the broken leg. |
| Ironic afterthought | A ski-jump champion needs nerve and skill. Todd is short on skill, but nerve he has. Or once had. |

Even for these purposes, sentence fragments become less successful the more formal and impersonal the writing is. If you doubt the wisdom of such a fragment, either avoid it or, on a school paper, write "intentional fragment" by it in the margin. At least then the teacher will know that the fragment was not a careless error.

Chapter 13

Complete Single Sentences

13a Complete sentences
13b Single sentences

To be acceptable, a sentence needs to be **complete,** not a fragment. And it needs to be a **single** sentence, not two sentences written as if they were one.

13a Complete Sentences

(1) Fragments caused by missing elements
(2) Fragments caused by subordinating words
(3) Semicolon fragments
(4) Permissible fragments

A **fragment** is an incomplete sentence wrongly punctuated as if it were a complete sentence. In most circumstances the sentence fragment is regarded as a serious error.

(1) Fragments caused by missing elements

Except for imperative sentences (which have understood subjects), all normal sentences have both subject and verb. The absence of either subject or verb produces a fragment.

Fragment: no subject	The Maya Indians are known for their architectural accomplishments. And also are famous for their advanced mathematical ideas.
Corrected	The Maya Indians are known for their architectural accomplishments and also for their advanced mathematical ideas.
Fragment: no verb	The Maya were a tiny people. The men only about 5'1" and the women about 4'8".
Corrected	The Maya were a tiny people. The men averaged only about 5'1" and the women about 4'8".
Fragment: no (finite) verb	Their greatest empire existed from A.D. 800 to 950. The empire collapsing at that time.
Corrected	Their greatest empire existed from A.D. 800 to 950, when it suddenly collapsed.
Fragment: no subject or verb	The Maya were accomplished in several other areas. Especially in the fields of agriculture and astronomy.
Corrected	The Maya were accomplished in several other areas, especially in the fields of agriculture and astronomy.

Notice that a fragment may be corrected by joining it to the preceding sentence or by supplying the missing elements.

(2) Fragments caused by subordinating words

A sentence must be able to stand on its own; that is, it must be (or contain) an independent clause. A subordinating word turns a would-be sentence into a fragment. Examples of subordinating words are the relative pronoun *which* and the subordinating conjunction *although*.

Fragment (dependent clause)	The Maya maintained some semblance of an empire until the coming of Cortez. *Which* resulted in their final overthrow by the Spaniards.
Correction	The Maya maintained some semblance of an empire until the coming of Cortez, which resulted in their final overthrow by the Spaniards.

As can be seen here, one way to correct a dependent-clause fragment is to connect it to the related sentence. Another way is to revise the fragment so that it does not contain a subordinating word:

Alternate correction	The Maya maintained some semblance of an empire until the coming of Cortez. His arrival resulted in the final overthrow of the Maya by the Spaniards.

● **Practice 13-1** On your own paper improve the following paragraph, changing the fragments to complete sentences.

Have you ever seen a budgerigar? People like these small parakeets for a variety of reasons. Their tameness, ability to mimic, and many color variations being a few. In the wild they live in flocks of thousands. They are beautiful to behold. Generally green with yellow head, back, and wings. And also a long slender blue tail. They are native to Australia. Where they can be found nesting in hollow trees near water or feeding on the ground in the fields. Introduced to the Western world in 1840, "budgies" are a favorite pet in many American homes.

(3) Semicolon fragments

Section **13a** began by defining the fragment: "an incomplete sentence wrongly punctuated as if it were a complete sentence." With most fragments, the wrong punctuation is a period. But also a wrongly used semicolon can create a fragment, or even a pair of fragments.

The correct uses of the semicolon are given in **10h.** Most often the semicolon appears between independent clauses, with or without a conjunctive adverb in the second clause.

| Independent Clause | ; | Independent Clause |

Now suppose a semicolon is used in a way not covered by **10h.** If what precedes or follows the semicolon is not an independent clause, it is a **semicolon fragment.** A semicolon fragment must be corrected.

Semicolon fragments	Some of the Maya ; however, never did submit to the Spaniards.
Correction	Some of the Maya , however, never did submit to the Spaniards.

• **Practice 13-2** Correct the semicolon fragments, and write *C* for any correct sentences.

1. Thomas Edward Lawrence was a British archaeologist, soldier, and author; we know him best as Lawrence of Arabia.
2. During World War I he was sent to Egypt by the British; since he had already mastered the Arabic language.
3. Supposedly, he quit the British service to lead an Arab revolt against Turkey; yet he and his guerrillas continually received money and supplies from England.
4. He masterminded the guerrillas' strategy; which included hit-and-run raids and the destruction of vital railways.

5. After the revolution achieved its success; however, Lawrence returned to England to write about his escapades.

(4) Permissible fragments

Fragments are common (and acceptable) in conversation, particularly in answer to questions. Although written fragments look like mistakes, skillful authors do sometimes use a fragment effectively. See **12e(4)** for more information.

13b Single Sentences

(1) The comma splice
(2) The fused sentence

It is important that what we punctuate as a single sentence really *be* a single sentence—not two sentences masquerading as one.

(1) The comma splice

A comma splice consists of two sentences incorrectly joined by only a comma. A comma splice is a serious sentence error.

| Comma splice | Peace is not the absence of conflict, it is the ability to cope with conflict. |

There are three main ways to correct comma splices:

| Two sentences | Peace is not the absence of conflict. It is the ability to cope with conflict. |

| Coordinating conjunction | Peace is not the absence of conflict, **but** it is the ability to cope with conflict. |

| Semicolon | Peace is not the absence of conflict; it is the ability to cope with conflict. |

Sometimes another possibility is to make one of the clauses into a phrase or a dependent clause: Peace is not the absence of conflict, but the ability to cope with conflict.

● **Practice 13-3** Correct the comma splices, using a variety of methods. Write *C* for a correct sentence. These sentences deal with the terms *bulls* and *bears* as they relate to the stock market.
  1. Bulls believe that stock prices will rise, bears believe that prices will fall.
  2. Bulls act on optimism, they are always buying more stocks.
  3. A rising market is a bull market, a falling market is a bear market.
  4. Because the stock market reflects the attitude of investors, a bull market often precedes the end of a recession.

To see how conjunctive adverbs fit into the picture, study **10c(2-3).**

(2) The fused sentence

A fused sentence consists of two sentences incorrectly joined without any punctuation at all. A fused sentence is a serious sentence error.

Fused sentence	Peace is not obtained by throwing rocks at hornets such action only produces irritation.

Fused sentences are corrected in the same three main ways as comma splices:

Two sentences	Peace is not obtained by throwing rocks at hornets. Such action only produces irritation.
Coordinating conjunction	Peace is not obtained by throwing rocks at hornets, **for** such action only produces irritation.
Semicolon	Peace is not obtained by throwing rocks at hornets; such action only produces irritation.

Furthermore, sometimes one of the clauses can be made into a dependent clause: Peace is not obtained by throwing rocks at hornets, *since* such action only produces irritation.

Be very careful not to try to correct a fused sentence by inserting only a comma—the resulting comma splice would be no improvement.

- **Practice 13-4** Correct the fused sentences, using a variety of methods. Write *C* for a correct sentence.
  1. William Sydney Porter is a well-known writer of short stories you may know him only as O. Henry.
  2. He began writing fiction while in a penitentiary he had been imprisoned for embezzlement.
  3. His favorite writing technique was the surprise ending his favorite setting was the big city.
  4. He has delighted many a reader with such favorites as "The Cop and the Anthem" and "The Gift of the Magi."
  5. O. Henry was considered a recluse he avoided publicity and had no close friends.

Chapter 14
Lively Sentences

14a Verbs that act
14b Details
14c Accuracy
14d Pauses for breath
14e Figurative language

How nice it would be if all our writing were not only correct, but also interesting. Here we look at how to make a sentence come alive.

14a Verbs That Act

Action verbs are more interesting than state verbs. (For an explanation of state verbs, see the second paragraph of **7b**.) The most colorless state verb, the verb *be,* can often be replaced by a verb with more color and life.

| State verbs | The weather *had been* wet for two days. The cold, heavy rain *would* probably *last* another day at least. The storm drains *were* nearly full, and pedestrians *were* at the mercy of the splashing water from passing cars. |

| Action verbs | It *had* already *rained* for two days. The cold, heavy rain *would* probably *fall* for at least another day. Water *poured* down the storm drains, and passing cars *splashed* the pedestrians mercilessly. |

Do not feel that you must replace every state verb with an action verb, but do look critically at verbs like *be*. A sentence is often more lively with a verb that acts.

4b Details

Lively sentences give the reader the details he needs in order to imagine the situation.

| Few details | Janet waited for a bus at a drugstore. The rain let up, and she got on the bus. Her feet were cold and wet. |

| More details added | Janet took momentary shelter in the entrance to a Rexall drugstore as she waited for a bus. The rain let up just as the bus approached, but the bus stopped too far from the curb. As she stepped down into the running water, Janet wished she had not worn open-toed shoes. |

The secret to giving details is to visualize the scene or the situation completely. Then give the reader the important details that will help him visualize it too.

14c Accuracy

    (1) Accurate words
    (2) Accurate phrasing
    (3) The right connotation
    (4) Specific, concrete words

Lively writing is accurate writing—using just the right words in the right way.

(1) Accurate words

Be sure that the words you choose have the meaning you intend. If in doubt, consult your dictionary.

| Wrong word | The British took Australia from the *descendants* of today's aborigines. |
| Corrected | The British took Australia from the *ancestors* of today's aborigines. |

(2) Accurate phrasing

Sometimes a sentence misses the mark because a whole phrase is misused or misstated. Correct the phrasing and the sentence flashes home to the target.

| Inaccurate phrasing | Mr. Johnson will *open us* in prayer. |
| Corrected | Mr. Johnson will *open our meeting* in prayer. |

Here is another example.

| Inaccurate phrasing | Utterly unconcerned, Sadie said she *could care less* what we do. |
| Corrected | Utterly unconcerned, Sadie said she *could not care less* what we do. |

(3) The right connotation

Connotation, the emotional coloring of a word, can at times be as important as denotation (the word's actual meaning). For example, the phrase *my male parent* has the same meaning as *my father,* but not the same connotation. It is important to recognize differences in connotation and to use them to create the effect you want.

| Neutral (less favorable) connotation | I received a birthday card from *the preacher at my church.* |
| More favorable connotation | I received a birthday card from *my pastor.* |

Dictionaries sometimes alert users to unfavorable connotations by the use of labels such as *derogatory* or *offensive.* The kinds of synonyms given for a word can also indicate the word's connotation.

(4) Specific, concrete words

A colorless sentence may become more vivid when a specific word is substituted for a general one.

| General | As he thought about the hunt to come, Jay finished his *food* quickly. |
| More specific | As he thought about the hunt to come, Jay finished his *bacon and scrambled eggs* quickly. |

Even a statement that presents a generalization may become more interesting when specific words are used to suggest the whole category.

| General | Our treasure is in heaven, yet we all are in danger of caring too much about *material possessions.* |
| More specific | Our treasure is in heaven, yet we all are in danger of caring too much about *stylish clothing, a late-model car, or a fine home.* |

Similarly, concrete words are usually more interesting than abstract ones.

Abstract	Mr. Owings usually had good ideas, but he disliked *opposition*.
More concrete and specific	Mr. Owings usually had good ideas, but he disliked *arguments* or even *questions* about his ideas.

14d Pauses for Breath

A long, loosely strung-out sentence leaves the reader gasping for air—and perhaps wondering what the main point was. A **stringy sentence** should usually be broken into two or more sentences.

Stringy sentence	It is a good idea to be neat, and I like neatness as much as anyone, but it is just hard to remember to put things away as soon as I have finished with them, and not to leave them lying around in a handy position.
Split into three sentences	It is a good idea to be neat, and I like neatness as much as anyone. However, I have a hard time remembering to put things away as soon as I have finished with them. Too often I fall for the temptation to leave things lying around in a handy position.

4e Figurative Language

An occasional touch of metaphor can add color to your writing. For instance, let's start with the revised example above in **14d.**

Now we add a sentence to the end of it:

> Metaphor added
>
> . . . .Too often I fall for the temptation to leave things lying around in a handy position. *Then I realize I am about to drown in all those handy things.*

Section **15f** gives suggestions for the use of metaphors.

Chapter 15
Logical Sentences

Sentences can seem illogical because either the grammatical constructions or the meanings do not fit together quite right. In this chapter you will find ways to correct and improve the logic of your sentences.

15a Saying Things Directly

This section is first aid for overblown sentences. Are your sentences full of "built nouns," nouns like *persistence, discovery, investigation, separation,* and *difficulty?* (Built nouns, covered in **3b(4.2),** are nouns built from simpler words by the use of noun-forming suffixes.) Sentences that are full of built nouns need to be simplified. It often helps to look for "who did what to what."

| Overblown sentence | Mme. Curie's *discovery* of radium happened because of her *persistence* in the *investigation* of natural radioactivity. |

Who did what to what? Mme. Curie discovered radium. Here the built noun *discovery* is peeled back to its root verb, *discover.* The sentence contains two other built nouns, *persistence* and *investigation.* Find the verb in each of these and ask yourself who did the action.

| Revised sentence | Mme. Curie *discovered* radium because she *persisted* in *investigating* natural radioactivity. |

The phrase *persisted in investigating* is still a bit heavy, so we might try again.

| Alternate versions | Mme. Curie *discovered* radium because she *kept on investigating* natural radioactivity. |
| | Mme. Curie *discovered* radium because she *persistently investigated* natural radioactivity. |

When a noun is built on an adjective, try asking what that adjective describes.

| Overblown sentence | Great *difficulty* was involved in the *separation* of radium from pitchblende. |

What was *difficult?* The separation of radium from pitchblende. And what about *separation*—can we use it in the form of a verb (or verbal)?

| Revised version | *Separating* radium from pitchblende was very *difficult.* |

Of course, not every built noun needs to be peeled back. For instance, *natural radioactivity* is more concise than *substances that are naturally radioactive.* But if you have too many built nouns, you may need to ask WDWW—**Who Did What to What?**

- **Practice 15-1** Simplify the following sentences.
  1. Paul's establishment of the church at Philippi occurred because of his obedience to a vision from God.
  2. Paul's evangelization of Philippi resulted in the conversion of a Jewish merchant, a Greek slave, and a Roman jailer.
  3. A difficulty was encountered by the new church: the persecution and imprisonment of Paul and Silas.
  4. Then God's deliverance of Paul and Silas from prison became a great encouragement to the believers.

15b Saying What You Mean

It is important to say exactly what you mean. First, do your subjects and verbs work together logically?

Illogical predication	S LV PN *Using a good dictionary* can be a guide for spelling.
Corrected	S LV PN *A good dictionary* can be a guide for spelling.

The dictionary, not the using of it, is the guide.

Illogical predication	S People (who hold tickets issued by the TrV-P now-bankrupt airline) will be honored by other airlines.
Correction	S Tickets (issued by the now-bankrupt TrV-P airlines) will be honored by other airlines.

It is the tickets that will be honored, not the people.

Looking for the sentence pattern elements will help you become aware of this kind of problem.

Second, are your examples really examples?

Illogical exemplification	While the men of the tribe hunt, the women collect *food* in the area, **such as** *picking* berries or *going* to the beach and *digging* clams.
Correction	While the men of the tribe hunt, the women collect *food* in the area, **such as** the *berries* they pick or the *clams* they dig on the beach.

The phrase *such as* tells the reader that examples will follow. Therefore, in what comes next, the examples should be the main words.

Other kinds of illogical sentences are possible, of course. Correct all such sentences by looking for the main sentence elements and making them work together logically.

● **Practice 15-2** Revise the following sentences to make them say what was intended.
1. Finding a tree cavity is a good place for hornbills to build their predator-proof nests.
2. Once the female is inside the cavity, the male provides everything she needs, such as finding mud for plastering shut the opening to the nest and finding and bringing berries and fruit for her and the young to eat.
3. People who have observed the hornbills roosting in large flocks will be noisy and boisterous.

15c Saying Things Consistently

In conversation it is not uncommon to begin a sentence with one construction and then mistakenly end it with a different one. In writing, though, we want to catch that kind of problem.

Mixed constructions	In the Middle East, herding no longer has *the* important part *as* it once had.
Possible corrections	In the Middle East, herding no longer has *the* important part *that* it once had. In the Middle East, herding no longer has *as* important a part *as* it once had.

Usually there are two possible corrections for a sentence with mixed constructions. Sometimes one of the two is more formal than the other:

Mixed constructions	That is one problem *for which* we have found no answers *for*.
More formal correction	That is one problem *for which* we have found no answers.
Less formal correction	That is one problem that/which we have found no answers *for*.

● **Practice 15-3** Revise the following sentences to correct any mixed constructions that you find.
1. Participation in extracurricular activities still plays the necessary role as it always has.
2. For all those students who enjoy activities that teach something, join the drama or debate team.
3. Another activity in which a student develops character is the joys of playing sports.
4. Those who participate in extracurricular activities the events are usually educational and stimulating.
5. By making the most of every opportunity to participate in extracurricular activities will help a student to develop a well-rounded personality.
6. Extracurricular activity is one area for which we have found no substitute for.

15d Making Clear and Logical Comparisons

(1) Comparing separate things or groups
(2) Comparing things of the same type
(3) Making the second element clear
(4) Completing the construction before *or*

When two similar things are being compared with reference to some quality, the comparison should be stated in a clear and logical way. Most obviously, the comparative and superlative degrees of adjectives and adverbs must be used correctly. The comparative, of course, is for two things being compared (A is tall*er* than B), and the superlative is for three or more things being considered together at once (C is tall*est*). Further, as noted in **3d(1),** certain adjectives (like *perfect*) cannot logically be used in this way for comparisons.

(1) Comparing separate things or groups

Things to be compared must be separate. That is, one cannot be part of another.

| Faulty comparison | Our yard is bigger than any yard on our street. |

The comparison is illogically stated because "our yard" *is* one of the "yards on our street"—and a thing cannot be compared with itself.

| Correction | Our yard is bigger than any *other* yard on our street. |

The word *anyone* is often found in faulty comparisons:

| Faulty comparison | He played better than anyone on his team. |

| Correction | He played better than anyone *else* on his team. |

Did you notice?—the first version had him playing better than himself (since he obviously is on his own team). The word *else* solves the problem.

(2) Comparing things of the same type

The things to be compared must be things of the same type.

Faulty comparison	Spanish vowels are simpler than any other European language.

Spanish vowels should be compared with other vowels, not with "any other European language."

Corrections	Spanish vowels are simpler than *the vowels of* any other European language.
	Spanish vowels are simpler than *those of* any other European language.

The second correction, which has the advantage of brevity, uses *those* to stand for *the vowels.*

Comparisons using *same* or *different* also must involve things of the same type.

Faulty comparison	A young girl's role is different from any other aged woman's role.

This comparison, using *other,* is illogical because the young girl's role is not a subtype of the aged woman's role.

Possible corrections	A young girl's role is different from any other female role.
	A young girl's role is different from an aged woman's role.

The choice between these corrections would depend on what the writer wanted to say. (Notice here the correct use of *different from,* rather than *different than,* before a noun phrase.)

- **Practice 15-4** Correct the faulty comparisons, writing *C* for correct sentences.
  1. A beaver's nest is probably bigger than any nest in the animal kingdom.
  2. The bubble nest of the Siamese fighting fish is different from any other mammal's or bird's nest.
  3. The fairy tern's nest is simpler than any other nest; the tern just lays its eggs in the fork of a tree, on a branch, or on top of a rock.
  4. The junk-filled pack rat's nest is more unique than any other rodent's nest.
  5. Megapodes' nesting habits are different than the nests of other birds; megapodes rely on the heat of decaying vegetation to hatch their eggs.

(3) Making the second element clear

Sometimes the last part of a comparison can be understood from the context.

> He plays hymns more than classical music. (more than *he plays* classical music)
> She has taken more math than Mary. (than Mary *has taken*)

It is acceptable, even advisable, to leave out the part that is not needed. However, nothing should be left out that is needed for clarity.

	?
Unclear Comparison	He calls Paul as much as Nate.

Here *Nate* could be intended as either the subject or the direct object of the understood verb *calls*. The sentence should be clarified.

Possible corrections	He calls Paul as much as Nate *does*.
	He calls Paul as much as *he calls* Nate.

(4) Completing the construction before *or*

Some comparisons state that one of the things may be *either* equivalent *or* superior with regard to some quality.

In such a construction, *as* is needed after the first adjective or adverb.

Incomplete construction	My little brother plays *as well* or *better than* I do.
Corrections	My little brother plays *as well as* or *better than* I do. My little brother plays *as well as* I do or *better*.

The corrections work the same way for an adjective like *tall* as for the adverb *well*.

Incomplete construction	Probably by next year he will be *as tall* or *taller than* I.
Corrections	Probably by next year he will be *as tall as* or *taller than* I. Probably by next year he will be *as tall as* I am, or *taller*.

(Rule 9 in **4a(2.6)** explains why "taller than *I*" is correct.)

- **Practice 15-5** Correct the faulty comparisons, writing *C* for correct sentences. All the problems from **15d(1-4)** may be included.
  1. Our baseball team's catcher is better than any catcher in the league.
  2. He throws and bats as well or better than the other players on the team.
  3. A baseball catcher's leadership responsibilities are the same as the leadership responsibilities of any football quarterback.
  4. Our catcher encourages us as much as Coach Roberts.
  5. His contributions to the success of the team are greater than any player's contributions.

15e Using Noun Clauses When Needed

(1) Noun clause, not adverb clause
(2) Dependent clause, not independent clause

A sentence sounds odd when one of the words in it is used as the wrong part of speech. Similarly (but not always so obviously), an unmet need for a correct noun clause may throw a whole sentence off course.

(1) Noun clause, not adverb clause

When the sentence construction calls for a noun or a noun clause, do not substitute an adverb clause. (In standard written English, clauses that begin with subordinating conjunctions like *because, when,** and *although* are always adverb clauses.)

Adverb clause as subject	Just because you want something does not mean that you will get it.
Corrected	The fact that you want something does not mean that you will get it.

The next example is an attempt at defining a noun. The definition of any noun must be a noun phrase, a gerund, or a noun clause—not an adverb clause.

Adverb clause as PN	A success is when everyone who worked on something is happy.
Corrected	A success is the achievement of what was attempted.

(2) Dependent clause, not independent clause

Never use an independent clause as the subject of a sentence. Instead, convert the independent clause to a

---

* For *when* as an indefinite relative, see **3e(7)**.

noun clause (or to some other noun-equivalent), or revise the sentence entirely.

Independent clause as subject	I studied hard this time was the reason I passed.
Corrections	The fact that I studied hard this time was the reason I passed. I passed because I studied hard this time.

Similarly, a direct question must be changed to an indirect question if it is to be used as a noun clause. See **8a(4)** for help in changing direct quotations to indirect.

Direct question as subject	How well do they adjust is the question.
Corrections	How well they adjust is the question. More important is how well they adjust. Here is the main question: How well do they adjust?

● **Practice 15-6** All of the following sentences have errors in what should be noun clauses. Correct each sentence in the way you think best.

1. Devaluation is when a country decreases the value of its currency.
2. A country has an imbalance of trade is the usual reason it devalues its currency.
3. Because there is a tendency toward rapid inflation after devaluation is one reason economists criticize such action.
4. An underdeveloped country with the ability to increase its exports can benefit from devaluation is a reason it may make such a move.
5. How much does a country depend on imports is the critical question.

15f Keeping Your Metaphors Straight

(1) Mixed metaphors
(2) Stretched metaphors
(3) Misused dead metaphors

Clarity and vividness often increase when we describe one thing in terms of another. The general term for all such comparisons is *metaphor.* In the narrow sense, metaphors are stated or implied comparisons like the following:

Stated comparisons	"The Lord is my *rock,* and my *fortress,* and my deliverer; my God, my strength, in whom I will trust; my *buckler,* and the *horn* of my salvation, and my *high tower.*" (Ps. 18:2)
Implied comparison	"The heathen are sunk down in the pit that they made: in the net which they hid is their own foot taken." (Ps. 9:15)

Implied in the second example is a comparison of the heathen enemy to a hunter who tries to catch his prey in a pit or a net. Other comparisons, technically called similes, are made in statements with *like* or *as:*

> "But the wicked are like the troubled sea, when it cannot rest, whose waters cast up mire and dirt. There is no peace, saith my God, to the wicked." (Isa. 57:20-21)

Such comparisons show metaphor to be a valuable tool. However, this tool can easily slip in our hands.

(1) Mixed metaphors

The most obvious problem to avoid is the metaphor that points in two directions at once. For instance, here is a poor version of the preceding sentence:

Mixed metaphors	The most obvious trap to avoid is a comparison that swims both upstream and down.

Are we talking about a trap or a fish? (A trap that swims?) Here the original statement is preferable. The next example is even more ludicrous.

Mixed metaphors	When Mr. Smith was put out to pasture, he had to tighten his belt and pinch pennies.
Possible improvements	When Mr. Smith was retired, he had to tighten his belt a notch or two.
	When Mr. Smith was retired, he had to be more careful with his money.

(2) Stretched metaphors

Another problem is the overly elaborate metaphor. A metaphor that tries too hard is more of a hindrance than a help.

Stretched metaphor	The acid of bitterness can eat deep into the soul. It never etches an agreeable image on its container, but instead pits and mars it. Without the neutralizing effect of forgiveness, it only becomes more and more potent with the passage of time.

The basic comparison here is fitting, but the way it is presented turns our attention away from the subject (bitterness) and to the comparison (acid). Furthermore, the metaphor breaks down in some of its details. (Acid is used in etching, but not when it is in "its container."

And forgiveness would *replace* bitterness, not just make it weaker.)

| Simplified, improved metaphor | Bitterness always destroys its own container. The only remedy for bitterness is a forgiving spirit. |

A metaphor can be developed at greater length, but care is needed: extended metaphors are hard to write well. In a good example, like Psalm 23, the metaphor illuminates without getting in the way.

(3) Misused dead metaphors

Many of our common expressions originated as metaphors. For instance, we can *grasp* an idea, *pick up* new ideas, *hold* them in mind, and even *tear* them *apart*. We may *tear into* or *wade into* a problem without ever thinking of the picture that these words once called to mind. The metaphor, we say, is now dead. Dead metaphors are usually harmless, but sometimes they suddenly come to life and make trouble.

The most frequent problem is an unthinking use of two dead metaphors that clash. The clash often revives the original meaning, creating the mixed-metaphor problem discussed above in **15f(1)**.

| Dead metaphors mixed | He waded into the problem and tackled it at the source. (making a tackle against something that can be waded in?) |
| Corrected | He attacked the problem at its source. |

| Dead metaphors mixed | He got to the root of the problem right off the bat. (finding the root of a plant that has just been batted?) |
| Corrected | He found the root of the problem right away. |

Dead metaphors may also come to life disconcertingly when something in the context makes us think of their literal meaning.

Inappropriate dead metaphor	Before he presented his report on caterpillars, Tommy had butterflies in his stomach.

Here it would be better to say that Tommy "was nervous."

So far, dead metaphors sound like a problem, but they need not be. They can be used appropriately, and even turned to advantage.

1. Try to be aware of dead metaphors, especially when you do revisions. If one creates a problem, change it.
2. Revive a dead metaphor on purpose occasionally. For example, see the last two sentences before **15f(1).**

• **Practice 15-7** Revise any sentences that contain a clash of dead metaphors. Write *C* for a correct sentence.

1. Old Jake is finally on the wagon, walking the straight and narrow.
2. Part of a President's job is to ride shotgun on the ship of state.
3. Though Tom was dead on his feet, he still tried to fill his father's shoes.
4. You can't keep your ear to the ground if you have a chip on your shoulder.
5. His defeat was a bitter pill to swallow, but he was a good soldier through it all.

Three

Other Helps for Writing

Chapter 16
Writing Words Correctly

16a Capitalization
16b Spelling
16c Apostrophes
16d Hyphens
16e Numbers
16f Abbreviations

This chapter is all about writing words correctly. It will help you with capitalization and with spelling, including apostrophes and hyphens. It will also help you to know when to spell out numbers and when to use various abbreviations.

16a Capitalization

   (1) Proper nouns
   (2) Proper adjectives
   (3) Titles of works
   (4) First words
   (5) Parts of a letter
   (6) Personifications
   (7) Single letters as words
   (8) Epithets for proper nouns
   (9) Parts of a book
  (10) What not to capitalize

Most words that need capitalization are proper nouns, important words in titles of works, or the first words of certain units like sentences and parts of an outline.

(1) Proper nouns

(1.1) Persons
(1.2) Personal titles
(1.3) Geographical names
(1.4) Nationalities
(1.5) Organizations
(1.6) Large constructions
(1.7) Times and historical items
(1.8) Religion
(1.9) Brand names

Capitalize proper nouns, that is, specific names for particular persons, places, or things. Compare **16a(10).**

(1.1) Persons Capitalize names of persons, including titles and initials, and words for family relationships when they are used as proper nouns.

Dr. Charles **L.** Linton, **J**r.
Paul **W.** **R**obinson, **M.D.**
Does your **m**other actually think **D**ad is a lawyer?

If a word like *mother* is modified by a determiner, it is not being used as a proper noun and should not be capitalized.

(1.2) Personal titles Capitalize any title when it is used before a person's name.

I think **S**enator Jones and a few other **s**enators met with **P**rime **M**inister Thatcher during her visit.

You may also capitalize the titles of the highest officials in all countries; just be consistent in whether or not you do this.

The **P**resident entertained the **P**remier in the White House.
The **p**resident entertained the **p**remier in the White House.

(1.3) **Geographical names** Capitalize specific geographical names and names of heavenly bodies. Compare **16a(10),** Rules 4-7.

Continents and countries: **A**sia, **C**anada
States and cities: **O**hio, **A**lbany
Streets and roads: **M**arshall **A**venue, **B**lue **R**idge
Parkway
Bodies of water: **H**udson **B**ay, **M**ississippi **R**iver,
Atlantic **O**cean
Public areas: **G**reat **S**moky **M**ountains **N**ational
Park
Natural wonders: **C**arlsbad **C**averns
Sections of the country: the **M**idwest, the **S**outh
Heavenly bodies: **V**enus, the **M**ilky **W**ay, the
North **S**tar

(1.4) **Nationalities** Capitalize nationalities, races, languages, and flags.

Many **G**ermans also speak **F**rench.
Most **E**uropeans are **C**aucasian.
England's flag, the **U**nion **J**ack, once flew over a
vast empire.

(1.5) **Organizations** Capitalize the names of businesses, governmental departments, political parties, other organizations, and members of most organizations.

University of **I**owa	a **B**oy **S**cout
Library of **C**ongress	a **R**epublican
Department of	**C**ampbell **S**oup
Commerce	**C**ompany

(1.6) **Large constructions** Capitalize the names of buildings, monuments, ships, trains, aircraft, and spacecraft.

Empire **S**tate **B**uilding	the **O**rient **E**xpress
Washington **M**onument	*Spirit of St. Louis*
S.**S**. *United States*	*Apollo II*

(1.7) **Times and historical items** Capitalize calendar items, historical and special events, periods of time, historical documents, and awards.

January, Monday, Easter, 4 B.C., A.D. 1066,
World War I, Battle of the Bulge, Victorian Age,
Treaty of Versailles, Pulitzer Prize

The abbreviations *a.m.* and *p.m.* may be either capitalized or not.

10:00 **p.m.**, 10:00 **P.M.**

(1.8) Religion Capitalize certain words related to religion.

Names of religions: Islam
Words referring to the one God, but not to
mythological gods:
"Lest there should be among you [anyone]
whose heart turneth away this day from the
Lord our God, to go and serve the gods of these
nations" (Deut. 29:18).
Personal pronouns (but usually not other
pronouns) that refer to God:
Since God is our Lord, we should follow Him.
Paul preached of Christ, who had saved and
called him.
The Bible and its parts: Old Testament, Joshua.

(1.9) Brand names Capitalize brand names but not the products.

Firestone tires, Crest toothpaste, Ford automobile

(2) Proper adjectives

Capitalize most adjectives that are made from proper nouns.

the British colonies, Christian fellowship,
American liberties

(3) Titles of works

Capitalize the first and last words in a title, as well as all other important words. Do not capitalize articles, coordinating conjunctions, the *to* of the infinitive, or prepositions of fewer than five letters.

Literary works: "The Fall of the House of Usher," *The Old Man and the Sea*
Works of art: *The Last Supper*
Specific courses of study: Algebra I (*But:* She likes **a**lgebra.)

(4) First words

(4.1) Beginning a sentence
(4.2) Beginning a line of dialogue
(4.3) Beginning a line of poetry
(4.4) Beginning a topic in an outline
(4.5) Beginning a resolution
(4.6) Beginning a statement after a colon

Capitalize the first words of certain units.

(4.1) Beginning a sentence Capitalize the first word in a sentence.

Many people like "The Rime of the Ancient Mariner."

(4.2) Beginning a line of dialogue Capitalize the first word in a line of dialogue.

Joe asked, "**W**hy do you like this poem?"
"**B**ecause it's so vivid," Pam answered.

(4.3) Beginning a line of poetry Usually capitalize the first word in a line of poetry.

Water, water everywhere,
And all the boards did shrink;
Water, water everywhere,
Nor any drop to drink.

(4.4) Beginning a topic in an outline Capitalize the first word of a topic in an outline.

    I. The first campaign
       A. The battle for the delta
       B. The conquest of the seas

(4.5) Beginning a resolution Capitalize the first word of a resolution following the word *resolve* or *resolved*.

Because of the recent action of that organization, we do hereby resolve:
    That said organization can no longer participate in the activities of this council.

(4.6) Beginning a statement after a colon You may capitalize or not capitalize the first word of a formal or explanatory statement following a colon, as long as you are consistent.

The novel has a familiar theme: **M**an's faith in himself is a hopeless faith.

(5) Parts of a letter

(5.1) Salutation
(5.2) Complimentary closing

Capitalize words in certain parts of a letter.

(5.1) Salutation Capitalize the first word and all nouns in the salutation of a letter.

Dear **M**onica and **F**riends,
Dear **S**ir:

(5.2) Complimentary closing Capitalize the first word in the complimentary closing.

Sincerely yours,

(6) Personifications

Capitalize the names of things that are personified.
In the darkness, **W**inter had placed his cold hands over the window panes.

(7) Single letters as words

Capitalize the words *I* and *O*.

What if **I** come early?
We rest, **O** Lord, in Thee.

Capitalize letters used for academic grades, vitamins, musical notes, and major musical keys. Also capitalize letters used to clarify a following word.

a **B** average	**T**-square
vitamin **A**	**I**-beam
middle **C**	**V**-neck
C major	**L**-shaped

(8) Epithets for proper nouns

Capitalize epithets used with, or in place of, proper nouns.

Wild **B**ill Hickock
the **F**ather of our **C**ountry

(9) Parts of a book

Capitalize the parts of a book or other long work.

Chapter 10	Act II	Foreword
Appendix D	Index	Volume III

(10) What not to capitalize

Do not capitalize common nouns—or any other words without good cause.

Rule 1. Do not capitalize seasons, unless they are personified.

spring, **a**utumn

Rule 2. Do not capitalize names of flowers, trees, games, food, musical instruments, and so on.

rose, **o**ak, **t**ag, **p**izza, **o**boe

Rule 3. Do not capitalize types of animals and birds.

skunk, **c**ollie, **r**obin

Rule 4. Do not capitalize directions on a compass.

This road runs **e**ast and **w**est.

Rule 5. Do not capitalize a word modified by a proper adjective, unless the words together form a proper noun. See also **16a(1.9)**.

> After World War II many **B**ritish **c**olonies became independent of the **B**ritish **E**mpire.
> He bought an **A**merican **p**ainting of Shetland **p**onies grazing by an old **B**aptist **c**hurch.

Rule 6. Do not capitalize a geographical noun unless it is part of a proper noun.

> Is that **l**ake in the distance **L**ake **E**rie?

Rule 7. Do not capitalize the words *earth, sun,* and *moon* except in the phrase *planet Earth.*

> The **e**arth revolves around the **s**un.

Rule 8. Do not use capital letters for the members of an academic class.

> **f**reshmen, the **s**ophomore class

Rule 9. Do not capitalize the first word of a sentence that is in parentheses within another sentence.

> The desire to rule the world (**t**his is an age-old dream) can cause powerful men to commit horrible crimes.

16b Spelling

> (1) Ways to improve your spelling
> (2) Regular noun plurals and present third-person singular verbs
> (3) Four other spelling rules
> (4) Comparing related words

For at least two hundred years people have been judging other people's education and intelligence by the quality of their spelling. Those judgments may not be fair, but still people make them. A further problem with poor spelling is that readers often find it distracting, even confusing.

That's the bad news. The good news is that with a reasonable amount of the right kind of effort, you can conquer most—perhaps all—of your remaining problems with spelling.

(1) Ways to improve your spelling

1. **"Care enough to do your very best."** The reasons are mentioned above, and the remedies below.

2. **Look up the spelling of doubtful words.** Use your desk dictionary or one of the handy secretarial aids that lists only the words, "spelled, divided, and accented for quick reference." Every time you look up a word, put a small check mark beside it in the margin of your dictionary or secretarial wordbook.

3. **Proofread your work carefully.** See **17e** for suggestions.

4. **Keep a list (or a card file) of words that are problems for you.** A word should go on your list when you find that you have misspelled it or when you put the second check mark beside it in your dictionary or secretarial wordbook.

5. **Look for possible groupings among your problem words.** If you find a group of similar words, try to either figure out or find a rule for that group. For instance, if you have problems with *ie* and *ei,* study the rule in **16b(3.4).**

6. **Spell by syllables.** Mentally "sounding out" a long word by syllables will often help you spell correctly. Thinking about prefixes, suffixes, and other word parts can be helpful here.

un + necessary	unnecessary
under + rate	underrate
under + age	underage
mis + spell	misspell
personal + ly	personally
green + ness	greenness

7. **Study your list of problem words systematically.** Begin by writing a word several times, concentrating on its appearance and perhaps also exaggerating its pronunciation.

Repeat this procedure on three or four different days within the next week. Then, the day after your last study, have someone quiz you on that word and on any others you have been studying. If you can write the word correctly and without hesitation, transfer it to your "learned" list (or file). If a problem or a doubt remains, keep working on the word.

8. **To ensure permanent mastery, review the words on your "learned" list after about a month, and again after the second and third months.** (Keep track by putting the dates beside these words until you have three dates written there.) You can have someone quiz you each month, on the day after your review. If a problem should turn up, the word can be temporarily moved back to the problem list. The principle behind this method of study is that short periods of concentration can be effective if they are spaced out over a period of time.

(2) Regular noun plurals and present third-person singular verbs

(2.1) The general rule
(2.2) Proper nouns
(2.3) Words ending in *o*
(2.4) Compounds
(2.5) Other plurals

The plurals of regular common nouns are formed in the same way as the third-person singular forms of present-tense verbs. There are also a few minor rules for the plurals of certain types of nouns.

(2.1) The general rule Add *-es* to words ending in *ch, sh, s, x,* or *z,* if the ending makes an extra syllable.

march**es**	genius**es**	box**es**
push**es**	the Davis**es**	quizz**es**

(See **16b(3.1)** for the doubling of the final *s* or *z*. One-syllable words ending in *s,* however, may or may not double the *s: buses* and *busses* are both correct.)

Add *-es* to words whose final *y* has been changed to *i* according to **16b(3.2).** That is, "change *y* to *i* and add *es.*"

| marri**es** | deni**es** | poppi**es** | poni**es** |

Add *-s* to other words.

| look**s** | bug**s** | menu**s** | bone**s** |
| jump**s** | hybrid**s** | ski**s** | paw**s** |

(2.2) Proper nouns The plurals of proper nouns are made by adding *-s* or *-es* according to the preceding rules, but without any other spelling changes. Never use an apostrophe in making the plural of a proper name.

| two Tom**s** | two Betty**s** | the Smith**s** | the Jones**es** |

(2.3) Words ending in *o* Consult your dictionary for words ending in *o*. Musical terms are likely to require *-s* rather than *-es*.

| echo**es** | solo**s** |
| tomato**es** | photo**s** |

(2.4) Compounds Attach the suffix to the **end** of most compounds.

Nouns	*Verbs*
cease-fire**s**	babysit**s**
cupful**s**	brainwash**es**
five-year-old**s**	freeze-drie**s**
madm**en**	sidestep**s**
standby**s**	water-ski**s**

Instead, pluralize the **first** element of certain compound nouns—those in which the first element is felt to be the most important part of the compound. When in doubt, consult your dictionary.

| sister**s**-in-law | passersby |
| commander**s** in chief | poet**s** laureate |

(2.5) Other plurals Consult your dictionary for irregular noun plurals.

crisis/crises	medium/media	criterion/criteria
larva/larvae	alumnus/alumni	species/species

For the plurals of numerals, letters, and so on, see **16c(3)**.

Some of the plurals of personal titles are irregular.

General or Formal	*General or Informal*
Messrs. Smith and White	Mr. Smith and Mr. White
Mmes. Davis and Ryan	Mrs. Davis and Mrs. Ryan
Misses Diane Black and Susan Dill	Miss Diane Black and Miss Susan Dill
Drs. Poll and Truman	Dr. Poll and Dr. Truman

A plural title can be used also when the same title applies to two or more persons with the same name.

Formal	*General*
the Messrs. Smith	the Mr. Smiths
the Drs. Jones	the Dr. Joneses

The informal, general, and formal varieties of standard English are described in the table found in section **1b**.

(3) Four other spelling rules

(3.1) Doubling a final consonant
(3.2) Changing final *y* to *i*
(3.3) Dropping final silent *e*
(3.4) Spelling with *ie* or *ei*

(3.1) Doubling a final consonant Double the final consonant before adding a suffix only if **all three** of the following are true.

1. The original word has only one syllable, or has its main accent on the final syllable.   (oc**cur**)
2. The final consonant is preceded by a single vowel.   (occur)
3. The suffix begins with a vowel.   (**-ing**)

occur—occur**r**ing, occurred
wrap—wrap**p**ed, wrapper
confer—confer**r**ing, conferrer
snob—snob**b**ery, snob**b**ish

Exceptions:

1. The consonant does not double when the suffix causes the main accent to shift away from the final syllable: *conference* vs. *conferring*.
2. Final *l* sometimes doubles regardless of the location of the main accent, especially in British usage: *counselor* or (mainly British) *counsellor*. Consult your dictionary.

(3.2) Changing final *y* to *i* Change final *y* to *i* before adding a suffix if **both** of the following are true.

1. A consonant precedes the *y*. (like**l**y)
2. The suffix begins with any letter other than *i*. (-**h**ood)

poppies	likelihood	babied
dries	plentiful	sixtieth

(In the first column notice that after *y* becomes *i*, the *-es* spelling, not *-s*, is used for either the regular noun plural or the present verb suffix. "Change *y* to *i* and add *-es*.")

Exceptions:

1. Some words keep the *y: babyhood, shyness.*
2. In a few established spellings, the *y* has become *i* in spite of the preceding vowel: *daily, paid.*

(3.3) Dropping final silent *e* Drop the final silent *e* before adding a suffix if **both** of the following are true.

1. A consonant precedes the silent *e*. (name)

2. The suffix begins with a vowel.   (**-i**ng)

    name**—**naming (*but* nameless)
    lik**e—**likable (*but* lik**e**ly)

Exceptions:

1. The *e* is kept to signal the "soft" pronunciation of *c* or *g* before a suffix beginning with *a* or *o: noticeable, courageous.*
2. A word ending in *ue* normally drops the *e* even when the suffix begins with a consonant: *truly, argument.*
3. Words ending in *dge* lose their *e* (in American English) before *-ment: judgment, acknowledgment.*
4. A few other words are exceptional, some of them to distinguish homonyms: *awful, mileage, dyeing* (vs. *dying* from *die*), *singeing* (vs. *singing*).

    (3.4) Spelling with *ie* or *ei* Several words with *ie* or *ei* cannot be covered by any simple rule; check these words in your dictionary. The three principles below, however, cover most *ie/ei* words.

1. When the sound is "long *e*"—
    Put *i* before *e*—
        believe, chief, shield, niece, wield
    Except after *c*—
        receive, ceiling, deceive, receipt
    Exceptions: *caffeine, leisure, protein, seize, weird, financier. Either* and *neither,* in their more common American pronunciation, are also exceptions to this rule.

2. When the sound is "long *a*"—
    Spell *e* before *i*—
        eight, freight, neighbor, vein, weigh

3. When the two vowels are pronounced separately, spell according to the pronunciation of the first vowel.

atheist	variety	quiet
deist	science	proprietor

(4) Comparing related words

Often the sound of a related word can be a clue to the spelling of an unclear vowel.

Unclear Vowel	Clue Word	Unclear Vowel	Clue Word
president	presidential	grammar	grammatical
occupant	occupation	heresy	heretical
specify	specific	similar	similarity
exhibit	exhibition	rapid	rapidity
observatory	observation	repetition	repetitive
transitive	transition		

However, some related words are spelled differently. Correct pronunciation helps with the spelling of many of these.

pronounce	pronunciation	proclaim	proclamation
similar	simulate	space	spatial
example	exemplify		

16c Apostrophes

(1) Contractions
(2) Possessives
(3) Special plurals
(4) Omission of figures

Apostrophes were once used in English only to indicate that one or more letters had been omitted from a word. Today they are used mainly with contractions and possessives.

(1) Contractions

The apostrophe replaces missing letters in contractions. It appears at the spot where the missing letter or letters would have been.

don't	I'm	let's
aren't	it's	o'clock
can't	she'll	ma'am
won't	they've	man-o'-war bird

Any noun or pronoun subject can form a contraction with an appropriate form of *be, have, will,* or *would.*

> Tom's coming in, and someone's apparently told him.
> It's Mary who'll have the best answer.

The contraction *it's* (for *it is* or *it has*) should not be confused with the possessive *its.*

(2) Possessives

(2.1) Forming the possessive of nouns and indefinite pronouns
(2.2) Joint and separate possession

(2.1) Forming the possessive of nouns and indefinite pronouns Nouns and many indefinite pronouns can be made possessive by the addition of *-'s* or sometimes just the apostrophe. (See **4a(2.4)** for the possessive of personal pronouns.)

1. For **most singular nouns or indefinite pronouns,** add *-'s* for the possessive.

   > Joe's aunt
   > an hour's trip
   > someone's book
   > your son's hat
   > a dollar's worth
   > his son-in-law's job

2. For the possessive of **singular nouns that end in s,** some variation is possible. Add *-'s* to a particular word if you would pronounce the possessive suffix as a separate syllable. Use

just the apostrophe otherwise. (Though this rule allows you some choice, you should be consistent within a single piece of writing.)

> John Keats' poems *or* John Keats's poems
> the waitress's help
> in Jesus' name (*or possibly* in Jesus's name)
> for conscience' sake

In the last example, there were two *s* sounds already, because of *s*ake.

3. For **regular plural nouns,** make the possessive by adding just an apostrophe to the end of the plural word.

> her in-laws' house
> two days' rest
> the Smiths' car (owned by the Smiths)
> three dollars' worth

4. For **plural nouns not ending in *s*,** add -'s for the possessive.

> your children's toys
> his two sons-in-law's houses
> the policemen's actions

(2.2) Joint and separate possession When two or more persons possess something together, the possession is expressed just once, at the end of the series.

> Sam and June's house is light yellow with tan shutters.

When the possession is separate, each noun or pronoun should be possessive.

> Sam's and June's ideas are sometimes very different.

(3) Special plurals

(3.1) Plurals of letters being discussed
(3.2) Plurals of words being discussed
(3.3) Plurals of numbers

For the sake of clarity, an apostrophe is often used to make certain special plurals, mostly plurals of items being discussed. The italic print (or underlining) used for the items being discussed does not extend to the plural suffix.

Do not use an apostrophe for the plurals of proper nouns or with other types of nouns not mentioned here.

(3.1) Plurals of letters being discussed Use -'s to indicate the plural of a lower-case letter being discussed.

the *b*'s   *typed:* the b's

Use -'s for the plural of capital letters if omission of the apostrophe might cause confusion with a word ending in *s*.

two *A*'s

When no confusion would result, use -*s* alone for the plurals of capital letters and abbreviations made of capital letters. (It is also acceptable, but less usual today, to use -'s for these.)

the three Rs   their IQs

(3.2) Plurals of words being discussed Use -'s for the plural of a word being discussed. (It is also acceptable to use -*s* alone, as long as no confusion would result.)

too many *very*'s

(3.3) Plurals of numbers Use -*s* alone for the plural of a number that is expressed in figures. (It is also acceptable, but less usual today, to use -'s.)

the 1920s   your 7s

Never use an apostrophe for a number that is spelled out.

(4) Omission of figures

In informal writing, an apostrophe may be used to replace the first two figures for a year.

the '74 recession   the class of '89

In less informal contexts, no figures should be omitted.

> the 1974 recession   the class of 1989

16d Hyphens

(1) Omission of connecting word
(2) Word division at the end of a line
(3) Numbers and fractions
(4) Prefixes
(5) Compounds
(6) Multiword modifiers as temporary compounds
(7) Hyphenated words with a common element

The hyphen, about half as long as the dash, is used to join the parts of words, or sometimes to join separate words together.

(1) Omission of connecting word

A hyphen can be used in place of a single connecting word, especially between figures.

> Romans 12:1-2   June 5-9   the Rome-Paris Express

A hyphen can replace a single connecting word, but it cannot be used when there is a *pair* of connecting words, such as *from* and *to* or *between* and *and*.

> He traveled from Rome to Paris, between June 5 and June 9.

(2) Word division at the end of a line

When necessary, use a hyphen to divide a word at the end of a line. The hyphen, of course, goes at the end of a line, not at the beginning of the next line.

A word to be divided must contain at least two actual (pronounced) syllables, but the accepted places for dividing the written word may not exactly follow the division between pronounced syllables. Consult the main dictionary entry to see the places where any specific word can be divided. You may divide the word at any of those spots as long as the following two rules are not violated:

1. At least two letters and the hyphen must remain on the first line.
2. At least three letters must appear on the second line.

> . . . . . in-
> put . . . . .

If you cannot satisfy these requirements, do not divide the word. For example, *ocean* (**o • cean**) should be carried entire to the next line.

(3) Numbers and fractions

When you spell out the multiword numbers from twenty-one through ninety-nine, use a hyphen between the parts. Also hyphenate these numbers when they are part of larger numbers spelled out, as on a check.

> *One hundred twenty-nine and no/100*   dollars

Use a hyphen between the numerator and the denominator of a spelled-out fraction, unless either of these already contains a hyphen.

>   two-thirds   forty-two hundredths
>
>   four and one-half

(4) Prefixes

(4.1) Prefixes that require hyphens
(4.2) Prefixes before figures and proper names
(4.3) Prefixes hyphenated to differentiate words
(4.4) Prefixes before the same vowels

(4.1) Prefixes that require hyphens Some prefixes are always hyphenated: *all-, ex-* (meaning "formerly"), *half-,* and *self-.*

>   all-inclusive   ex-waitress   self-evident

Certain other prefixes, like *non-* and *anti-,* are hyphenated by some publishers but not by others. Both styles are permissible, but the trend is toward writing these words solid rather than with a hyphen.

The remaining prefixes, like *un-* and *over-,* are normally not hyphenated except under the conditions described below.

(4.2) Prefixes before figures and proper names Hyphenate any prefix before a figure, a proper noun, or a proper adjective.

post-1989   pre-Christmas   un-Christian

(4.3) Prefixes hyphenated to differentiate words Sometimes a prefixed word needs a hyphen to distinguish it from a word spelled similarly.

re-creation	recreation
re-collect	recollect
un-ionized	unionized

(4.4) Prefixes before the same vowels Sometimes a hyphen is used after a prefix in order to separate identical vowels.

co-owner   re-enter   anti-inflationary
                    (*or* reenter)

In keeping with the general trend away from hyphens, some words of this type can be written either way. Other words are now regularly written without hyphens: *cooperate, coordination.* Follow a reliable recent dictionary. (If the word is not listed, follow the analogy of similar words there.)

(5) Compounds

The typical compound is a pair of words that conveys a single special concept. (Some compounds, like *father-in-law,* contain more than two words.) Usually the first word is accented more strongly than the last. Certain compounds require hyphens, some are written solid, and others are written as separate words.

Hyphenated compound	high-test

Solid compound	highway
Open compound	high school

The trend is away from hyphenated compounds in favor of the other two types, but only your dictionary can tell you how to write a particular compound. And because dictionaries sometimes differ, it is best to choose just one reliable recent dictionary to follow.

(6) Multiword modifiers as temporary compounds

When two or more words function as a single unit to modify a following noun, this "temporary compound" should be hyphenated.

Multiword modifier of following noun	Other uses
the first-grade room	He is in first grade.
a know-it-all attitude	Do you know it all?
a thank-you note	Thank you for the help.
a well-known idea	The idea is well known.
a spelled-out number	The number is spelled out.

(7) Hyphenated words with a common element

If two or more hyphenated words have the same final element, that element may be omitted from all but the last word. In that case, you should hyphenate and space the words as follows:

the first-, second-, and third-grade rooms
in pre- or post-Revolutionary days

435

16e Numbers

(1) Numbers spelled out
(2) Numbers expressed in figures
(3) Roman numerals

There are several special rules for writing numbers, but the main question is when to spell them out and when to use figures. In technical writing usually all numbers are expressed in figures, but in other situations certain numbers are spelled out.

(1) Numbers spelled out

(1.1) Exact numbers under one hundred
(1.2) Round numbers
(1.3) Numbers that begin sentences

In general, numbers that can be expressed briefly are spelled out. (See **16d(3)** for the hyphenation of certain spelled-out numbers.) The exceptions to the first two rules below are listed in **16e(2).**

(1.1) Exact numbers under one hundred Spelling out numbers under one hundred is a safe rule to follow, although other rules do exist for various purposes. (Newspapers, for example, generally spell out only the numbers below ten.)

> So far there are still **forty-five** vacancies for Friday night.

(1.2) Round numbers Spell out approximate numbers, and any numbers that can be expressed as even hundreds, thousands, or millions.

> **Twelve thousand** people attended the rally.
> The football game drew **thirty-five hundred** spectators.

(1.3) Numbers that begin sentences Any number that begins a sentence must be spelled out. Sometimes it may be worthwhile to avoid the problem by rewording the sentence.

> **Nineteen seventy-six** was a year of bicentennial observances.

During **1976** many bicentennial observances were held.

(2) Numbers expressed in figures

(2.1) Years and usually days
(2.2) Pages and other parts of a book
(2.3) Numbers in lists and outlines
(2.4) Numbers used for identification and location
(2.5) Numbers used with abbreviations and symbols
(2.6) Mixed numbers, decimal fractions, and percentages
(2.7) Numbers associated with other numbers expressed in figures

Regardless of the size of the number, all of the following types of numbers should be expressed in figures.

(2.1) Years and usually days Dates may be expressed in the following ways:

July 4, 1776	4 July 1776 *(no comma if day is first)*
July 4	the Fourth of July *(established holiday)*

An exception to the use of figures is found in the extremely formal language of a wedding invitation.

(2.2) Pages and other parts of a book Use figures for locations in a book.

Chapters 2-3	page 11	footnote 2 on page 37

(2.3) Numbers in lists and outlines Any kind of numbered list or outline requires figures. See **17a(5.2)** for outline form.

1. The executive branch
2. The legislative branch
3. The judicial branch

(2.4) Numbers used for identification and location Use figures for such things as house numbers and other parts of an address (except possibly for low-numbered street names), telephone numbers, and various identification numbers.

Apartment 3B, 1411 Sixth Avenue	Delta Airlines flight 466
130 W. 104th Street (*or* 104 Street)	Mastercharge card 43-177-0999

(2.5) Numbers used with abbreviations and symbols Figures are used with abbreviations and symbols. (Most of the abbreviations and symbols themselves are more likely to be used in writing that is either technical or informal, or both.)

Technical or Informal	*Other*
3 mi.	three miles
78° F.	seventy-eight degrees Fahrenheit
60 mph	sixty miles an hour
4′ x 8′	four by eight feet

Exact time and amounts of money normally require figures and symbols: 9:15 p.m., $3.75.

(2.6) Mixed numbers, decimal fractions, and percentages Use figures for any kind of mixed number or percentage.

3½ minutes	27% *(technical writing)*
an average of 2.2 miles	27 percent *(other writing)*

(2.7) Numbers associated with other numbers expressed in figures In a paragraph, be consistent in writing numbers that deal with the same topic. If one of the numbers in some category must be written in figures, all should be.

> The City Parks Department is responsible for 3 large parks, 24 regional playgrounds, and 117 green-space areas. The department's twenty-six employees spend most of their time on the large parks and the 24 regional playgrounds.

> The first timed trial was 4½ minutes, the second 5 minutes, and the last 4¼ minutes.

(3) Roman numerals

Roman numerals appear with the major points of most outlines. In lower-case form (for example *iii* for three), they enumerate the preliminary pages of a book. They are sometimes used for chapters and larger parts of books, for acts and scenes of plays, and for volumes in a set or series. They are also used for dates on public buildings.

1	I	14	XIV	70	LXX	1000	M
2	II	15	XV	80	LXXX	1004	MIV
3	III	19	XIX	90	XC	1100	MC
4	IV	20	XX	100	C	1200	MCC
5	V	21	XXI	112	CXII	1300	MCCC
6	VI	24	XXIV	200	CC	1400	MCD
7	VII	25	XXV	300	CCC	1500	MD
8	VIII	29	XXIX	400	CD	1600	MDC
9	IX	30	XXX	500	D	1700	MDCC
10	X	31	XXXI	600	DC	1800	MDCCC
11	XI	40	XL	700	DCC	1900	MCM
12	XII	50	L	800	DCCC	1965	MCMLXV
13	XIII	60	LX	900	CM	2000	MM

16f Abbreviations

(1) Abbreviations always used
(2) When to use other abbreviations
(3) Spacing with abbreviations
(4) Abbreviations for the states

Abbreviations are convenient, but they should be used appropriately. The rules below may be supplemented by dictionary entries for certain individual abbreviations.

(1) Abbreviations always used

(1.1) Expressions of time
(1.2) Personal titles
(1.3) Abbreviations in company names

Certain abbreviations are correctly used in any type of writing.

(1.1) Expressions of time The following abbreviations are standard when used with numerical expressions of time.

7:15 a.m. (*or* A.M.)	8:45 EST (Eastern Standard Time)
1:00 p.m. (*or* P.M.)	A.D. 1066 (*A.D.* properly precedes the date)
2500 B.C.	

(1.2) Personal titles Always abbreviate the following titles when they accompany personal names.

Mr. Roberts	Dr. J. J. Roberts
Mrs. Roberts	Ms. Mary Roberts

Likewise abbreviate *Junior, Senior,* and academic degrees.

John J. Roberts, Jr.	Mary Roberts, Ph.D.

Other personal titles are abbreviated only when they precede the *full* name of the person.

Sen. David Patterson	Senator Patterson

Miss, of course, is not an abbreviation.

(1.3) Abbreviations in company names Abbreviations and symbols that are part of the official name of a company or other organization should be used as they stand.

> Pleasantburg Pets   Ironside Computer
> & Grooming Inc.   Corp.

(2) When to use other abbreviations

Additional abbreviations and symbols are often used in technical writing and in informal writing. However, in most writing it is best to avoid abbreviations not mentioned above in **16f(1)**. "When in doubt, spell it out."

(3) Spacing with abbreviations

Do not space within most abbreviations.

> Ph.D.   R.S.V.P.   CBS
> e.g.   D.C.   FBI

However, the initials of a person's name require spaces, as do most abbreviations consisting of more than single initials.

> R. C. Barbe   Lt. Gov.   W. Va. (*or*
>   W.Va.)

(4) Abbreviations for the states

The two-letter abbreviations for the states should be used only with Zip Codes in addresses. The traditional abbreviations should be used for other purposes, such as in lists and reference notes. Below are both types of abbreviations for the states, territories, and possessions of the United States.

	Zip	*Other*		*Zip*	*Other*
Alabama	AL	Ala.	California	CA	Calif.
Alaska	AK	—	Colorado	CO	Colo.
Arizona	AZ	Ariz.	Connecticut	CT	Conn.
Arkansas	AR	Ark.	Delaware	DE	Del.

District of Columbia	DC	D.C.	New Jersey	NJ	N.J.
			New Mexico	NM	N. Mex.
Florida	FL	Fla.	New York	NY	N.Y.
Georgia	GA	Ga.	North Carolina	NC	N.C.
Guam	GU	—	North Dakota	ND	N. Dak.
Hawaii	HI	—	Ohio	OH	—
Idaho	ID	—	Oklahoma	OK	Okla.
Illinois	IL	Ill.	Oregon	OR	Oreg.
Indiana	IN	Ind.	Pennsylvania	PA	Pa.
Iowa	IA	—	Puerto Rico	PR	P.R.
Kansas	KS	Kans.	Rhode Island	RI	R.I.
Kentucky	KY	Ky.	South Carolina	SC	S.C.
Louisiana	LA	La.	South Dakota	SD	S. Dak.
Maine	ME	—	Tennessee	TN	Tenn.
Maryland	MD	Md.	Texas	TX	Tex.
Massachusetts	MA	Mass.	Utah	UT	—
Michigan	MI	Mich.	Vermont	VT	Vt.
Minnesota	MN	Minn.	Virgin Islands	VI	V.I.
Mississippi	MS	Miss.	Virginia	VA	Va.
Missouri	MO	Mo.	Washington	WA	Wash.
Montana	MT	Mont.	West Virginia	WV	W. Va.
Nebraska	NE	Nebr.	Wisconsin	WI	Wis.
Nevada	NV	Nev.	Wyoming	WY	Wyo.
New Hampshire	NH	N.H.			

Chapter 17

Writing a Good Paper

17a The prewriting stage
17b The rough draft
17c Revision: a checklist
17d The clean copy
17e Proofreading

Good writing will just flow out if you wait for the perfect inspiration to strike—right? Wrong! Easy writing makes hard reading. Following the right process, though, can make writing a pleasure, especially as the results become better and better.

17a The Prewriting Stage

(1) Gathering information and ideas
(2) Thinking it over
(3) Determining the purpose
(4) Choosing the main idea
(5) Outlining the paper

What you do before you begin to write (that is, the prewriting stage) can be just as important as the actual writing. The two major parts of prewriting are getting your ideas together and planning your paper.

(1) Gathering information and ideas

Once you have decided to write something, whether for an assignment or for some other reason, your first step should be to jot down what you already know about the general subject area.

For example, let's suppose that the assigned subject area for a paper of three to five paragraphs is the unusual characteristics of some kind of animal. Several ideas for a topic might come to mind.

> Endangered species—blue whales, condors, whooping cranes
> Unusual animals—platypus, opossum, kangaroo
> Other ideas—the migration of lemmings, snakes' senses, whales beaching themselves

Having listed your ideas, you should next look for additional information. Besides encyclopedias and books, remember magazines, interviews, and discussion with others. Because the animal paper will be short, great amounts of information are not necessary. However, the information you find could very well help you decide which topic you will use. If you cannot find enough information on some topic, then you will have to cross that idea off your list. If you find too much information for one paper, then you will need to either drop that idea or narrow the topic.

(2) Thinking it over

After you have gathered some relevant information, you should think about the ideas and information you have. In this case, since "unusual characteristics" is the key to the paper, several of your possible topics may not be appropriate. For example, there may be nothing especially unusual about some of the endangered species listed.

Reflection is also helpful once you have found the right topic. As you think about the topic or tell someone else about it, additional ideas or examples may come to mind. Also, most writers find that as they mull over their ideas for a while, they see more clearly which things are most important and how they would like to handle the subject. (Of course, to have time for this step, you have to start early enough on the project.)

This is also a good time to consider the interests of your audience. First, who will your audience be? Will the whole class read (or hear) your paper, or will only your teacher read it? (If you are not sure, it may be best to write as if to your class.) What will be interesting to them? What is the best way to present this topic to them?

(3) Determining the purpose

It is important to decide early what your purpose will be. Is it to inform? to entertain? to persuade? Just what kind of information do you want to convey? Or just what do you want to convince your audience of or persuade them to do?

In our example, the paper is meant to inform the reader about some animal. Perhaps you decide specifically to inform your classmates about the unusual senses of snakes.

(4) Choosing the main idea

As you think about your information and what you will do with it, decide on the main idea. Try to make your main idea something that most of your audience will not already agree with or know. State your main idea in one sentence. (This sentence, summarizing the point of your whole paper, is sometimes called the **thesis** of your paper.) In this case, it might be that "snakes have unusual senses."

(5) Outlining the paper

(5.1) A scratch outline
(5.2) Outline forms

You should always outline a paper before you begin to write it, using at least a scratch outline. The outline will help you remember to cover the important things, and it will help you cover them in a logical order.

(5.1) A scratch outline A scratch outline is always helpful. Simply jot down the ideas you will include in your paper. After you have the ideas written down, you can rearrange them in the best order for the paper.

The following scratch outline was done after some research on the senses of snakes.

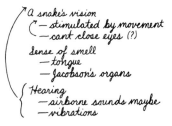

A snake's vision
— stimulated by movement
— can't close eyes (?)
Sense of smell
— tongue
— Jacobson's organs
Hearing
— airborne sounds maybe
— vibrations

(5.2) Outline forms A well-organized outline can be a real help in writing a paper. Sometimes you will be asked to hand in an outline along with a paper. Any outline that others will see should follow one of the two forms given below.

A **topic outline** uses phrases only—no sentences and no finite verbs. Points numbered or lettered in the same series should have the same grammatical form (nouns or adjectives or prepositional phrases or participles, for instance).

Introduction: snakes' strange abilities
  I. A snake's sense of hearing
    A. Airborne sounds
    B. Ground vibrations
 II. A snake's sense of vision
    A. Unaided by eyelids for squinting
    B. Stimulated by movement
    C. Supplemented by heat sensitivity
      1. In pit vipers only
      2. Even at night
III. A snake's sense of smell
Conclusion: senses as aids to survival.

A **sentence outline** includes more information than does a topic outline, for every point in it is a complete sentence.

> Introduction: Although snakes are fearful to many, their senses are fascinating.
>   I. The snake's sense of hearing is doubtful.
>   A. Snakes cannot hear airborne sounds.
>   B. They can hear ground vibrations.
>   II. The snake's sense of vision is unusual.
>   A. Snakes cannot close their eyes.
>   B. They cannot see still objects.
>   C. Some can "see" night victims.
>   III. The snake's sense of smell is incomparable.
> Conclusion: These senses are important to the snake's survival.

17b The Rough Draft

(1) The introduction
(2) Building good paragraphs
(3) The ending
(4) The title

Once you have planned your paper, you are ready to write your rough draft. The rough draft is simply your first try at writing the paper. You will have a chance to improve it later, and so you need not spend much time trying to find exactly the right word for something. It is usually better to write the whole paper fairly quickly, and then go back to improve it later.

(1) The introduction

Some writers like to write the whole rough draft straight through, beginning with the introduction. (Often they thoroughly rewrite the introduction later.) Others prefer to write the introduction after they have finished the rest of the paper. Whenever you do write your introduction, keep two things in mind.

First, an introduction should arouse the reader's interest or curiosity, compelling him to read on. People love a story, and so you might begin by telling an incident that can be tied to your subject. Another way is to refer to a common situation or problem. Sometimes a key quotation can help. But whatever you do, keep the introduction short and interesting.

Second, an introduction needs to introduce the subject. Usually the best plan is to begin the paragraph with the arouser of interest and then to tie it to the subject of your paper. Do not say, "In this paper I will tell you about such-and-such"; instead simply mention the "such-and-such" in the very last sentence of the introductory paragraph.

Below are three sample introductions, any one of which could introduce the paper about the unusual senses of snakes.

Example 1

The field mouse froze in terror, suddenly aware of an enemy that could not yet be seen. There was a different movement in the waving of the tall grass, a subtle but deadly slithering that chilled the heart. Suddenly, panic took over, and the mouse scurried for safety. That was a fatal mistake. Quickly and efficiently, the black snake struck it. Like most snakes, it rarely missed. But without the snake's unusual senses, perhaps none of this would have happened.

Example 2

Snake—the word itself makes some of us feel a special chill up our spine. The poet Emily Dickinson called him "a narrow fellow in the grass" that leaves us with "a tighter breathing, and zero at the bone." Our initial fear, though, should not keep us from recognizing that God has given snakes special senses to help them find food.

Example 3

Jesus instructed His disciples to be "wise as serpents." What special traits has God given

snakes, calling this attention from their Creator?
Certainly their senses are unusual.

Notice that the last sentence of each example contains
in some way the thesis mentioned in **17a(3):** snakes have
unusual senses.

(2) Building good paragraphs

(1) Topic sentences
(2) Methods of development

The body (main part) of the paper should consist of
well-developed paragraphs, each one dealing with a
single division of the subject. These divisions, of course,
come from your outline. You may want to begin by
marking the paragraph divisions on a copy of your
outline.

(2.1) Topic sentences Not all good paragraphs
contain topic sentences, but many paragraphs in
informational or persuasive writing do. A topic sentence
embodies the topic of the paragraph. Usually the topic
sentence begins the paragraph, and then everything else
in the paragraph relates to the subject matter of that
sentence.

If you used just a scratch outline or a topic outline
to organize your paper, you will probably compose each
topic sentence right along with the rest of the paragraph.
On the other hand, a sentence outline can, with some
adjustments, furnish the topic sentences for your paper.
(Any prewritten topic sentences are likely to need some
modification as you write the paper.)

For the paper outlined in **17a(5),** you might come
up with these three topic sentences:

- There is some question about whether snakes
  can hear at all.
- A snake's vision is unusual in several ways.
- Believe it or not, a snake's best "smeller" is its
  tongue.

(2.2) Methods of development

Paragraphs may be developed in several ways. One obvious way is to back up the topic sentence by examples, details, or reasons. Another way is to explain the topic further, perhaps even defining a key term. You may also compare or contrast two things or ideas.

For our snake essay, it would be natural to use examples. Since the purpose of the paper is to show that a snake's senses are unusual, the paper needs examples of their unusual qualities.

(3) The ending

The purpose of the ending—usually a final paragraph—is to clinch the main idea and to give a sense of completeness. Therefore, you need to restate or at least somehow refer to the main idea. Then you may go on to draw some logical conclusion from the main idea or to show the reader why that idea is important. Occasionally a short quotation may help you end your paper strongly.

The sense of completeness can be obtained simply by your echo of the idea stated at the end of the introductory paragraph. If you did begin the paper with a little attention-getting incident, you might even be able to tie the ends together by some further reference to the incident. Whatever method you use, though, keep the ending short.

Below are three possible endings for the snake paper. They can be paired with the sample introductions in **17b(1).**

Example 1

The field mouse probably would have survived unseen a bit longer if it had not moved. However, the snake still could have used its tongue to follow the scent of the mouse. Such abilities make the snake a deadly enemy indeed. What other animal can smell with its tongue and "hear" with its whole body?

Example 2

Now, the next time you are being chased by a snake, there are several evasive maneuvers you need to consider. First, to counteract its sense of hearing, try flying or swinging on a vine. Just don't touch the ground! Next, to confuse its sense of sight, sit perfectly still. Don't move at all! Finally, to escape its sense of smell—oh well, you can't win them all. Do you feel that chill up your spine again?

Example 3

A snake's senses are indeed unusual. Yet those senses are perfectly suited to the reptile's life. Its senses of sight, smell, and hearing all help the snake avoid danger and catch its prey.

(4) The title

A good time to write the title is just after you have finished the rough draft of the paper. The title, of course, should give at least a hint of the paper's subject matter. It should be **short,** usually no more than five or six words. If possible, it should be **interesting,** inviting the audience to read on. Finally, a title should be **specific.** Rather than just the general subject area, it should suggest the subject and perhaps the approach of that particular paper.

Too general	Snakes
	Unusual Characteristics of Animals

Good possibilities	How the Snake Locates the Mouse Unusual Senses of Snakes "Wise as Serpents" A Snake's Senses How a Snake Knows What's Happening

17c Revision: A Checklist

(1) Fulfilling the purpose
(2) Interest
(3) Clarity
(4) Unity
(5) Coherence
(6) Emphasis
(7) Conciseness
(8) A smooth and pleasing sound
(9) Precise words
(10) Fresh words
(11) Correctness

Revision of the first draft should always be *re-vision*—seeing the material again. That is, you look at the rough draft again after a day or so, to see whether you have said what you wanted to say and to see how you can improve the saying of it. The lapse of time helps you see it more objectively, as other people will see it.

No experienced writer skips the process of revision, nor should you. Revision is the way you improve whatever you are writing at the time, and it will gradually help you turn out better first drafts too.

Examples in this section will be drawn from the following two drafts of the body of the paper on snakes.

Original: Rough Draft
[1]Thier is some question about whether snakes can hear at all. [2]Most scientists are convinced that they cannot hear airborn sounds at all. [3]Yet they

Revised: Final Draft
[1]There is some question about whether snakes can hear at all. [2]Most scientists are convinced that these reptiles cannot hear airborne sounds.

are convinced that snakes can sense vibrations from the ground. [4]Which is actually all the "hearing" they need. [5]Their prey travels along the ground, and they can readily sense the approach of danger.

[6]A snake's vision is unusual in several ways. [7]First, it can never blink, squint, or close its eyes. [8]A snake's eyesight is stimulated by movement. [9]If the prey it is seeking sits perfectly still, the snake cannot find it with its eyes. [10]Some snakes, pit vipers, have an extra sense to help them "see" in the dark. [11]The pits, which are situated near their eyes, are heat-sensitive, so that they can spot the presence of a warmblooded prey, even at night. [12]Snakes like to eat a variety of things.

[13]Believe it or not, but a snake's best "smeller" is its tongue. [14]Special glands called Jacobson's organs allow a snake to follow the coldest trail to the hiding place of its meal. [15]A snake can put any bloodhound to shame in its ability to find its prey.

[3]Yet they are just as convinced that snakes can sense vibrations from the ground. [4]Actually, this is all the "hearing" they need. [5]Using these vibrations, snakes can "hear" their prey moving and also sense the approach of danger.

[6]A snake's vision is unusual in several ways as well. [7]First, a snake can never blink, squint, or close its eyes. [8]In addition, a snake's eyesight is stimulated by movement. [9]If its quarry sits perfectly still, the snake cannot see it. [10]Some snakes, pit vipers, have an extra sense to help them "see" in the dark. [11]Situated near their eyes, the pits are heat-sensitive, so that the vipers can spot the presence of a warm-blooded animal, even at night.

[13]Surprisingly, a snake's best "smeller" is its tongue. [14a]When trailing game, the snake uses its flicking tongue to transfer scents from the ground and the air to special glands in the mouth called Jacobson's organs. [14b]These sensitive glands detect the odors and enable a snake to follow even the coldest trail to the hiding place of its next meal. [15]Consequently, in its ability to find its prey, a snake can put any bloodhound to shame.

(1) Fulfilling the purpose

Check your composition to see whether you have fulfilled your purpose in writing it. Have you informed, or perhaps persuaded, your readers as you intended to? A paper that has not zeroed in on its purpose probably also lacks unity and clear organization.

(2) Interest

If a paper is not interesting, it will not do its job well. But how can you tell whether it is interesting? Even the most lively piece of writing may seem dull after you have worked on it for a while. One solution is to let one or more friends read it for you and give you their reactions. You can also try writing an alternate introductory paragraph (or final paragraph) and ask a friend to help you decide which one is more interesting and effective.

(3) Clarity

Problems of clarity are among the hardest to find—after all, *you* know what you meant. It is here perhaps that a lapse of time between writing and revision is most important. Possibly a friend can also help you spot confusing sentences. Look particularly for the problems dealt with in Chapter 9, "Clear Links."

Three examples of lack of clarity can be found in the rough draft at the beginning of **17c.** In sentence 2 *they* has unclear reference. (Who cannot hear the sounds—the snakes or the scientists?) In sentence 7 *it* is unclear, seeming to refer to the snake's vision instead of to the snake itself. Also, in sentences 13 and 14 the relationship between the tongue and the Jacobson's organs is not made clear. Notice the improvements in the final version of the sample paper.

(4) Unity

Everything within a paragraph should relate to the topic of that paragraph. Leave out anything that does not belong. (The same principle applies to the paper as a whole: every paragraph should relate to the main idea of the entire paper.)

In the sample rough draft for **17c,** one of the sentences of the second paragraph does not belong there. The topic sentence for that paragraph deals with a snake's vision, but sentence 12 has nothing to do with vision. Because the sentence disrupts the unity of the paragraph, it should be omitted.

(5) Coherence

The principle of coherence is that the parts should cohere (stick together) well. Logical, clear transitions are an important element in good writing. Transitions between sentences and transitions between paragraphs are both important.

In the sample rough draft for **17c,** a transitional device is needed between sentences 7 and 8 to suggest the addition of another characteristic of a snake's vision. The revision uses *in addition;* other words and phrases can be found in **9e(5).** Sentence 15 is improved by the addition of *consequently,* indicating the result or consequence of the facts mentioned before it.

The sample rough draft has no transition between the first two paragraphs. A word or phrase showing similarity is called for, such as *also* or *as well.*

(6) Emphasis

Always we want to emphasize whatever we consider most important. The most effective way to attain emphasis is by position; the most important point of a paragraph usually appears at the end or at the beginning. Also, more important ideas usually receive more space.

After we remove the unrelated sentence, sentence 12, the sentences of the second paragraph of the rough draft in **17c** show good ordering. The beginning of the paragraph is used for the topic sentence. Then the supporting ideas are arranged from least important to most important. Thus the two most significant ideas are in the two positions of most emphasis.

Within a sentence, the final position gives a natural emphasis, as explained in **9h(3.1)** and **12a.** Compare the old and new versions of sentence 15 to see how much difference rearrangement can make.

(7) Conciseness

(7.1) Elimination of obvious redundancy
(7.2) Reduction of clauses

In general, concise writing is more effective than wordy writing.

(7.1) Elimination of obvious redundancy All writing contains a certain amount of redundancy, but we want to get rid of any that is noticeable. When it is clear that fewer words will do the job, then fewer words should be used.

For example, in sentence 2 of the sample rough draft, the *at all* is unnecessary repetition from sentence 1. In sentence 9 ("the prey it is seeking"), the word *prey* includes the meaning of being sought, and so *it is seeking* can be omitted. Also in sentence 9, *cannot find it with its eyes* can be stated more simply as *cannot see it.*

(7.2) Reduction of clauses You can often help a problem sentence by reducing a dependent clause to a shorter, simpler element (see **8b**). Often the reduced clause is not only more concise but also more flexible in sentence position.

For example, consider the adjective clause in sentence 11. Reducing the clause *which are situated near their eyes* to a participle phrase is an aid to conciseness. Then moving the phrase to the beginning of the sentence adds sentence variety to the paragraph.

(8) A smooth and pleasing sound

We all want our writing to read smoothly. Some people can "listen" for problems as they read silently, but others find this hard to do. A good way to judge the flow of your writing is to read the paper aloud. You can also ask someone to read it aloud while you listen. Then revise any phrase or sentence that sounds awkward.

There are several reasons why a sentence might be awkward.

1. Language that is not fully natural. See **11a** and **11b** for help with this problem.

2. A subject that is too long. See **12d(2)** for help.

3. A long interruption between subject and verb.

Awkward	Musicians, *it has always seemed to me though I am no expert,* should begin performing early in life.
Improved	It seems reasonable that musicians should begin performing early in life.

4. An interruption between a verb and its object.

Awkward	My brother played *at age nine* his first violin solo.
Improved	My brother played his first violin solo at age nine.

5. A string of modifying nouns in the sentence.

Awkward	Mr. Martin did research on college students' *pre-college music performance experience.*
Improved	Mr. Martin studied college students' *earlier experience in performing music.*

See **15a** for additional help in simplifying sentences.

6. Excessive complexity.

Awkward	Mrs. Fields practiced a scientific procedure when she observed that people in front of large audiences tend to lose their composure and then devised a plan using that observation.
Improved	Mrs. Fields practiced a scientific procedure based on observation. After noticing that people in front of large audiences often lose their composure, she devised a plan using that observation.

Also, see **9i(6)** for help in clarifying parallelism.

7. The same structure appearing more than once in a sentence, apart from intentional parallelism.

Awkward	*In* the first place, *in* a good performance there is variety.
Improved	First, in a good performance there is variety.

(9) Precise words

One purpose of revision is to correct the inaccurate or imprecise words. Though your words may be either general (like *glands*) or specific (like *Jacobson's organs*) according to your need, they should express the right meaning.

Sentence 14 of the rough draft for **17c** contains an inaccurate verb. Do the Jacobson's organs really *allow* (give permission or opportunity to) the snake to follow the trail? A more precise word is *enable* (give the means or ability to).

(10) Fresh words

Overused words or phrases can drain vitality from a paper. Find a fresh replacement for a word that is repeated too often in your paper. A thesaurus may help you find suitable synonyms. A similar problem is the cliché, a worn-out phrase that has lost its effectiveness. Substitute simpler expressions or new comparisons for clichés like *cool as a cucumber, stick out like a sore thumb, pride and joy, first and foremost,* and *to the bitter end.*

In the sample rough draft one noun is overused, the word *prey.* Words that might be substituted, according to the context, are *victims, quarry, animals,* and *game.* Of course, not all repetition is bad, just noticeably frequent repetition. The final version keeps *prey* in two sentences, numbers 5 and 15. (Also, *snake* or *snakes* appears fairly often, because it is the only available common word. *These reptiles, they,* and *it* have limited usefulness.)

A cliché appears in sentence 13. An adequate substitute for *believe it or not* might be *surprisingly* or *amazingly.*

(11) Correctness

(11.1) Sentence structure and grammatical forms
(11.2) Spelling and other conventions

The final step in revising your paper is a careful check of its correctness. Errors distract your reader from what you have said. They may also reduce his confidence in your ideas.

(11.1) Sentence structure and grammatical forms Be sure that you have corrected any fragments, comma splices, or fused sentences, according to **13a** and **13b.** Also be sure that the grammatical forms in the paper are correct; check such problem areas as agreement, pronoun case, and so on.

For example, in the sample rough draft for **17c,** sentence 4 is a fragment. In the revised version it is rewritten as a sentence.

(11.2) Spelling and other conventions

Check your final draft carefully for spelling; do not wait until you have made the clean copy to hand in. Look up every word you are not completely sure of. For example, the sample rough draft contains three spelling errors: *thier* for *there; airborn* for *airborne;* and *warmblooded* for *warm-blooded.*

Also check other areas of correctness—punctuation, capitalization, underlining, and so on. Chapters 10 and 16 contain the rules you need. Remember that the more you work on these areas now, the less you will need to in the future.

17d The Clean Copy

(1) Form on the page
(2) Neatness

Once you have revised your paper, you are ready to make a neat copy of the final draft, the copy to turn in.

(1) Form on the page

Be sure you know what form the teacher expects, and then follow that form carefully.

Handwritten papers usually must be written on 8½-by-11-inch lined notebook paper, on one side only, in blue or black ink. The teacher may prefer that you use the standard wide-lined paper or that you write on every other line of the narrow-lined paper. Leave even margins on the right and the left sides, and leave the last two lines blank.

Typewritten papers should be typed with a black ribbon on standard typing paper. Double-space your paper, leaving at least one-inch margins on all four sides.

Follow your teacher's instructions about the placement of your name, the date, and the name of the class.

(2) Neatness

Your final copy must be neat. If you have too many errors on part of what was supposed to be the clean copy, recopy the page. Even a good paper makes a poor impression if it is not done neatly.

17e Proofreading

(1) What to look for
(2) How to proofread

At last you have a clean copy. Now it is time for a last check, to make sure that no errors have crept in as you made the final copy. Mistakes can occur accidentally as you rewrite or type your paper, but you need to find and correct them. If someone else types your paper, you are still responsible for any errors.

(1) What to look for

As you proofread your final copy, look especially for the following types of errors:

1. Repeated or omitted words
2. Accidentally misspelled words, such as *the* for *they*
3. Omitted or incorrect punctuation
4. Incorrect division of words at the end of a line

These are the errors that writers often make as they copy a paper. Other errors should have been caught during revision; but if one has been overlooked, correct it now.

If proofreading reveals several errors on one page, you should recopy the page.

(2) How to proofread

Good proofreading takes practice, but you can learn to do it well. Unless you are already an expert proofreader, the most important principle is this: do not expect to find every error (or every kind of error) in a single reading. Read in different ways to find different things.

First read your paper slowly and carefully, thinking about the meaning as you go. This reading will help you catch errors like the substitution of *threw* for *through;* both are correct words, but one cannot replace the other. Then examine the paper even more slowly, looking deliberately at each word to see whether it is spelled correctly. This kind of proofreading is not easy, because we normally take in whole phrases at a time when we read. Some people make themselves slow down by using a blank card or sheet of paper to cover what has not yet been examined. Others read the paper aloud. Still others look at the words in reverse order, as if they were reading backwards.

Finally, you may want to read the paper through more quickly a few times, looking each time for some particular problem area that has been difficult for you in the past. For instance, it is fairly easy to spot comma problems when you read looking only for commas.

Careful proofreading does take some time. It is only a little more time, however, in comparison with what you have already invested in your project. And it can make an important difference in people's impression of your work.

Writing Letters

Even in this day of easy telephoning, a letter is often needed. When it is, you want to present yourself at your best.

18a Personal Letters

(1) General appearance and style
(2) Form

Personal letters include those that send personal news and renew friendly contact, those that convey an invitation or respond to one, and those that say thank you for a kindness. They also include notes that send congratulations or express sympathy.

(1) General appearance and style

Personal letters do not follow as many rules as do business letters, but there are some guidelines.

> *General appearance:* legible, preferably
> handwritten, on white or pastel stationery
>
> *Style:* warm, friendly, informal, showing an
> interest in the other person

(2) Form

The standard parts of a personal letter appear in the example below. Notice that there is a margin on all four sides.

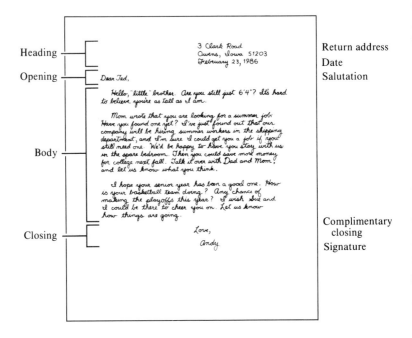

Heading — | 3 Clark Road | — Return address
Owens, Iowa 51203 | Date
February 23, 1986

Opening — Dear Ted, | Salutation

Hello, "little" brother. Are you still just 6'4"? It's hard to believe you're as tall as I am.

Mom wrote that you are looking for a summer job. Have you found one yet? I've just found out that our company will be hiring summer workers in the shipping department, and I'm sure I could get you a job if you still need one. We'd be happy to have you stay with us in the spare bedroom. Then you could save more money for college next fall. Talk it over with Dad and Mom, and let us know what you think.

Body —

I hope your senior year has been a good one. How is your basketball team doing? Any chance of making the playoffs this year? I wish Sue and I could be there to cheer you on. Let us know how things are going.

　　　　　Love, — Complimentary closing

Closing — 　　　　*Andy* — Signature

18b Business Letters

> (1) General appearance
> (2) Style and content
> (3) Form

Business letters include letters to ask for information, letters to order merchandise, letters to request the correction of a problem, and letters to apply for a job. The business letter format is also used in expressing an opinion to a government official or to an editor (for possible publication). There are strong expectations concerning the appearance, style, and form of all business letters.

(1) General appearance

Unless you are writing for a business or organization on its letterhead stationery, you should use white unlined paper, normally 8½ by 11 inches. (A sheet 5½ by 8½ inches is acceptable for a very short letter.) Business correspondence should be typed if at all possible, and only one side of the paper should be used. Your letter should be neat, without strikeovers or obvious corrections. If you cannot type it, write it on unlined paper as neatly as possible.

Keep your letter to one page if you can. If you need a second page, use a continuation heading:

Name *(of person written to)*
Page 2
September 12, 19—

This heading is typed at the left margin, beginning on the seventh line of the page. Then your message continues three lines below the heading.

(2) Style and content

Your letter should use clear, simple language. It should be courteous and free of errors. In style, it should be neither chatty nor stiffly formal.

Assume that you are writing to a busy person. Keep your letter as brief as possible, but do include all the needed information. Use short paragraphs, and make sure that your first paragraph clearly presents the purpose of your letter.

(3) Form

(3.1) A sample letter
(3.2) The salutation
(3.3) The complimentary closing
(3.4) Signature and writer's identification

(3.1) A sample letter The sample letter below illustrates the parts of the business letter. It is typed in the blocked style, the most common style for business letters. In the blocked style there is no indentation for paragraphs, and both the heading and the closing begin at the center. (On letterhead stationery the letterhead would substitute for the return address. The date would be typed at least three lines below the letterhead, beginning at the center.)

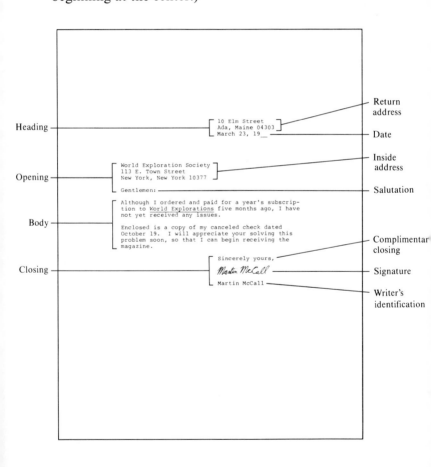

Heading —
   10 Elm Street
   Ada, Maine 04303 — Return address
   March 23, 19__ — Date

Opening —
   World Exploration Society
   113 E. Town Street
   New York, New York 10377 — Inside address

   Gentlemen: — Salutation

Body —
   Although I ordered and paid for a year's subscription to World Explorations five months ago, I have not yet received any issues.

   Enclosed is a copy of my canceled check dated October 19. I will appreciate your solving this problem soon, so that I can begin receiving the magazine.

   Sincerely yours, — Complimentary closing

Closing —
   Martin McCall — Signature
   Martin McCall — Writer's identification

(3.2) The salutation Always use the name of the person you are writing to if you know it. If you do not, use one of the following salutations.

To a company or organization	Gentlemen:
To a person, name unknown	Dear Sir: Dear Madam: Dear Sir or Madam:

(3.3) The complimentary closing The best closing for most business letters is *Sincerely yours.* Somewhat more personal are *Sincerely, Cordially yours,* and *Cordially.* More formal are *Yours very truly, Very truly yours,* and *Respectfully yours.*

Do not precede the complimentary closing with any such phrase as these: "Thanking you in advance," or "Hoping to hear from you soon, I remain." Simply finish your final paragraph and then move on to the complimentary closing.

(3.4) Signature and writer's identification A woman should give the appropriate courtesy title with her name: *Miss* or *Mrs.* (some use *Ms.*). The courtesy title usually appears either before her typed name or within parentheses before her signature.

Sincerely yours,

Helen Farmer

Mrs. Helen Farmer

Sincerely yours,

(Mrs.) Helen Farmer

Helen Farmer

For social correspondence, a married woman may use her full married name. In that case she would use the form given below.

> Sincerely yours,
>
> *Helen Farmer*
>
> Mrs. Bruce Farmer

A woman always signs her own given name, never her husband's.

A man does not use *Mr.* with his name unless his given name could be either a man's or a woman's. In that case he should use *Mr.* when he writes to a person for the first time.

> Sincerely yours,
>
> *Shane Barber*
>
> Mr. Shane Barber

> Sincerely yours,
>
> *(Mr.) Shane Barber*
>
> Shane Barber

18c The Résumé

(1) Content and general appearance
(2) Form
(3) The cover letter

If you want to create a fuller display of your qualifications than is convenient in a letter of application, you can use a résumé. A résumé would hardly be needed by a teenager applying for his first summer job, but it is expected for many full-time jobs, especially those requiring extensive training.

(1) Content and general appearance

A résumé is a brief summary of your personal data, experience, and other qualifications for the job. It is organized under certain headings such as *Education,*

Areas of Knowledge, and *Significant Achievements*—whatever will best cover the essential areas and help you present your strong points. Within individual sections of the résumé, chronological ordering begins with the present.

A résumé is typed (or printed) on 8½-by-11-inch white unlined paper. Above all, your résumé should be clear and easy to read. Follow these guidelines as you plan your résumé:

1. Be positive, but totally honest—avoid negatives, but do not exaggerate your qualifications.
2. Be concise—use no long sentences or paragraphs. Brief phrases are usually best.
3. Be specific—show in what ways you are qualified for this particular type of job.

(2) Form

The accompanying sample shows one effective form for the résumé. Variations in form are common. For instance, the personal data at the upper right on the sample might instead appear partway down under its own heading, *Personal.* If so, that information can be consolidated into two or three lines. Also, the headings could be pulled out to appear entirely within a narrow left column; each heading would begin to the left of the first line of its section. In either position, the headings can be typed in all capitals with no underlining.

```
                LYNN JOHNSON                    Birthdate:   June 19, 19__
                413 Clover Avenue               5'7"         122 lbs.
                Lakeland, Wisconsin 53891        Single
                Telephone:  289-4214            Excellent health


        Objective

            Computer operator and programmer trainee

        Areas of Experience

            Office operations                Simple accounting
            Secretarial procedures           Public contact

        Education

            Lake Shore Christian High School, Lakeland, Wisconsin,
                college preparatory curriculum, June 19__
                One year typing (speed:  40 wpm)
                One semester business machines
                One semester introduction to data processing

            Lake County Technical School
                Computer Languages I:  Fortran (ten-week evening
                course), fall 19__

        Work Experience

            Cashier and office assistant, Woolworth Department Store,
                Lakeland, Wisconsin, summer 1987

            Youth-group treasurer (elective office), Lakeland Baptist
                Church, Lakeland, Wisconsin, 1986-87

            Camp counselor and water safety instructor, Wild Haven
                Camp, Marlow, Michigan, summer 1986

            Volunteer secretary-receptionist, Lakeland Baptist Church,
                part-time 1985-86

        Availability

            June 4, 19__ (full time; but can begin now part time)

        References

            References will be provided upon request.
```

(3) The cover letter

A résumé should always be accompanied by a letter addressed to the appropriate person in the company.

Use the person's name if you can, but by all means use his title. Type the cover letter on white unlined 8½-by-11-inch paper.

Keep the cover letter short. Do not repeat the material that is on your résumé, but do mention something positive to invite further interest. Begin by stating the position you hope to fill, and end by requesting an interview.

413 Clover Avenue
Lakeland, Wisconsin 53891
February 23, 1984

Personnel Manager
Control Data Corporation
1305 Main Street
Lakeland, Wisconsin 53890

Dear Sir or Madam:

Because of your company's reputation in data processing, I would like to apply for a position at Control Data as a computer operator and programmer trainee. I am interested in working full-time with the company for the next three or four summers while I am in college.

I believe I can soon become an asset to the corporation. My background will allow me to learn your procedures quickly, and I know how to work hard. My résumé is enclosed.

My intended college major is Mathematics Education, since I plan to teach high school math and computer science. My work at Control Data would mesh well with my studies, and it would provide valuable experience to share later with my students.

May I come and talk with you?

Sincerely yours,

(Miss) Lynn Johnson

Lynn Johnson

18d The Envelope

The sample business envelope below is in the standard blocked style with single-spacing.

```
Lynn Johnson
413 Clover Avenue
Lakeland, WI 53891




                    Personnel Manager
                    Control Data Corporation
                    1305 Main Street
                    Lakeland, WI 53890
```

The most common envelope size for business correspondence is 9½ by 4⅛ inches (No. 10), but No. 6¾ (6½ by 3⅝ inches) is also acceptable. Depending on the size of the stationery and the envelope, the letter may be folded in thirds, or else first in half and then in thirds.

The envelope for personal correspondence has the same format, but it is usually handwritten. The envelope is normally sized to match the letter paper in such a way that the personal letter can be folded either in half or in thirds.

When you fold a letter in half or in thirds, leave about three-eighths of an inch so that the letter will be easy to open.

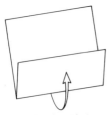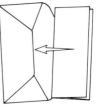

Folding in thirds

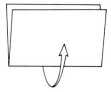

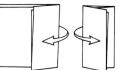

In half   In half, then thirds

Research Skills

Part of education is knowing how to find the information you need and then knowing how to use it. The first sections of this chapter will help you find information, and the rest will help you use that information in a research paper.

19a Using the Dictionary

An ordinary hard-cover desk dictionary contains a wealth of helpful information—more than you may realize.

(1) Finding the word

The **entry words** are those in boldface type set slightly to the left of the text column. Whether the entry is one or more words, it is alphabetized according to each letter throughout the whole boldface entry.

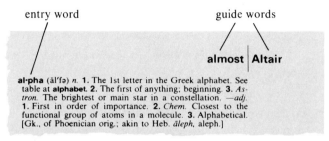

entry word   guide words

almost | Altair

al·pha (ăl′fə) *n.* **1.** The 1st letter in the Greek alphabet. See table at **alphabet. 2.** The first of anything; beginning. **3.** *Astron.* The brightest or main star in a constellation. —*adj.* **1.** First in order of importance. **2.** *Chem.* Closest to the functional group of atoms in a molecule. **3.** Alphabetical. [Gk., of Phoenician orig.; akın to Heb. *āleph,* aleph.]

Guide words help you determine which words are on a specific page. A pair of guide words appears at the top of each page, in boldface type, opposite the page number. In the example, the word to the left of the vertical bar, *almost,* is the first entry on the page. The word to the right of the bar, *Altair,* is the last entry on the page.

Even if you are unsure of the exact spelling of a word, you should be able to find it in the dictionary by guessing at its likely spelling. If your dictionary has a table of correspondences between sounds and spellings, you can use the table to help you think of other ways the word might be spelled.

(2) Understanding the entry

(2.1) Pronunciation
(2.2) Parts of speech
(2.3) Inflected forms
(2.4) Variant spellings

(2.1) Pronunciation The pronunciation usually appears just after the entry word. The pronunciation symbols are given in the pronunciation guide at the bottom of the page and in a fuller table in the front of the dictionary.

The following symbols are perhaps the most common in dictionaries:

(ə) A schwa represents an obscure vowel sound found in an unstressed syllable.

(′) or (') An accent mark shows which syllable receives the most stress:

ocean (ō′shən)   **ocean**\'ō-shən\

(ˉ) A macron indicates a "long" vowel sound.

(˘) A breve may indicate a "short" vowel sound, or such a vowel may be left unmarked.

Some words have two (or more) noticeably different acceptable pronunciations. Both pronunciations are listed for these words. In one leading dictionary, the first pronunciation is more common when the second is preceded by *also;* the two are equally common when they are joined only by a comma. If your dictionary follows a different system, you will find it explained in the introductory material.

pronunciation   parts of speech

a·loof (ə-lōof′) *adj.* Distant, esp. in one's relations with other people; indifferent. —*adv.* At a distance, but within view; apart. [Obs. *aloof,* toward the wind : ʌ-² + obs. *loof,* luff.] —**a·loof′ly** *adv.* —**a·loof′ness** *n.*

(2.2) Parts of speech All the parts of speech of each entry word are listed along with the definitions. For example, the word *aloof* can be either an adjective or an adverb.

The part-of-speech names used to identify words in your dictionary may differ somewhat from those used in this handbook. The terms used by the compilers of each dictionary can usually be found in the front of the book.

Because the meaning of a verb may vary according to whether it is transitive or intransitive or linking, dictionaries usually classify verb meanings into two groups. Transitive verb meanings are labeled *tr.v.* (or *v.tr.* or *vt*). Intransitive and linking verb meanings are both labeled *intr.v.* (or *v.intr.* or *vi*). Every verb has at least one of these labels along with its meanings. For instance, *alphabetize* is labeled as a transitive verb. Certain other verbs (like *harden*) have both labels.

verb type   inflected forms

al·pha·bet·ize (ăl′fə-bĭ-tīz′) *tr.v.* **-ized, -iz·ing, -iz·es. 1.** To arrange in alphabetical order. **2.** To supply with an alphabet. —**al′pha·bet′i·za′tion** (ăl′fə-bĕt′ĭ-zā′shən) *n.* —**al′pha·bet·iz′er** *n.*

(2.3) Inflected forms The inflected forms of a word are forms that differ from the main entry because of the addition of suffixes or because of other changes to the word. Usually included are the irregular plurals of nouns, certain verb forms, and the suffixed comparative and superlative forms of adjectives and adverbs.

At the end of the entry there may be additional words in boldface type, words that are derived from the entry words by certain common suffixes. (These derived words may be called "run-on entries.") For example, *alphabetization* and *alphabetizer* are derived from *alphabetize*.

(2.4) Variant spellings

Some words can be spelled in two ways. In general, the spelling listed first is more common if the second is preceded by *also*. The two are equally acceptable if they are joined by *or*.

variant spellings   definitions

al·pac·a (ăl-păk′ə) *n., pl.* **alpaca** or **-as. 1.** A domesticated South American mammal, *Lama pacos,* related to the llama, and having fine, long wool. **2. a.** The silky wool of the alpaca. **b.** Cloth made from alpaca. **3.** A glossy cotton or rayon and wool fabric, usually black. [Sp. < Aymara *allpaca.*]

(2.5) Definitions, idioms, and synonyms A word may have several definitions. Each of these will be listed and numbered. If one definition includes closely related meanings, these are labeled a. b. c. rather than with new numbers. Some dictionaries (such as the one sampled here) put the most central or basic meanings first; other dictionaries put the most frequent meanings first; and still others put first the earliest meanings that are still used. The introductory material in your dictionary will tell which ordering system your dictionary uses.

Dictionaries also list the various idioms used with a word. An **idiom** is an expression whose meaning we learn individually; its meaning is not the same as the usual meaning of the words by themselves. For example, *let alone* (meaning "not to mention") has little to do with letting or with aloneness.

a·lone (ə-lōn′) *adj.* **1.** Apart from anything or anyone else. **2.** Excluding anyone else; sole; only. **3.** With nothing further added: *The drive alone takes four days.* **4.** Without equal; unique: *alone in his ability to unite all factions of the party.* **—idioms. leave alone.** To refrain from interrupting or interfering with (someone). **let alone.** Not to speak of or think of: *I haven't a minute to spare, let alone an hour.* **let well enough alone.** To be satisfied with things as they are. **stand alone.** To be without equal. [ME < *al one,* all one.] **—a·lone′** *adv.* **—a·lone′ness** *n.*

    Synonyms: *alone, lonely, lonesome, solitary.* These adjectives are compared as they describe lack of companionship. *Alone* emphasizes isolation from others and does not imply unhappiness. *Lonely* adds to isolation the painful consciousness of it. In *lonesome,* the desire for companionship is more plaintive, but less profound: *lonely for a lover; lonesome for a friend. Solitary* stresses physical isolation, sometimes self-imposed.

idioms

synonyms

For certain words like *alone* there is also a list of synonyms, with the relevant distinctions of meaning.

(2.6) Capitalization The correct capitalization of a word is found in a dictionary entry, even for words like *alpine* that are capitalized for one meaning and not for another.

> **al·pine** (ăl′pīn′) *adj.* **1. Alpine.** Of, pertaining to, or characteristic of the Alps or their inhabitants. **2.** Of or pertaining to high mountains. **3.** *Biol.* Living or growing on mountains above the timberline. **4.** Intended for or concerned with mountaineering. **5. Alpine.** Of or pertaining to competitive downhill racing and slalom skiing events. **6. Alpine.** Of or pertaining to a subdivision of the Caucasian race predominant around the Alps. [Lat. *Alpinus* < *Alpes*, the Alps.]
> **al·pin·ist** also **Al·pin·ist** (ăl′pə-nĭst) *n.* A mountain climber. **—al′pin·ism** *n.*

capitalization

(2.7) Miscellaneous information in entries A dictionary usually provides such additional information as the scientific names for plants and animals, special usage notes, illustrations, and cross references. The introduction to a dictionary lists and explains these and any other types of information it provides.

(2.8) Etymology The etymology of a word is the word's life history—where it came from and sometimes where it has been at various stages. Instead of starting at the beginning, though, dictionary etymologies start with the recent past and work backward in time.

Sometimes knowing a word's history can make the word come alive for you. For instance, *aloft* was made from two words meaning "in air," a good description of where the sailor aloft in the rigging is.

> **al·most** (ôl′mōst′, ôl-mōst′) *adv.* Slightly short of; very nearly. [ME < OE *ealmæst* : *eall*, all + *mæst*, most.]
> **alms** (ämz) *pl.n.* Money or goods given to the poor in charity. [ME *almes* < OE *ælmesse* < LLat. *eleemosyna* < Gk. *eleēmosunē* < *eleēmōn*, pitiful < *eleos*, pity.]

etymologies

> **a·loft** (ə-lôft′, ə-lŏft′) *adv.* **1.** In or into a high place; high or higher up. **2.** *Naut.* At or toward the upper rigging. *—prep.* On top of: *birds perching aloft telephone wires.* [ME < ON *ā lopt* : *ā*, in + *lopt*, air.]

Some words, like *almost,* are **native words**—words that have always been English words, as far back as we can trace them. Other words, like *alms* and *aloft,* we call **borrowed words,** because they came from other languages.

Below are some common abbreviations for languages and their historical stages. Other abbreviations are explained in the front of your dictionary.

Ancient	Gk. (Greek)	Lat. (Latin)	
Early		LLat.	OE (Old
Medieval		(Late Latin)	English)
Late		OFr.	ME (Middle
Medieval		(Old French)	English)
Modern		Fr. (French)	

Names in the same column refer to different stages of the same language. The approximate dates for Old English are A.D. 450-1100, and for Middle English, 1100-1500.

When you read an etymology, try to remember the difference between changes within the same language and borrowing from a different language. For instance, the word *parsley* has a long history, including two borrowings. It started out as a word made up long ago by Greeks who noticed a similarity between parsley and celery:

Greek   *Latin*   *English*

Gk. petroselinon ——borrowed——▶ Lat.
(petra "rock" +   petroselinum
selinon "celery")   ↓
     LLat.
     petrosilium ——borrowed——▶ OE petersilie
                           ↓
                           ME persely
                           ↓
                           parsley

As you can see, the greatest changes in the word have happened in the thousand years since the word came into Old English from Late Latin. (Many common words were shortened in the old days, when few people knew how to read and write.)

Remembering that a dictionary etymology starts at the end of the process, not the beginning, see how the history of *parsley* is written:

> **parsley** [ME *persely* < OE *petersilie* < LLat. *petrosilium* < Lat. *petroselinum* < Gk. *petroselinon* : *petra,* rock + *selinon,* celery.]

Compare this with the diagram above, and you will see that the symbol "<" means "from."

For practice, let's look at one more. The etymology of *charity* mentions two languages other than English: Latin and Old French. However, the word was borrowed just once, since French is one of the languages that Latin gradually turned into.

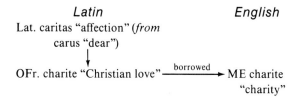

Here it is dictionary-style:

> **charity** [ME *charite* < OFr., Christian love < Lat. *caritas,* affection < *carus,* dear.]

Etymologies can be interesting, but don't fall into the trap of thinking that the "original" meaning of a word must be its "real" meaning today. Most words have more than one meaning, and these meanings are based on the way people today (especially educated people) actually use the words. For instance, in its earliest recorded uses *girl* had the meaning "young man or young woman," but a person would be foolish to use *girl* that way today.

Etymologies not only tell us about the early forms of words with long histories, but they also explain the origin of many newer words. For example, during World War II the word *radar* was made from *ra*dio *d*etection *a*nd *r*anging. (You can look up *emcee, sonar* and *laser* for other examples.)

Finally, you can use etymologies to help you avoid "minced" (weakened) oaths. You probably do not need a dictionary to tell you that *darn* is an alteration of *damn,* used by many people as a way of swearing in polite company. But if you wonder about the interjections *gee, gosh,* and *golly,* the dictionary will tell you that the first is an alteration of *Jesus* and the other two are from the word *God.* Words like these, of course, should be avoided by anyone wanting to back up his Christian faith by pure speech.

(2.9) Usage labels   Each dictionary applies usage labels to certain entry words. These labels may differ somewhat from one dictionary to another. Check the introduction to your dictionary to find the meaning of the terms it uses. Below are some commonly used types of labels.

1. **Field labels** point out definitions that apply to a special area such as music or physics or sports. For example, the second definition of *aloft*, in **19a(2.8),** is for the nautical term. Also, the third definition of *alpine*, in **19a(2.6),** applies to the field of biology.
2. **Geographic labels** limit usage to a particular region. Some examples of geographic labels are *regional, dialect, New England,* and *chiefly British.*
3. **Stylistic labels** limit a word or a definition to a particular usage level. Some examples follow:

    nonstandard/substandard (words or expressions generally not used by the educated) *informal* (words perfectly acceptable in conversation but generally not used in formal writing)

usage label
/

al·so-ran (ôl′sō-răn′) *n. Informal.* One that is defeated in a race, election, or other competition; loser.

slang (showy or humorous words, often faddish and short-lived)

vulgar/obscene (words that violate standards of decency)

archaic/obsolete (words that were once common but are now rarely seen except in old writings)

Unlabeled words are standard usage.

A Christian would certainly not want to use words that are labeled as vulgar or obscene. The worldly associations of some slang expressions should also cause us to avoid their usage. If you are unsure of a term or expression, find out its usage level and its meaning and associations. This information can help you decide whether or not to make it part of your own vocabulary.

(3) Using special sections of the dictionary

Most dictionaries have various special sections: abbreviations, biographical names, geographical names, colleges and universities, foreign words and phrases, rules for punctuation and capitalization, the ways to address certain officials, and so on. A look at the index or the table of contents will tell you what special sections are found in your dictionary.

19b Finding Information in the Library

The name *library* comes from the Latin word for book, but today's library could better be called something like an "information-ary"—a place of information. Some of that information is in books, and some of it is in other media. What follows is a brief guide to finding information in the library.

(1) Arrangement of books

(1.1) Fiction
(1.2) Nonfiction: the Dewey decimal system
(1.3) Nonfiction: the Library of Congress system
(1.4) Reference books

(1.1) Fiction You can expect to find fiction books all in one place in the library, shelved alphabetically according to the authors' names. If you know the author and the title of a novel, you should be able to find it easily on the shelves. After you find the section of books by that author, look alphabetically for the title.

If the book you want is not on the shelf, you can check the library catalog to see whether the library owns that book. (Section **19b(2)** explains the library catalog.) If the book appears in the catalog but is not on the shelf, ask at the circulation desk whether it has been checked out. If so, you may be able to put your name on a list to be notified when the book comes in. (There may be a small charge for this service.)

Another reason a book may not be on the shelf is that it is "on reserve." Sometimes fiction or nonfiction books may be put on reserve during periods of time when many people need access to them. Books on reserve may be used in the library, but they cannot be checked out for the usual period of time (or perhaps not at all). If your library uses this system, the reserve books will be in a special section.

(1.2) Nonfiction: the Dewey decimal system In most school libraries and many college libraries, the nonfiction books are classified and arranged on the shelves according to the Dewey decimal system. This system, devised by the American librarian Melvil Dewey (1851-1931), gives every nonfiction book a number according to its subject matter. This number appears on the spine of the book and is the key to finding the book on the shelves.

The number of a specific book can be found by looking in the library catalog, as is explained in **19b(2).** However, once you know the Dewey number of the subject that interests you, you can find most of the books on that subject in the one location in the shelves.

It is helpful to be familiar with the ten large classifications in the Dewey system.

000-099	General works (including reference books, collected essays, and journalism)
100-199	Philosophy (including psychology, logic, and ethics)
200-299	Religion (including church history and pagan religions)
300-399	Social sciences (including politics, economics, government, education, and customs)
400-499	Languages (including phonetics, English, and foreign languages)
500-599	Pure science (including mathematics, physics, chemistry, and biology)
600-699	Applied science (including medicine, engineering, and home economics)
700-799	Fine arts (including architecture, drawing, photography, and music)
800-899	Literature (including works about the drama, fiction, and poetry of many countries)
900-999	History (including geography, biography, and ancient and modern history)

The topics in parentheses give just a rough idea of what is included in each of the large classifications. Each of the ten large classifications is divided again into ten categories. For example, the 600s have these subdivisions:

600-699	Applied science
600	Applied science in general
610	Medicine
620	Engineering
630	Agriculture
640	Home economics
650	Communication, business
660	Chemical technology
670	Manufacturing
680	Mechanical trades
690	Building

The beauty of this system is that we can keep dividing by ten as long as needed. For instance, a subdivision of 630 (agriculture) is 634—orchards, fruit, and forestry. Further levels of subdivision use a decimal point:

634.3   Citrus fruit   *(subdivision of 634)*
634.31   Oranges   *(subdivision of 634.3)*

The Dewey system is called a decimal system because of its repeated divisions by ten.

Under a book's Dewey decimal number is a number that identifies the book by its author and perhaps by one or more letters of its title. For example, Paul Roberts might have the author number R543. His book *Understanding Grammar* would have the Dewey decimal number 425, for grammars of English. These two numbers together make up the **call number** of the book.

425   (Dewey decimal number)
R543   (author number)

If a library already had another 425 book by Paul Roberts, then it would probably add a "work letter" to the second book to differentiate it. In this case the work letter would probably be *u* from *Understanding Grammar*.

425   (Dewey decimal number)
R543u   (author number and work letter)

In this way every book in the library has a different two-line call number.

(1.3) Nonfiction: the Library of Congress system Some large libraries use the Library of Congress system rather than the Dewey decimal system. Instead of using only numbers, the Library of Congress classification system uses a combination of letters and numbers. Because there exist more letters than numerals, more subjects can be classified without going to excessively long numbers.

There are twenty-one basic categories in the Library of Congress system:

A General works (including reference works and collected essays)
B Philosophy and religion
C History and related sciences
D Foreign history and topography
E American history
F Local American history
G Geography, anthropology, and folklore
H Social sciences
J Political science
K Law
L Education
M Music
N Fine arts
P Language and literature
Q Science
R Medicine
S Agriculture and forestry
T Technology and engineering
U Military science
V Naval science
Z Bibliography and library science

A typical Library of Congress number is CB245.K28, for *The Western Heritage,* a history of Western civilization. The first letter is C because the book is a broad work of history, and B245 further specifies the subject.

After the period, K28 identifies the main author, Donald Kagan.

(1.4) Reference books Every library has certain very useful books that stay in the library permanently for general use. Such books are in the library's reference collection. They are marked with an *R* above or below the regular classification numbers. For example, the twenty-eighth volume of the *Encyclopedia Americana* might have this on its spine:

031	(Dewey decimal number)
En19	(author number)
1980	(date)
v. 28	(volume number)
R	(reference collection)

Usually the books in the reference collection are in a special part of the library.

(2) The library catalog

The library catalog is the most important key to finding information in the library. In a school or public library, the library catalog will be either a **card catalog** or something else that works in much the same way.

Every nonfiction book in a library is represented by at least three cards in the card catalog. There is an **author card,** one or more **subject cards,** and a **title card.** (Works of fiction have only author cards and title cards.) As the examples show, everything from the author's name on down is the same on all three types of cards. The subject card has an extra line at the top for the subject, typed either in red or in all capitals (newer style) to show that it is the subject. On the title card, the extra line at the top is the title of the book, typed with just the first letter of the title capitalized.

All three pictured cards say that the library owns a book by Joseph Gies called *Bridges and Men,* with drawings by Jane Orth Ware. Its call number is 624 / G363. This is the first edition, published in Garden City, New York, by Doubleday & Company in 1963.

It has 15 pages of front matter, 343 pages of text, and 32 pages of plates (unnumbered pages of photographs or art). It also contains illustrations and maps. It is 24 centimeters high. It has a bibliography, from the unnumbered page 328 through page 334; and it contains an index.

Author card

author

```
624      Gies, Joseph.
G363          Bridges and men / Joseph Gies with
         drawings by Jane Orth Ware. -- 1st ed. --
         Garden City, N.Y. : Doubleday & Co., 1963.
             xv, 343 p., 32 p. of plates : ill., maps ;
         24 cm.

             Bibliography: p. [328]-334.
             Includes index.
```

Subject card

subject

```
         BRIDGES--HISTORY.
         Gies, Joseph.
             Bridges and men / Joseph Gies with
         drawings by Jane Orth Ware. -- 1st ed. --
         Garden City, N.Y. : Doubleday & Co., 1963.
             xv, 343 p., 32 p. of plates : ill., maps ;
624      24 cm.
G363
             Bibliography: p. [328]-334.
             Includes index.
```

title

```
624          Bridges and men.
G363     Gies, Joseph.
             Bridges and men / Joseph Gies with
         drawings by Jane Orth Ware. -- 1st ed. --
         Garden City, N.Y. : Doubleday & Co., 1963.
             xv, 343 p., 32 p. of plates : ill., maps ;
         24 cm.

             Bibliography: p. [328]-334.
             Includes index.
```

Title card

Your library probably has all three kinds of cards alphabetized together in one large catalog. Some libraries, though, have a separate file for the subject cards.

The cards are alphabetized by the top line of each card. Author cards come before subject cards, and subject cards before title cards (the same order as in the illustration). For example, author cards for writers named Bridges would come before subject cards for books about bridges or about the man Robert Bridges. And all of these would come before the title card for a book named *A Bridge of Understanding*. The articles *a/an* and *the* are disregarded in alphabetizing.

The individual drawers of a card catalog are labeled to indicate their alphabetical contents. Within a drawer are guide cards to help you find the alphabetical location quickly. In the photograph both of these can be seen. In the pictured drawer the subject cards for bridges are found several cards behind the guide card for Leonard Bridges, since subject cards come after author cards. On one of those subject cards is Joseph Gies' book *Bridges and Men*. A little farther back in the drawer is the title card for that same book.

Instead of catalog cabinets, some libraries have catalog scanners or computer terminals to give catalog information. With either of these newer methods, the user does not handle actual catalog cards, but he does get the same information in about the same format.

(3) The periodical indexes

The card catalog will help you find books on your subject, but it will not help you find articles in magazines and newspapers. To find these articles, you need to consult a periodical index.

The most generally useful periodical index is the *Reader's Guide to Periodical Literature.* Articles from over 170 magazines are listed in it by subject and by author. Articles are listed soon after publication, in one of the twenty-one issues during the year. At the end of the year all of these are combined and reissued in the single large annual volume.

Let's suppose you want to find some articles about the building of bridges. You start with one of the recent annual volumes and find the following information. After some author entries for people named Bridges, you find the subject heading "Bridges." Under it are three "see also" entries to suggest other places you can look in this volume. First, though, you look to see whether either of the articles listed here might be helpful.

Bridges
    See also
  Brooklyn Bridge (New York, N.Y.)
  Covered bridges
  San Francisco (Calif.)—Bridges
  In disaster's wake, an expert warns of America's aging
    bridges: cross at your own risk [interview with G.
    Mair] il por People Wkly 17:44-6 My 3 '82
          Accidents
  A bridge too near [collapse of unfinished highway
    bridge in East Chicago, Ind.] il Newsweek 99:36
    Ap 26 '82
        Great Britain
    See also
  London (England)—Bridges
  Thames River (England)—Bridges

The article listed under the subheading "Accidents" looks helpful, and so you write down the information. To save space, the listing uses a number of abbreviations, explained in the front of each volume of the *Reader's Guide*. This entry says that an **il**lustrated article on the subject "Bridges: Accidents" entitled "A Bridge Too Near" will be found in volume **99** of *Newsweek*. It is on page **36** of the issue for **April 26, 1982.** The article is about the collapse of an unfinished highway bridge in East Chicago, Indiana.

When you look up the "see also" entry "Covered bridges," you find an article in *Southern Living* that may or may not help you, and one in the November-December issue of the 1982 *Americana* that looks promising.

Covered bridges
Georgia's covered bridges. il South Living 17:17 Ag
'82
He builds them to last [work of M. Graton] G. Walther.
il pors Americana 10:40-6 N/D '82

To see whether your library carries these two magazines, you can check the library catalog or a special periodical listing. Of course, to find articles published in other years, you would look in other volumes of the *Reader's Guide*.

At times you may want to check other periodical indexes for special subjects or for periodicals not included in the *Reader's Guide*. These other indexes are similar in form to the *Reader's Guide*. Examples are the *Social Sciences Index* and the *Humanities Index,* both of which cover scholarly journals in certain fields of study. The *New York Times Index* can help you find information in back issues of other newspapers as well as the *New York Times,* since it will help you discover the date of newsworthy events.

(4) Special reference tools

(4.1) Almanacs and yearbooks
(4.2) Atlases and gazetteers
(4.3) Bible commentaries and concordances
(4.4) Biographical sources
(4.5) Dictionaries
(4.6) Encyclopedias
(4.7) Indexes
(4.8) Thesauruses

We consult reference books for specific information, rather than reading them straight through. Their systematic arrangement makes it easy to find the facts they contain. Sometimes we get information directly from them, and sometimes they point us to the place where the information is available.

(4.1) Almanacs and yearbooks Both almanacs and yearbooks supplement encyclopedias by giving current information about statistics and recent events. Most almanacs, and all yearbooks, are published every year. Widely used almanacs include the *Information Please Almanac* and the *World Almanac*. Yearbooks tend to concentrate on special subjects. For instance, the *Statesman's Year-book* gives information about the governments of countries around the world.

(4.2) Atlases and gazetteers Atlases are books of collected maps. Examples are *The Times Atlas of* *the World* (by the *Times* of London), the U.S. Geological Survey's *National Atlas of the United States of America,* and Shepherd's *Historical Atlas.* Gazetteers are indexes of place names. The *Columbia Lippincott Gazetteer of the World* includes much additional information for each place. The (London) *Times Index Gazetteer of the World* includes over 345,000 place names, of which slightly over half appear in the five-volume *Times Atlas* mentioned above.

(4.3) Bible commentaries and concordances Commentaries are explanations of the Bible, going through part or all of the Bible, verse by verse or section by section. There are some good commentaries on individual books of the Bible, and there are longer works such as Matthew Henry's commentary on the whole Bible and the one-volume *Wycliffe Bible Commentary.*

Bible concordances are alphabetical indexes to the words of the Bible. They are helpful for locating a passage and sometimes for studying a subject through the Bible. Young's *Analytical Concordance to the Bible* and Strong's *Exhaustive Concordance of the Bible* list every word of the King James Version of the Bible. They also make it possible to find out which Greek or Hebrew word is being translated (Young's more conveniently than Strong's).

(4.4) Biographical sources Besides book-length biographies of particular people, the library contains a number of sources for more concise biographical information. People living today appear in such works as *Current Biography, Contemporary Authors,* and the various *Who's Who* biographical dictionaries. Persons no longer living are described in sources such as the well-known *Dictionary of American Biography* and the British *Dictionary of National Biography.*

(4.5) Dictionaries Dictionaries, of course, are alphabetical listings of words. As explained in **19a,** even an ordinary desk dictionary contains a variety of facts about the words it lists. In addition to these dictionaries, your library contains larger dictionaries and special-purpose dictionaries. The large unabridged dictionaries, such as *Webster's Third New International Dictionary,* contain several hundred thousand words. The most complete dictionary in any language, though, is the *New English Dictionary on Historical Principles,* originally published in ten volumes (1888-1933). Now usually called the *Oxford English Dictionary,* it and its later supplements contain a full history of nearly every word used in England since A.D. 1150.

In addition, libraries contain a number of special-purpose dictionaries, such as dictionaries of synonyms, Bible dictionaries, foreign language dictionaries, and dictionaries of areas like sports or the sciences.

(4.6) Encyclopedias Encyclopedias give brief introductions to many subjects, in articles that are arranged alphabetically. Well-known examples include the *New Encyclopaedia Britannica,* and the somewhat simpler *Encyclopedia Americana* and *Collier's Encyclopedia.* The *World Book Encyclopedia* is intended particularly for young people.

(4.7) Indexes Indexes are listings that make it easy to find information. Most useful are the periodical indexes, described in **19b(3).** Other indexes include the *Book Review Index,* the *Essay and General Literature Index,* and books of quotations such as Bartlett's *Familiar Quotations.*

(4.8) Thesauruses A thesaurus is a treasury of synonyms. Some thesauruses list the main words alphabetically, and others group all words by meaning, directing you to the meaning groups from a detailed index in the back. In either case, you choose a synonym from the words you find listed. A dictionary and a thesaurus are often well used together—the thesaurus to help you think of a word, and the dictionary to confirm that the word is in fact the one you need. *Roget's II,* though, defines the entry word and then gives synonyms for each definition.

(5) Other library resources

Besides the obvious—books and periodicals and ways to find them readily—libraries contain a variety of resources.

Nonprint media should not be overlooked. Most libraries contain speech and music records and perhaps cassette tapes; these can often be checked out as well as used at the library. Some libraries have circulating copies of filmstrips, slides, and even educational films. Special displays and collections, along with temporary exhibits, add interest and educational value. And nearly every library has at least one world globe for viewing.

The **vertical file** consists of one or more filing cabinets containing recent pamphlets and newsletters on various subjects. It may also contain pictures and newspaper clippings. At least the first time, ask a librarian for help in using the vertical file.

To save space and expense, certain books or periodicals may be available only on **microfilm** or **microfiche.** These materials can be used in the library on special magnifying readers.

Finally, your library may have a **reference librarian,** a professional with special training in finding information. If you have reached a blind alley in your search for information, speak with a librarian (a reference librarian if possible). You may be surprised at the help you get.

19c Researching a Topic

(1) Exploratory reading
(2) The working bibliography
(3) Initial planning
(4) Note-taking
(5) Writing the paper

Let's assume that you need to do a research project in the library. Perhaps you have been assigned—or have decided—to write a short paper about comets or about some particular comet.

(1) Exploratory reading

Your first step is to go to the library and do some exploratory reading. If you know almost nothing about comets, you can look in a general source like an encyclopedia. (Some general knowledge about the subject will help you proceed more intelligently.) Mainly, though, you need to find out what other information your library contains and where it is. Section **19b** will help you find good sources of information.

Now you are ready to make a working bibliography of the sources that you may use.

(2) The working bibliography

A bibliography is simply a list of sources about some subject. Your finished paper will no doubt include your final bibliography, a list of the sources you used for the paper. For now, though, you need a working bibliography—a list of likely-looking sources for your paper.

Because your final bibliography will need to be in alphabetical order, it is a good idea to write your sources on index cards, one source to a card. Then you can easily add or subtract cards and put them in alphabetical order.

To save unnecessary work later, go ahead and write your bibliography cards in the form you will need for your final bibliography. Details about this form are given in section **19d(4).** You should also include the complete call number of every book, so that later you can easily locate the book. In addition, you can add a note about how helpful the book or article seems to be.

Bibliography Card

```
523.6      Brown, Peter Lancaster. Comets, Meteorites
8 814          and Men. New York : Taplinger, 1974.

           Fairly technical, but has a good
        chapter on Halley's comet ( p. 22— )
```

(3) Initial planning

Having located some possible sources, you are ready for the planning stage. Even though your paper will be based on research, the planning stage is essentially the same as the prewriting stage described in **17a:**

1. Gathering information and ideas—do enough reading to get a good idea of the subject.
2. Thinking it over—add ideas of your own, and decide what aspects of the subject will be most interesting to you and to your audience.
3. Determining the purpose—decide what you will try to do in the paper (inform? persuade?).
4. Choosing the main idea—from what you know now, decide what one main idea you will probably try to present.
5. Outlining the paper—make a rough plan for the paper, including all the support you can think of for your main idea.

Your plan may change, but having one can save you a good bit of wasted effort as you take notes.

(4) Note-taking

Most of the information you use in your paper will come from the notes you take from your sources. Many experienced researchers take their notes on 4-by-6-inch cards, so that these cards can be shuffled and rearranged as the paper takes shape.

When you take notes, remember that what you are looking for is information—not usually how someone else worded that information. So normally you should take down the information in your own words. There are two methods:

1. You can summarize the information, leaving out examples and unneeded details. Be careful to use your own wording. (If you should need to use a phrase of the author's, you must put quotation marks around it.)

2. On the other hand, you may need all of the information given in a short passage. To keep from just copying the author's words, take notes in your own brief phrases rather than in whole sentences.

If your notes are brief phrases rather than entire sentences, you will later find it easier to weave them into a paragraph that does what you want. After all, the purpose of the paper you write will be different from the purpose of any of your sources.

Below are examples of both methods of note-taking. The original follows each note card.

Summary

Halley's Comet — history ———————— slug

J. R. Hind (British astronomer, 1823-95) looked in early records, mainly Chinese. Found appearances of Halley's Comet back to 12-11 B.C. ———— note

Brown, p. 31 ———————— source

Almost a century after the death of Halley, another Englishman appeared on the scene who was equally interested in this particular comet. J. R. Hind (1823-1895) in his own right discovered three comets and ten minor planets from the private observatory of Mr. Bishop, which was then (in the middle of the nineteenth century) situated in Regent's Park, London. Hind is one of the few Englishmen to have gained prize money from his comet and minor planet discoveries. He became fascinated by comets at an early age, and apart from his observational work and the computation of the orbits of new comets he systematically examined old records, especially the Chinese Annals, to find out all he could about comets that had appeared in the past. From this research he was able to trace with fair probability many previous appearances of Halley's Comet as far back as 12-11 B.C.

Brief Phrases

> ### A Comet's Tail
>
> Comet's tail — transparent, very long, very small mass.
>
> Example: Halley's (when longest in 1910) — if dust, one million tons; if gas, one thousand tons (actually is part gas, part dust). Even if use large figure, still like a cubic inch of our air spread over 200 cubic miles! No such vacuum on earth.
>
> Brown, pp. 67-68

Generally, comet tails are described as being highly transparent, and stars can be observed through them without any diminution of brilliance. In spite of their volume the mass of a tail must be infinitely small. When the tail of Halley's Comet reached its greatest length in 1910, Schwarzschild estimated that if it were composed of only fine dust particles, it might possibly weigh 1,000,000 tons, but if it were gas, it would be considerably less—perhaps not more than 1,000 tons. We know now that both kinds of material are present; if we use the larger figure, which still sounds like a great deal of material, and take into account its dimensions, this would imply that it contains one cubic inch of air at atmospheric pressure disseminated throughout a volume of 200 cubic miles! No modern vacuum-pumping technique can hope to simulate this tenuous density on Earth.

The "slug" at the top of a note card makes it easy for you to see at a glance what the note is about. If possible, the slug should be the point on your tentative outline that the note supports. The page reference to the source is absolutely necessary, so that you can give credit properly later.

Rarely, you may find it necessary to quote all or part of a sentence. If so, be sure to put quotation marks around what you have quoted.

Quotation

Newton on regularity of solar system

Isaac Newton said in his *Principia*:

"This most beautiful system of the Sun, planets and comets, could only proceed from the counsel and dominion of an intelligent and powerful Being, . . . This Being governs all things, not as the soul of the world, but as Lord of all."

"Principia," *Encyclopedia Americana*

Implied here is the need to avoid plagiarism. As **19d(1.1)** points out, plagiarism (a type of dishonesty) is the use of someone else's ideas or words as if they were your own. Good note-taking is the key to avoiding plagiarism:

1. If you ever need to use someone's phrase or sentence, put quotation marks around it.
2. Write down the source for every note card, and show the source in your paper.

You may later find that a fact is "common knowledge," as explained in **19d(1.1).** But until you know that, you need to record the source. In other words, every note card must have a reference to the source.

(5) Writing the paper

Once your notes are taken, you should rethink your outline once more to be sure it is still a good plan for the paper. When you are satisfied with your plan, arrange your note cards in the order of the outline.

Now you can write the rough draft, following your plan and using your notes. Apply the suggestions given in **17b,** but also remember to note in your rough draft the sources for all information you take from your cards. After you complete the rough draft, go to section **19d** for help with how to indicate these sources in your finished paper.

Let your completed rough draft sit for a while—at least a day. Then go on to revision (**17c**), making a clean copy (**17d**), and proofreading (**17e**).

19d Acknowledging Your Sources

(1) The purposes of notes
(2) Three options for notes
(3) The bibliography page
(4) Forms: first footnotes, with corresponding bibliography entries
(5) Form of later footnotes
(6) Form of parenthetical reference notes

A completed research paper gives clear recognition to the sources used in preparing it. This section will show you how to use notes and a bibliography for this purpose.

(1) The purposes of notes

(1.1) Reference notes
(1.2) Content notes

(1.1) Reference notes Anyone writing a research paper makes use of some facts or ideas that he found in doing his research. Unless a fact is **common knowledge** —something mentioned by nearly everyone who writes about the subject—the writer of the research paper should tell where he learned it. He does so by using a reference note.

Reference notes serve two main purposes.

1. The most important purpose of reference notes is to preserve the **honesty** of the writer. (1) Do not make it appear that you discovered the facts yourself; instead, give the source. (2) Do not make it appear that someone else's words are your own; instead, put them inside quotation marks and then give the source. Failure to do these things is **plagiarism,** a type of dishonesty.
2. Reference notes also make it easy for the reader of your paper to **find out more** about the subject. If you note your sources adequately, your reader will know where to look for more information about any part of your paper.

Item 1 above, concerning honesty, distinguishes between using someone else's facts only and using someone else's words. It is important to make a clear difference between these two ways of handling the material. (1) When you reword the information (that is, when you *paraphrase* it), be careful to put the material entirely into your own words. (2) If you ever need to quote (and so use quotation marks), be careful to copy the person's words exactly. See **10i(6.1, 7.1)** for the allowable ways to make adjustments in quotations.

Below are examples of acceptable and unacceptable paraphrase. The footnote number (⁴) is a reminder of the need for a reference note.

The original material	The schoolhouse I attended consisted of one room, roughly thirty feet square, with a large entryway where outdoor clothing, rubbers, and dinner pails could be left during the day. —*K. W. Carter, "I Remember . . . my Little White Schoolhouse"*
Acceptable paraphrase (change in words and structure)	Carter attended a one-room schoolhouse about thirty feet by thirty feet. There was a large area at the entrance for coats and overshoes.[4]
Two kinds of **unacceptable** paraphrase (plagiarism underlined)	Carter attended a schoolhouse with just one room. It was about <u>author's words</u> <u>author's structure</u> <u>thirty feet square</u>, <u>with a large entrance</u> <u>where outer clothing, overshoes, and</u> <u>lunch buckets could be kept during</u> <u>the school day.</u>[4]
Acceptable paraphrase of part and quoting of part	Carter attended a thirty foot by thirty foot one-room schoolhouse, "with a large entryway where outdoor clothing, rubbers, and dinner pails could be left during the day."[4]

An acceptable paraphrase changes the sentence structure (the arrangement of the words), and it changes the main words themselves.

Remember: to avoid plagiarism—

1. Give reference notes for all facts, ideas, and quotations taken from another person. Most of your information should be expressed in your own words; be sure that you have paraphrased it completely.
2. Put quotation marks around a phrase or a sentence taken from someone else, as well as giving a reference note.

(1.2) Content notes Most notes in a paper or a book are reference notes, serving the purposes mentioned above. Another type of note is the content note. The content note gives information that seems too important to leave out but too much of an interruption for the text itself.

An example of the content note can be seen in the sample research paper in **19e(1):**

> [7] Halley was so convinced of the value of Newton's <u>Principia</u> that he paid to have it published.

In that paper the source for the latter part of the paragraph, including this content note, is given in the footnote at the end of the paragraph. If the source were not given in that way, it could appear in the content note:

> [7] Halley was so convinced of the value of Newton's <u>Principia</u> that he paid to have it published. Oppenheimer and Haimson, p. 58.

Likewise, a sentence of information can be added after the period of a regular reference footnote.

A word of caution is in order. Many good papers have no need of content notes, and no paper should use so many as to cause distraction. If the material is important enough to mention, it usually will fit into the paper itself.

Content notes are usually footnotes, although they could also be part of a series of endnotes. See **19d(2.1, 2.2).**

(2) Three options for notes

(2.1) Footnotes
(2.2) Endnotes
(2.3) Parenthetical reference notes

Today there are three possible ways to handle the reference notes in a paper, each with its own advantages. For a student, of course, the crucial question is which one his instructor requires (or which ones he allows).

(2.1) Footnotes

"HE WHO MAKE FOOTNOTES GET SORE FEET."

Traditionally, reference notes have usually appeared as footnotes. Footnotes have the advantage of giving full information on the page where it is first relevant. The main disadvantage for the writer is the need to plan ahead for the right amount of space at the bottom of the paper. (However, rough-typing all the footnotes first will make it clear how much room should be saved for them on each page.)

In a paper, the presence of a footnote below is signaled by a raised footnote number in the text. This number is a regular Arabic numeral, with no period or other punctuation. The footnote number comes after the sentence (or small group of sentences) to which it refers. There is no space between the footnote number and the preceding word or mark of punctuation. For illustration, notice the correct use of the footnote number ([4]) in all three examples of paraphrase above in **19d(1.1)**. The footnotes are best numbered consecutively throughout the paper, rather than starting over again on each page.

The footnotes themselves appear in numerical order at the bottom of the page to which they refer. That is, if the text of a certain page contains raised-number references to footnotes 3-5, then those three footnotes must be at the foot of that page. However, although footnote 5 must begin on that page, it can be continued at the beginning of the footnote section on the next page.

The footnote section of a page should be divided from the text section by a 1½-inch line that begins at the left margin. In a typed paper, double-space as usual after the last line of text. Beginning at the left margin, type fifteen strokes of underline. Double-space again, and indent to begin the first footnote. The footnotes themselves are single-spaced, but there is a double space between the notes. (The handwritten equivalent of double-spacing is to leave one blank line.) See the sample paper in **19e(1).**

To save room, two or three consecutive short footnotes may be combined on the same line.

[5] Harris, p. 14.   [6] Harris, pp. 37-38.   [7] Jackson, p. 209.

This space-saving form can be used only when all of the footnotes will be complete on that one line, and when at least three spaces can be left between the notes.

Sections **19d(4-5)** give the correct forms for footnotes.

(2.2) Endnotes Endnotes have the same form as footnotes, but they all come in one list, starting on a new page at the end of the paper. Placing the notes at the end is more convenient for the writer, but it is obviously less convenient for the reader. Do not use endnotes without your teacher's permission.

Begin an endnote page with the centered heading, Notes, two inches from the top. Triple-space down and begin the notes, using the same form and indentation and spacing as at the foot of the page. Every endnote should begin on a new line.

(2.3) Parenthetical reference notes The third, and most recent, option is to give all reference notes in very brief form inside parentheses in the text itself.

These brief parenthetical notes are easily written and typed, and they do give the essential information at the point where it is relevant. A possible disadvantage is that the reader must turn back to the bibliography for full information about any source.

Since the parenthetical note is considered part of the sentence to which it refers, the end-punctuation of the sentence comes *after* the parenthetical note.

> Experiments showed that most of the forgetting took place within the first five hours (Norris 37).
> Norris reported that most of the forgetting took place "before the end of the fifth hour" (37).

See **19d(6)** for the form of parenthetical reference notes, and see **19e(2)** for a sample paper using them.

(3) The bibliography page

At the end of the paper is the bibliography page, an alphabetical listing of the sources used in the paper. A sample can be seen at the end of the paper reproduced in **19e.**

Begin the bibliography with a centered heading, either Bibliography or Works Cited, two inches from the top of the page. Then triple-space down for the first entry. Single-space within the entries, but double-space between them.

The usual forms of the bibliography entries are shown on the righthand pages in **19d(4).** These entries, of course, would be arranged in alphabetical order in an actual bibliography. If a bibliography contains two or more sources by the same author, a line of ten unspaced hyphens replaces the author's name after the first entry:

```
Doe, John.  Awareness of Life.  Boston: Heritage, 1979.

----------.  Memories of Churchill: The War Years and Beyond.
    London: Preakness, 1965.

----------, and Howard Blank.  How Hitler Lost.  Boston: Heritage,
    1975.
```

The last book listed here is by John Doe and Howard Blank; works done by an author alone precede any that he co-authored.

(4) Forms: first footnotes, with corresponding bibliography entries

(4.1) Books
(4.2) Well-known reference books
(4.3) Periodicals with volume numbers
(4.4) Periodicals without volume numbers
(4.5) Other sources
(4.6) Secondary sources

In this section the footnote forms on the left page will be matched by bibliography forms on the right page. The forms given, including the punctuation, are well established and should be followed exactly unless your teacher directs otherwise. On the other hand, if some aspect of your specific source is not covered, you should choose a form in line with these general principles and follow that form consistently.

First Footnotes

In general, the first footnote reference to a particular source contains the following basic information.

1. **Author.** The person's name is given, first name first, followed by a comma. (Personal titles and degrees are omitted.)
2. **Title of the source.** This title may be simply a book title, or it may be the title of an article.
3. **Facts of publication.** For a book, the facts of publication are enclosed in parentheses; see the general footnote pattern numbered 1 for the arrangement and punctuation inside the parentheses. For a periodical article, the name of the periodical, the volume number (if any), and the date are included; see the general footnote patterns numbered 18 and 21.
4. **Page numbers.** After a comma, the specific page numbers are given. Except for a periodical with a volume number, the page number or numbers are preceded by the abbreviation *p.* (for *page*) or *pp.* (for *pages*). The footnote ends with a period.

The first line of each footnote is indented. The footnote begins with a slightly raised number, with no following punctuation. This number, of course, corresponds with the number at the end of the relevant passage in the paper itself. Section **19d(2.1)** gives information about the placement of footnotes.

At the beginning of the first four footnote sections (on the following lefthand pages), there is a general pattern. See the actual examples for more specific information.

Bibliography Entries

The typical bibliography entry contains the following types of information. The information in each of these sections ends with a period.

1. **Author.** The last name of the author is given first, since the entries are arranged alphabetically by author. If there is more than one author, reverse the name of the first one only.

2. **Title of the source.** This title may be a book title, or it may be the title of an article.

3. **Facts of publication.** (a) For a book, there may first be information about the edition or the volume(s), followed by a period. Then come the city, publisher, and year of publication, arranged as shown in the first general pattern below. (b) For a periodical article, the facts of publication include the name of the periodical, perhaps a volume number, the date, and the total pages of the article.

To help the user find an entry in the bibliography, "underhung" indentation is used. That is, the first line of an entry extends five spaces farther to the left than do the other lines. Section **19d(3)** explains the arrangement of a bibliography page.

At the beginning of the first four bibliography sections (on the following righthand pages), there is a general pattern. See the actual examples for more specific information.

(4.1) Books

General pattern

[1] Author, <u>Title Underlined</u> (City: Publisher, date), pp. 10-12.

Book: one author

[2] Gilbert Mueller, <u>Nightmares and Visions</u> (Athens: Univ. of Georgia Press, 1972), p. 106.

Book: two or three authors

[3] Chandler S. Robbins, Bertel Bruun, and Herbert S. Zim, <u>Birds of North America</u> (Racine, Wis.: Western Publishing, 1966), p. 64.

The state is added for further identification of the city, except for well-known cities and those made clear from the name of the publisher, as in footnote 2.

Book: more than three authors

[4] Harry Shaw et al., <u>A Complete Course in Freshman English</u>, 6th ed. (New York: Harper and Row, 1967), pp. 901-902.

Book with translator

[5] Aleksandr Isaevich Solzhenitsyn, <u>The First Circle</u>, trans. Thomas P. Whitney (New York: Bantam, 1973), p. 502.

Book with editor

[6] <u>The Music Makers</u>, ed. Victor Stevenson and Clive Unger-Hamilton (New York: Abrams, 1979), p. 159.

[7] Edmund Spenser, <u>The Faerie Queene</u>, ed. Thomas P. Roche, Jr. (New York: Penguin Books, 1978), pp. 39-40.

Translator and editor

[8] <u>The Travels of Marco Polo</u>, trans. William Marsden, ed. Manuel Komroff (New·York: Dutton, 1946), p. 400.

Later edition

[9] Jan Karel Van Baalen, <u>The Chaos of Cults</u>, 4th ed. (Grand Rapids: Wm. B. Eerdmans Publishing Company, 1969), p. 34.

(4.1) Books

General pattern

```
Last, First Middle.  Title Underlined.  City:  Publisher, date.
```

Book: one author

```
Mueller, Gilbert.  Nightmares and Visions.  Athens: Univ. of
     Georgia Press, 1972.
```

Book: two or three authors

```
Robbins, Chandler S., Bertel Bruun, and Herbert S. Zim.  Birds of
     North America.  Racine, Wis.: Western Publishing, 1966.
```

Book: more than three authors

```
Shaw, Harry, et al.  A Complete Course in Freshman English.  6th
     ed.  New York: Harper and Row, 1967.
```

Book with translator

```
Solzhenitsyn, Aleksandr Isaevich.  The First Circle.  Trans.
     Thomas P. Whitney.  New York: Bantam, 1973.
```

Book with editor

```
Stevenson, Victor, and Clive Unger-Hamilton, eds.  The Music
     Makers.  New York: Abrams, 1979.

Spenser, Edmund.  The Faerie Queene.  Ed. Thomas P. Roche, Jr.
     New York: Penguin Books, 1978.
```

Translator and editor

```
The Travels of Marco Polo.  Trans. William Marsden.  Ed. Manuel
     Komroff.  New York: Dutton, 1946.
```

Later edition

```
Van Baalen, Jan Karel.  The Chaos of Cults.  4th ed.  Grand Rapids:
     Wm. B. Eerdmans Publishing Co., 1969.
```

Corporate author

[10] Insight team of the London Sunday Times, The Yom Kippur War (New York: Doubleday, 1974), p. 59.

Anonymous

[11] The Earth and Man (New York: Rand McNally, 1976), pp. 86-87.

A short work in an edited collection

[12] Dwight Macdonald, "Too Big," in Short Model Essays, ed. Ann M. Taylor (Boston: Little, Brown, 1981), p. 22.

A volume

[13] T. Rice Holmes, The Roman Republic and the Founder of the Empire 58-50 B.C., II (New York: Russell and Russell, 1967), p. 152.

The volume number of a book is given in Roman numerals.

A book in a series

[14] George N. Boyd and Lois A. Boyd, eds., Religion in Contemporary Fiction, Checklists in the Humanities and Education Series, No. 1 (San Antonio: Trinity Univ. Press, 1973), p. 43.

(4.2) Well-known reference books

General pattern

[15] Author if known, "Article," Book Title, edition.

Encyclopedia: unsigned article

[16] "Nightmares," Encyclopedia Americana, 1980 ed.

For a signed article, the author's name should be given first:
[16]John Doe, "Nightmares," . . . .

Dictionary

[17] "Coliseum," American Heritage Dictionary, 2nd ed. (1982).

If there is no edition number, identify the edition by year as in footnote 16.

Corporate author

Insight team of the London <u>Sunday Times</u>. <u>The Yom Kippur War</u>.
New York: Doubleday, 1974.

Anonymous

<u>The Earth and Man</u>. New York: Rand McNally and Company, 1976.

A short work in an edited collection

Macdonald, Dwight. "Too Big." In <u>Short Model Essays</u>. Ed. Ann
M. Taylor. Boston: Little, Brown, 1981, pp. 21-24.

A volume

Holmes, T. Rice. <u>The Roman Republic and the Founder of the Empire
58-50 B.C.</u> Vol. II. New York: Russell and Russell, 1967.

A book in a series

Boyd, George N., and Lois A. Boyd, eds. <u>Religion in Contemporary
Fiction</u>. Checklists in the Humanities and Education Series,
No. 1. San Antonio: Trinity Univ. Press, 1973.

(4.2) Well-known reference books

General pattern

Last, First (if author is known). "Article." <u>Book Title</u>. Edition.

Encyclopedia: unsigned article

"Nightmares." <u>Encyclopedia Americana</u>. 1980 ed.

For a signed article, the author's name appears first: Doe, John.
"Nightmares." . . . .

Dictionary

"Coliseum." <u>American Heritage Dictionary</u>. 2nd ed. (1982).

(4.3) Periodicals with volume numbers

General pattern

[18] Author, "Article," <u>Periodical Title</u>, volume, issue number if needed (date), 10-12.

Journal paged consecutively throughout its annual volume

[19] John Hawley Roberts, "Vision and Design in Virginia Woolf," <u>PMLA</u>, 61 (1946), 837.

The volume number of a periodical is given in Arabic numerals; here the volume is number 61. Because this periodical has a volume number, the date is given within parentheses and then the page numbers simply follow a comma, with no *p.* or *pp.* (When the page numbers run throughout the whole volume, it is not necessary to identify the specific issue.)

Journal paged separately for each issue within its annual volume

[20] Phyllis A. Whitney, "Help Your Characters Be Themselves," <u>The Writer</u>, 94, No. 3 (1981), 7.

Because of the separate pagination, the issue number is needed.

(4.4) Periodicals without volume numbers

General pattern

[21] Author, "Article," <u>Periodical Title</u>, date, pp. 10-12.

Monthly magazine (no volume number)

[22] Gordon S. Wood, "The Bigger the Beast the Better," <u>American History Illustrated</u>, Dec. 1982, pp. 30-31.

Because there is no volume number, no parentheses surround the date, and the abbreviation *pp.* for *pages* is used.

(4.3) Periodicals with volume numbers

General pattern

```
Last, First.  "Article."  Periodical Title, volume, issue number
    if any (date), inclusive pages.
```

Journal paged consecutively throughout its annual volume

```
Roberts, John Hawley.  "Vision and Design in Virginia Woolf."
    PMLA, 61 (1946), 835-47.
```

Recent MLA format:

```
Roberts, John Hawley.  "Vision and Design in Virginia
    Woolf."  PMLA 61 (1946): 835-47.
```

Although the footnote refers just to p. 837, the bibliography entry states that the article extends from p. 835 through p. 847.

Journal paged separately for each issue within its annual volume

```
Whitney, Phyllis A.  "Help Your Characters Be Themselves."  The
    Writer, 94, No. 3 (1981), 7-11.
```

Recent MLA format:

```
Whitney, Phyllis A.  "Help Your Characters Be Themselves."
    The Writer 94.3 (1981): 7-11.
```

(4.4) Periodicals without volume numbers

General pattern

```
Last, First.  "Article."  Periodical Title, date, inclusive pages.
```

Monthly magazine (no volume number)

```
Wood, Gordon S.  "The Bigger the Beast the Better."  American
    History Illustrated, Dec. 1982, pp. 30-37.
```

Recent MLA format:

```
Wood, Gordon S.  "The Bigger the Beast the Better."
    American History Illustrated, Dec. 1982, 30-37.
```

Weekly magazine

[23] "What Makes Great Schools Great," <u>U.S. News & World Report</u>, Aug. 27, 1984, p. 47.

Dates may also be given in the British style, without internal commas: 27 Aug. 1984.

Daily newspaper

[24] Reese Fant, "Of Mongolian Bike Tours and Other Joys," <u>Greenville</u> (S.C.) <u>News</u>, Dec. 12, 1982, p. 1E, cols. 1-3.

Cols. here stands for *columns.*

Letter to the editor

[25] S. Hoechstetter, Letter, <u>American Heritage</u>, 33 (1982), 10.

(4.5) Other Sources

Personal communication

[26] Letter received from President Ronald Reagan, Aug. 12, 1984.

The writer of the paper received this letter.

[27] Gregory F. Paton, Jr., Letter to Richard Kingsley, May 3, 1977.

Someone other than the writer of the paper received this letter.

[28] Personal interview with Jeffrey Maynor, pastor of Calvary Baptist Church, Little Falls, Pa., Nov. 20, 1985.

[29] Telephone interview with Strom Thurmond, United States Senator, May 5, 1984.

Speech or lecture

[30] Jeffrey Maynor, "Christians and Citizens," sermon at Calvary Baptist Church, Little Falls, Pa., Feb. 5, 1984.

Unpublished work

[31] Jane C. Gray, "Churches in Indianapolis Before 1850," unpublished master's thesis, Indiana Univ., 1980.

Film or filmstrip

[32] <u>Ancient Egypt: Discovering Its Splendors</u>, National Geographic Society, 1978.

Weekly magazine

"What Makes Great Schools Great." <u>U.S. News & World Report</u>, Aug. 27, 1984, pp. 46-49.

Recent MLA format:

"What Makes Great Schools Great." <u>U.S. News and World Report</u>, 27 Aug. 1984, 46-49.

Daily newspaper

Fant, Reese. "Of Mongolian Bike Tours and Other Joys." <u>Greenville</u> (S.C.) <u>News</u>, Dec. 12, 1982, p. 1E, cols. 1-3.

Recent MLA format:

Fant, Reese. "Of Mongolian Bike Tours and Other Joys." <u>Greenville</u> (S.C.) <u>News</u>, 12 Dec. 1982, 1E, cols. 1-3.

Letter to the editor

Hoechstetter, S. Letter. <u>American Heritage</u>, 33 (1982), 10.

Recent MLA format:

Hoechstetter, S. Letter. <u>American Heritage</u> 33 (1982): 10.

(4.5) Other Sources

Personal communication

Reagan, Ronald. Letter to author. Aug. 12, 1984.

Paton, Gregory F. Letter to Richard Kingsley.

Maynor, Jeffrey. Personal interview. Nov. 20, 1985.

Thurmond, Strom. Telephone interview. May 4, 1984.

Speech or lecture

Maynor, Jeffrey. "Christians and Citizens." Sermon at Calvary Baptist Church, Little Falls, Pa., Feb. 5, 1984.

Unpublished work

Gray, Jane C. "Churches in Indianapolis Before 1850." Unpublished master's thesis, Indiana Univ., 1980.

Film or filmstrip

<u>Ancient Egypt: Discovering Its Splendors</u>. National Geographic Society, 1978.

Record or Tape

[33] Linda Jones Haught, <u>Creative Conditioning</u>, performed by the Bob Jones Univ. music organizations, Bob Jones Univ. Press, 021113 (cassette), 1984.

(4.6) Secondary sources

Primary and secondary source: main interest in original source

[34] John Dewey, "Science as Subject-Matter and as Method," <u>Science</u>, 36 (Jan. 28, 1910), 127, as cited by David A. Hollinger, "The Problem of Pragmatism in American History," <u>Journal of American History</u>, 67, No. 1 (1980), 94.

Primary and secondary source: main interest in secondary (later) source

[35] David A. Hollinger, "The Problem of Pragmatism in American History," <u>Journal of American History</u>, 67, No. 1 (1980), 94, citing John Dewey, "Science as Subject-Matter and as Method," <u>Science</u>, 36 (Jan. 28, 1910), 127.

Record or tape

Haught, Linda Jones. <u>Creative Conditioning</u>. Performed by the
  Bob Jones Univ. music organizations. Bob Jones Univ.
  Press, 121113 (cassette), 1984.

(4.6) Secondary Sources

Primary and secondary source: main interest in original source

Dewey, John. "Science as Subject-Matter and as Method." <u>Science</u>,
  36 (Jan. 28, 1910), 127. Cited by David A. Hollinger, "The
  Problem of Pragmatism in American History." <u>Journal of
  American History</u>, 67, No. 1 (1980), 94.

Primary and secondary source: main interest in secondary (later) source

Hollinger, David A. "The Problem of Pragmatism in American
  History." <u>Journal of American History</u>, 67, No. 1 (1980), 94.

---

(5) Form of Later Footnotes

Only the first footnote reference to a work gives the
full information for that work. Later references to it
state only what is necessary to clearly identify the work
and the location within it.

Below are later references to the books that appear
in footnotes 2-4 and 6 in **19d(4).**

[7] Mueller, p. 109.

[8] Robins, Bruun, and Zim, p. 69.

[9] Shaw et al., p. 203.

[10] <u>The Music Makers</u>, pp. 163-64.

Notice that all footnotes end with a period.

Regardless of the first footnote, second and later references to any periodical do use the abbreviations *p.* (for *page*) and *pp.* (for *pages*). The reason is that volume numbers are not restated in the later footnotes. Compare the following footnote with note 19 in **19d(4.3)**.

[11] Roberts, p. 838.

If you are using two or more sources written by the same person, then any later reference to either of them should include the title as well as the author.

[12] Solzhenitsyn, The First Circle, p. 201.

[13] Solzhenitsyn, Cancer Ward, pp. 78-79.

Similarly, if you quote two persons with the same last name, you will need to continue using their full names.

[7] Gilbert Mueller, p. 109.

[8] Ralph Mueller, pp. 302-319.

Until recently, *ibid.* (abbreviating Latin *ibidem,* "in the same place") was used in place of any information that would otherwise be repeated from the footnote *immediately* before it.

Older style, for same work and same page	[3] Ibid.

Older style, for same work and different page	[4] Ibid., p. 109.

Today, however, it is recommended that *ibid.* not be used unless a teacher requests it. Instead, use the regular forms shown above in footnotes 7-13 of this section.

(6) Form of parenthetical reference notes

Parenthetical reference notes, mentioned above in **19d(2.3),** are simple to write. They include only what is needed to clearly identify (1) the specific item listed in the bibliography and (2) the location within that listed source.

1. Either the text or the parenthetical note should identify the **author.** Use only the last name unless two of your authors have the same last name.

2. Normally the title is not needed. However, if two or more works by the same author are used, either the title should be mentioned in the text or a short version of it should appear in the reference note. In a parenthetical note, a comma would separate author and short title.

3. The **page reference** should appear either in the text or in the parenthetical note. Do not use the abbreviations *p.* ("page") and *pp.* ("pages") unless they are needed to avoid confusion. For a multivolume work, a colon and one space separate volume and page numbers (for example, 2: 85-87 means volume 2, pages 85-87). Otherwise no punctuation appears before page numbers.

If it should be convenient to mention all the vital information in the text, no parenthetical note is needed.

A few examples follow. In the first version both author and page appear within parentheses. The second version has only the page in parentheses since the author is mentioned in the sentence itself.

The houses built on London Bridge were popular dwellings during the sixteenth century (Gies 45).
According to Joseph Gies, the houses built on London Bridge were popular dwellings during the sixteenth century (45).

If the paper used two or more books by Gies (let's say *Bridges and Men* and *A Matter of Morals*), then the title would be needed:

> According to Joseph Gies in *Bridges and Men,* houses on London Bridge were very popular at that time (45).
>
> According to Joseph Gies, houses on London Bridge were very popular at that time (*Bridges* 45).
>
> Houses on London Bridge were very popular at that time (Gies, *Bridges* 45).

A volume number is used only when it is necessary to guide the reader to the correct location. For instance, if *Bridges and Men* were a two-volume work, we might be quoting from the first volume:

> In the sixteenth century, houses built on London Bridge were popular dwellings (Gies 1: 45).

The sample paper in **19e(2)** contains additional examples of parenthetical reference notes.

19e A Sample Research Paper

(1) Version with footnotes or endnotes
(2) Version with parenthetical reference notes

The short sample paper in this section appears in two versions, so that you can look just at the style you will use. (If your teacher has left the choice of documentation style up to you, see **19d(2)** for help in making that choice.)

If you plan to use either footnotes or endnotes, see the first version below. Look at the second version if you will use parenthetical reference notes.

(1) Version with footnotes or endnotes

This first version of the sample paper has the footnotes in place on each page. To use endnotes instead, simply omit the fifteen-space line and the notes at the foot of each page, and then use a final page of notes. A sample endnote page follows this paper.

Once Every Seventy-Six Years

Gerald Brown

English 11B
Mr. Trenton
November 14, 19__

If an outline page is requested, it takes this form. In addition, an instructor might request that the paper's thesis statement accompany the outline. If so, triple-space down from the heading and type the thesis statement single-spaced with no indentation; then triple-space down again before beginning the double-spaced outline.

Outline

I.   Common characteristics of Halley's Comet

    A.   Makeup

        1.   Head

        2.   Tail

    B.   Definite orbit

II.   Unique characteristics of Halley's Comet

    A.   Its orbit

    B.   Its brightness

    C.   Its known history

    D.   Its name

III.   Reactions to Halley's Comet

    A.   Amazement

    B.   Personal superstition

    C.   Fears

Once Every Seventy-Six Years

The year Mark Twain was born it paid the earth a visit. The United States, Europe, Japan, and Russia will all spend millions of dollars to study it[1]--about every seventy-six years. Scientists have called it a "dirty snowball," but it has showered fame upon a variety of people, from scientists to the German farmer who was the first person to spot its 1758 appearance. What is this hero-maker and scientific marvel? None other than the famous Halley's Comet.

Halley's Comet has many of the same characteristics as other comets. Like other comets, it has two main parts, a head and a tail. The solid nucleus of the head is very small, probably just a few miles in diameter.[2] The tail of any comet is created by the tiny dust particles and gases that have melted away from the head of the comet as it neared the sun. A comet's tail can become millions of miles long when the comet comes close to the sun. However, the tail contains little material--less than in the purest vacuum man can achieve on earth.[3] Also like other comets, Halley's

---

[1] Stephen P. Maran, "Getting Ready for Halley," _Natural History_, 90 (1981), 35.

[2] "Comet," _Encyclopedia Americana_, 1981.

[3] Peter Lancaster Brown, _Comets, Meteorites and Men_ (New York: Taplinger, 1974), p. 68.

2

Comet has a definite orbit. All comet orbits are either
short-period or long-period. Short-period comets have orbits that
take less than one or two hundred years to complete. Halley's
Comet, of course, is a short-period comet.

Halley's Comet has some characteristics, though, that set it
apart from other comets. Unlike many short-period comets,
Halley's goes around the sun in the opposite direction from the
planets.[4] Halley's is also the brightest of the short-period
comets.[5] Furthermore, because of its brightness, Halley's Comet
has been traced back in history as far as 240 B.C.[6] Finally,
Halley's Comet received its name in an unusual manner. Generally,
it is a comet's discoverer who gives his name to it. Halley's
Comet, though, received its name instead from the man who first
calculated that its orbit is about seventy-five to seventy-six
years in length. This astronomer, Edmund Halley, based his concept of the predictability of a comet's orbit on Isaac Newton's
book Principia. This scientific masterpiece discusses the law of
gravity and the laws of motion governing the movement of heavenly
bodies.[7] Using this information and using some historical
accounts of the comet's past appearances, Halley predicted that

---

[4] "Comet."

[5] Michael Oppenheimer and Leonie Haimson, "The Comet
Syndrome," Natural History, 89 (1980), 58.

[6] Brown, pp. 31-32.

[7] Halley was so convinced of the value of Newton's
Principia that he paid to have it published.

3

the comet would return in 1758. Although Halley died in 1742, when his comet returned on schedule scientists unanimously gave it his name.[8]

The reactions to Halley's Comet have been mixed, and often surprising. The ancient philosopher Seneca once exclaimed, "When one of these fiery bodies . . . appears . . . [men] know not whether to wonder or to tremble."[9] Mark Twain thought that since he had come in with Halley's Comet he might well go out with it. So he did, dying in the year of its 1910 appearance. When Halley's Comet came in 1910, some were even afraid that it would poison the inhabitants of the earth, or that it would hit the North Pole and electrocute everyone, or that it would eliminate earth-dwellers with laughing gas.[10]

Each time Halley's Comet returns, people may both wonder and tremble at this ball of ice and rock that speeds through space and appears in our skies every seventy-six years. We can certainly agree with Newton that such precision and order "could only proceed from the counsel and dominion of an intelligent and powerful Being, . . . This Being governs all things, not as the soul of the world, but as Lord of all."[11]

---

[8] Oppenheimer and Haimson, pp. 58-59.

[9] Oppenheimer and Haimson, p. 55.

[10] Oppenheimer and Haimson, pp. 59-60.

[11] Isaac Newton, _Principia_, cited by Herbert Westren Turnbull, "Principia," _Encyclopedia Americana_, 1976.

Bibliography

Brown, Peter Lancaster. Comets, Meteorites and Men. New York:
    Taplinger, 1974.

"Comet." Encyclopedia Americana. 1981 ed.

Maran, Stephen P. "Getting Ready for Halley." Natural History,
    90 (1981), 32-39.

Oppenheimer, Michael, and Leonie Haimson. "The Comet Syndrome."
    Natural History, 89 (1980), 55-60.

Turnbull, Herbert Westren. "Principia." Encyclopedia
    Americana. 1976 ed.

This sample endnote page would substitute for the footnotes of the preceding paper. In a paper its page number would reflect its position just before the bibliography page.

Notes

¹ Stephen P. Maran, "Getting Ready for Halley," <u>Natural History</u>, 90 (1981), 35.

² "Comet," <u>Encyclopedia Americana</u>, 1981.

³ Peter Lancaster Brown, <u>Comets, Meteorites and Men</u> (New York: Taplinger, 1974), p. 68.

⁴ "Comet."

⁵ Michael Oppenheimer and Leonie Haimson, "The Comet Syndrome," <u>Natural History</u>, 89 (1980), 58.

⁶ Brown, pp. 31-32.

⁷ Halley was so convinced of the value of Newton's <u>Principia</u> that he paid to have it published.

⁸ Oppenheimer and Haimson, pp. 58-59.

⁹ Oppenheimer and Haimson, p. 55.

¹⁰ Oppenheimer and Haimson, pp. 59-60.

¹¹ Isaac Newton, <u>Principia</u>, cited by Herbert Westren Turnbull, "Principia," <u>Encyclopedia Americana</u>, 1976.

(2) Version with parenthetical reference notes

Here now is the body of the sample paper using parenthetical reference notes. See **19e(1)** for the title page and the outline page. The form for the parenthetical notes is explained in **19d(6)**.

Once Every Seventy-Six Years

The year Mark Twain was born it paid the earth a visit. The United States, Europe, Japan, and Russia will all spend millions of dollars to study it--about every seventy-six years (Maran 35). Scientists have called it a "dirty snowball," but it has showered fame upon a variety of people, from scientists to the German farmer who was the first person to spot its 1758 appearance. What is this hero-maker and scientific marvel? None other than the famous Halley's Comet.

Halley's Comet has many of the same characteristics as other comets. Like other comets, it has two main parts, a head and a tail. The solid nucleus of the head is very small, probably just a few miles in diameter ("Comet"). The tail of any comet is created by the tiny dust particles and gases that have melted away from the head of the comet as it neared the sun. A comet's tail can become millions of miles long when the comet comes close to the sun. However, the tail contains little material--less than in the purest vacuum man can achieve on earth (Brown 68). Also like other comets, Halley's Comet has a definite orbit. All comet orbits are either short-period or long-period. Short-period comets have orbits that take less than one or two hundred years to complete. Halley's Comet, of course, is a short-period comet.

Halley's Comet has some characteristics, though, that set it apart from other comets. Unlike many short-period comets,

---

Halley's goes around the sun in the opposite direction from the planets ("Comet"). Halley's is also the brightest of the short-period comets (Oppenheimer and Haimson 58). Furthermore, because of its brightness, Halley's Comet has been traced back in history as far as 240 B.C. (Brown 31-32). Finally, Halley's Comet received its name in an unusual manner. Generally, it is a comet's discoverer who gives his name to it. Halley's Comet, though, received its name instead from the man who first calcu- lated that its orbit is about seventy-five to seventy-six years in length. This astronomer, Edmund Halley, based his concept of the predictability of a comet's orbit on Isaac Newton's book <u>Principia</u>. This scientific masterpiece discusses the law of gravity and the laws of motion governing the movement of heavenly bodies.[1] Using this information and using some historical accounts of the comet's past appearances, Halley predicted that the comet would return in 1758. Although Halley died in 1742, when his comet returned on schedule scientists unanimously gave it his name (Oppenheimer and Haimson 58-59).

The reactions to Halley's Comet have been mixed, and often surprising. The ancient philosopher Seneca once exclaimed, "When one of these fiery bodies . . . appears . . . [men] know not whether to wonder or to tremble" (Oppenheimer and Haimson 55). Mark Twain thought that since he had come in with Halley's Comet he might well go out with it. So he did, dying in the year of its 1910 appearance. When Halley's Comet came in 1910, some were even afraid that it would poison the inhabitants of the earth; or that

3

it would hit the North Pole and electrocute everyone, or that it
would eliminate earth-dwellers with laughing gas (Oppenheimer
and Haimson 59-60).

Each time Halley's Comet returns, people may both wonder and
tremble at this ball of ice and rock that speeds through space
and appears in our skies every seventy-six years. We can certainly
agree with Newton that such precision and order "could only proceed from the counsel and dominion of an intelligent and powerful
Being, . . . This Being governs all things, not as the soul of
the world, but as Lord of all" (Principia, cited by Turnbull).

Many papers contain no content notes. In them the final page is devoted entirely to the list of sources, beginning with the heading *Works Cited* two inches below the top of the page.

Notes

[1] Halley was so convinced of the value of Newton's <u>Principia</u> that he paid to have it published (Oppenheimer and Haimson 58).

Works Cited

Brown, Peter Lancaster. <u>Comets, Meteorites and Men</u>. New York: Taplinger, 1974.

"Comet." <u>Encyclopedia Americana</u>. 1981 ed.

Maran, Stephen P. "Getting Ready for Halley." <u>Natural History</u> 90 (1981): 32-39.

Oppenheimer, Michael, and Leonie Haimson. "The Comet Syndrome." <u>Natural History</u> 89 (1980): 55-60.

Turnbull, Herbert Westren. "Principia." <u>Encyclopedia Americana</u>. 1976 ed.

Appendix 1
Glossary of Usage

accept, except *Accept* is a verb meaning "to receive." *Except* is usually a preposition meaning "not including." *Except* can also be a verb meaning "to leave out." —*She will **accept** any small gift **except** money. When the teacher asked for clean-up volunteers, he **excepted** the class officers.*

affect, effect *Affect* is usually a verb meaning "to influence." *Effect* is usually a noun meaning "the result of some action." *Effect* can also be a verb meaning "to cause or bring about." —*That rule would **affect** all of us, and its **effect** might not always be good. Can we **effect** any change in that rule?*

ain't *Ain't* is nonstandard for *isn't* or for other contractions. Use the standard words, not *ain't*. —*John **isn't** here right now.*

among, between Usually *among* should be used in speaking of three or more persons or things, and *between* is used when there are only two. —*The missionary lived **among** the Indians, in the valley **between** Deer Mountain and Two Horn Mountain.*

and etc. See **etc.**

as, like See **like, as.**

bad, badly *Bad* is the adjective and *badly* is the adverb. See **6d(3.1).** —*He would feel **bad** if he did **badly** on that test.*

between, among See **among, between.**

between you and . . . Pronouns that follow any preposition must be in the objective case. Therefore it is correct to say "between you and me," never "between you and I." See rules 1 and 2 in **4a(2.6).**

could of, would of Expressions like *could of, might of,* and *would of* may sound all right to the ear, but they are incorrectly written. For example, the correct contraction for *could have* is *could've.* —*She **would've** been more careful if she'd known anyone cared.*

different When a noun or pronoun object follows, use *different from*, not *different than*. —*How is soccer **different from** football?*

double negative Avoid double negatives like *can't hardly, not no,* and *hardly no*. For these examples the correct forms are *can hardly, not any,* and *hardly any*. —*I **can hardly** believe that there are **not any** empty seats left.*

effect, affect See **affect, effect.**

except, accept See **accept, except.**

etc. *Etc.* is the abbreviation of *et cetera,* meaning "and others." Because *etc.* includes the meaning "and," it is never correct to say *and etc. Etc.* (and *et cetera*) should not be used in formal writing;

they are generally appropriate only in informal writing or in technical or business writing. Substitute an English phrase such as *and others* when needed, or else introduce the list with *such as.* —*My uncle grows **such** vegetables **as** celery, lettuce, and onions. Before lunch I've got to go buy celery, lettuce, **and so on.***

fewer, less *Few, fewer,* and *fewest* should be used with count nouns; and *little, less,* and *least* are used with noncount nouns. See **3b(3.2)** for count and noncount nouns, and **11c** for the use of these words with them. —*Next winter we'll need **less feed,** because we'll have **fewer animals.***

good, well *Good* is the adjective, and *well* (except when it means "not sick") is the adverb. See **6d(3.1)**. —*I feel **good** about doing **well** this morning.*

hisself Do not use *hisself* for the correct pronoun *himself.* See **4a(7-8)**. —*Terry did so well that he surprised **himself.***

infer, imply *Infer* means "to draw a conclusion." *Imply* means "to suggest indirectly." —*From her expression, Joe **inferred** that his mother was pleased with his idea. In his remarks the speaker **implied** that he had always supported conservative causes.*

its, it's *Its* is the possessive of *it,* and *it's* is the contraction of *it is* or *it has.* (Remember that personal pronouns never have apostrophes in their possessive forms.) —***It's** odd that the committee has not announced **its** decision.*

less, fewer See **fewer, less.**

lie, lay *Lie* usually means "to rest in a flat position." As an intransitive verb, *lie* never takes an object. Its principal parts are *lie, lay, lain. Lay* is normally a transitive verb that means "to put or place something"; it does take objects. The principal parts of *lay* are *lay, laid, laid.* —*The children **are lying** down; they usually **lie** down after lunch. The book **is lying** on the shelf; it **lay** there yesterday; it **has lain** there all week. Ken **is laying** the book on the shelf; he **laid** it there yesterday; he **has laid** it there before.*

like, as Both *like* and *as* have a variety of uses, but only one causes problems: the use of *like* as a subordinating conjunction. Although this use has a long and respectable history, many people object to it very strongly. You would therefore be wise to stick with *as,* not *like,* as the subordinating conjunction. Instead of "he did it like he should," say "he did it as (*or* in the way) he should." —*Sherry made the pie **as** the recipe suggested. Little Billy acted **as if** he had never heard of table manners.*

might could In standard English only one modal auxiliary is used in a single complete verb. (See **4b(4)** for the modal auxiliaries.) Use *might be able to* for *might could,* use *perhaps should* for *might should,* and leave out the *would* of *might would.* —*I **might be able to** come if you really need me.*

principal, principle *Principal* can be an adjective meaning "main, or most important." It can also be a noun meaning "the most important person in some situation, such as the head of an elementary or secondary school." *Principle* is a different noun, meaning "a basic truth or guiding policy." —*"Wisdom is the **principal** thing; therefore get wisdom" (Prov. 4:7). During chapel the **principal** reminded the students of several Bible **principles**.*

rise, raise *Rise* means "to go up." As an intransitive verb, *rise* never takes an object. Its principal parts are *rise, rose, risen*. *Raise* is a transitive verb that usually means "to make something go up." Its principal parts are *raise, raised, raised*. —*The balloon **is rising** now; it **rose** yesterday; it **has risen** before. Al **is raising** the window; he **raised** it yesterday; he **has raised** it before.*

sit, set *Sit* usually means "to rest in an upright (sitting) position," and it usually does not take an object. Its principal parts are *sit, sat, sat*. *Set* is normally a transitive verb that means "to put or place something." Its principal parts are *set, set, set*. —*The vase **is sitting** on the shelf. The baby **is sitting** up; he **sat** up yesterday; he **has sat** up before. Jan **is setting** the vase on the shelf; she **set** it there yesterday; she **has set** it there before.*

theirself, theirselves Do not use *theirself* or *theirselves* for the correct pronoun *themselves;* see **6d(3.1)**. However, if the antecedent is singular, a singular pronoun like *himself* is needed; see **9b(1)**. —*They tried not to involve **themselves** in someone else's business. Either Joe or Bob must have recognized **himself** in that story.*

this here (that there, these here, those there) Instead of "this here book," for example, say "this book" or "this book here." The same goes for *that there, these here,* and *those there*. —***These** sunglasses are really nice.*

this kind, these kind Although *these kind* and *those kind* are often heard in conversation, many people object to them as illogical and incorrect. The safe rule is never to mix singular and plural. That is, say either "these (those) kinds are . . . " or "this (that) kind is . . . ." —***This kind** of grape (or grapes) is my favorite.*

used to could Instead of *used to could,* say something like *used to be able to* or *once could*. —*I **once could** do back flips, but I seem to have forgotten how.*

well, good See **good, well**.

who, whom For the correct use of *who* and *whom*, see rules 6 and 7 of **4a(2.6)**.

would of See **could of, would of**.

your, you're *Your* is a possessive form of *you*, and *you're* is the contraction of *you are*. —***You're** coming very close to **your** goal.*

Appendix 2
Sentence Diagrams

Sample diagrams are given under the following major headings:

Subject and verb, with simple modifiers and appositives (1-5)
Sentence patterns with complements (6-16)
Compound sentence elements (17-20)
Independent sentence elements (21-24)
Verbals and verbal phrases (25-34)
Dependent clauses / complex sentences (35-45)
Compound and compound-complex sentences (46-48)

Subject and verb, with simple modifiers and appositives

1. Subject, complete verb (S InV)
   Christ is coming.

2. Understood subject of imperative, prepositional phrase
   Rejoice in the Lord.

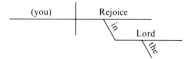

3. Modifiers (determiner, adjective, modifying
   noun, adverb, qualifiers)
   The most faithful Bible characters prayed
   very confidently.

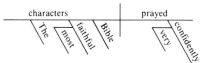

4. Possessive phrase
     The man of God delights in his Lord's Word.

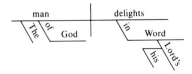

5. Appositive with modifiers
     David, a man after God's own heart, meditated daily in the Scriptures.

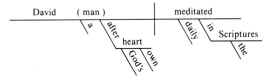

Sentence patterns with complements

6. Predicate noun (S LV PN)
     David is the author of many Psalms.

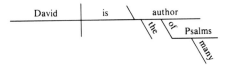

7. Predicate adjective (S LV PA)
     The Bible is faultless.

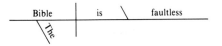

8. Direct object (S TrV DO)
     God's Word reveals His will.

9. Indirect object (S TrV IO DO)
   God gave Moses the law.

10. Adverbial after *be* (S *be* Advl)
    God's truth is there.

11. Prepositional phrase as adverbial after *be*
    (S *be* Advl)
    His commandments are in its pages.

12. Adjective as objective complement
    (S TrV DO OC)
    Bible study makes the Christian wise.

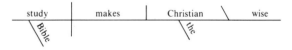

13. Noun as objective complement
    (S TrV DO OC)
    God renamed Jacob Israel.

| God | renamed | Jacob \ Israel |

14. Retained object (passive of S TrV IO DO)
    Moses was given the law.

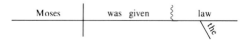

15. Predicate adjective with passive (retained objective complement)
    The Christian is made wise by Bible study.

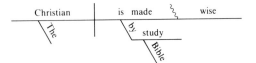

16. Predicate noun with passive (retained objective complement)
    Jacob was renamed Israel.

Jacob	was renamed ⸾⸾ Israel

Compound sentence elements

17. Compound subject, compound predicate
    Both the best students and the best teachers listen attentively and communicate ideas clearly.

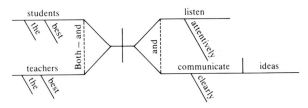

18. Compound verb with a shared auxiliary and adverb and a shared direct object
    Tom, Jack, and Barbara have already read and understood that assignment.

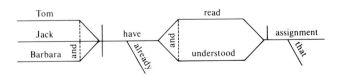

19. Compound adjectives, compound direct object
with shared modifier
    An effective and dedicated Christian teacher
bases his values and philosophy on the Bible.

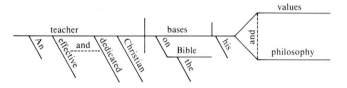

20. Compound adverbs
    Modern office machines operate faster and
more reliably.

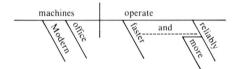

Independent sentence elements

21. The subject substitutes (expletives) *there* and *it*
    There is time now for your homework.

    It is good to study early.

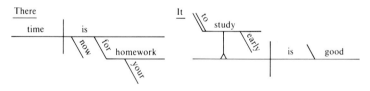

22. Isolates
    Oh, sure, I still have plenty of time.

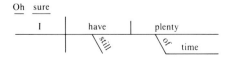

23. Noun of address
    Joan, have you finished yet?

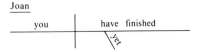

24. Absolute phrase (with and without participle)
    Her work being complete, she slept peacefully.

    Her work complete, she slept peacefully.

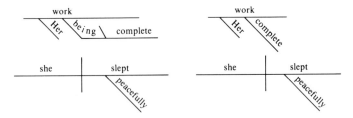

Verbals and verbal phrases (Participles)

25. Participle
    We once saw the flooding Amazon River.

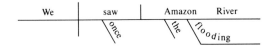

26. Participle phrase
    The Amazon, placidly crossing four countries, almost follows the equator.

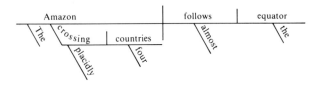

(Infinitives)

27. Infinitive phrase as subject
   To live on the Amazon requires a boat for transportation.

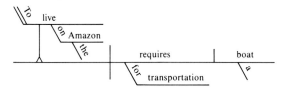

28. "Subject" of the infinitive
   We asked the pilot to fly over some large islands.

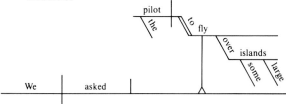

29. Infinitive phrase as object of the preposition, sign of the infinitive understood
   In that area people can do nothing except travel by boat.

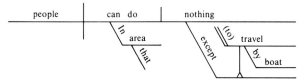

30. Adverbial infinitive phrase
   Roads are now being built to decrease the area's isolation.

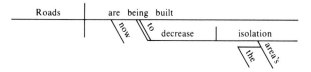

31. Infinitive modifying predicate adjective
    A road through that jungle would be hard to build.

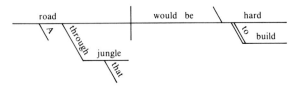

(Gerunds)

32. Gerund as subject
    Running is good exercise.

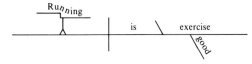

33. Gerund phrases as direct object and object of preposition
    Paul compared living for Christ to running a good race.

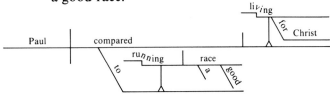

34. Gerund phrase as appositive, possessive "subject" of the gerund
    The Christian life, our running of the race, requires obedience to Christ.

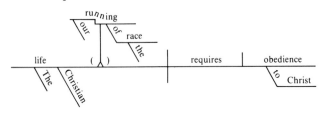

**Dependent clauses / complex sentences
(Adjective clauses)**

35. Adjective clause
    The coach who wants the best for his
    athletes teaches them self-discipline.

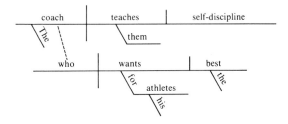

36. Adjective clause containing *whom* as direct
    object
    Such coaches will patiently instruct their
    athletes, whom they can help a great deal.

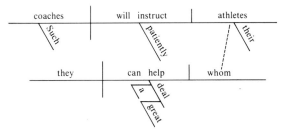

37. Adjective clause with understood relative
    pronoun
    The lazy student is not the kind they want
    on their teams.

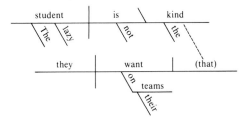

38. Adjective clause with relative adverb *when*
I can hardly remember a time when the coach was so happy with our effort.

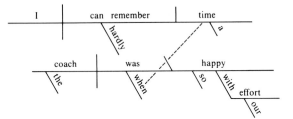

(Adverb clauses)

39. Adverb clause modifying the verb
The coach rejoiced because we won the sportsmanship trophy.

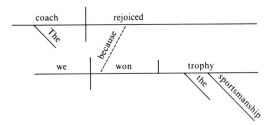

40. Adverb clause of comparison modifying the comparative word
The star player is six inches taller than the coach.

The coach is more experienced than he is.

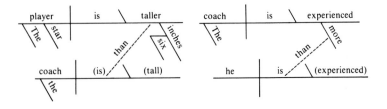

41. Adverb clause of comparison modifying *as*
    The coach deserved as much credit for our victory as we did.

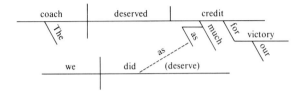

(Noun clauses)

42. Noun clause as subject (introduced by subordinating conjunction *that*)
    That the Pony Express quickly failed has not lessened its impact on American history.

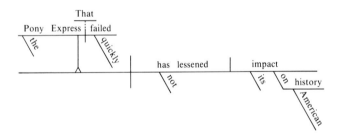

43. Noun clause as direct object (introduced by the indefinite relative adverb *how*)
    Have you ever studied how the Pony Express was formed and financed?

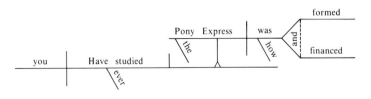

44. Noun clause as object of preposition
    The investors were stunned by how much money they lost.

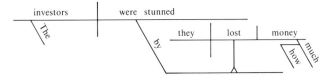

45. Noun clause as appositive
    The owners' idea that they could succeed financially died with the establishment of the telegraph.

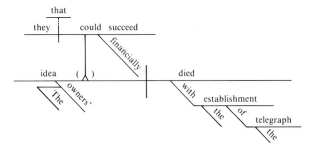

Compound and compound-complex sentences

46. Compound sentence with conjunction
    President Franklin Pierce was from the North, but he denounced the anti-slavery movement of his day.

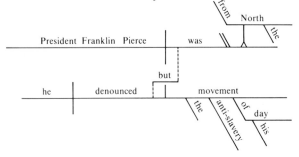

47. Compound sentence with semicolon instead of conjunction

His decisions and policies as President accomplished little; consequently, his party did not nominate him for re-election.

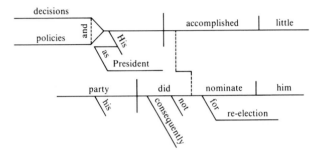

48. Compound-complex sentences

Above all, he wanted to avoid a civil war; and in later years he strongly criticized President Lincoln, whom he saw as the instigator of that conflict.

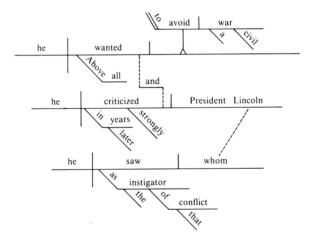

Glossary of Grammatical Terms

Absolute comparative and superlative The comparative or superlative degree used without any intention of specific comparison to other things. **3d(3.3)**

Absolute phrase A phrase that only loosely modifies the rest of the sentence. Because the phrase has no close connections with any other part of the sentence, it is called "absolute." Often an absolute phrase consists of a noun modified by a participle or participle phrase. **8b(3.4)**

Abstract noun A noun that refers to mental, nonmaterial things. **3b(3.4)**

Action verb A verb that expresses action. It is not necessarily either transitive or intransitive. **7b, 14a**

Active voice The verb forms which signal that the subject acts or is identified or described. All the basic sentence patterns incorporate active verbs. **7e**

Adjective A word that usually modifies a noun and can be compared using -er/-est or more/most. Any word that fits *both* blanks in this test frame sentence is an adjective: The _____ thing (person) is very _____ . **3d(1)**

Adjective clause A dependent clause that modifies a noun or a pronoun. Also called an "adjectival clause" or a "relative clause." Most adjective clauses contain relative pronouns. **8a(1)**

Adverb A word that usually modifies a verb. It adds information about the action or state of being expressed by the verb. See **qualifier** for most modifiers of adjectives and adverbs. **3e(1)**

Adverb clause A dependent clause that modifies a verb. Also called an "adverbial clause." Adverb clauses are introduced by subordinating conjunctions. **8a(2)**

Adverbial noun A noun that modifies a verb. **6b(7)**

Antecedent The word or word group that a pronoun stands for. The antecedent nearly always appears before the pronoun. **9b**

Appositive A word or phrase that renames a preceding noun or pronoun. The appositive usually comes right after the word renamed. **6b(4)**

Article A determiner that shows whether a noun is being used in a definite or an indefinite sense. **4c(2)**

Auxiliary A "helping verb" that may join the true verb in making the complete verb of a sentence or clause. **4b(1)**

Basic sentence pattern See **Sentence pattern.**

Case The form of a noun or a pronoun that reflects the way the word is used in the sentence. Pronouns have three case forms—subjective, objective, and possessive. **4a(2.4)**

Clause A group of words that has both a subject and a predicate. **4f(1.3), 8a(intro.)**

Close appositive A short appositive that is necessary to identify the word it follows. A close appositive can also be called a restrictive appositive. **6b(4)**

Collective noun A noun that refers to a group. **3b(3.3)**

Comma splice Two sentences incorrectly joined by only a comma. **13b(1)**

Common noun A general word for a person, place, thing, or idea. The opposite of **proper noun. 3b(3.1)**

Comparative degree The form of an adjective or adverb that shows comparison of two things. It can be made with *-er* or *more.* **3d(3.1)**

Complement A "completer" of any of the sentence patterns. Complements include predicate nouns, indirect objects, and so on. Both finite verbs (simple predicates) and verbals can have complements. **6b(8)**

Complex sentence A sentence made of one independent clause and at least one dependent clause. **8a(5.3)**

Compound noun A noun formed by joining two or more words to make a new word. Also called simply a "compound." **3b(4.1)**

Compound sentence A sentence made of two or more independent clauses. **8a(5.2)**

Compound sentence element Two or more items of the same kind of sentence element joined by a coordinating conjunction. For example, a sentence may have a compound subject. **4f(1.1)**

Compound-complex sentence A sentence made of two or more independent clauses and at least one dependent clause. **8a(5.4)**

Concrete noun A noun that refers to physical, material things. **3b(3.4)**

Conjugation A systematic listing of all the forms of a verb. **7g**

Conjunction A connecting word that joins words or groups of words in the sentence. **4f**

Conjunctive adverb An adverb that modifies the verb in an independent clause and serves as a meaning-link to another independent clause. **3e(7)**

Coordinating conjunction A connecting word that joins sentence parts of the same type. **4f(1)**

Coordination The joining of sentence elements on an equal basis. **9e(2.1)**

Correlative conjunctions A separated pair of words used to join equal sentence parts together. **4f(1.4)**

Count noun A common noun that can be made plural. **3b(3.2)**

Dangling modifier A modifier that has nothing in the sentence that it can logically modify. **9d(3)**

Demonstrative determiner A determiner that shows whether the noun it modifies names something near or far, and also whether there is one or more than one. **4c(4)**

Demonstrative pronoun A pronoun that points out the position of something. **4a(5)**

Dependent clause A clause that cannot stand alone as a sentence. A dependent clause has a subject and a predicate but is subordinate to an independent clause. **8a**

Determiner A word that points out, or limits, the following noun. In general, a determiner signals that a noun is coming in the sentence. Determiners come before any descriptive adjectives that may modify the same noun. **4c(1)**

Direct object A word in the predicate that receives the action of the verb. Except when the direct object is a reflexive pronoun, the direct object names something different from the subject of the sentence. **5d, 6b(2)**

Expletive A word in the sentence that is a mere "place-holder" for the subject, which comes later. Two English words can be expletives: *it* and *there*. **8a(3.1)**

Finite verb A verb whose form allows it to be used as a simple predicate in a sentence or clause. The opposite of *finite verb* is *nonfinite verb,* or *verbal.* **7f(1)**

Fragment An incomplete sentence wrongly punctuated as if it were a complete sentence. **13a**

Function What a word or phrase does in the sentence; how it is related to other parts of the sentence. **6a**

Fused sentence Two sentences incorrectly joined with no punctuation and no conjunction. **13b(2)**

Future perfect tense A verb expressing action that will be completed before a certain time in the future. **4b(3.1), 7b(3)**

Future progressive tense A verb that expresses continuing action that will take place in the future. **4b(3.2), 7b(3)**

Future tense A verb expressing what is going to happen in the future. **4b(2), 7b(3)**

Gender The classification of third-person singular pronouns into masculine, feminine, and neuter. **4a(2.3)**

Gerund A verbal noun: a verb form ending in *-ing* that performs one of the functions of nouns. **7f(4)**

Indefinite determiner One of a group of determiners that can be used instead of articles in the noun phrase. They give a somewhat indefinite meaning to the noun modified. **4c(5, 10)**

Indefinite pronoun A pronoun that refers to persons and things in general terms. It refers to a large category, or part of a large category, without definitely specifying the particular individual or the particular part. **4a(6)**

Independent clause A clause that can stand alone as a sentence. **4f(1.3)**

Independent possessive A possessive word or phrase that by itself is used like a noun phrase (for instance, as a subject or a direct object). **6b(3.2)**

Indirect object A word or phrase that (without a preposition) tells to whom or for whom an action is done. It appears before the direct object. **5e**

Infinitive A phrase made up of *to* and a following verb. Infinitives may modify nouns or verbs, or they may perform the functions of nouns. **7f(2)**

Intensive pronoun A pronoun ending in *-self* or *-selves* that emphasizes some noun or pronoun already in the sentence. Grammatically it functions as an appositive to the noun emphasized. **4a(8)**

Interjection A word used to express strong feeling. The interjection is one type of isolate. **4g**

Interrogative adverb An adverb that asks a question. **3e(7.1)**

Interrogative determiner A determiner that asks for more information about the noun modified. **4c(7)**

Interrogative pronoun A pronoun that asks a question; the answer would be a noun or a pronoun. **4a(4)**

Intransitive verb A verb that occurs in the pattern *S InV.* An intransitive verb does not require anything to complete it (that is, it is an active verb without a complement). **7a(2)**

Isolate A word that can stand alone, punctuated as a sentence, or can appear along with a regular sentence in which it takes no real part. It is not a necessary part of any regular sentence. Isolates express strong feeling, agreement or disagreement, greetings, politeness, and hesitation or introduction of a subject. **4g**

Limiter One of a certain small group of determiners *(all, both, half)* that often precede other determiners. They further limit, or specify, the meaning of the total noun phrase. **4c(8, 10)**

Linking verb A verb that appears in either pattern, *S LV PN* or *S LV PA*. A linking verb is something like an equal sign, linking the subject with a predicate noun or a predicate adjective. **7a(3)**

Major parts of speech The four large classes of words that carry most of the meaning of sentences. The major parts of speech are nouns, verbs, adjectives, and adverbs. **3a**

Minor parts of speech The small classes of words that mainly show how the nouns, verbs, adjectives, and adverbs are related to one another in sentences. The minor parts of speech are pronouns, auxiliaries, determiners, qualifiers, prepositions, conjunctions, and isolates. **3a**

Misplaced modifier A modifier whose position makes it seem to modify the wrong word in the sentence. The sentence should be revised so that the modifier is by the word it modifies. **9d(1)**

Modal auxiliary An auxiliary that expresses the speaker's attitude toward the action or state of being he is talking about. **4b(4)**

Modifier A grammatical relationship in which one word is dependent on another. In meaning, a modifier describes whatever is named by the word it modifies. **6a**

Modifying noun A noun that modifies another noun. **6b(5)**

Noncount noun A common noun that cannot be made plural (cannot be counted). **3b(3.2)**

Nonfinite verb A verb whose form allows it to be used in a way other than as a simple predicate. Nonfinite verbs are also called verbals. There are three types: infinitives, participles, and gerunds. **7f**

Nonrestrictive modifier A modifier that adds extra information but is not necessary for identification of the particular item described. **10d(5)**

Noun The name of a person, place, thing, or idea. Most nouns can be made plural or possessive or both. **3b(1)**

Noun clause A dependent clause that functions in the sentence as if it were a noun. Also called a "nominal clause." Most noun clauses are introduced by the subordinating conjunction *that*. **8a(3)**

Noun of address A noun that identifies the person being addressed. **6b(6)**

Noun phrase A noun or a pronoun and any modifiers it may have. **6c(1)**

Number The classification of personal pronouns into singular and plural. Also, the singular and plural forms of nouns. **4a(2.2), 3b(2)**

Object of preposition The word or phrase that the preposition relates to the rest of the sentence. The preposition and its object together make up the prepositional phrase. **4e(1)**

Objective case The form of a pronoun when it is an object: direct object, indirect object, object of preposition. Words with certain other functions may also be in the objective case. **4a(2.6), 6b(2)**

Objective complement A word or phrase that comes after the direct object and either renames or describes it. An objective complement completes the information about the direct object as a result of the action of the verb. **5g**

Parallel elements Words or phrases that have the same grammatical form and are joined on an equal basis (usually by a coordinating conjunction). **9i**

Part of speech One of the kinds of words (noun, verb, preposition, etc.) that we use to make sentences. The parts of speech are recognized most reliably by their form and the typical ways they are used in sentences, but they also tend to express certain areas of meaning. **3(intro.), 3a**

Participle A verbal adjective. A participle, made from a verb, modifies a noun. Many participles end in *-ing, -en,* or *ed.* **7f(3)**

Passive voice The verb forms which signal that the subject is acted upon. Only transitive verbs can be made passive. **7e**

Past perfect tense A verb expressing action that was completed before a certain time in the past. **4b(3.1), 7b(2)**

Past progressive tense A verb expressing continuing action that took place in the past. **4b(3.2), 7b(2)**

Past tense A verb expressing action that has already happened. **7b(2)**

Personal pronoun One of the group of pronouns that are distinguished by person, number, and sometimes gender. The personal pronouns are *I, we, you, he, she, it,* and *they,* along with their other case-forms. **4a(2)**

Phrase A word group that does not contain both a subject and a predicate. Compare **noun phrase. 4f(1.2)**

Possessive A word that expresses ownership or some other kind of "belongingness." Most possessive nouns and pronouns function as determiners, modifiers of nouns. **3b(2), 4a(2.4), 4c(3)**

Possessive determiner A possessive word or phrase that modifies a noun. **6b(3.1)**

Appendix 3

Possessive phrase A group of words that contains a possessive noun and shows ownership. When a possessive phrase modifies a noun, it does so as a unit, acting as a single determiner. **4c(3)**

Predicate The part of the sentence that asserts something about the subject. The complete predicate consists of a verb (the simple predicate) and usually other words. **2a-2c**

Predicate adjective An adjective in the predicate that describes the subject. **5c**

Predicate noun A noun (or noun-substitute) in the predicate that renames or identifies the subject. **5b, 6b(1)**

Preposition A word that relates its object (normally a noun or a pronoun) to another word in the sentence. **4e(1)**

Prepositional phrase A preposition and its complete object (a noun phrase). **4e(1)**

Present perfect tense A verb expressing action that has been done within the present time period. **4b(3.1), 7b(1)**

Present progressive tense A verb expressing action going on (action in progress) in the present. **4b(3.2), 7b(1)**

Present tense A verb expressing action that normally happens (in the general present), or a present state of affairs. **7b(1)**

Principal parts The three basic forms of a verb from which all other forms of that verb can be made. **7c**

Pronoun A word that substitutes for a noun or for an entire noun phrase. **4a(1)**

Pronoun reference The relation of a pronoun to its antecedent, an earlier word or phrase. **9c(intro.)**

Proper noun A specific name for a certain person, place, or thing. Proper nouns must be capitalized. **3b(3.1)**

Qualifier A special kind of word that modifies an adjective or an adverb, either strengthening or weakening the idea of the adjective or adverb. **4d**

Quantity word One of the group of determiners that can be used after other determiners like articles, possessives, and demonstratives. (Most words in this group have meanings of quantity or numerical ordering.) **4c(6, 10)**

Reciprocal pronoun A pronoun that expresses a mutual relationship among the persons mentioned in the subject. There are two reciprocal pronouns, *each other* and *one another*. **4a(10)**

Reflexive pronoun A pronoun ending in *-self* or *-selves* that is used as an object to refer to the same person or thing as the subject. **4a(7)**

Relative adverb An adverb that modifies the verb in a dependent clause, introducing the clause and relating the clause to the rest of the sentence. (A relative adverb introduces an adjective clause that modifies a noun of time, place, or reason.) **3e(7)**

Relative pronoun A pronoun, in a dependent clause, that relates the dependent clause to the rest of the sentence. The relative pronoun has a function such as subject or direct object in its own clause. **4a(9)**

Restricter One of the small group of determiners that are used at the very beginning of the noun phrase. **4c(9, 10)**

Restrictive modifier A modifier that is necessary for identification of the particular item described. **10d(5)**

Retained object A direct or indirect object that is retained in object position when an active sentence is made passive. **6b(11)**

Sequence of tenses How the tenses of two clauses work together to relate the times of two events. **9f(1.2)**

Simple sentence A sentence made of one independent clause only. **8a(5.1)**

State verb A verb used to describe a state or a condition. It is not necessarily a linking verb. **7b, 14a**

Subject The word or phrase that the sentence is about. It may refer to the doer of the action or to the person or thing described or identified by the predicate. **2a, 2b, 6b(1)**

Subject-verb agreement Correct use mainly of singular subjects with singular verbs and of plural subjects with plural verbs. The first word of the complete verb agrees with the person and number of the subject. **9a(1)**

Subjective case The form of a pronoun when it is a subject. Words with certain other functions may also be in the subjective case. **4a(2.6), 6b(1)**

Subjective complement A word or phrase in the predicate that either renames or describes the subject. The two kinds of subjective complement are the predicate noun and the predicate adjective. **5c**

Subordinating conjunction A conjunction that joins a dependent clause (a subordinate clause) to an independent clause. A subordinating conjunction is part of the dependent clause, but its only function in that clause is to introduce it in a fitting way. **4f(2)**

Subordination Changing certain independent clauses to dependent clauses to express the relations between clauses and make the paragraph flow more smoothly. **9e(2.2)**

Superlative degree The form of an adjective or adverb that shows comparison of three or more things. It can be made with *-est* or *most*. **3d(3.1)**

Tag question A phrase like *didn't he* or *would you* that is "tagged" on to the end of a sentence to make it into a question. **10d(4.6)**

Tense Forms of a verb that indicate time, continuing action, or completed action or state of being. (Strictly speaking, tense has to do only with time: past, present, future. For convenience, though, we usually speak of the progressive and perfect forms as being tenses too.) **7b, 4b(2-3)**

Test frame A formula used to determine the part of speech. There is a test frame for verbs and one for adjectives. **3c(1), 3d(1)**

Transitive verb A verb that appears in any pattern that includes a direct object, such as *S TrV IO DO*. Only a transitive verb can be made passive. **5d, 7a(1)**

Two-way modifier A modifier that is unclear because it stands between two sentence elements that it could modify. **9d(2)**

Verb A word that expresses action or state of being. A true verb can be identified by form: it can take the *-ing* suffix, and in the present tense it has a change in form for the third-person singular. It can also be identified by the use of the test frame in **3c(1)**.

Verb-adverb combination (VAC) A verb and a following adverb used to express a single meaning. The adverb is movable, appearing right after the verb or after the direct object. **3e(6.1)**

Verbal See **Nonfinite verb**

Voice The verb-form differences that signal the role of the subject in relation to the verb. English has two voices, active and passive. **7e**

Answers to Practice Exercises

Chapter 2

Practice 2-1
Numbers 1, 3, 7, and 10 are complete sentences.

Practice 2-2
1. The rainbow | reminds us of God's promise in Genesis 9:11-17.
2. Rainbows | are produced by sunlight and raindrops.
3. Many drops of water | reflect the sun's rays.
4. A bright arch of colors | appears in the sky.
5. Every rainbow | has the same colors, from true red through violet.

Practice 2-3
1. <u>Glass</u> | <u>has</u> many uses.
2. Glass <u>jars</u> | <u>preserve</u> food safely.
3. Bullet-resisting <u>glass</u> | <u>can stop</u> even heavy bullets.
4. Glass <u>windows</u> | <u>admit</u> light.
5. Art <u>objects</u> of fine glass | <u>have</u> a special beauty.

Chapter 3

Practice 3-1
The nouns: dream, Christian, Vanity Fair, Hopeful, companion, person, testimony, truth, ashes, pilgrimage, men, fair, time.

Practice 3-2

Singular	man	boy	wife	runner
Singular Possessive	man's	boy's	wife's	runner's
Plural	men	boys	wives	runners
Plural Possessive	men's	boys'	wives'	runners'

Practice 3-3
Count nouns: family, van, trip, house.
Noncount nouns: furniture, luggage, gravel.

Practice 3-4
The verbs: strolled, yearned, barked, landed, learned. Without the *-ed* suffix, they all fit into at least one test-frame sentence.

Practice 3-5
1. cold, white   3. Hungry   5. Warm, old
2. Small, round   4. icy

Practice 3-6
1. earlier   3. worse   5. dirtier
2. more practical 4. more helpful

Practice 3-7
1. smaller   3. rich (*or* richest) 5. better
2. short   4. tangy   6. most refreshing

Practice 3-8

Adverb	Classification	Adverb	Classification
silently	manner	around	place
Earlier	time	clearly	manner
constantly	time or manner	not	negative
now	time	even	manner (extent)
already	time	Everywhere	place
away	place	deeply	manner (extent)

Practice 3-9
2. called off   6. makes up   10. (should) give up
5. (Did) look up 7. (Have) filled out

Note concerning numbers 3 and 8: Dictionary definitions are not a reliable guide as to whether a pair of words is a VAC. Dictionaries do normally define VACs (like *look up*), but they also include some combinations of verb and preposition (like *look for* or *look after*). Their purpose in doing so is to clarify meaning, not to make a grammatical point.

Practice 3-10
The verb-adverb combinations: (can) bring about, found out, filled out, turned in, put across, think through. The two improved sentences: (1) All the production-line workers filled out one of the comment sheets last week. (2) Now how can we put across a better attitude toward them?

Chapter 4

Practice 4-1
1. He   2. me   3. her   4. him

Answers to Exercises

Practice 4-2
1. I   2. him   3. I

Practice 4-3
1. We   2. we   3. us   4. We

Practice 4-4
1. she   2. they   3. he

Practice 4-5
1. who   2. who   3. who   4. whom   5. who

Practice 4-6
1. Who   2. who   3. whom   4. who   5. who

Practice 4-7
1. he   2. he   3. I   4. me

Practice 4-8
1. my   2. Her   3. his   4. His

Practice 4-9
Numbers 3 and 5 may sound awkward; after the correct answer for each of these, one possible revision is given.
1. us   3. she (She must be the next speaker.)
2. me   4. him
               5. her (No one thought she would be the loser.)

Practice 4-10
1. Whom, who   5. which (indirect form of the question, "Which of us
2. (none)   shall be the greatest?")
3. who, What   6. Which
4. (none)   7. Whose

Practice 4-11
1. that   2. (none)   3. This   4. (none)   5. These, those

Practice 4-12
1. Everyone   2. Many,few 3. all   4. something, nothing

Practice 4-13
1. himself   3. yourself   5. itself   7. themselves
2. themselves 4. himself   6. yourselves 8. himself

Practice 4-14
1. herself   4. myself   6. themselves
2. yourself   5. herself   7. himself (*or* yourself)
3. (none; *herself* is reflexive, an object of preposition)

Practice 4-15
1. who   4. who, that, that
2. who   5. that
3. who   6. which

Practice 4-16
1. Whatever   3. which   5. whichever
2. what   4. (none; *who* is interrogative)

Practice 4-17

A. 1. past
   2. past
   3. future
   4. present

B. 1. past perfect
   2. present perfect
   3. future perfect

C. 1. past progressive
   2. past progressive
   3. future progressive
   4. present progressive

D. 1. present perfect
   2. present
   3. present
   4. past
   5. past perfect
   6. past progressive
   7. past
   8. past
   9. present
  10. present perfect
  11. future progressive
  12. future

Practice 4-18
1. would like   4. may become
2. might study   5. would study
3. is calling   6. become

Practice 4-19
Passive verbs are found in numbers 2, 3, 4, and 6.

Practice 4-20
1. was walking   6. can come
2. thought   7. have missed
3. will do   8. is
4. will shoot ('ll shoot)   9. do make—emphatic
5. do hope—emphatic

Practice 4-21
1. our neighbor's   2. His   3. A   4. our other neighbor's, a, the

Practice 4-22
1. This cup, that saucer   6. these smaller plates
2. those glass dishes   8. these dishes, these days
4. these two plates   (The other demonstratives are pronouns.)

Practice 4-23
1. Many useful corn <u>varieties,</u> <u>America,</u> one interesting <u>type,</u> <u>popcorn</u>
   Det   Adj ModN   Det   Adj
2. its small pearl <u>kernels,</u> delicious white <u>puffs</u>
  Det Adj ModN   Adj   Adj
3. Most <u>scientists,</u> these tiny <u>explosions,</u> steam <u>pressure</u>
  Det   Det Adj   ModN
4. All the <u>kernels,</u> just enough <u>moisture,</u> the <u>corn</u>
  Det Det   Det   Det   Det

Practice 4-24

1. somewhat, rather
2. quite, even
3. much
4. very, almost

Practice 4-25

1. *to* the door, *of* the cage
2. *on* his face, *in* the cage
3. *With* his wooden chair, *at* a safe distance
4. *of* laughter, *from* the audience
5. *of* shiny false fangs, *from* the lion's mouth

Practice 4-26

1. *among* the world's great inventors
2. *During* his lifetime, *of* useful inventions
3. *Without* a doubt, *above* all the others
4. *with* a cylinder, *on* the top
5. *around* the cylinder, *with* a crank
6. *toward* the mouthpiece
7. *along with* his assistant
8. *After* a brief pause
9. *According to* the story, *with* astonishment

Practice 4-27

1. (of the prettiest things (in our yard)) [OP, OP]
2. (of blue flowers), (to the blooms (of the lilac)) [OP, OP, OP]
3. (to butterflies) [OP]
4. (In northern winters), (to the roots) [OP, OP]
5. (on the new wood (of the current year)) [OP, OP]

Practice 4-28

1. (for the butterfly bush) [OP]
2. (on new wood), (in the winter) [OP, OP]
3. (into its new growth), (in late spring) [OP, OP]
4. (to about six inches), (in the winter) [OP, OP]
5. (Except for its winter trim), (from any (of us)) [OP, OP, OP]

Practice 4-29

1. Watch **and** pray
2. Many are called, **but** few are chosen.
3. friend **or** brother
4. All the rivers run into the sea; **yet** the sea is not full.
5. to the right hand **nor** to the left
6. Alpha **and** Omega, the beginning **and** the end, the first **and** the last

Answers to Exercises

Practice 4-30
1. in Paris **and** in New York
2. **Both** the Eiffel Tower in Paris **and** the Statue of Liberty in New York
3. freedom **and** brotherhood (In this sentence *both* is a determiner, not a correlative conjunction.)
4. **Neither** the Eiffel Tower **nor** the Statue of Liberty
5. The Statue of Liberty was dedicated in 1886, **yet** it did not become a national monument until 1924.
6. **Either** too tall **or** too ugly
7. slowly **but** surely, **both** national **and** international

Practice 4-31
1. because she desired a son
2. if He would grant her request
3. After she had borne Samuel
4. When she would come to offer sacrifice
5. once she had kept her vow

Practice 4-32
1. unless in her heart she fears the Lord
2. While it is yet night
3. so that their needs will be met
4. as she would act toward the Lord
5. Since her husband safely trusts in her
6. so that she is found worthy of the praise of her husband and her children

Practice 4-33
1. When the Canaanites afflicted Israel
2. lest he lose courage
3. that not one of the enemy escaped
4. as if she were a friend of Sisera, the Canaanite captain
5. that Deborah and Barak composed a song to commemorate the battle

Practice 4-34
1. that new farming methods could use less seed and yet produce greater yields
2. that root-crop rotation could provide both nitrogen for the soil and winter fodder for livestock
3. That Robert Blackwell's cattle-breeding methods worked
4. that seeds be planted in rows
5. (no noun clause)
6. that small farmers could not afford to enclose their land with the required fences
7. that unemployed village farmers would become the factory workers for the Industrial Revolution

Practice 4-35
1. Hello
2. Yes (*Why* is not an isolate in this sentence.)
3. Well, please
4. Why, yes, uh (*Right* is not an isolate here or in the next sentence.)
5. Okay
6. Right
7. Thanks

Chapter 5

Practice 5-1

1. The general finally arrived.
   S   InV

2. Now the ceremony could begin.
   S   InV

3. The valiant young lieutenant stepped to the front.
   S   InV

4. He looked into his commander's eyes.
   S InV

5. A tear rolled down the old general's cheek.
   S   InV

6. Such rewards belong only to the brave.

Practice 5-2

1. Carnegie was working in the telegraph office of a railroad company.
   S   InV

2. Later he moved into the steel industry.
   S   InV

3. His wealth increased through hard work and wise investment.
   S   InV

4. By 1900 he had become a millionaire.
   S   LV   PN

5. In his later years he was a generous contributor to worthy causes.
   S LV   PN

6. Carnegie's financial success sprang from America's free-enterprise system.
   S   InV

Practice 5-3

1. The doctors were helpless.
   S   LV   PA

2. Finally Lazarus died.
   S   InV

3. After four days the Lord Jesus came to the tomb.
   S   InV

$\overset{S}{\text{Lazarus}}$ had $\overset{LV}{\text{been}}$ $\overset{PN}{\text{His friend.}}$

4. Lazarus had been His friend.

5. Jesus called with a loud voice.

6. Lazarus walked out of the grave.

7. Jesus Christ is the resurrection and the life.

Practice 5-4

1. The groundhog saw his shadow on the snow.

2. He became a very worried creature.

3. He hid himself deep in his burrow.

4. Afterward the people had six more weeks of winter.

5. Today the groundhog story has become a legend.

6. The second day of February is Groundhog Day.

Practice 5-5

1. The children took the old radio to school.

2. They showed it to their friends.

3. Jack offered them ten dollars for it.

4. They suggested a higher price.

5. In the end they sold the radio to Jill.

Practice 5-6

1. One of the worst natural disasters in our history happened in Johnstown in 1889.

2. Johnstown is a city in western Pennsylvania.

3. Joseph Johns gave the city its name.

4. The valley setting of the city is very beautiful.

5. In 1889 a heavy rainfall swelled the reservoir behind the South Fork Dam.

6. The earthen dam finally burst under the pressure.

7. The flood waters covered the city.

8. Approximately 2100 people died in the flood.

        S   TrV   IO   DO

9. Clara Barton of the Red Cross offered the survivors her help.

                         S   LV

10. High-water markers on certain downtown buildings are

            PN

present-day reminders of the historic disaster.

Practice 5-7

    Advl   *be*   S

1. Where are the mysterious Galapagos Islands?

               S   *be*   Advl

2. The Galapagos Islands are (in the Pacific Ocean).

    S LV   PN

3. They are a part of Ecuador.

          S   TrV   IO   DO

4. Herman Melville gave them a different name, the

Enchanted Islands.

             S   S   TrV   DO

5. English buccaneers and whalers first discovered these islands.

             S   LV   PA

6. The land turtles on these islands are gigantic.

    S   TrV DO

7. Sailors used them as a source of fresh meat.

              S   TrV   DO

8. Didn't Charles Darwin develop his preposterous theory of

evolution after a visit to these islands?

            S InV

9. When did he visit there?

          S   *be* Advl

10. In 1835 he was there.

Practice 5-8

                S   TrV   DO

1. In A.D. 330 Constantine the Great made Constantinople the

    OC

new capital of the Roman Empire.

                      S   TrV   IO   DO

2. During this time Constantine gave the Christians relief from

years of persecution.

         S   *be*   Advl

3. Constantinople is (on the shores of the Bosporus River).

                                       S   LV

4. During the Middle Ages this large European city was

    PA

magnificent.

                              S   InV

5. By the tenth century one million people lived in this city.

             S   LV PN

6. Constantinople's church Hagia Sophia, Holy Wisdom, is one

of the supreme architectural masterpieces of the Middle Ages.

7. Historians call this period the Byzantine period.
   S   TrV   DO   OC

8. The people, however, considered themselves "Romans."
      S   TrV   DO   OC

9. A triple wall of fortification and the use of Greek fire protected
      S   S   TrV
   this city from most invaders.
    DO

10. Eventually, though, the Turks captured the city.
                    S   TrV   DO

11. They renamed it Istanbul.
   S   TrV   DO OC

Chapter 6

Practice 6-1
1. spirit *(subject),* team   3. team, member *(subject),* teammates
2. captain *(subject),* player

Practice 6-2

1. <u>Howler monkeys</u> abound throughout South and
    S   InV

   Central America.

2. <u>They</u> make loud resounding calls.
   S   TrV   DO

3. <u>They</u> are <u>the largest New World monkeys.</u>
   S   LV   PN

4. <u>The treetops</u> provide howlers food and protection.
    S   TrV   IO   DO   DO

5. Consequently, <u>they</u> rarely descend to the ground.
             S   InV

6. <u>Howlers</u> can be black, brown, or red.
   S   LV PA   PA   PA

7. <u>Fifteen to eighteen animals</u> are <u>a typical howler clan.</u>
              S   LV   PN

Practice 6-3

1. This is our farmhouse (on <u>the left</u>).
  S LV   PN   (OP)

2. The house is old-fashioned but comfortable.
   S   LV   PA   PA

3. Dad built <u>my mother</u> <u>a porch swing.</u>
  S   TrV   IO   DO

4. (In <u>late fall</u>,) Mom plants <u>tulips</u> (along <u>the front walk</u>).
     (OP)   S   TrV DO   (OP)

5. (In <u>the spring</u>,) Dad plants <u>sweet corn</u> (beyond <u>the barn</u>).
     (OP)   S   TrV   DO   (OP)

Answers to Exercises

6. He gives <u>us</u> <u>the lawn mowers</u>.
   <small>S TrV IO DO</small>

7. We feel privileged, of course.
   <small>S LV PA</small>

Practice 6-4
1. My brother's
2. its
3. Bobby's, his
4. my brother's, my

Practice 6-5
1. Whose
2. (none)
3. mine
4. the teacher's
5. (none)
   The other possessives are determiners.

Practice 6-6
1. The Lord restored <u>the servant's</u> health.
   <small>S TrV DO</small>

2. <u>Peter's</u> mother-in-law was sick with a fever.
   <small>S LV PA</small>

3. The Lord healed her with the touch of <u>His</u> hand on <u>hers</u>.
   <small>S TrV DO (OP)</small>

4. <u>A widow's</u> sobs for <u>her</u> dead son reached <u>the Lord's</u> ears.
   <small>S TrV DO</small>

5. <u>His</u> tender heart responded to the <u>the widow's</u>.
   <small>S InV (OP)</small>

6. The young man became alive at <u>the Lord's</u> command.
   <small>S LV PA</small>

Practice 6-7
1. The Lord restored *his* health.
4. *Her* sobs for her dead son reached *His* ears.
5. His tender heart responded to *hers*.
6. The young man became alive at *His* command.

Practice 6-8
The sentence patterns are labeled for your convenience.

1. Herman Melville, <u>the famous American novelist,</u> based his
   <small>S TrV</small>
   stories on his experiences at sea.
   <small>DO</small>

2. In 1841 he became a seaman on the whaling ship <u>*Acushnet*</u>.
   <small>S LV PN</small>

3. Later he spent some time in the Marquesas Islands,
   <small>S TrV DO</small>
   <u>a group of islands in the South Pacific.</u>

4. *Typee,* <u>Melville's first novel,</u> draws its inspiration from his
   <small>S TrV DO</small>
   adventures on these islands.

5. After a month on the islands, he took another whaler, $\overset{S}{} \overset{TrV}{} \overset{DO}{}$

   an Australian vessel, to Tahiti.

6. His most famous whaling story is the novel *Moby-Dick.* $\overset{S}{} \overset{LV}{} \overset{PN}{}$

Practice 6-9
1. Gray rain clouds, the noonday sun
   Adj ModN   ModN
2. Hungry sea gulls, brown pelicans, the water, a fish dinner
   Adj ModN   Adj   ModN
3. An autumn storm, the sandy beach
      ModN   Adj

Practice 6-10
Children (6:1), ye fathers (6:4), servants (6:5), ye masters (6:9)

Practice 6-11
1. every morning, all summer
2. the first day
3. the whole month of June
4. the second day
5. home

Practice 6-12
1. to be his ambassador to England   (PN)
2. Being sympathetic to the Confederate cause   (PA)
3. preventing British recognition of the South   (DO)
4. Faithfully serving the American people   (DO)

Practice 6-13
1. Taking control of the social life of her husband's administration

2. rearing her son, John Quincy Adams; <u>him</u> to become a
   president of the United States

3. <u>her grandson's</u> publishing of her many letters

4. contributing to America as a wife, mother, and historian

Practice 6-14
1. a tremendous defeat
2. embarrassing setbacks
3, 4. (none)
5. the name of John Zizka
6. its first hint of modern motorized tank warfare

Practice 6-15
1. Christina Rossetti
2. (none; *poet* is object of the preposition *as*)
3. high *marks*

4. a deep *insight* into her devout Christian character and love for God
5. us

Practice 6-16

1. The Waldenses ^S were ^{LV} a strictly biblical group who were active
during the Middle Ages.
2. They ^S were severely persecuted ^{TrV-P} by the Roman Catholics.
3. Continuous persecution ^S was dealt ^{TrV-P} these people ^{RO} for four centuries.
4. By their own members they ^S were named ^{TrV-P} "The Poor of Christ," ^{SC}
based on Christ's teaching in Matthew 5:3.
5. The Bible, ^S translated into the common language, was made ^{TrV-P}
available ^{SC} to the people by the Waldenses.
6. The Roman Catholic church ^S was called ^{TrV-P} the "Babylonian house ^{SC}
of lies" by these forerunners of the Reformation.
7. Later they ^S gave ^{TrV} the Reformation ^{IO} their full support. ^{DO}

Practice 6-17

1. The old wall, the orchard
2. The pink blossoms, many bees, the orchard
3. A lizard, the tree
4. red apples, the tree
5. Each limb, the weight
6. Men, the ripe fruit
7. The harvest, a good one

Practice 6-18

1. The ^{Det} rusty ^{Adj} screen ^{ModN} door; the ^{Det} wind
2. Faded ^{Part} green ^{Adj} shutters; the ^{Det} decaying ^{Part} walls
3. The ^{Det} abandoned ^{Part} shack; many ^{Det} hikers; some ^{Det} welcome ^{Adj} shelter
4. Dust; the ^{Det} first ^{Det} raindrops
5. Blowing ^{Part} tree ^{ModN} limbs; the ^{Det} dented ^{Part} tin ^{ModN} roof
6. The ^{Det} thunderstorm; the ^{Det} empty ^{Adj} cabin; the ^{Det} woods

Answers to Exercises

Practice 6-19
The adjectives are in bold print.

1. Five **flabby** fish flopped from the **flat** pan into the **fierce, fateful** fire.
    - S: flabby, InV

2. Granny's **green** gourds grew **golden** in the **grassy** glen.
    - S, LV, PA

3. **Happy** Harry hands his **hefty** hounds **hearty** hamburgers after each hunt.
    - S, TrV, IO, DO

4. The **infamous** insects were **inactive** inside the **icy** igloos.
    - S, LV, PA

5. A **jolly** jogger jerked the jackrabbit from the **jagged** jaws of the **jumpy** jackal.
    - S, TrV, DO

Practice 6-20
The adverbs are in bold print.

1. In 1789 Justin Morgan, a Vermont schoolteacher, **reluctantly** accepted a stubby colt as partial payment from a debtor.
    - S, TrV, DO

2. He would **certainly** have preferred cash.
    - S, TrV, DO

3. The short-legged horse was **not** Morgan's idea of a good deal.
    - S, LV, PN

4. **Soon** he was thinking **differently** about his little horse Figure.
    - S, InV

5. His sturdy animal's capacity for work **clearly** surpassed that of other horses.
    - S, TrV, DO

6. **Gradually,** Morgan's horse became famous for his tireless strength.
    - S, LV, PA

7. Demand for Figure's offspring grew **steadily** throughout America.
    - S, InV

8. During the nineteenth century the Morgan horse served our country **faithfully** on farms, battlefields, and frontiers.
    - S, TrV, DO

Practice 6-21

1. Man's <u>greedy</u> craving for gold <u>truly</u> became <u>evident</u> in the gold rushes of the nineteenth century.
    - S, LV, PA

2. In 1849 a <u>sudden</u> ^Sflood of humanity in search of the <u>precious</u>

   metal poured <u>rapidly</u>^{InV} into California.

3. A <u>similar</u>^S event <u>briefly</u>^{TrV} shook <u>Australia</u>^{DO} during the 1850s.

4. <u>Later</u>, the desire for <u>easy</u>^S wealth drew many <u>eager</u>^{TrV} prospectors^{DO}

   <u>northward</u> during the <u>Alaskan</u> gold rush.

5. These <u>frenzied</u> rushes <u>never</u>^S brought their <u>participants</u>^{TrV} any^{IO}

   <u>permanent</u>^{DO} satisfaction.

6. <u>Certainly</u> God's <u>eternal</u>^S Word is^{LV} more <u>desirable</u>^{PA} than "much

   <u>fine</u> gold."

Practice 6-22
1. nice (adjective modifying *manner*)
2. nice (predicate adjective); nicely (adverb modifying *speaks*)
3. well (adverb modifying *did*); well (adverb modifying *studied*)
4. good (adjective modifying *knowledge)*
5. well (*adverb* modifying *likes*)

Chapter 7

Practice 7-1
After each answer the sentence pattern is given to help you understand any verb types you may have missed. (See Chapter 5 for additional help in identifying sentence patterns.)

1. transitive (S TrV DO)
2. linking (S LV PN)
3. transitive (S TrV DO)
4. intransitive (S InV)
5. intransitive (S InV)
6. intransitive (S InV)
7. intransitive (S InV)
8. transitive (S TrV DO)
9. intransitive (S InV)
10. linking (S LV PA)
11. intransitive (S InV)
12. transitive (S TrV DO)
13. transitive (S TrV DO)
14. transitive (S TrV DO)
15. transitive (S TrV DO)

Answers to Exercises

Practice 7-2
1. brought   3. will be helping   5. lie/lies
2. had gone   4. have/has fallen

Practice 7-3
1. active   4. passive   7. active (both clauses)   10. active
2. active   5. active   8. passive
3. passive   6. active   9. active (all three verbs)

Practice 7-4
Other answers may be possible.
1. First the horses pulled the logs about twenty yards.
2. Then Brown stopped the horses for a rest.
3. During the break, the horses' considerate owner threw stones out of the way.
4. He petted the horses on their noses, and then he told them to pull again.
5. All the while, the watching crowd said not a word. (*or* did not say a word)

Practice 7-5
The second sentence needed revision: During the final pull, the horses were kept to their work by the calm logger with the soft but firm voice.

Chapter 8

Practice 8-1
1. who made a living by writing novels
2. which contains five novels
3. that he had read to his ailing wife
4. which is a part of the Leatherstocking Saga
5. who rose to prominence in the American literary circles of the late nineteenth century

Practice 8-2
1. whose reputation exceeds real life
2. that number nearly 150,000 ants
3. that are injured or trapped
4. which are sensitive to bright light
5. for whom they serve as pest exterminators

Practice 8-3
1. *surface*—where they are constantly on the lookout for insects
2. *insects*—that are either at rest nearby or in flight near the water's surface
3. *mouth*—which it raises above the surface of the lake
4. *fish*—to whom God has given such a remarkable skill
5. *instant*—when the "shot" insect hits the surface of the water

Practice 8-4
1. that it is useless to worry about yesterday or tomorrow (direct object)
2. (This sentence contains an adverb clause, but no noun clause.)
3. whatever we did yesterday (subject)
4. how He can turn yesterday's failures into victories (direct object)
5. that the God of infinite love also controls our tomorrows (appositive to *fact*) Here is an additional example of a noun clause used as an appositive: I was surprised by John's belief [that his cat could learn to do tricks].
6. what God would have us do today (object of preposition)
7. whoever would question us (indirect object), why we need to worry (direct object)
8. if we will ever learn to live in the present and leave our yesterdays and our tomorrows with God (direct object) Some would prefer *whether* to *if* in this sentence; but you should be able to recognize both.

Practice 8-5
1. The quarterback explained that the coach had sent in a play with him.
2. I asked why he [*or* they] changed [*or* had changed] it.
3. He answered that the other team's defensive backs had been [*or* were] in a zone defense.
4. Mark, the right end, added that he had been open the whole game against their zone.
5. The quarterback asked happily whether we noticed how much time the linemen gave [*or* had given] him to throw.
6. With a laugh, Mark said that he caught the ball in full stride and just sailed into the end zone.

Practice 8-6
1. complex   2. compound   3. simple   4. complex

Practice 8-7
1. simple   4. complex
2. complex   5. compound
3. compound-complex

Practice 8-8
Other answers may be possible.
1. Catherine the Great deposed her husband Peter III and then became empress of Russia.
2. She wrote plays and historical papers.
3. In wars fought during her reign, Poland was conquered but Turkey was not.

4. Catherine suppressed the commoners and even gave some peasants as gifts to the nobility.
5. Obviously, the nobility supported Catherine but the commoners did not at all.

Sentences 1, 2, and 4 are now simple sentences. (The other two are elliptical compound sentences.)

Practice 8-9

1. Easter Island, located in the South Pacific, is actually a part of Chile.
2. The island, discovered on Easter Sunday in 1722, contains three extinct volcanoes.
3. Hand-carved stone statues weighing up to seventy tons are found all over the island.
4. Many people visit the island to wonder at these four-story-high lava statues and to speculate about their still unknown purpose.
5. The builders of these eyeless images also left behind wooden tablets carved in an undecipherable script.

Practice 8-10

1. The Yoruba, the third largest ethnic group in Nigeria, have a common language and culture.
2. Many of these people, captured during the Slave Wars, were sent to Brazil.
3. The Yoruba in Brazil still speak their native language and worship their old idols.
4. In Africa these people with skill in most crafts are especially well known for their work with bronze. (*Or:* skilled in most crafts)
5. (This sentence is probably better in its original form.)
6. Cacao, Nigeria's most important cash crop, is produced primarily by the Yoruba.

Practice 8-11

1. The Cavalier Poets, fiercely devoted to Charles I, wrote during the seventeenth century.
2. These English poets were known as the "tribe of Ben" (Jonson).
3. Sir John Suckling, in exile at the end of his life, had spent his fortune for the royalist cause.
4. Richard Lovelace, possibly the best-known Cavalier poet, was even imprisoned for a time.
5. Their poetry, often written in a lighter vein, emphasized the pleasures of this world.

6. Their lyrical poems, still read today, are considered to be primarily love songs. (This sentence is perhaps better in its original form.)

Practice 8-12
1. In the seventeenth century, monarchs stressed the divine right of kings in order to suppress the revolutionary ideas growing in Europe.
2. Having become dissatisfied with the Pope's political and religious power, the nobility during the Middle Ages had transferred that authority to their kings.
3. Being supposedly ordained by God, the monarchy could not be abolished.
4. (no change)
5. In addition, kings considered themselves to be above the law, thinking they were accountable only to God.

Practice 8-13
1. An earthquake having shifted the ocean floor, a great wave called a tsunami starts out across the surface.
2. The ocean being so large, these hundred-mile-long waves are not easily spotted.
3. The waves being of such tremendous size, a tidal effect is produced on the shore.
4. Because of their excessive speeds (350 to 500 m.p.h.), these "tidal waves" are devastating when they reach the shore.
5. A tsunami having reached the shore, men are helpless before its might.

Practice 8-14
1. Although educated at home,
2. (no change, unless the main clause is changed too—otherwise it will sound as if his father was the student)
3. (no change)
4. While observing a young crippled girl picking berries in a field,
5. . . . known as well today as ever.

Practice 8-15
Other answers are possible.
1. A novelist's success depends upon his understanding of other people and himself.
2. (no change)
3. His goal was to be a morally and socially responsible novelist.
4. Dickens' hope was for society to be governed by human compassion and not by commercial interests.

5. Did you know about Dickens visiting America and being extremely critical of slavery? *Or:* Did you know about Dickens' visit to America and his strong criticism of slavery?
6. In his later years people asked him to do readings of his own works for the public.

Chapter 9

Practice 9-1
1. dawns
2. hear
3. has
4. shows
5. are
6. sound
7. brightens
8. throw

Practice 9-2
1. reward is
2. stores are
3. hour is
4. words have
5. cook has
6. each wants

Practice 9-3
1. has
2. is
3. is
4. are
5. is
6. is

Practice 9-4
1. seems
2. has
3. remind
4. offers
5. promises
6. assure

Practice 9-5
1. thunders
2. are
3. are
4. blares, has
5. are
6. have
7. cut
8. is

Practice 9-6
1. is
2. is
3. take
4. are
5. has
6. is

Practice 9-7
1. totals
2. are
3. perform
4. give
5. occurs
6. are
7. is
8. form

Practice 9-8
1. is
2. have
3. means
4. was
5. was
6. have
7. was

Practice 9-9
1. was
2. trouble
3. rise
4. was
5. were (*Was* would require a different meaning and different punctuation.)
6. was
7. was

Practice 9-10
1. were
2. is
3. is
4. has
5. is
6. were

Practice 9-11

1. everyone, his
2. Marsha and Kelly, their
3. Each person, his
4. Lassie, her
5. the only one, his
6. The others, their

Practice 9-12

1. his
2. it
3. its, their
4. its
5. its
6. their
7. their
8. their
9. his

Practice 9-13

Other answers are possible.

1. Mr. Varner said to Jerry, "You (*or* I) can attach the bicycle to the trunk of the car."
2. After putting it on the rack, tie the bicycle securely to the bumper.
   After putting the bicycle on it, tie the rack securely to the bumper.
3. Tom rode in the "Little 500" race in Bloomington, Indiana, and then sold his bicycle to Jerry.
   In the "Little 500" race in Bloomington, Indiana, Jerry rode the bicycle that Tom sold him.
4. After taking Susie to the "Little 500," Linda decided to go to Europe for the annual "Tour de France" race.
   After Linda took her to the 'Little 500," Susie decided to go to Europe for the annual "Tour de France" race.
5. When they sped by the crowds on the outskirts of Paris, the cyclists knew that the race was almost over.
   When the cyclists sped by, the crowds on the outskirts of Paris knew that the race was almost over.

Practice 9-14

Other answers are possible.

1. As Natasha walked onto the wharf after the long voyage from Russia, she shouted to her mother.
2. Mr. Raymond said to Harvey, "You will have to work the late shift tonight."
3. In a country dominated by Communism a person is sometimes put in prison for practicing his religion.
4. When I got to the bank window, the teller said I had waited in the wrong line.

Practice 9-15

Other answers are possible.

1. In his science class Mr. Vent said that the tornado is the most violent type of storm found in nature.

2. Last year I found a diary that belonged to my grandmother, and I read about how she survived a tornado almost forty years ago.
3. A neighbor's telephone call warned Grandmother to seek shelter, but the neighbor himself died when the storm destroyed his house.
4. Her barn roof flew off, but the barn remained standing with no damage to the walls or contents.
5. When God creates a whirlwind, His power and sovereignty are very evident.

Practice 9-16
Other corrections are possible.
1. My biology lab manual says that microscopes should be moved carefully.
2. In class we were told that bumping a microscope hard may put its lenses out of adjustment.
3. C
4. C
5. In our class we can prepare our own slides to examine.
6. A person must know what he is doing in order to prepare slides correctly.

Practice 9-17
Other answers are possible.
1. The ability of kangaroos to thrive and multiply even under harsh conditions creates problems for Australian sheep herders. Australian sheep herders have problems with kangaroos, which can thrive and multiply even under harsh conditions.
2. Because of the weightless conditions experienced during orbit, early space voyagers had to eat food pastes and concentrates squeezed from tubes.
3. Bob decided to give up a career as an insurance salesman in order to study for the ministry. His decision came as a surprise to everyone.
4. Julie gets up at five o'clock every day in order to jog four miles before breakfast.
5. On rare occasions Larry's dog stands up on his hind legs and begs.

Practice 9-18
1. I bought only three books because I could hardly afford any more.
2. She puts even tennis shoes in her new washer.
3. Since he is on a diet, he wants just a small piece of cake.

4. They spent hardly any time grading the road surface before they paved it.
5. My little four-year-old sister can write almost the entire alphabet by herself.

Practice 9-19
Other answers are possible.
1. Near the tour guide was a plant sculptured like an elephant with long, floppy ears.
2. I saw scores of such bushes and trees scattered throughout the park.
3. Our tour guide explained that the park gardeners who patiently trim and prune each plant had become very adept at topiary.
4. In the tour bus he told us about ancient Egypt, where topiary was first practiced.
5. At the end of the tour he pointed out an exotic dog-shaped tree that had a peculiar bark.

Practice 9-20
Other answers are possible.
1. Scientists who constantly study bird migration admit that they understand little about how birds accurately navigate to distant locations.
2. One species that lives during the summer months in the Arctic regions wings its way to Antarctica to spend the winter.
3. Bird watchers explain that when the days begin to grow shorter birds sense the arrival of migration time.
4. Many migrating birds frequently use the sun and stars for navigation.
5. On several occasions Christ tells his followers that God cares for them more than He does the birds: "Behold the fowls. . . ."

Practice 9-21
Other answers are possible.
1. By standing on your toes, you can easily reach the top shelf.
2. To ride a unicycle, one needs a good sense of balance.
3. When an electron microscope was used, the virus became visible to human eyes for the first time in history.
4. The matchbook cover should be closed before one strikes a match.
5. If the milk and eggs are left unrefrigerated, Joe will soon have a quart of sour milk and a carton of rotten eggs.
6. To pilot a commercial airliner, one needs years of training and flight experience.

Practice 9-22
Sometimes another answer is possible, but its meaning may or may not fit as well.

1. furthermore
2. In addition
3. nevertheless
4. Indeed
5. at that time; Later; likewise

Practice 9-23
Other answers may be possible.

1. Because the nation faced a huge financial deficit, Congress raised taxes substantially; but it was unfortunate that they cut hardly any spending plans.
2. After William McKinley was assassinated in 1901, the leadership of the United States fell into the hands of Theodore Roosevelt.
3. You can observe a short meteor shower if you get up at three o'clock tomorrow morning and watch the northeastern sky.
4. Although leaders of oil-rich countries appear unified in their desire to raise the price of oil, they often quarrel among themselves over how to attain their goal.
   Leaders of oil-rich countries appear unified . . . oil, although they often quarrel. . . .
5. The Lord sent prophets to the land of Israel so that the people could learn about the coming judgment and turn from their idolatry.

Practice 9-24
Other answers are possible.

   Each completed auto body is chemically cleaned, and then the lower part of the body is dipped into an anti-corrosion primer. Next, the joints in the sheet metal are sealed in order to prevent corrosion caused by leaks. After that, two coats of primer are applied and baked on the whole car body. To protect against stone chips, sometimes an anti-chip vinyl material is applied to the lower body sides. Finally, two coats of color are applied and baked.

Practice 9-25
1. flowed
2. realized, was being carried
3. was being crushed
4. was horrified, was carried
5. was saved

Practice 9-26
1. After he had shouted that
2. people who had died
3. had given birth
4. had caused the chaos
5. had fully realized that

Practice 9-27
The corrections are in italics, and the past perfect verbs are in bold print.

> I began shouting, "Form chains! Form chains!" I *started* to join neighboring hands together by force. Some tough young men began to help me. Gradually people understood. They *joined* hands and *formed chains.* The crowd was ceasing to be a savage beast.
>
> "Women and children into the trucks!" yelled one of the young men. And women and children, passed from hand to hand, *sailed* over our heads into the trucks. The whirlpool was slowing down.
>
> The police too finally began to help us.
>
> At last, the tide **had turned** and everything was calm.
>
> Somehow, I no longer felt like going to see Stalin's remains. Instead, I *left* with one of the boys who **had been organizing** chains. We walked to my place.
>
> "Did you see Stalin?" my mother *asked* me.
>
> "Yes," I said, too weary to explain.
>
> I **had**n't really **lied** to my mother. I **had seen** Stalin. Because everything that **had** just **happened**—that was Stalin.

Practice 9-28
Other answers may be possible.
1. Tall oaks from little acorns grow.
2. You can do anything you ought to do.
   We can do anything we ought to do.
3. He who has one enemy will meet him everywhere.
4. C
5. Never look a gift horse in the mouth.
6. Pygmies placed on the shoulders of giants see more than the giants themselves.
7. "Train up a child in the way he should go: and when he is old, he will not depart from it."
8. If you can't say something good, you shouldn't say anything.
   If you can't say something good, don't say anything.
   If we can't say something good, we shouldn't say anything.

Practice 9-29
Other answers are possible.

> Spiders are one of the world's most common species. Spiders can be found from the Arctic to the Antarctic. They are, however, most abundant in the topics. We picture them as brown or black, but spiders can also be green, yellow, red, or white. They feed mainly on insects, but they fear their enemy the wasp. Although spiders are good for killing bugs in the garden, we do not appreciate them in our homes.

Practice 9-30
Other answers are possible.
1. The Chinese were the first to mint coins.
2. Coins have been made from nonmetals like porcelain and plastic, as well as from silver, nickel, platinum, and gold.
3. The American colonies made the continental dollar from lead.
4. In 1865 the United States first minted coins from nickel.
5. Throughout the centuries, the main metal used for coinage has been silver.

Practice 9-31
Other answers are possible.
1. William Jennings Bryan was called "The Great Commoner."
2. He ran three times for the presidency of the United States and lost.
3. According to Bryan, the cause for World War I was a godlessness promoted by the theory of evolution.
4. In Bryan's opinion, before the nation could go to war a public vote should be taken.
5. Because of his belief in a literal interpretation of the Bible, he was hated by many scientists.

Practice 9-32
Other answers are possible.
1. The book of Judges is a picture of the misery that results from spiritual compromise.
2. It was not spiritual knowledge that the people lacked, but wisdom.
3. Their sin of spiritual apathy was difficult to overcome.
4. God left some of their enemies in the land to test Israel's faithfulness.
5. The result of their worldly associations was unrighteous living.

Practice 9-33
Other answers are possible.
1. Basketball teams know the importance of being aggressive on both offense and defense.
2. Good offensive basketball includes a well-balanced attack, patient self-discipline, and precise execution.
3. A good defensive team knows the value of tenacity, intensity, and hard work.
4. An effective defensive player is always aware of the position of the ball, of his opponent, and of the basket.
5. Winning basketball teams usually show respect for teammates, coaches, opponents, and officials.

Practice 9-34
1. President Grover Cleveland is portrayed as courageous, ingenious, and strong-minded.
2. C
3. To perform the necessary surgery, the doctors had to sneak scalpels, retractors, and other operating instruments onto a yacht.
4. C
5. The facts about the operation were known by just a few men, including those who performed the surgery and those who guarded the yacht.

Practice 9-35
Other corrections may be possible.
1. The American grizzly bear is pictured as aggressive, voracious, and fearsome.
2. The existence of the grizzly bear is threatened by exploration, exploitation, and the construction of roads and towns.
3. C
4. Grizzlies are intelligent, strong, and quick.
5. C
6. Immediately after hibernation, the bears are lazy, passive, and sleepy.
7. Grizzly bears are expert diggers, climbers, and hunters.

Practice 9-36
Other answers are possible.
1. Many of the great minds of America's past thought cities to be loathsome, fearful, and valueless.
2. Thomas Jefferson feared the city because it produced dependence, ambition, and corruption.
3. Herman Melville perceived city people as shameful, decadent, and uncivilized.
4. What a contrast to the praise for the city of God in Psalm 48 and the love for it in Psalm 87!

Practice 9-37
Other answers are possible.
1. The men who fight forest fires must learn to parachute into trees, to work sixteen-hour days, and to put up with intense heat.
2. These firefighters become experts at digging fire lanes, felling burning trees, and giving first aid.
3. Firefighters learn to accept parachuting into creeks on a cold day, untangling themselves from treetops after a bad jump, and sleeping in holes in the chilly ground.

4. The hot air and the updraft from a forest fire have been known to blister firefighters' lungs, to produce 35,000-foot smoke columns, and to uproot entire trees. (*or*: to blister . . . , produce . . . , and uproot)
5. Helicopters are used for transporting firefighters to the blaze, bombarding "hot spots" with water, and transferring gear for the crews.

Practice 9-38
Other corrections are possible.
1. Samson's parents demonstrated not only a desire to please the Lord but also a desire to oppose the Philistines.
2. Samson demonstrated great personal courage, and he could not have succeeded without it.
3. C
4. The Philistines tried to assimilate the Israelites by trading with them and by encouraging intermarriage.
5. Samson chose the wrong company, and he ended up in failure.
6. C
7. God's discipline of Samson shows His desire to restore us completely and His longing to make us useful.

Practice 9-39
Other corrections may be possible.
1. C
2. By the time of the Civil War the wild turkey was faced with both the loss of woodland habitat and the danger of extinction.
3. The Civil War sent many farmers to the West, making possible both the restoration of the Eastern woodlands and the revival of the wild turkey population.
4. Since turkeys are both elusive and intelligent, hunters sometimes spend hours trying to bring a gobbler within shooting range.
5. Devices named either wing-bone yelpers or peg-and-slate scratchers can be used to call turkeys toward a hunter.

Practice 9-40
Other answers may be possible.
1. In dealing with the general public, in medical diagnosis, and in "cures" prescribed, the medical quack totally ignored honesty.
2. The traveling medicine show of the past used either tales of miraculous cures or testimonials of personal healings to sell its so-called medicine.
3. The medicine man's financial success and his system of appealing to the emotions were clearly connected.
4. A medicine show quack would learn to "diagnose" known ailments and to invent diseases that did not even exist.

5. We deplore these quacks' thievery and their unscrupulous methods that endangered the health of others.

Chapter 10

Practice 10-1
1. I will be your guide on this tour through Monticello.
2. What a beautiful estate this is!
3. Who built it?
4. Monticello was designed and built by Thomas Jefferson.
5. Jefferson, our third President, worked on his home between 1768 and 1809.

Practice 10-2
Notice the periods after the numbers 1-5.
1. Dr. and Mrs. Winston will be speaking to the science lab classes at 3:10 p.m.
2. The Winstons arrived from Richmond, Va., about 7 a.m.
3. T. F. Winston, Jr., is an expert in archeology, especially archeology of the Middle East from 586 B.C. to A.D. 476.
4. Mrs. Winston has worked at NASA.
5. They open every lecture by reading II Pet. 3:4.

Although they are not incorrect, the abbreviations *Va.* and *Pet.* are preferably spelled out when used in sentences, except inside parentheses.

Practice 10-3
1. I want to learn all about caves, for my brother and I recently discovered one nearby.
2. Perry wanted to explore it immediately, but I reminded him of the danger.
3. In his opinion I could wait outside, or I could go in right away with him.
4. Just inside the entrance, water dripped on our heads, and strange noises echoed in the darkness.
5. We weren't afraid, but we both decided to call off our exploration.

Practice 10-4
1. Visitors to Africa may explore the Sahara Desert or the Nile River; they may even go on a big-game hunting expedition.
2. Africa used to be called the Dark Continent; many parts of it were mysterious and unknown to outsiders.

Answers to Exercises

Practice 10-5

1. Most of the world's diamonds come from Africa's mines; furthermore (*or* also), a large amount of the world's cacao, palm oil, peanuts, and sisal comes from Africa's farms.
2. Cocoa and chocolate come from cacao; therefore, cacao is a popular export.
3. Many people have never seen a sisal plant; however, everyone has used its products, rope and twine.

Practice 10-6

Other answers are possible.

1. In order to find moisture, prairie grasses must sink their roots deep into the soil: there is only moderate to low rainfall on the prairie.
2. These grasslands support running and clustering animals like antelope, and they provide homes for burrowing animals like prairie dogs and gophers.
3. Prairie farms and farm ponds provide a suitable habitat for woodland animals; such forest creatures as raccoons and opossums are being attracted to these locations.
4. In earlier years people called America's vast grasslands the "great American desert"; however, today the area produces much of our country's food.

Practice 10-7

1. When Hank passed, Phil slowed down.
2. For dessert we have harvest cake, sweet potato pie, and gingersnaps.
3. When the teacher asked for John, Mark came forward instead.
4. It is your turn to cook, Cheryl.
5. Dad, our accounting teacher stressed the need for a calculator.
6. Just beyond the dark cave, water could be heard roaring over the falls.
7. For inspecting, George will use a flashlight, tape measure, and operating manual.

Practice 10-8

1. With my vast understanding of the various problems involved in lawn care, I will assume the responsibility of organizing the work projects.
2. Well, the twins may cut the grass after lunch.
3. Connie, our young helper, will water the flowers and wash the lawn chairs.
4. Over there, Leroy, you will find a garden hoe and some fertilizer.
5. Using the electric trimmer, Grover should easily finish the hedges by suppertime.

6. The proper care of a yard, as you can see, can be quite demanding.
7. Supervising the whole operation is, however, the most difficult job, don't you think?

Practice 10-9
1. Many of the old legends and myths that we have read and enjoyed since childhood are stories about giants.
2. In classical Greek mythology, with all of its fictional superheroes, there were giant men who eventually revolted against the gods and were destroyed.
3. The giant lumberjack Paul Bunyan, who has always been a favorite American folk hero, had a giant blue ox named Babe.
4. We even get the adjective *gargantuan* from *Gargantua and Pantagruel,* which is a novel about two giants.

Practice 10-10

518 Windbrook Street
Millerton, Vermont 05999
June 4, 19—

Dear Sarah,

Matthew, Cheryl, and I are still planning to come up to your house at the end of the month. All three of us look forward to the quiet, calm atmosphere of the country.

When we checked with Dad about being away at the end of June, he said, "I really wish I could take my vacation then!"

"To go with us?" I asked.

"No," he said, "to stay home to enjoy the silence!" We all laughed.

By the way, our address is *518* Windbrook Street, Millerton, Vermont, not 815. However, our town is so small that the address hardly matters; we got your note anyway.

We can't wait to see you, your family, and (of course) the horses!

Sincerely yours,

Kathy

Practice 10-11
1. Correct
2. Remove the comma between the modifier (*best*) and the noun (*reason*). 10d(7.4)
3. Remove the comma after the conjunction (*and*). 10d(7.3)
4. Remove the comma between the subject (*no one*) and the verb (*found*). 10d(7.2)
5. Remove the comma before *and,* a conjunction that joins only two words (*happiness* and *contentment*). 10d(7.1)
6. Remove the comma after the conjunction (*and*). 10d(7.3)

Practice 10-12
1. Derham was owned at various times by different medical doctors—a situation he used to his advantage.
2. His last owner—his name has been forgotten—allowed him to purchase his freedom.
3. Shortly afterwards John Derham—and this is important—became America's first Black doctor.

Practice 10-13
1. "But you—you really should pay attention to where your horse is going," Sue yelled into the wind.
2. "I can't—I can't hear you. What did you say?" he called back, turning his mount down a forest trail.
3. "Look out for the—oh, no—look out for that branch, Ron!" she shouted.
4. "What? Look at the ranch? I don't see a—."

Practice 10-14
1. The handsome new science teacher—and believe me, the number of coeds taking biology had greatly increased—was a strong believer in lab work.
2. "Today," he began, "we are going to begin dissecting and—is something wrong, Sharon?"
3. "Okay. Pigs, cats, and frogs—these are the three types of animals we will be dissecting in the lab."
4. "Dissecting these animals—this will be one of our most important experiments—will teach us much about the marvelous structure and workings of the body. Let's begin, shall we?"
5. The three students who turned green—the boys' basketball star, the soccer goalie, and Sharon—were all quickly excused from the lab.

Practice 10-15
1. The American poet Robert Frost (1874-1963) read two of his poems at the inauguration of President Kennedy in 1961.
2. Although more will be said about the dinosaur (see below), we must now focus our attention on the duckbilled platypus.
3. According to Senator Strom Thurmond (South Carolina), the announcement was to be made at a news conference.
4. Sodium chloride (NaCl) is the chemical name for common salt.
5. You have a choice of (1) Algebra II first hour or (2) American History or Personal Typing third hour.

Practice 10-16
1. C
2. Proverbs 31:20 kind to the poor:
3. at 5:30
4. five things:
5. Titus 2:4

Practice 10-17

1. Jesus called twelve men to be his disciples; these men came from varied backgrounds and occupations.
2. Many were fishermen, such as Peter, Andrew, James, and John; and Matthew, the Levite, was a tax collector.
3. We remember Thomas because of the times he questioned Jesus; consequently, he is often referred to as Doubting Thomas (John 11:16; 14:5; 20:25).
4. C
5. The others are not as familiar to us: Nathaniel, sometimes called Bartholomew; Philip, friend of Peter and Andrew; Simon Zelotes; Jude; and James, son of Alphaeus.

Practice 10-18

1. C
2. "There is nothing more thrilling to me than sitting on a wall," declared Humpty.
3. "It gives me a feeling of superiority," he said proudly.
4. "When I'm up here," he continued, "everyone has to look up to me."
5. "It appears that we will have scrambled eggs for supper tonight," said one of the king's men.
6. "It is always true," added another gravely, "that pride goes before a fall."

Practice 10-19

1. For Monday we will read "The Necklace," a short story by the French author Maupassant.
2. "The Raven" and "The Bells" are two of Edgar Allan Poe's best-known poems.
3. Frank Gauche's article entitled "Politics as Usual" presents a one-sided view.
4. The final examination will cover all the chapters from "Climates and Weather" to the end of the book.

Practice 10-20

1. "Well," said Chuck, "I read the chapter entitled 'The Language of Bees' last night."
2. "What did you think of it?" asked Marcia.
3. "I was amazed to learn that bees communicate with each other by means of various 'dances.' "
4. "What do you mean?"
5. "To direct other bees to some newly-discovered food," Chuck explained, "a bee will perform certain patterned movements on the floor of the hive."
6. "How fascinating!" exclaimed Marcia.

Practice 10-21

"And he [Jahaziel] said, Hearken ye, all Judah, and ye inhabitants of Jerusalem, and thou king Jehoshaphat. . . . the battle is not yours, but God's" (II Chron. 20:15).

"Ye shall not need to fight in this battle [against the children of Ammon and Moab]: set yourselves, stand ye still, and see the salvation of the Lord with you, O Judah and Jerusalem: . . . to morrow [*sic*] go out against them: for the Lord will be with you" (II Chron. 20:17).

Practice 10-22
1. *Morning Sun*
2. *within*
3. the *Titanic*
4. *The Red Badge of Courage*
5. *Freedom 7, Eagle*
6. the U.S.S. *Hornet*
7. *Inside Outer Space*

Chapter 12

Practice 12-1
Other answers are possible.

Genghis Khan was also a great warrior. His Mongol cavalry would quickly surround an enemy and destroy it. The Mongols used other military tactics as well. They used spies, and often they led the enemy into an ambush by pretending to retreat. They used terror as they spread tales of their viciousness. They even adopted certain methods of their enemies. Although ruthless, they were not like Hitler or Stalin, since the Mongols never tried to exterminate any certain group of people.

Practice 12-2
Other answers are possible.

Twenty-four years after leaving Venice, Marco Polo returned. A few years later, while he was a prisoner of war in Genoa, he told his adventures to a fellow-prisoner. The fellow-prisoner, a scribe, wrote them down in French. Until the nineteenth century, many considered the stories either fiction or exaggeration. Yet a copy of Marco's book inspired Columbus. In 1492 the queen of Spain sent Columbus in search of Polo's Cathay. Thus, the discovery of America came about because of the friendship between a Mongolian ruler and an Italian adventurer.

Practice 12-3
Other answers are possible.

His slave parents named him "Dog." When the people were freed from slavery, they chose him as one of their leaders. They sent him and several others to spy out a land for conquest. The country was as marvelous as God had told them it would be. However, giants and fierce warriors occupied the land. Afraid, the people outvoted this man and his friend, who wanted to attack the enemy. Their countrymen threatened them with execution, but these two men would not join the rebellion against God's promises. God judged the people by making them wander in the wilderness for forty years. When the people finally entered the land, this eighty-five-year-old man asked for permission to attack the giants. For forty years he had wanted to test God's promises. Is there any doubt who won? Here was a man who "wholly followed the Lord God of Israel" (Josh. 14:15). Today, God needs more men like Caleb, His faithful friend.

Practice 12-4

2. There were many ideas common to all the tribes, regardless of their environment or customs.
4. He also taught the tribe the myths and legends of their gods.
(Sentence 4 needed indirect-object revision more than sentence 5 did.)

Practice 12-5

Other answers are possible.

Aaron Burr was a politician and adventurer. A few years after he served under George Washington during the American Revolution, he became a New York politician. He made a powerful political machine out of the Tammany Society, which he used as a power base to seek the presidency in 1800. Because he tied with Thomas Jefferson, at seventy-three electoral votes each, a special election was held in the House of Representatives. Alexander Hamilton helped Jefferson win. Later, Burr fought and killed Hamilton in a duel over charges made in an election campaign. Several years later Burr was tried for treason, accused of planning to start his own empire in the West and the South. He was acquitted, and he then spent five years in Europe. Finally, he returned to New York and served as a lawyer until his death.

Practice 12-6

Other answers are possible.

1. Iroquois crops were planted in flood plains, in natural clearings, and in areas cleared by burning.
2. During the colonial wars, the Iroquois Indians fought for the British twice, against the French once, and against the American colonies once.
3. The Iroquois aided the early English settlers in their struggles for survival and defended them in their wars with the French.

Practice 12-7

Other answers are possible.

By 1722 the Iroquois Indians, *the "People of the Longhouse,"* were a loose confederation of six tribes. Maize (corn), beans, and squash were the three crops on which their *agricultural* economy was based. Men cleared the land, but women did everything else *necessary,* such as the planting, weeding, and harvesting. The men helped to supplement the diet *by fishing and hunting.* In addition, *gathering berries, mushrooms, and maple sugar* added more variety to their menu.

Practice 12-8

Other revisions may be possible.

1. Loose. (Periodic: In order to claim the Twenty-third Psalm as our own, we must first admit to being sheep of His pasture.)
2. Loose. (Periodic: Sheep, because they are oblivious to the dangers around them, are always falling off ledges and placing themselves in hopeless situations.)
3. Periodic. (Loose: Sheep are also quite defenseless, since "baaa" has never yet intimidated a wolf.)

Practice 12-9

Other answers are possible.

No one will care if I take another helping. It looks so delicious just sitting there all alone in the middle of that pie pan. Won't its feelings be hurt if it's the only piece not taken? "Pass the lemon meringue pie, please." A paragon of self-control I am not.

Chapter 13

Practice 13-1

Other answers are possible.

Have you ever seen a budgerigar? People like these small parakeets for a variety of reasons. Their tameness, ability to mimic, and many color variations are just a few of their delightful qualities. In the wild they live in flocks of thousands. They are beautiful to behold, being generally green with yellow head, back, and wings and a long slender blue tail. They are native to Australia, where they can be found nesting in hollow trees near water or feeding on the ground in the fields. Introduced to the Western world in 1840, "budgies" are a favorite pet in many American homes.

Practice 13-2

1. C
2. During World War I he was sent to Egypt by the British, since he had already mastered the Arabic language.
3. C
4. He masterminded the guerrillas' strategy, which included hit-and-run raids and the destruction of vital railways.
5. After the revolution achieved its success, however, Lawrence returned to England to write about his escapades.

Practice 13-3

Other answers are possible.

1. Bulls believe that stock prices will rise, but bears believe that prices will fall.
2. Bears act on optimism, and so they are always buying more stocks.
3. A rising market is a bull market; a falling market is a bear market.
4. C

Practice 13-4

Other answers are possible.

1. William Sydney Porter is a well-known writer of short stories, but you may know him as O. Henry.
2. He began writing fiction while in a penitentiary. He had been imprisoned for embezzlement.
3. His favorite writing technique was the surprise ending, and his favorite setting was the big city.
4. C
5. O. Henry was considered a recluse; he avoided publicity and had no close friends.

Chapter 15

Practice 15-1

Other answers are possible.

1. Paul established the church at Philippi because he obeyed a vision from God.
2. Paul evangelized Philippi, converting a Jewish merchant, a Greek slave, and a Roman jailer.
3. The persecution and imprisonment of Paul and Silas was difficult for the new church.
4. The believers were encouraged when God delivered Paul and Silas from prison.

Answers to Exercises

Practice 15-2
Other answers are possible.
1. A tree cavity is a good place for hornbills to build their predator-proof nests.
2. Once the female is inside the cavity, the male provides everything she needs, such as mud for plastering shut the opening to the nest and berries and fruit for her and the young to eat.
3. Hornbills roosting in large flocks are noisy and boisterous.

Practice 15-3
Other answers are possible.
1. Participation in extracurricular activities still plays the necessary role that it always has.
2. For all those students who enjoy activities that teach something, I recommend joining the drama team or the debate team.
3. Another activity in which a student develops character is sports.
4. Those who participate in extracurricular activities usually find the events educational and stimulating.
5. Making the most of every opportunity to participate in extracurricular activities will help a student to develop a well-rounded personality.
6. Extracurricular activity is one area for which we have found no substitute.

Practice 15-4
Other answers are possible.
1. A beaver's nest is probably bigger than the nest of any other animal.
2. The bubble nest of the Siamese fighting fish is very different from a mammal's or a bird's nest.
3. C
4. The junk-filled pack rat's nest is more unusual than any other rodent's nest.
5. Megapodes' nesting habits are different from the nesting habits (*or*: those) of other birds; megapodes rely on the heat of decaying vegetation to hatch their eggs. (Note: different *from*)

Practice 15-5
Other answers are possible.
1. Our baseball team's catcher is better than any other catcher in the league.
2. He throws and bats as well as or better than the other players on the team.

3. C
4. Our catcher encourages us as much as Coach Roberts does.
5. His contributions to the success of the team are greater than those of any other player.   (than any other player's)

Practice 15-6
Other answers are possible.
1. Devaluation is a planned decrease in the value of a country's currency.
2. A country is most likely to devalue its currency because of an imbalance of trade.
3. One reason economists criticize such action is the tendency toward rapid inflation after devaluation.
4. An underdeveloped country with the ability to increase its exports can benefit from devaluation, and therefore it may make such a move.
5. The critical question is how much the country depends on imports.

Practice 15-7
Other answers are possible.
1. Old Jake has finally quit drinking and is walking the straight and narrow.
2. Part of a President's job is to protect the United States.
3. Though Tom was exhausted, he still tried to fill his father's shoes.
4. C
5. His defeat was a great disappointment, but he was a good soldier through it all.

Correction

¶	Begin a new paragraph here. **17b(2)**, p. 449
dev ¶	Develop this paragraph more fully. **17b(2.2)**, p. 450
no ¶	Do not begin a new paragraph here. **17b(2)**, p. 449
//sm	Improve the parallelism of these elements. **9i**, p. 301
2-way	Move the modifier so that the reader will know which of the two words it modifies. **9d(2)**, p. 274
adj	Use an adjective here, not an adverb. **6d(3)**, p. 157
adv	Use an adverb here, not an adjective. **6d(3)**, p. 157
awk	Improve this awkward phrasing. **17c(8)**, p. 456
cap	Follow the rules for capitalization. **16a**, p. 414
case	Use the proper case form of this pronoun. **4a(2.6)**, p. 54
cl rel	Show the relationship between these clauses more accurately. **9e(5)**, p. 282
CS	Correct this comma splice. **13b(1)**, p. 389
DM	Dangling modifier: let the reader know who or what is being described. **9d(3)**, p. 276
frag	Correct this sentence fragment. **13a**, p. 385
FS	Correct this fused sentence. **13b(2)**, p. 390
gl	Consult the Glossary of Usage to correct this word or phrase. **Appendix 1**, p. 536
inf	Informal: use a more suitable expression or form. **1b-1c**, p. 3
ital	Underline for italics here. **10j**, p. 358
MM	Put this misplaced modifier next to the word or phrase it modifies. **9d(1)**, p. 271
nat	Use the natural English wording for this phrase. **11a-11b**, p. 362
no cap	Do not capitalize here. **16a(10)**, p. 420
P/A agr	Make this pronoun agree with the singular or plural word it replaces. **9b**, p. 254
pct	Use correct punctuation. **10a-10i, 16c-16d**
/'	apostrophe **16c**, p. 428
[/]	brackets **10i(7)**, p. 356
/:	colon **10g**, p. 344

Symbols

/,	comma **10d**, p. 322
/—	dash **10e**, p. 337
/. . .	ellipses **10i(6)**, p. 354
/!	exclamation mark **10b(3)**, p. 316
/-	hyphen **16d** p. 432
(/)	parentheses **10f**, p. 341
/.	period **10b(1, 4)**, pp. 315, 317
/?	question mark **10b(2)**, p. 316
"/"	quotation marks **10i(1-5)**, p. 349
'/'	single quotation marks **10i(4)**, p. 353
/;	semicolon **10h**, p. 347

pers Make the nouns and pronouns consistent in person. **9g(1)**, p. 293

prin pt Use the correct principal part of this verb. **7c-7d**, p. 169

pr phr Phrase this idea more precisely. **14c(2)**, p. 394

pr wd Try to find a more precise word. **17c(9)**, p. 458

ref Make this pronoun refer clearly to a particular word. **9c**, p. 262

sent log Make the parts of your sentence relate to each other more logically. **15b-15c**, p. 400

s/mood Use the subjunctive mood here. **7i(3)**, p. 194

sp Spell this word correctly. **16b**, p. 421

S/V agr Make this verb agree with its singular or plural subject. **9a**, p. 238

tns Make the tenses of these verbs consistent. **9f(1)**, p. 287

var Work on sentence variety in this paragraph. **12b-12c**, p. 372

voice Use the active voice unless the situation calls for the passive. **7e(3)**, p. 178

WDWW Make your sentence more direct and clear by telling "Who Did What to What." **15a**, p. 398

wdy Wordy: try to say the same thing in fewer words. **17c(7)**, p. 456

w wd Wrong word: replace it with a better one. **14c(1)**, p. 394

Correction

Correct Word Forms

4a(2.6) Pronoun case
6d(3)   Adjectives vs. adverbs

Verbs

7d   Troublesome verbs
7e(3)   Using active and passive
7i(3)   Subjunctive mood

Indirect Quotations

8a(4)   Changing direct
         quotations to
         indirect

Agreement, Reference

9a   Subject-verb agreement
9a(2)   Finding the real subject
9a(3)   Problem subjects
9a(4)   Compound subjects
9b   Pronoun-antecedent
         agreement
9c   Pronoun reference

Modifiers

9d(1)   Misplaced modifiers
9d(2)   Two-way modifiers
9d(3)   Dangling modifiers

Joining Clauses

9e(1)   Need for connective words
9e(2.3) Faulty subordination
9e(4)   Need for subordination

Avoiding Shifts

9f(1.1) Consistent tenses
9f(1.2) Sequence of tenses
9f(2)   Consistent voice
9g   Nouns and pronouns:
         consistent person
         and number

Placement in the Sentence

9h(1)   Sequence of subjects
9h(2-3) Ending sentences well

Parallelism

9i(2)   Logical use
9i(3)   Parallel parts of speech
9i(4)   Parallel structures
9i(5)   Correlative conjunctions
9i(6)   Clarifying parallelism

Basic Punctuation

10a   Punctuation for clarity
10b(1-3) Ends of sentences
10b(4) Other uses of the period
10c   Punctuating compound
          sentences

Commas

10d(2) Using *pairs* of commas when
          needed
10d(3) Commas after introductory
          elements
10d(4) Commas to set off other
          elements
10d(5) Restrictive and nonrestrictive
10d(6) Other uses of the comma
10d(7) Incorrect commas

Other Punctuation and Italics

10e   The dash
10f   Parentheses
10g   The colon
10h   The semicolon
10i(1-4) Quotation marks
10i(5) Other punctuation with
          quotation marks
10i(6) Ellipses
10i(7) Brackets
10j   Underlining for italics

Guide

Index

A

close appositive (restrictive), 132-33, 325, 328, 553
  defined, 132-33, 151, 552
  in the noun phrase, 151
  punctuation of, 132-33, 325, 328
Appropriateness, adjusting for (*see* Levels of usage)
Article, definite and indefinite, 82-83, 552
as, 537
Audience, adjusting for (*see* Levels of usage)
Auxiliary, 72-81, 553
  be for the passive, 79
  be for the progressive, 76-77
  do for emphasis, question inversion, etc., 80-81
  have for the perfect, 75-76
  will, shall, 74-75
  defined, 19, 72-74
  modal, 73, 78, 194, 556
  types of (table), 73
Awkwardness, 456-58

B

bad, badly 536
Basic sentence patterns, 108-20 (*see also* Sentence patterns)
be, passive auxiliary, 79
be, progressive auxiliary, 76-77
between, 536
Bibliography card, 498
Brackets, 356-57
  for insertions or replacements in a quotation, 356-57
  how to make, 356
  to replace parentheses inside other parentheses, 357
Built nouns, avoiding overuse of, 398-400

C

Capitalization, 415-21
  dictionary as a guide for, 479
  incorrect, 420-21
  of *I* and *O,* 419-20
  of brand names, 417
  of calendar items, 416-17
  of complimentary closing of a letter, 419
  of epithets for proper nouns, 420
  of first word of sentence, poetic line, resolution, etc., 418-19
  of geographical names, 416
  of God (words for), 417
  of historical events, periods, documents, 416-17
  of large constructions, 416
  of letters used for musical notes, grades, etc., 420
  of names of persons, 415

of nationalities and languages, 416
  of organizations and members, 416
  of parts of a book, 420
  of personal titles, 415
  of personifications, 419
  of proper adjectives, 417
  of proper nouns, 415-17
  of religions and related terms, 417
  of salutation of a letter, 419
  of titles for persons, 415
  of titles of works, 417-18
Card catalog, of a library, 488-91
Case of pronouns, 50-52, 54-60, 125-31, 553
  (*see also* Subjective case, Objective case, Possessive case)
Clarity, 238, 409, 454
  of comparisons, 403, 405
  punctuation for, 315, 323
Clause
  adjective clause, 151-52, 199-204, 547-48, 552
  adverb clause, 199, 204-6, 548-49
  defined, 98, 553
  dependent, defined, 199, 200, 204, 554
  independent, 214-16, 319-22, 379-80
  independent, defined, 98, 214, 555
  modified by an adverb, 157
  noun clause, 199, 206-11, 549-50, 556
  of condition (subjunctive), 195-96
  reducing clauses to simpler structures, 216-33, 379-80
Clean copy of a paper, form and neatness of, 460-61
Cliché, 459
Close appositive, 132-33, 325, 328, 553
Coherence, 455
Collective noun, 24, 553
Combining sentence-ideas, 199-211
Colon, 322, 344-47
  after the salutation of a business letter, 344
  before an appositive at the end of a sentence, 345
  before a series at the end of a sentence, 344-45
  between a formal introduction and a quotation, 345
  between title and subtitle of a book, 346
  general effect of, 344
  how to type, 344
  in Bible references, 344
  in certain compound sentences, 322, 346
  in expressions of time, 344
  position with parentheses, 342
  position with quotation marks, 353
  to give emphasis, 344-45
Comma, 319, 322-37
  after certain parts of a letter, 332

M

N

distinguished from a direct modifier, 145
Predicate nominative (*see* Predicate noun)
Predicate noun, 110-11, 113
  case of, 56, 59-60, 126
  defined, 110-11, 114, 126, 558
Preposition, 91-96, 558 (*see also* Prepositional phrase)
  defined, 19, 91-92
  distinguished from adverb, 92
  idiomatic use of, 362-64
  meanings (with lists), 93-94
  multiword, 93
  nine most common, 91
  object of, 91-92, 557
Prepositional phrase
  defined, 91, 558
  effect of, compared with indirect object, 376-
  77
  in a noun phrase, 147-48
  included or separate, 95-96
  modifying an adjective, 234
Present-tense family, 166-67
Prewriting, 443-47
Principal parts
  defined, 169, 558
  how to use, 169-71
  of troublesome verbs (list), 171-73
principal, principle, 538
Progressive verb forms, 76-77, 165-69
Pronoun, 47-72, 558 (*see also* Pronoun-antecedent agreement)
  case form and usage, 50-52, 54-60
  compound personal (intensive, reflexive), 64-
  66, 558
  consistent person and number, 293-95
  defined, 19, 47, 558
  demonstrative, 48, 62-63, 554
  functions of, 125-43
  indefinite, 48, 63-64, 555
  indefinite relative, 70-71, 209-10
  intensive, 48, 66, 555
  interrogative, 48, 61-62, 555
  personal, 48, 41-61, 557
  reciprocal, 48, 71-72, 558
  reference of, 262-71, 558
  reflexive, 48, 64-65, 113, 115, 558
  relative, 48, 67-71, 200, 559
  types of (table), 48
Pronoun-antecedent agreement, 254-61
  antecedent defined, 254, 552
  basic principle, 254-56
  with collective nouns, 260-61
  with indefinite pronouns, 256-57
  with nouns joined by *or,* 259-60
  with nouns modified by indefinite determiners, 258-59

Proofreading, 461-62
  how to proofread, 462
  what to look for, 461-62
Punctuation, 314-58 (*see also* Apostrophe,
  Hyphen, Italics)
  brackets, 356-57
  colon, 322, 344-47
  comma, 319, 320, 322-37
  dash, 337-40
  ellipses, 354-56
  ends of sentences, 315-16
  exclamation mark, 316
  for clarity, 315, 323
  of compound sentences, 319-22
  parentheses, 341-43
  period, 315, 317-18
  question mark, 316
  quotation marks, 349-54
  semicolon, 320-21, 347-49, 388
Purpose, of a composition, 445, 454

Q

Qualifier, 90, 558
  defined, 19, 90, 558
  position with adjective in the noun phrase,
  149
Question
  direct and indirect, 211-13, 316, 408
  rhetorical, 382
  tag question, 14, 326-27, 559
Question mark, 316
  incorrect with indirect questions, 316
  incorrect with requests stated as questions,
  316
  position with parentheses, 342
  position with quotation marks, 354
  use of, 316
Quotation
  brackets for insertion in, 356-57
  capitalization of first word in, 418
  changing direct quotation to indirect, 211-
  13, 316, 408
  correct omission of comma before, 336-37
  ellipses for omission in, 355-56
  quotation marks with, 350-51
  use of colon before, 345
  use of comma with, 330-31
  within another quotation, 353
Quotation marks, 349-54
  for direct quotations, 350
  for titles of short works, 351
  for words used in a special sense, 352-53
  incorrect for indirect quotations, 351
  other punctuation with, 353-54
  single, 353

R

raise, 538
Reciprocal pronoun, 48, 71-72, 558
Reducing clauses to simpler structures, 216-33, 379-80
Redundancy, 456
Reference of pronouns, 262-71, 558
  basic principle, 262
  indefinite use of *they, it, you,* 266-69
  to a broad idea, 270-71
  to an implied noun, 264-65
  to a noun that modifies, 265-67
  unclear reference, 263-64
Reflexive pronoun, 48, 64-65, 113, 115, 558
Relations between sentence-ideas, expressing (table), 283-84
Relative adverb, 45, 203-4, 558
Relative clause (*see* Adjective clause)
Relative pronoun, 48, 67-71, 200, 559
  case of, 56-57, 68
  choice of *who, which,* or *that,* 68-69
Research
  exploratory reading, 497
  initial planning, 498
  taking notes, 498-502
  using the library, 483-96
  working bibliography, 497-98
Research paper, 497-535
  bibliography
    format, 508
    forms, 509-21
    working bibliography, 497-98
  content notes, 505
  endnotes, 507, 509-20
  footnotes, 506-7, 509-22
  note-taking, 498-502 (*see also* Plagiarism)
  outline page, 526
  parenthetical reference notes, 507-8, 523-24
  planning, 498
  reference notes, 503-8
  researching a topic, 497
  sample paper, 524-35
  title page, 525
  writing the paper, 502
Restricter, 87-88, 559
Restrictive modifier, 327-28, 559 (*see also* Close appositive)
  adjective, 31
Résumé, 468-71
Retained object, 141-42, 541, 559
Revision, 452-60
Rhetorical question, 382
rise, 538
Rough draft, 447

S

S *be* Advl, 116-19, 541

S InV, 109-10, 539
S LV PA, 112-13, 540
S LV PN, 110-11, 540
S TrV DO, 113-14, 540
S TrV DO OC, 119-20, 541
S TrV IO DO, 114-15, 541
Semicolon, 320-21, 347-49, 388
  before the conjunction in certain compound sentences, 347
  between items in a series, 347-48
  between two independent clauses, 347
  general effect and use of, 347
  incorrect, 349, 388
  overuse of, 347
  position with parentheses, 342
  position with quotation marks, 353
Semicolon fragment, 388
Sentence (*see also* Lively sentences)
  comma splice, 389-90, 553
  defined, 9-11
  diagrams, 539-51
  division into subject and predicate, 11-13
  end of, managing well, 296-300, 371-72
  end punctuation, 315-16
  fragment, 383-84, 385-88
  fused sentence, 390-91, 554
  inverted, 81, 118-19, 383
  logical, 398-412
  patterns, 108-20
  periodic, 381-82
  placement in, 295-300
  stringy, 396
  types by clause structure (compound, etc.), 213-16
  types by purpose (declarative, etc.), 14
  variety in paragraph, 372-74
Sentence-ideas, relationships between, 277-84
Sentence logic
  comparisons, 403-6
  dependent clause, need for, 407-8
  examples, 401
  metaphors, 409-12
  mixed constructions, 401-2
  noun clause, need for, 407
  subjects and verbs, 400-401
Sentence patterns, 108-20, 540-41
  basis for all clauses, 108-9
  basis for all verbal phrases, 136-39, 182, 185, 188
  S *be* Advl, 116-19
  S InV, 109-10
  S LV PA, 112-13
  S LV PN, 110-11
  S TrV DO, 113-14
  S TrV DO OC, 119-20
  S TrV IO DO, 114-15